I0042258

Marriage Records of

SCIOTO COUNTY, OHIO

1803-1860

Marriage Records of
SCIOTO COUNTY, OHIO

1803-1860

By
Caryn R. Fuller Shoemaker
&
Betty J. Sisler Rudity

CLEARFIELD

Reprinted for
Clearfield Company, Inc. by
Genealogical Publishing Co., Inc.
Baltimore, Maryland
2003

Copyright © 1987
Genealogical Publishing Co., Inc.
Baltimore, Maryland
All Rights Reserved
Library of Congress Catalogue Card Number 86-82404
International Standard Book Number 0-8063-1170-3
Made in the United States of America

INTRODUCTION

Scioto County marriage records derive not only from the traditional marriage register, but also from applications for the license, letters of consent, and the original returns. The compilers have abstracted marriage records and references from all of these sources. In many cases, one or more of the papers are missing, or information varies between sources. To decide on the preferred spelling of a name, priority was given to a legible signature by the groom and/or the minister's return, and variant spellings were set off in parentheses.

The marriage affidavits are the applications for a license. In most cases, the groom signed a statement that he was over 21, his intended wife was over 18 and a county resident, neither had a former spouse living, and they were not nearer of kin than first cousins. Frequently a letter of consent is attached, giving parental permission for a minor to marry. In abstracting these, care was taken to note whether a relationship is stated exactly through the use of the terms "son" or "daughter." In 1900, these affidavits were riveted together by year and filed in drawers high on a Probate Court wall. The dusty packets were discovered in 1981, containing prime evidence of relationships (none of which is entered in the marriage record volumes), but they are still unindexed and inaccessible to researchers.

The original returns are likewise riveted together by year and filed in packets in the Probate Court's wall files. In most cases, they were copied verbatim into the marriage record volumes; however, there are nearly a hundred that were never entered, and hundreds more that were copied carelessly, with misinterpretations of handwriting. The returns that were omitted from the volumes are shown here with the name of the officiating Justice of the Peace or minister.

The marriage record volumes are used daily by researchers and courthouse staff. They have been indexed into a large card file which is generally accurate but does contain errors in spelling, interpretation, and filing.

The sources for each marriage record are provided in abbreviated form to allow the reader to check interpretations, request copies, or see what exists for each marriage. Marriage affidavits are referenced **MA**; original returns, **R**; and volume and page are given thus: A-283, B-151, etc. Other abbreviations used here are:

att.	attest
Co.	County
cons.	consent
dau.	daughter
J.P.	Justice of the Peace
pars.	parents
res.	residence
Tp.	Township
witn.	witness

August 1986

Caryn R. Fuller Shoemaker
Betty J. Sisler Rudity

Marriage Records of
SCIOTO COUNTY, OHIO

1803-1860

Abbot, Allen & Martha A. Hatfield. 20 Aug. 1857. R, D-56.
Abbots, Ambrose & Ann Coney. 24 Nov. 1850. MA, B-196.
Abbott, Ebenezer & Nancy Burk (Buck?). 13 Feb. 1817. MA, R, A-26.
Abbott, James Jr. & Dolly Chamberlain. Wyatt Chamberlin att.
    Dolly is over 18. 18 Aug. 1812. MA, R, A-328.
Abbott, Jeremiah & Betsy Chamberlain. 1 Apr. 1818. MA, R, A-38.
Abbott, Orrin H. & Angeline McMannus. 29 Sep. 1852. MA, B-250.
Abbott, Samuel & Aurella Chamberlin. James Abbott att. he heard
    Dolly Chamberlin, widow, and mother of Orrilla, cons. 1 Oct.
    1812. MA, R, A-318.
Abby, William & Margaret McLoud. 25 Sep. 1838. MA, R, A-260.
Able, John & Mary C. Row. 1 Dec. 1860. MA, R, D-125.
Adair, Lewis D. & Lavina Kendall. 15 Oct. 1857. R, D-67.
Adair, Smilie R. & Lucy C. Whitcomb. 2 Sep. 1850. MA, R, B-187.
Adams, Austin & Mary B. Morgan. His father Simpson Adams, and
    her father Isim Morgan cons. 5 May 1853. MA, B-265.
Adams, Calvin & Letitia Moore. 15 Feb. 1855. MA, R, D-15.
Adams, Edward & Eveline Dixon. 26 Jan. 1854. D-7.
Adams, Fannin & Elizabeth Garret. 9 Sep. 1842. MA, R, B-34.
Adams, Frank & Barbara Peter. 11 Nov. 1852. MA, B-250.
Adams, Frank & Catharine Out. 31 May 1846. MA, R, B-87.
Adams, George W. & Nancy Gard. 15 July 1858. MA, R, D-93.
Adams, Henry & Nancy Pugh. Henry is 21, born Bulford C.P.(sic),
    son of William. Nancy is 16, born Meigs Co., Ohio, dau. of
    Peter. 7 June 1857. R, C-15, D-56.
Adams, Ira & Nancy Williams. Ira is 22, born & res. Harrison Tp.,
    son of John & Nancy (Fanny). Nancy is 18, res. Porter Tp.,
    dau. of H. & Jane. 28 Mar. 1857. R, C-13, C-14, D-51.
Adams, Jacob & Mary Anne Norman. Her father William Norman cons.
    20 Oct. 1853. MA, B-271.
Adams, Jesse & Rebecca Jones. 24 Oct. 1860. MA, R, D-123.
Adams, John & Fanny Cole. Edmund & Phebe Cole cons. 3 Feb. 1825.
    MA, R, A-88.
Adams, John B. & Eveline Shunkwiler. 22 Jan. 1839. MA, R, A-266.
Adams, John G. & Mary Wallborn. 21 Dec. 1839. MA, R, A-278.
Adams, John Q. & Nancy Jane Gunn. 14 Dec. 1847. R, B-111.
Adams, Joseph & Sarah White. 20 Aug. 1854. R, D-9.
Adams, Louis & Margaret Smith. 5 May 1859. MA, R, D-91.
Adams, Martin & Mary Yerkins. 11 Nov. 1841. MA, R, B-37.
Adams, Nathan & Maria Jane Bennett. 19 Nov. 1846. MA, R, B-98.
Adams, William & Sarah M. Bennet. 4 July 1858. MA, R, D-87.
Addeley, James & Sarah Ann Liggett. 11 June 1838. MA, R, A-256.
Addis, Lewis E. & Harriet Horner. 10 Feb. 1848. William Aucker-
    man att. ages. MA, R, B-122.
Addis, Nathaniel & Barbara A. Davis. 6 May 1849. MA, R, B-148.
Adkins, David & Anna Stewart. Both of Upper Tp. 14 Dec. 1814.
    MA, R, A-343.
Adkins, Lewis & Polly Massey. Thomas Massey cons., witn. John
    Snorgrass, Matison Crump. 24 Oct. 1832. MA, R, A-168.
Adkins, William & Martha McGraw. 31 Mar. 1844. MA, R, B-58.
Adwill, Andrew & Anna McAuley. 11 Sep. 1849. MA, R, B-157.
Aeh (Oeh), Martin & Caroline Glass (Klages). 12 Apr. 1852. MA,
    B-237.
Aikins, Charles & A.M. Brewer. 30 June 1855. B-286.
Aitken, Alexander & Sarah Yeager. 9 Aug. 1848. MA, R, B-129.
Aitken, Alexander & Margaret A. Giles. 29 Nov. 1851. MA.
Akin, John & Hannah Wright. 19 Dec. 1805. R, A-9, A-279.
Albertson, Abraham H. & Sarah M. Marsh. 22 Mar. 1838. R, A-251.

1

Albrecht, Michael & Magdalena Wurth (Wits). 6 Apr. 1850. MA, R, B-176.

Aldrich, Arbaces & Elizabeth Boren. He is 19, born and res. Scioto Co., son of H.T. & Louisa Aldrich. She is 17, born Beaver, Pa., dau. of A.H. & Hannah Boren. 23 Aug. 1857. R, C-8, D-64.

Aldrich, Asa & Martha J. Turner. 1 Nov. 1837. R, A-234.

Aldrich, Gustavus M. & Eliza Tubbs. 11 June 1841. MA.

Aldrich, Gustavus M. & Susannah Rollins. 18 Oct. 1842. MA, R, B-39.

Aldrich, Huron T. & Louisa Searl. 6 Oct. 1836. MA, R, A-223.

Aldrich, Luke & Elizabeth Lowery. 4 Feb. 1818. R, A-33.

Aldrich, Mark & Lucretia Belli. 9 Dec. 1821. R, A-62.

Alexander, Peyton & Mahala Hensly. 20 Apr. 1835. MA.

Alexander, Traverse & Jula (Jude) Bush. 12 Mar. 1846. MA, R, B-84.

Alferd, Roswell B. & Martha Lodge. 16 Nov. 1836. R, A-221.

Allan, David & Lucretia Fisher. 15 Feb. 1859. MA, R, D-80.

Allard, Joseph & Susanna Dillen. 9 Feb. 1833. MA, R, A-174.

Allard, William & Frances Ann Cole. 10 Mar. 1853. MA, B-264.

Allen, David & Sarah Mead. 13 Sep. 1819. MA, R, A-49.

Allen, Elihu & Minerva Smith. 14 Dec. 1854. MA, R, D-12.

Allen, Isaac & Julia Ann Irwin. 25 Apr. 1860. Elizabeth Irwin cons., witn. Margaret Dodge & William Allen. MA, R, D-120.

Allen, James A. & Nancy Wheeler. 8 Oct. 1840. MA, R, B-12.

Allen, Jesse & Mary Yeley. 2 Aug. 1838. R, A-259.

Allen (Allard), John & Mary Taylor. 22 Dec. 1836. MA, R, A-238.

Allen, John & Mary Cox. 1 Nov. 1856. R, D-42.

Allen, Moses H. & Mary M. Huston. 21 Mar. 1857. R, D-50.

Allen, Oren T. & Hannah Randell. 9 Dec. 1849. MA, R, B-165.

Allen, Thomas H. & Mary L. Turner. 27 Oct. 1842. R, B-36.

Allen, William & Sarah Worley. He res. Mason Co., Ky. His father Robards Allen cons., witn. Benjamin Allen, Thomas Allen, & John Allen. 7 Dec. 1818. MA, R, A-61.

Allen, William & Mary J. McGowen. Her father, James McGowen cons. 18 July 1860. MA, R, D-132.

Allen, William & Mrs. P.S. Slocumb. 5 Apr. 1855. R, D-17.

Allender, George & Sarah A. Thompson. 28 Mar. 1850, by Noah Tracy, J.P. MA, R.

Allison, David & Fetamar (Fatama) Smith. 10 Mar. 1842. MA, R, B-29.

Allison, George H. & Elizabeth Rickards (Richards). He is 21, born Beaver Co., Pa., res. Madison Tp., son of James B. & Catherine Allison. She is 20 (21), res. Madison Tp., dau. of John M. & Rebecca Richards. 17 Nov. 1857. R, C-9, C-11, D-66.

Allison, James & Nancy Boggs. 16 Mar. 1845. MA, R, B-69.

Allison, James M. & Mary Ann Feurt (Fort). 10 Apr. 1850. MA, R, B-177.

Allman, Jesse & Lovina Jenkins. 9 Sep. 1838. MA, R, A-259.

Allmonge, John & Jane Nolder. 22 Nov. 1837. R, A-235.

Althouse, Andrew & Elizabeth Rope. Washington Partlow att. ages. 8 Dec. 1851. MA.

Altman, Samuel & Catherine Crabtree. Her father William W. Crabtree cons. 24 May 1860. MA, R, D-119.

Altman, Solomon & Narcissis Marshall. 15 Nov. 1860. MA, R, D-127.

Altman, Solomon & Mary Thocmorton. 29 Jan. 1856. R, D-25.

Altring, Frances & Emma Comer. 8 June 1858. D-86.

Amberg, John & Anna Hauberth (Herbert). 30 Jan. 1855. MA, R, D-15.

Amberg, John & Catherine Smith. 28 Aug. 1858. MA, R, D-81.

Ambrose, Ambrose & Ann Perry. 14 June 1838. MA, R, A-255.

Amburg, Conrad & Ann Clark. 20 Mar. 1858. MA, R, D-71.

Ames, Nicklas & Francis Stigerwolt. 25 Aug. 1860. MA.

SCIOTO COUNTY MARRIAGES

Ammon, Charles & Roane Winett. 4 Jan. 1857. R, D-60.
Amos, John & Mary Will. 8 Sep. 1855. MA, R, D-27.
Anderson, Abner & Elizabeth Haynes. 18 Nov. 1855. R, D-64.
Anderson, Abner & Nancy Hodges. Cons. of Samuel Cawins & Polly
    Cawins for "..my daughter Nancy Hodges...about 15 years old,
    born a daughter of Polly Cowins before she was mared to
    Cowins." Witn. A.D. Hodges & Ransom Hodges. 12 June 1812.
    MA, R, A-117.
Anderson, Abner & Martha Atkins. 30 Oct. 1849. MA, R, B-163.
Anderson, Benjamin & Isabel Harmon. 4 Feb. 1853. MA.
Anderson, Benjamin & Louisa Brown. Her pars., Thomas & Levicy
    Remy of Junior Furnace, cons., witn. William Barnett & John
    L. Turner. 29 Oct. 1843. MA, R, B-66.
Anderson, Benjamin & Julia Ann Wilcox (Wilson). 26 Dec. 1830,
    by Ezra Osborn, J.P. MA, R.
Anderson, David & Elizabeth Milam. 16 Dec. 1852. MA, B-254.
Anderson, Gabriel T. & Sarah R. Dickson. 12 July 1854. B-284.
Anderson, Jacob & Julia Huston. 11 Aug. 1814. MA, R, A-338.
Anderson, James M. & Elizabeth Scott. 22 Nov. 1860. MA, R, D-126.
Anderson, Marshall & Rachel J. Pyle. Her father Samuel Pyle cons.
    Witn. Samuel Anderson. 11 Dec. 1859. MA, R, D-120.
Anderson, Robert & Elizabeth Nogle. 24 Dec. 1860. MA, R, D-124.
Anderson, Samuel J. & Sydney Anne Huston. 23 Nov. 1829. R, A-137.
Anderson, Thornton F. & Eleanor Evans. 11 Apr. 1833. MA, R,
    A-175.
Anderson, William & Matilda Price. 30 Sep. 1852. MA, B-250.
Anderson, William & Elizabeth Wallsinger. 28 July 1842. MA.
Andre, Augustus & Almira California Chaffin. Her father Phineas
    Chaffin cons., witn. Francis Andre. 12 Mar. 1860. MA, R, D-129.
Andre, Francis & Abigail Chafin. 13 May 1860. MA, R, D-118.
Andre, Francis & Sophia Dutiel. 28 Mar. 1830. R, A-142.
Andre, Jacob & Jane Dutiel. 4 Sep. 1823. R, A-77.
Andre, John & Chloe Randall. 11 Dec. 1831. R, A-160.
Andre, Peter & Juliann Randell. 6 July 1826. MA, R, A-99.
Andre, Peter & Mary L. Hudson. 13 Jan. 1859. MA, R, D-94.
Andrews, James & Milly Clark. 20 Apr. 1835. MA.
Andrews, James & Nancy Clark. 14 Sep. 1835. MA, R, A-205.
Andrews, James & Esther Powers. 29 Dec. 1814. R, A-344.
Andrews, William & Louisa Cumpston. 24 Oct. 1858. MA, R, D-94.
Andrews, William & Caroline M. Barker. 20 June 1848. R, B-128.
Andrews, William & Sarah A. Russell. 3 June 1852. MA, B-240.
Angel, Joshua & Eliza Monk. 21 Nov. 1850. B-197.
Angele, Andrew & Ursena Kopf. 25 Dec. 1859. MA, R, D-111.
Antis, Samuel & Nancy Spence. His father John Antis cons.
    18 Dec. 1838. MA.
Apel, Georg & Mary Ministt (Minster). 4 Apr. 1848. MA, R, B-121.
Apel, George & Maria Sherer. 22 May 1852. MA, B-241.
Appel, Peter & Sophie Bez. 28 July 1849. R, B-154.
Appel, Phillip & Catharine Bender. 4 May 1848. MA, B-244.
Applegate, Andrew & Sally Bond (Brand). 20 Sep. 1827. MA, R, A-110.
Applegate, Jacob & Lucinda Home. 4 May 1848. MA, R, B-122.
Applegate, Jacob & Rosanthe Bostwick. 9 June 1858. MA.
Applegate, John & Sally Rose. 20 May 1822. MA, R, A-66.
Applegate, Joseph & Sarah Spriggs. 1 Aug. 1844. MA, R, B-61.
Applegate, Richard & Lucy J. Bostwick. 7 Feb. 1860. MA, R, D-112.
Applegate, Richard & Rebecca Spriggs. 1 Apr. 1847. MA, R, B-100.
Applegate, William & Mary Campbell. Philip K. Weller att. her
    age over 18. 12 Apr. 1837. MA, R, A-240.
Appler, Jesse J. & Eunice E. Melcher. 25 Apr. 1837, at the home
    of Benjamin Melcher. MA, R, A-241.
Appler, Washington C. & M. Emma Gilbert. 13 Sep. 1858, by E. P.
    Pratt. MA, R.
Archbold, David & Rebecca Williams. 4 May 1850. R, B-178.

3

Archer, Francis & Elizabeth Mason. His mother Betsey Farley
    cons., witn. William Douglas. 13 Feb. 1834. MA, R, A-191.
Arder, Lowis & Patsey Carpenter. 5 June 1809. R, A-296.
Arend, William & Elizabeth Spelman. 18 Dec. 1842. MA, R, B-38.
Argo, William V. & Nancy Sisler. 8 Sep. 1850. MA, R, B-191.
Armitage, John & Susanna Rupe. 7 Sep. 1828. R, A-122.
Armstrong, Aaron & Eleanor Burns. 19 Mar. 1818. R, A-34.
Armstrong, Aaron & Christeane Waggoner. 26 July 1821. MA, R,
    A-61.
Armstrong, George L. & Jane Armstrong. 7 May 1842. MA, R, B-33.
Armstrong, John & Jane Stewart. 18 Feb. 1845. R, B-68.
Armstrong, Joshua & Margret McCann. 10 Nov. 1831. MA, R, A-158.
Armstrong, Wilson & Elizabeth Cese (Case? Cox?). Nathan Hughes
    att. her age over 18. 14 Feb. 1836. MA, R, A-208, A-228.
Arnold, Daniel & Cynthianne Hazlebaker. 17 Apr. 1853. MA, B-266.
Arnold, George W. & Eliza A. Holt. 12 June 1856. R, D-31.
Arnold, Isaac & Sarah Brown. Her mother Hetty Brown cons.
    28 June 1835. MA, R, A-202.
Arnold, Isaac & Polly Hesler. 19 Jan. 1823. MA, R, A-71.
Arnold, William & Sarah Shelpman. Thomas Arnold cons., witn.
    James Rankins, Isaac Arnold. 7 May 1835. MA, R, A-202, A-209.
Arthur, James S. & Hester Richardson. 2 Feb. 1860. MA, R, D-164.
Arthur, Joseph & Fanny Bennett. Matthias Bennett att. ages.
    24 Mar. 1853. MA, B-258.
Arthurs, Tompkins & Hannah Gennis. 8 Aug. 1857. R, D-65.
Artist, David & Elizabeth Bush. 10 May 1849. MA, R, B-148.
Artist, Thomas & Elizabeth L. Smedley. 10 May 1849. MA, R, B-148.
Ashley, Holt & Catharin Hise (Hin?). 3 Apr. 1824. MA.
Ashley, Jeremiah & Luceba Conklin. 29 Mar. 1845. R, B-70.
Ashley, John & Elizabeth Thompson. 24 Dec. 1843. MA, R, B-52.
Ashley, John & Matilda Louderback. 31 Oct. 1822. MA, R, A-70.
Ashmore, Thomas & Louisa Kisor. Jacob Kiser cons., witn. Samuel
    Cable, Salathiel Millirons. 11 June 1840. MA, R, B-12.
Atkins, Francis & Jane F. Bonser. 9 June 1858, by Henry Comer,
    J.P. MA, R.
Atoff, Adam & Mary Shetel. 14 Nov. 1855. D-22.
Auckerman, Samuel & Anne Hinkley. Frederick Herron att. ages.
    27 Nov. 1859. MA, R, D-102.
Ault, George G. & Margaret A. Oakes. 21 Oct. 1849. MA, R, B-162.
Austin, Charles K. & Susan Fowler. 10 Oct. 1850. MA, R, B-191.
Austin, Nelson & Mary Yonkin. 10 Aug. 1849. R, B-154.
Austin, Richard M. & Jane Madison. 18 Aug. 1841. MA, R, B-23.
Austin, Samuel & Ann Eliza Kirkpatrick. 9 Oct. 1854. R, D-10.
Austin, Walter & Sarah Nurse. 12 July 1827. R, A-101.
Ayres, Nathan T. & Mary C. Black. 16 Oct. 1843. R, B-52.
Baccus, Amaziah, of Porter Tp. & Melissa Salladay, of Green Tp.
    31 Dec. 1833. R, A-186.
Baccus, David & Mary Burk. William Burk & Sally Burk cons.,
    witn. Jesse Baccus. 23 Jan. 1845. MA, R, B-67.
Baccus, Eza & Eunice Higgans. 7 Jan. 1841. R, B-15.
Baccus, Isaac & Nancy Littlejohn. Henry Littlejohn att. her age
    over 18. 26 May 1836. MA, R, A-215, A-233.
Baccus, Isaiah & Rachel Mariah Townsend. His father James Baccus
    of Porter Tp. cons., witn. C.W. Alford, Samuel Baccus. Her
    mother Elizabeth Moore of Porter Tp. cons., witn. C.W. Alford.
    10 Apr. 1836. MA.
Baccus, Jesse & Cinthia Burk. 31 Jan. 1844. MA, R, B-53.
Baccus, John & Elizabeth Faurty (Faverty?). 25 Dec. 1831. R,
    A-160.
Baccus, Mathias & Catherine Gohean (Coheenes). 3 Dec. 1840. MA,
    R, B-7.
Baccus, Samuel & Rhoda Townsend. 6 May 1841. MA, R, B-18.
Baccus, Thomas J. & Julia Ann Patton. 2 July 1850. MA, R, B-184.

4

Baccus, William & Mary Littlejohn. 25 Jan. 1827. R, A-103.

Bacom, James & Sarah Roberts. 21 Mar. 1822. R, A-65.

Bader, Samuel & Mrs. Sarah E. Thompson. 29 June 1856, by J. Nichols. R.

Baesler, Frederick & Marian Schaffer. 15 Apr. 1847. MA, R, B-101.

Baesler, Frederick & Elizabeth Pelhank. 19 June 1855, by E.P. Pratt. R.

Bagby, Lewis & Elizabeth Littlejohn. 11 Dec. 1824. R, A-85.

Bagley, James & Elizabeth Harr. Matthew J. Thompson att. her age over 18. Mrs. Sarah Bagley cons., witn. James Gibbs. 29 June 1838. MA, R, A-256.

Bagley, John & Elizabeth Pierce. Horace Pierce cons., att. William Kelly. 22 Dec. 1850. MA, B-199.

Bahler, Louis (Ludwig) & Mary J. Noel. 6 Aug. 1859. MA, R, D-100.

Bailey, Albert G. & Mary Smith. 17 Mar. 1833. MA, R, A-175.

Bailey, Albert G. & Eliza Oard. 6 Dec. 1837. A-236.

Bailey, Andrew & Henrietta Horner. 17 Apr. 1845. MA, R, B-72.

Bailey, David & Catherine Vinson. 18 Dec. 1836. MA, R, A-241.

Bailey, Joseph & Cassandra Paxson. 13 Sep. 1851. MA.

Bailey, William & Eliza Willson. 28 May 1840. R, B-9.

Baird, Abner & Louisa Lewis. 25 Dec. 1836. R, A-220.

Baird, Moses & Phebe Goodrich. 5 Feb. 1845. MA, R, B-68.

Baird, Moses B. & Maria McMasters. Joseph Chester att. ages. 9 Apr. 1838. MA, R, A-253.

Baker, Dwight M. & Narcissa Voorhees. 16 June 1844. MA, R, B-60.

Baker, George & Sally Stephenson. 26 Dec. 1837. MA, R, A-235.

Baker, George W. & Nancy Martin. 25 Dec. 1856. R, D-46.

Baker, Isaac & Rebeccah Sheward. His father Abraham Baker cons., witn. William Baker. Her father James Sheward cons., witn. her brother Nathan Sheward. 3 Feb. 1814. MA, R, A-330.

Baker (Backer), Jacob & Margaretha Siahl. 24 Aug. 1849. MA, R, B-156.

Baker (Beoker), Jacob & Caroline Rau (Row). Henry Rowe att. ages. 17 Oct. 1850. MA, R, B-190.

Baker, John & Minerva Lane. 24 Sep. 1856. MA, R, D-36.

Baker (Backer), Joseph & Emily Hall. 6 May 1859. MA, R, D-91.

Baker, Michael & Catharine Weesner. 26 Oct. 1840. MA, R, B-8.

Baker, Robert & Cornelia Wilson. He is 25, born Kent, England, son of Robert & Harriet, res. Portsmouth. She is 17, born New York, dau. of Moses, res. Portsmouth. 28 Mar. 1856. R, C-3, D-27.

Baker (Barker), Thomas & Catherine Dawson. 12 June 1817. MA, R, A-29.

Baker, Washington & Diana Massey. 2 Aug. 1860. MA, R, D-132.

Baker, William & Patty (Polly) Monrow. 19 June 1817. MA, R, A-29.

Baker, William & Margaret Warden. 5 Dec. 1841. MA, R, B-25, B-37.

Balcom, Henry & Caroline (Catherine) Reeve. Charles P. Tracy att. ages. 4 June 1860. MA, R, D-121.

Baldridge, Robert & Margaret Hodge. 24 June 1850. MA, R, B-181.

Baldridge, Samuel J. & Susan Kendall. 21 Nov. 1850. MA, B-195.

Ball, David & Mary Eliza Sikes. 10 Mar. 1844. R, B-57.

Ball, Demosthenes & Clarinda Chapman. 5 Aug. 1845. R, B-75.

Ball, George & Margaret Noel. 21 Apr. 1858. R, D-73.

Ball, George & Jane Gillett. 2 June 1853. MA, B-262.

Ball, Henry & Julia Ann Smith. 31 Oct. 1847. MA, R, B-114, B-119.

Ball, John & Hester Ann Haskins. 27 Aug. 1838. R, A-259.

Ball, Orlando & Harriet Bliss. 4 Mar. 1827. MA, R, A-103.

Ball, Oscar & Amanda Nurse. 20 Dec. 1855. R, D-25.

Ball, William H. & Sarah M. Barber (Barker). 9 Dec. 1851 (1850 on MA). MA, B-226.

Ballenger, Asa & Amanda Swaar (Swan). 28 Sep. 1815. R, A-283.

Ballenger, Evy & Elizabeth Nolder. 14 July 1833. R, A-180.

Ballenger, J.W. & Isabella Stewart. 2 Sep. 1860. MA, R, D-170.

5

Ballenger, Levi & Rebecca Pile (Piat?). 3 Nov. 1853. B-271.
Baly, James & Mary Smith. 19 Mar. 1832. R, A-160.
Banes, James & Elizabeth Ates. His father A.B. Banes of Morgan
    Tp. cons. "Elizabeth is a girl living at Philip Noel Senior's
    house." Att. Isaac Eulitt, Henry Utt. 25 Apr. 1844. MA, R,
    B-59.
Banion, Henry & Mary Elizabeth Lupius. 20 Apr. 1854 at Pinegrove
    in Lawrence Co. R, D-7, D-94.
Baraham, John & Lucretia Jane George. Her father Robert A.J.
    George cons. 13 May 1858. MA, R, D-76.
Barbee, Elias & Elizabeth Baise. 18 Nov. 1851. MA, B-225.
Barbee, Joshua & Eliza Mitchell. 20 Jan. 1850. R, B-171.
Barbee, Wesley & Lucy Ball. 19 Sep. 1850. MA, R, B-189.
Barber (Barbee), Elias & Mary Elizabeth Hayale (Hyett). 18 Oct.
    1837. R, A-235.
Barber, James & Mary Ann Queen. 15 Nov. 1838. MA, R, A-263.
Barber, James & Urania Lindsey. 30 Jan. 1842. R, B-28.
Barber, John & Violet Swords. 5 Sep. 1816. MA, R, A-22.
Barber, Joseph & Rebecca J. Worley. 12 Jan. 1860. MA, R, D-111.
Barber, Joseph L. & Mahala Colley, both of Vernon Tp. Edward
    Colly att. her age over 18. 5 Jan. 1837. MA, R, A-238.
Barber, Nathaniel & Ann Eliza Shoemaker. 27 May 1850. R, B-182.
Barber, Samuel & Margie B. Fink. 21 Dec. 1859. MA, R, D-105.
Barber, Samuel & Nancy Tomlinson. John Tomlinson att. her age
    over 18. 12 Sep. 1812. MA.
Barber, Uriah & Rachel Beard. 7 Oct. 1806. R, A-283.
Barber, Uriah Jr. & Rachel Barber. 18 July 1844. R, B-61.
Barber, Washington & Razilly Gellim (Kazilla Gillim). 16 Dec.
    1829. R, A-137.
Barber, William E. & Caroline Cole (Noel). 25 Dec. 1851. MA,
    B-227.
Barkeloo, Edward & Rutha Patten. Thomas Pattan of Green Tp. cons.
    Witn. Thomas Patten Jr., Jermiah Patten. 24 Sep. 1806. MA, R,
    A-281.
Barkelow, Benjamin & Margaret Foster. Valentine Littlejohn att.
    her age over 18. Jesse Hitchcock att. he has known Barklow's
    father's family for years and believes Benjamin to be over
    21. 27 Feb. 1817. MA, R, A-26.
Barker (Barber?), Isaac & Lucy Dennis. 4 Mar. 1827. R, A-104.
Barker, John & Anna Jane Gregg. Thomas C. Lewis att. ages.
    30 Nov. 1853. MA, B-270.
Barker, John F. & Aurilla M. Porter. 12 Sep. 1847. MA, R, B-107.
Barker, Levi C. & Nancy Leonard. 1 May 1823. MA, R, A-74.
Barker (Baker), Nikolas & Sophia Zergebel (Zergild). 12 Feb.
    1850. MA, B-244.
Barkis, Henry & Sarah Lindsey. 20 June 1841. MA, R, B-21.
Barkley (Bradley), Georg & Charity Artis. 6 Aug. 1856. R, D-34.
Barklow, Edward & Malissa E. Cox. 7 Mar. 1858. MA, R, D-75.
Barklow, James Johnson & Isabella Rose. 27 May 1858 (1854?).
    R, D-79.
Barklow, Stout & Sarah Jane Jeffords. 15 Aug. 1844. R, B-62.
Barklow, William F. & Sarah Crain. 5 Dec. 1859. MA, R, D-106.
Barnes, Robert & Julia Gillis. 18 May 1820. R, A-52.
Barnet, Jacob D. & Anna Melvina Wyatt. 14 Jan. 1837. MA, R, A-227.
Barnet, William & Elizabeth Stone. Her father John Stone cons.,
    att. John M. Fuqua, James Stone. 17 Dec. 1833. MA.
Barnhous, John & Nancy McNeal. Edman Napp att. ages. 12 Feb.
    1847. MA, R, B-101.
Barns, David & Nancy Ann Cloud. 5 Dec. 1842. MA.
Barr, Andrew & Jane Liggett. 13 Mar. 1844. R, B-56.
Barr, John P. & Mary Martin. 19 June 1842. MA, R, B-32.
Barr, Joseph C. & Mary Jane Grovin. 27 July 1850. MA, R, B-184.
Barr, William H. & Cynthia M. Dean. 17 Apr. 1853. MA, B-260

SCIOTO COUNTY MARRIAGES

Barrett, Henry & Eliza Anderson. 27 Oct. 1853. MA, D-2.
Barrett, Henry Jr. & Jane F. Forny. 26 Nov. 1856. R, D-41.
Barrett, John H. & Ruby G. Hatch. 2 Jan. 1849. MA, R, B-149.
Barrett, Thornton & Jennyetta Ball. 5 Mar. 1840. R, B-3.
Barrett, William & Ellen Kelly. 14 Apr. 1856. R, D-28.
Barrick, Henry & Mary A. Eifort. 5 Dec. 1851. MA, B-243.
Barriman, Jacob & Jemima Hartman. 10 Feb. 1848. MA, R, B-120.
Bartels, Peter & Maria Snook. 15 Nov. 1838. MA, R, B-6.
Bartholamew, William & Elizabeth Lope. 30 Dec. 1858. MA, R, D-96.
Bartlett, M.R. & Mary McCague. 20 Apr. 1843. R, B-44.
Bartlow, William F. & Sarah Ann Johnson. 15 Feb. 1844. R, B-58.
Barton, Charles A. & Mary J. Maddock. He is 33, born Maine, res.
    Portsmouth. She is 21, born & res. Portsmouth, dau. of William
    & Mary Maddock. 25 Feb. 1858. R, C-13, D-66.
Barton, Joseph & Elizabeth Rector. 1 Oct. 1805. R, A-8, A-278.
Barton, Sharp & Elsa Lewis. 16 Sep. 1828. MA, R, A-122.
Bartrum, Thomas & Charlotte Robinson. 10 Nov. 1836. MA.
Basampag, Michael & Rosina Sheret (Shred). 7 Mar. 1854. D-6.
Basette, William & Mary Kelly. He is 35, born Ireland, res.
    Portsmouth, son of William. She is 20, born Ireland, res.
    Portsmouth, dau. of Michael. 14 Apr. 1856. C-6.
Basford, Henry & Amelia Ann Bertholf. 31 May 1859. MA, R, D-96.
Basham, James & Rachel Miller. Hiram Miller att. her age over
    18. Cons. of John Basham, witn. Notingham Bradburn, Nathan (?)
    Basham. 22 Jan. 1842. MA, R, B-28.
Basham, John & Mary Clark. 16 Nov. 1843. MA, R, B-50.
Basham, William & Sarah Ann Buckley. Her father Thomas Buckly
    cons., witn. William Rowley, Madison Price. 16 May 1842. (MA
    is dated 1843.) MA, R, B-47.
Basler, Jacob & Margaret Adam. 19 Nov. 1847. MA.
Basset, Amos & Susannah Colgin. 5 Sep. 1811. A-313.
Basset, Isaac & Elizabeth McCollister. 27 Oct. 1841. R, B-24.
Bassett, Isaac N. & Cyanda Moore. 4 Mar. 1847. MA, R, B-100.
Bassett, Luke A. & Sarah (Laura) J. Copen. 12 Apr. 1850. R, MA,
    B-177.
Batterson, Addison & Sarah Sikes. 27 Oct. 1850. MA, B-194.
Batterson, Addison & Dorothy Oakes. 4 Dec. 1851. MA, B-227.
Batterson, Franklin & Mary Stockham. 8 Apr. 1841. R, B-17.
Batterson, James & Polly Squires. 6 Mar. 1819. MA, R, A-45.
Bauer, Jacob & Philipena Lair. 25 Mar. 1853. MA.
Bauer, John Friedrich & Anna G.T. Wolf. 13 Sep. 1857. R, D-62.
Bauer, Peter & Anna Catharine Bergman (Catrena Berexman).
    17 Aug. 1859. MA, R, D-109.
Bauers (Barnes?), Thomas J. & Frances Bennet (Barnett). 23 Oct.
    1834. R, A-193, A-243 (shows his name Baccus).
Baum, Michael & Sarah M. Archbold. 16 Feb. 1851. B-202.
Baumgarner, Daniel & Amey Brush. 15 Mar. 1832. R, A-162.
Baumont (Bowman), Joseph & Louisa Usbee (Husbee). 26 Oct. 1851.
    MA, B-221.
Bausch, Michal & Anna Blechner. 28 Mar. 1859. MA, R, D-89.
Bayler, Daniel & Elizabeth L. Huston. 26 Apr. 1842. MA, R, B-30.
Bayner (Beohner), George & Margaret Ammon. 16 Sep. 1850. MA, R,
    B-188.
Bays (Bayse), Robert & Esther Eldridge. 26 Jan. 1841. MA, R, B-1.
Beaman, Gamaliel C. & Emelia Creichton. 27 Sep. 1836. R, A-224.
Bean, Benjamin & Minerva Jackson. 9 Nov. 1837. R, A-236.
Beard, Henry C. & Mary E. Noel. 25 Dec. 1860. MA, R, D-130.
Beard, Jacob & Catherine Masters. 28 Mar. 1841. R, B-17.
Beardslee, Nehemiah & Elizabeth Collins. 22 Aug. 1833. MA, R,
    A-180.
Bears, Harvey & Charlotte Woodruff. 3 Feb. 1848. MA, R, B-120.
Beatty, Alexander & Ruth Drury. 21 Mar. 1821. MA, R, A-59.
Beatty, L.T. & Aury Larkin. 29 Sep. 1853. MA, B-270.

7

Beatty, Samuel & Lydia Bradshaw. 4 Dec. 1852. MA.
Beaty, Rhynard C. & Amelia Ann Criss. Hiram Jones (Janes?) att.
    ages. 12 Dec. 1852. MA, B-253.
Beavers, Andrew & Mary Ann Clifford. 16 May 1858. MA, D-76,
    D-166, D-169.
Bebee, Carey T. & Rebecca Williams. 29 Aug. 1850. MA, R, B-189.
Beck, Jacob & Mary E. Norton. He is 20, born & res. Pike Co.,
    Oh., son of John & Rebecca. She is 18, born & res. Gallia
    Co., Oh. 20 Sep. 1857. C-9.
Becker, Conrad & Sally Dolch. 29 Aug. 1839. MA.
Beebe, Isaac & Nancy Burriss. 4 May 1823. R, A-74.
Beebee, William A. & Lucinda Allen. 25 May 1849. R, B-190.
Beechler (Beacher), John & Barbara Spate. 6 Nov. 1848. MA, B-244.
Beeghler, John & M. Hottes. 14 May 1854. R, D-8.
Beeles (Beals), Asa Gideon & Mahala Black. 10 Apr. 1853. MA,
    B-259.
Beeshler, Henry & Mary J. Batman. 11 June 1848. MA, R, B-127.
Beeson, Martin & Selinda Baccus. Her mother Nancy Baccus cons.,
    "Celinda was 15 years old the 10th of October last." Witn.
    W.J. Finton, Porter Tp. 5 Feb. 1846. MA, R, B-85.
Behrens, J. Henry & Margaret Stacel. 15 June 1858. MA, R, D-86.
Behrwind, George & Mary Raynor. 15 Aug. 1856. MA, R, D-34.
Beierlein, Georg & Druzilla Thomason. 30 Jan. 1847. MA.
Beigler, Christian & Christina Houser. 14 Mar. 1857. R, D-50.
Beirhoop (Beuhoop?), Henry & Eda Hemmlipp. 2 Feb. 1857. R, D-46.
Bekum, Charles & Phebe Kelly, persons of colour. 18 June 1841.
    R, B-20.
Belcher, Jesse & Elizabeth Roberts. His brother Joseph Belcher
    witn. cons. of her father Lewis Roberts. 21 July 1833. MA,
    R, A-180.
Belcher, Joseph & Lucy Blair. Her father John Blair cons., witn.
    Richard Belcher (Joseph's brother), John Squires. 4 July
    1833. MA, R, A-180.
Belcher, Mailon & Kaziah Carter. 16 Feb. 1845. MA.
Belcher, Richard & Maria Zirkel (Fukel? Fiche?). 15 Sep. 1833.
    MA, R, A-183.
Bell, Charles & Mary Sewell. 18 Sep. 1831. MA, R, A-155.
Bellamy, William & Clarissa Calhoun. 26 June 1836. MA, R, A-219.
Bellar, Elias & Catherine Toland. 11 Feb. 1841. MA, R, B-15.
Bellomy, Bartley & Prudence Zorns. 7 May 1848. MA, R, B-126.
Bellomy, Joshua B. & Ethelinda Bibbey. Cons. of Catharine James
    and Sarah Bibby, witn. Jeremiah Piles, Charles Young, and
    Horatio Burriss. 21 Nov. 1843. MA, R, B-52.
Beloat, George & Mary Turner. 22 Apr. 1812. R, A-320.
Beloat, George W. & Sarah Allerd. 10 Apr. 1849. R, B-147.
Beloat, James & Susanah Free. 3 Aug. 1826. R, A-99.
Beloat, Joseph B. & Eleanor Patan. Not dated, filed with 1836.
    A-225.
Beloat, William Q. & Elizabeth Collins. His mother Mary Brown
    cons. "He will be 19 years old April 1, 1837." Witn. George
    W. Beloat, Joseph Beloat. 28 Jan. 1837. MA, R, A-245.
Belote, George & Mary Colines (Collins). 5 Apr. 1832. R, A-164.
Belur (Belan), Charles & Caroline Jaynes. 9 June 1845. R, MA,
    B-73.
Benage, John & Mahala (Rebecca) Osborne. 16 July 1851. MA, B-212.
Bengel, John & Luisa Jaeger. 27 Aug. 1855. R, D-20.
Bennet, Abraham & Priscilly McFaden. 19 Nov. 1821. R, A-62.
Bennet, Amaziah & Sarah Queen. 5 Mar. 1846. MA, R, B-85.
Bennet, Amos & Deany Lee. 8 Nov. 1814. MA, R, A-340.
Bennet, Benjamin & Mary Rawlins. Samuel Bennet, Esq. att. Benja-
    min is over 21. Her father William cons. 8 Nov. 1814. MA, R,
    A-341.
Bennet, Caleb & Rebeccah Bedal. 25 Nov. 1834. R, A-197.

SCIOTO COUNTY MARRIAGES

Bennet, Caleb & Eliza Stockham. Her father Joseph Stockham cons.,
witn. Aaron Stockham. 1 Mar. 1832. MA, R, A-162.
Bennet, Charles Junr. & Martha Bennet. 10 Dec. 1817. MA, R, A-33.
Bennet, Ephraim & Rachel Mead. His mother Elizabeth Bennet cons.
8 Jan. 1834. MA, R, A-201.
Bennet, Henry & Nancy Lowe. 4 Nov. 1814. MA, R, A-342.
Bennet, Ira G. & Rhoda Hayse. E.L. Gaston att. ages. 27 Mar. 1830.
MA, R, A-166 (gives year 1831).
Bennet, James M. & Susan Fullerton. 5 Jan. 1843. MA, R, B-40.
Bennet, Jesse & Lancy Hunter. 15 Feb. 1843. R, B-50.
Bennet, Jesse & Eliza Knapp. Benjamin F. Bennet att. ages. 11 Apr.
1850. MA, R, B-181.
Bennet, John & Catherine Lewis. 18 July 1826. R, A-98.
Bennet, John & Rebecah Bennet. 9 Dec. 1815. MA, R, A-17.
Bennet, John & Mary Jane Green. 22 Mar. 1842. R, B-29.
Bennet, Joshua J. & Elizabeth Higgins. John Higgins cons. 10 Aug.
1836. MA, R, A-225.
Bennet, Madison P. & Sarah Johnson. His father Samuel Bennet
cons. 15 Mar. 1853. MA, B-259.
Bennet, Nimrod J. & Nancy Crull. 21 Dec. 1848. R, B-138.
Bennet, Noah & Elizabeth Woolford. 14 Apr. 1825. R, A-88.
Bennet, Robert C. & Mary Ann Montgomery. 22 Nov. 1826. R, A-101.
Bennet, Samuel & Emily Powell. Her father Skelton Powell cons.,
witn. Gilbert Bennet, John Bennet. 20 Sep. 1838. MA, R, A-259.
Bennet, Samuel & Jane Hull. Her father Isaac Hull Senr. cons.,
witn. James W. Burt, Isaac Hull Jr., Henry Lewis. 7 June 1827.
MA, R, A-108.
Bennet, Thadeus & Rachel Cheney. 17 Aug. 1826. R, A-101.
Bennet, Thomas & Juliana Conley (Cauley?). 23 July 1836. MA, R,
A-226.
Bennet, Thomas & Francis Lower. 10 June 1810. R, A-302.
Bennet, William & Rebecca Jones. 9 May 1805. R, A-5, A-278.
Bennet, William & Hannah Culp. 17 Jan. 1847. MA, R, B-98.
Bennet, William H. Parmolee & Abigail Bonser. 10 Sep. 1846. MA,
R, B-91.
Bennett, Benjamin B. & Margaret Baynes. 12 Oct. 1847. MA, R,
B-109.
Bennett, Benjamin F. & Sarah Ann Snorgrass. 11 Mar. 1849. R,
B-146.
Bennett, Benjamin M. & Lucretia Utt. 13 Dec. 1827. R, A-113.
Bennett, Caleb C. & Elizabeth Trexler. 25 Aug. 1841. R, B-23.
Bennett, David & Margaret Byers. 18 Nov. 1830. MA, R, A-148.
Bennett, David F. & Hannah Crull. 9 Sep. 1847. R, B-106.
Bennett, Elias & Hannah Hayward. 11 Mar. 1852. B-235.
Bennett, G.W. & Martha Ross. 10 Dec. 1849. R, B-171.
Bennett, Hosea & Rebecca Woods. 21 Nov. 1841. MA, R, B-27.
Bennett, Jacob & Cynthia McKinney. 16 June 1825. R, A-90.
Bennett, John & Martha J. Cable. 26 Oct. 1851. B-224.
Bennett, Joshua & Sarah Craig. 20 May 1824. R, A-82.
Bennett, Joshua & Susannah Woolford. 7 Apr. 1814. MA, R, A-335.
Bennett, Josiah & Susan Shoemaker. Orsemus Canfield att. her age
over 18. 8 Apr. 1830. MA, R, A-144.
Bennett, Madison & Susan Powell. 7 Mar. 1840. MA.
Bennett, Rolley E. & Sarah Samson. Her father James Samson cons.
15 Dec. 1839. MA, R, A-275.
Bennett (Benight), Thaddeus & Abigail Wait. 2 Apr. 1820. MA, R,
A-52.
Bennett, Thadeus & Lucinda Neowell. 22 June 1837. R, A-244.
Bennett, Thomas & Hannah Burt. 27 Apr. 1828. R, A-117.
Bennett, Thomas & Nancy Fullerton. His mother Nancy Bennet cons.,
witn. John Fullerton. 16 Apr. 1829. MA, R, A-130.
Bennett, Thomas S. & Mary Jane Downey. He is 23, born Scioto Co.,
res. Madison Tp., son of Ephraim. She is 19, born Pa., res.
Madison Tp., dau. of Samuel. 6 July 1857. R, C-11, D-55.

9

Bennett, William & Sarah Mastin. 9 Nov. 1851. MA, B-223.
Bennette, Sylvester & Levina Cable. 4 July 1852. MA, B-241.
Bennit, Jehial & Mary Craine. 22 Dec. 1844. MA, R, B-71.
Bennitt, Hosea & Hannah Baldwin. 9 July 1822. MA, R, A-68.
Bensinger, Ferdinand & Eleanor Musser. 18 Aug. 1840. MA, R, B-10.
Bensinger, Frederick & Magdalina Jaiky (?). 27 July 1855. MA.
Benson, James & Delila Posten. 16 Jan. 1840. R, B-2.
Bentinck, Count William Frederick & Wilhelmina Sarah Gerdes
    (Giddis). 4 Oct. 1833. MA, R, A-183.
Bentley, George & Jane Allen. 14 Dec. 1848. MA, R, B-135.
Bentley, John H. & Elizabeth A. Davis. 11 Dec. 1848. R, B-135.
Bentley, Morrison A. & Elizabeth H. Davis. 14 Feb. 1856. R, D-26.
Benton, Anthony G. & Elizabeth Kittle. 14 Jan. 1847. MA, R,
    B-100.
Benton, Simon A. & Margaret Grow. 30 Apr. 1846. R, B-88.
Beormeister (Poormaster), Heinrich & Hannah K. Catsemire. 28 Apr.
    1853. MA.
Berdinc, John T. & Mary Roach. 12 Feb. 1850. MA, R, B-171.
Berg, Alois & Ludivica Hiltz. 21 July 1858. MA, R, D-87.
Beringer, William & Rosanne Winet. 1 Feb. 1857. R, D-61.
Bernd, Louis & Mary Elsiser. 7 July 1857. R, D-65.
Berndt, Daniel & Mary Benesser. 26 Aug. 1858. MA, R, D-81.
Berriman, Thomas & Sally Vannort. 12 Apr. 1807. R, A-285.
Berry, James & Mary Ann Reynolds. 26 Feb. 1836. R, A-208, A-229.
Berry, James & Catharine Rowley. 7 May 1845. MA, R, B-71.
Berry, John & Elizabeth Glaze. Her brother Andrew Glaze att. her
    age over 18. 28 June 1812. MA, R, A-321.
Berry, Jonathan & Hester Thoreman. 22 Nov. 1848. R, B-136.
Berry, Jonathan & Jerusha Henshaw. 29 July 1841. MA, R, B-21.
Bertram, Henry & Amelia Shuter. 20 Jan. 1844. MA.
Bertram, Henry Christian & Mary Lattermann. 8 Jan. 1855. MA, R,
    D-13.
Bertrand, Henry & Mary Sharp (Sherer). 13 Jan. 1848. MA, R,
    B-114, B-119.
Bertrand, John B. & Mary Hard. 29 Dec. 1835. MA, R, A-211.
Bertrand, William & Elizabeth Pettit. 1 Jan. 1846. MA, R, B-82.
Besco, John Lutor & Philipina Nail. 11 Dec. 1853. D-4.
Bescoe, Quincy & Catherine Nagel. 18 Jan. 1860. MA, R, D-108.
Besenbeck, Johan & Margaret Metz. 8 Sep. 1845. MA.
Beson (Leeson), Michael & Mary Leonard. 29 July 1852. MA, B-251.
Bess, John & Elizabeth Gillenwater. 21 May 1848. MA, R, B-127.
Best, Valentine & Mahetabel Bennett. 13 Oct. 1836. MA, R, A-223.
Bets, John & Malinda C. Masters. Her mother Sally Dole, of
    French Grant, cons., witn. Franz Kerr, Abraham Bets. 27 Oct.
    1859. MA, R, D-109.
Bettis, William & Catharine Young. 21 Jan. 1858. R, D-72.
Beverly, Herod & Amanda Keys. 19 Feb. 1853. MA, B-279.
Bevers, Thomas & Sarey Hickman. 17 Apr. 1804. R, A-1.
Beyer, John & Sarah Sheppart. 17 Sep. 1849. R, B-157.
Beyerly, George F. & Phillipina Hobstater. 26 May 1849. MA,
    B-244.
Bibbey, Abraham & Elizabeth Walker. 6 Jan. 1853. MA, B-256.
Bibbey, Isaac & Sarah Storer. 11 Mar. 1830. R, A-142.
Bibby, Abraham & Sarah Hutton. 30 Oct. 1823. R, A-78.
Bick (Bieck), Frederick & Catherine Sinn. 13 Apr. 1852. MA,
    B-237.
Biehlman, Kolaman & Catherine Haubert. C-2 shows he is 28, born
    Ireland, res. Portsmouth; she is 24, born Ireland, res. Ports-
    mouth. C-1 shows he is John Billman, 21, born Germany, son of
    K. & Agatha; she is 18, born Buffalo, N.Y., dau. of Nickolas
    & Anna, both res. Portsmouth. 1 June 1856. R, C-1, C-2, D-49.
Bieler, Georg & Laura Piesons. C-7 shows he is George Beeler, 24,
    born Germany, son of George; she is Eleanor Resons, 20, born
    Germany, dau. of Adam. 8 Dec. 1856. R, C-7, D-60.

SCIOTO COUNTY MARRIAGES

Biggs, Anthony & Christriam Ross. 2 June 1836. R, A-215, A-232.
Biggs, Daniel & Louisa Hickimbottom. 5 July 1858. MA.
Biggs, William W. & Capy Carroll. 9 May 1847. MA, R, B-105.
Bigley, Jonathan & Eveline J. Griffin. 5 July 1840. MA, R, B-9.
Bigly, Thomas & Eliza Jane Armstrong. D.W. Murphy att. ages.
    22 Nov. 1853. MA, D-4.
Bihlman, Joseph & Wilhelmina Baker. 5 Apr. 1858. MA, R, D-72.
Billian, George & Margaret Lehman. 24 Nov. 1859. MA, R, D-106.
Bilton, William H. & Matilda Dobbs. 19 May 1856, by E.P. Pratt.
    R.
Bingham, N. & Caroline Manny. He is 32, born New York, res.
    Cleveland, son of Simeon. She res. Cleveland, dau. of J.
    Nov. 1856. C-6.
Bishop, Jacob & Rebecca Windle. 23 Mar. 1848. MA, R, B-120.
Bishop, Lewis & Agnes Whistler. 23 Mar. 1846. MA, B-242.
Bishop, Stephen D. & Serena Kidd Lalendorf. 5 May 1860. MA, R,
    D-117.
Bishop, William & Keziah Zull. 9 Mar. 1856 by E.P. Pratt. R.
Bissett (Bassete), Alexander & Ann Mickey. 1 Mar. 1805. R, A-4.
Bivins (Bevins), John & Matilda Barton. 25 Nov. 1814. MA, R,
    A-346.
Black, John & Charlotte Wilcoxon. 23 Dec. 1832. R, A-171.
Black, Joseph D. & Mary Jane Thomas. 8 Oct. 1848. MA, R, B-133.
Blackburn, Jeremiah & Sylvia Kellogg. 1 Aug. 1833. R, A-179.
Blackburn, Thomas & Caroline Scott. 11 Aug. 1853. B-267.
Blackford, Joseph & Sarah Courtney. 30 Jan. 1855. MA, R, D-15.
Blagg, Adam & Liza (Louisa) Perry. Her father Samuel Perry cons.
    5 Aug. 1852. MA, B-242.
Blagg, John & Sarah Ann Bradshaw. Her father Isaac Bradshaw
    cons., witn. A. Jackson McFann, Hezekiah Reese. 29 Mar. 1845.
    MA, R, B-72.
Blagg, William & Mary Jane Cunningham. 6 May 1847. MA, R, B-104.
Blair, Jesse & Joanna Smedley. 18 July 1841. R, B-22.
Blair, John H. & Eliza Gorsute. 15 May 1852. B-257.
Blair, Joseph W. & Harriet Cole. 10 Feb. 1859. MA, R, D-87.
Blair, W.H. & Sarah Craycraft. 14 July 1856. R, D-41.
Blake, John & Charlotte Swabia. 15 Feb. 1860. MA, R, D-112.
Blakeman, Andrew J. & Mary J. Plumb. He is 23, born Kentucky,
    res. Madison Tp., son of Moses. She is 19, born Scioto Co.,
    res. Madison Tp., dau. of John Plum. 12 Nov. 1857. R, C-12,
    D-66.
Blankenship, Daniel J. & Mary Barber. Her father Samuel Barber
    cons., att. James Barber. 20 Jan. 1842. MA, R, B-36.
Blankenship, Ezekial & Mary Briggs (Biggs). 8 Mar. 1841 by
    Isaac Fullerton. MA, R.
Blankenship, Moses & Harriet Squires. 20 May 1859. MA, R, D-92.
Blankinship, John & Sarah White. 20 Nov. 1851. MA, B-225.
Blentlinger, James & Sarah Jane Burris. 11 Apr. 1844. MA, R,
    B-57.
Blentlinger, John & Margaret A. McCall. 6 Aug. 1845. MA, R, B-75.
Blessnig, John R. & Lucinda A. Shope. 29 Apr. 1850. R, B-179.
Bliss, Benjamin F. & Hannah Brown. 25 Feb. 1842. R, B-45.
Bliss, Charles & Josephine Williamson. 9 Oct. 1848. MA, R, B-132.
Bliss, George W. & Priscilla C. Poters (Peters). 22 Feb. 1842.
    MA, R, B-28.
Bliss, John & Manarcissa (Narissa) M.R. Turner. Jonathan Bliss
    cons. 2 Oct. 1823. MA, R, A-82.
Bliss, Jonathan & Anna Ellis. 25 Jan. 1829. R, A-129.
Bliss, Stephen & Rebecky Karr. 27 Jan. 1834. MA, R, A-185.
Bliss, Theodore & Nancy Dean. 19 May 1822. R, A-66.
Bliss, Theodore & Mary P. Flower. 1 May 1837. R, A-244.
Blobaum, William & Elizabeth Banker. 2 Nov. 1844. MA, R, B-64.
Blythe, Thomas & Eunice Chaffin. 9 Sep. 1814. MA, R, A-341.

11

Boardinghouse, Josiah & Elizabeth Young. 10 Oct. 1838. MA, R, A-261.
Bobst, Johann & Harriet Freidenmacher. 19 Mar. 1859. MA, R, D-90.
Bode (Kode?), John H. & Ann M. Slaver. 27 Apr. 1848. MA, R, B-122.
Bodmer, Jakob & Catharena Troxler. 11 Nov. 1854. MA.
Boetsch (Baze, Bayse, Bage), Joseph & Margarita Luther. 6 Jan. 1848. MA, R, B-112, B-117.
Bogert, George & Jane Cottrell (Cottel). 31 Aug. 1823. MA, R, A-76.
Boggs, Annesly W. & Cornelia Chaffin. His father Samuel Boggs att. ages. 3 Feb. 1847. MA, R, B-100.
Boggs, Anthony P. & Sobina McNamer. 25 Nov. 1849. MA, R, B-162.
Boggs, James W. & Nancy Arthur. 18 June 1840. MA, R, B-11.
Boggs, John & Martha Taylor. 25 Sep. 1856. R, D-36.
Boggs, Milton & Mary Lauderback. 24 Apr. 1840. MA, R, B-11.
Boggs, Samuel & Juliann Woods. 5 Jan. 1845. R, B-66.
Bohm, Casper & Lena Andress. 4 Aug. 1859. MA, R, D-109.
Boidston, Joshua & Winney ___. 10 Apr. 1806. R, A-11, A-279.
Bolan, Thomas & Susannah Maria Dusing. 9 Nov. 1845. MA.
Boldman (Baldman), Elijah & Ellendor Holt. 15 Mar. 1849. MA, R, B-145.
Boldman, Frederick & Phebe Hodges. 30 Aug. 1834. MA, R, A-190.
Boldman, James & Sarah Jane Holt. 30 Nov. 1849. MA, R, B-163.
Boldman, John & Julia Ann Holt. "Father of girl present and gave consent." 24 Dec. 1847. MA, R, B-114, B-118.
Boldman, John & Mary Jane Shively. He is 26, born Adams Co., son of Peter & C. She is 19, born Adams Co., dau. of John & Jane. 23 Apr. 1857. R, C-13, D-53.
Bolds (Rowls), George & Lucy Canary, of Jackson Furnace. 24 Dec. 1846 by William Howell, M.G. MA, R.
Bolen, Alexander & Lydia Fout. 18 May 1837. MA, R, A-242.
Bolen, Henry & Anna Thompson. 3 Oct. 1840. MA, R, B-8.
Boll (Ball), Frank X. & Dainer Stroble (Walertine Strabel). 3 Aug. 1852. MA, B-251.
Bollinger, Jacob & Francis Beinger (Beelenger). 9 Mar. 1855. MA, R, D-16.
Bollman, John & Josephine Besecon. 16 Apr. 1846. MA.
Boltz, Hartman & Mary Betz. 21 Jan. 1841. MA, R, B-14.
Boltz, Hartman & Catherine Belz. 17 May 1850. MA.
Boltz, William & Elizabeth Hosted (Hasted). 4 Sep. 1848. MA, B-244.
Bondenet, Tobias & Susan Smith. 15 July 1852. MA, B-240.
Bondraunt, Benton P. & Lydia Mead. V.L. Kent att. ages. 8 Apr. 1860. MA, R, D-114.
Bondurant, Joel & Lucy Jane Lyons. 22 Aug. 1858. MA, R, D-86.
Bonser, Isaac & Nancy Maria Huddleston. 11 Jan. 1857. R, D-45.
Bonser, Isaac Jr. & Mahittabel Burt, of Porter Tp. Her father Benjamin Burt, Esq. cons. 1 May 1817. MA, R, A-29.
Bonser, Jacob & Catharine Wolford. 4 Feb. 1830. R, A-138.
Bonser, John & Rebecca Halsted. 22 Mar. 1827. R, A-104.
Bonser, Joseph & Rebecca Patten. 27 Jan. 1820. R, A-51.
Bonser, Samuel & Hannah Mead. 5 Aug. 1819. MA, R, A-46.
Bonser, Uriah & Aveline A. Venhon (Avenhon). 13 Aug. 1829. R, A-134.
Bonser, Uriah & Sarah Annas Coriell. 18 July 1841. R, B-21.
Bonum, Benjamin R. & Leah Shelton. 10 Jan. 1850. R, B-173.
Bonzo, Joseph & Mary Wilson. 30 Nov. 1854. MA, R, D-12.
Booth, David & Rebecca Lantz. 21 Dec. 1845. MA, R, B-82.
Booth, James & Isabella Harmon. 3 July 1853. B-270.
Booth, Levi & Levora Laforgey. 1 Sep. 1860. MA, R, D-170.
Boothe, Valentine & Mary Eppenhimer. Her father Samuel Eppenhimer cons., witn. Samuel Applegate. 30 Aug. 1841. MA.

Border, Daniel & Sarah Ellen Thompson. He res. Columbus, Oh.,
     she res. Portsmouth, her second marriage. 29 Dec. 1856.
     C-3, D-45.
Boren, Jas. & Mary Kittles. He is 25, born Beaver Co., Pa., res.
     Bloom Tp., son of Stephen & Elizabeth. She is 22, born Scioto
     Co., res. Vernon Tp., dau. of W. & L. 14 May 1857. C-12.
Boren, John S. & An E. Kittle. 14 May 1857. D-57.
Born, Victor & Hannah W. Hamlibb. 15 June 1855. R, D-18.
Born, Wolfgang & Magdalena Beeler. 19 Aug. 1857. R, D-61.
Borum, John J. & Sarah J. Ward. 25 Nov. 1852. MA, B-251.
Bosman, Jan (Busmer, John) & Mary Ann Gonkler. 22 Mar. 1849.
     MA, R, B-143.
Bostwick, Thomas & Ellenor Campbell. 2 May 1833, by Benjamin
     Feurt. MA, R.
Bosworth, Marcus & Sarah Dole. 22 Feb. 1821. MA, R, A-59.
Both (Roth), John & Catharine Hartman. 24 July 1848. MA, R,
     B-128.
Botkin, James & Mary Frances Cockerell. 14 Nov. 1824. MA, R,
     A-84.
Bouker (Beoker, Baker), Henry & Louisa Pelhank. 29 Dec. 1851.
     MA, B-205.
Boultenhous, Daniel & Suanah Graves. 7 Mar. 1805. R, A-8.
Bourshaw (Bershaw), Victor & Josephine Livery. 16 Oct. 1856.
     MA, R, D-38.
Bousawine, Nicholas & Catherena Laneharten. Not dated, filed
     with 1853. MA.
Bowen, John & Rachel Feurt, of Green Tp. 2 Feb. 1815. R, A-346.
Bowen, John & Mary L. Nichols. 19 Mar. 1857. R, D-170.
Bowen, Thomas & Katharine Higgins. 15 Nov. 1825. MA, R, A-94.
Bowen, William & Susanah Triggs. 29 Jan. 1815. MA, R, A-344.
Bower, Henry & Elizabethe Bennett. 1 Sep. 1825. R, A-91.
Bower, Ludwig & Elizabeth Cook Mueller. 31 Jan. 1860. MA, R,
     D-112. [The name Cook is crossed through on the return.]
Bower, Peter & Mary Schwitzeren. 11 June 1859. MA.
Bower (Bowen), Philip & Charlotte C. Hickle. 12 Nov. 1845. MA,
     R, B-79.
Bower, William & Caroline Miller. Her pars. Friedrich & Louisa
     Miller (Muller) cons., witn. George Crawford. 25 Sep. 1859.
     MA, R, D-103.
Bowers, George & Mary Dever. 31 July 1823. R, A-76.
Bowman, Aaron & Melissa Squires. 4 Feb. 1847. MA, R, B-99.
Bowman, James & Elizabeth Mollies (Mullins). Foster Mullins att.
     his sister is over 18. 15 Nov. 1834. MA, R, A-199.
Bowman, John & Mahala Squires. Aaron Bowman att. ages. 13 Oct.
     1852. MA.
Bowman (Beuman), Lewis & Lucey Patten. 5 Nov. 1856. R, D-39.
Bowman, Lewis W. & Matilda Worley. 23 July 1834. MA, R, A-190.
Bowman, Runion & Catherine Hatfield. 16 June 1847. MA, R, B-103.
Boyce, Frederick & Mahala Ross. Joseph Ashton att. ages. 2 Apr.
     1860. MA, R, D-114.
Boyce, Richard & Lucinda Munnell. 2 July 1853. B-263.
Boyd, Jonathan & Levina Boyd. His pars. Jonathan & Elizabeth
     cons. 18 Mar. 1834. MA, R, A-193.
Boydston, John & Abigail Shupe. 13 Sep. 1855. MA, R, D-20.
Boyer, Alexander & Hannah K. Stockham. 10 Jan. 1844. MA, R, B-52.
Boyer, Alfred & Temperance Purdy. 11 Apr. 1856. R, D-28.
Boyer, Charles W. & Elizabeth McNelly. 20 Jan. 1850. R, B-142.
Boyer, Noah & Eliza Jane Shafer. 1 Jan. 1846. MA, R, B-84.
Boyle, Henry & Malvina Coryell. 26 Sep. 1852. MA, B-247.
Boyle, Henry & Harriet McCoy. Her father James McCoy cons., att.
     Pearson McCoy. 3 Mar. 1839. MA, R, A-266.
Boynton, Asa & Julia Bertrand. Her father John St. Bertrand, of
     French Grant, cons. 20 Dec. 1828. MA.

13

Boynton, Asa & Madalin Cadot. 1 Jan. 1855, by S.T. Cummins, M.G.
   MA, R.
Boynton, Charles & Rhoda Sumner, both of Upper Tp. 3 Mar. 1814.
   R, A-332.
Boynton, John & Eliza A. Copenhaver. 26 Mar. 1857. R, D-52.
Boynton, John L. & Felicity Bertrand. 23 Feb. 1837. R, A-240.
Boynton, Joseph E.J. & Elizabeth Wheeler. Portius Wheeler att.
   her age over 18. 16 Jan. 1813. MA, R, A-329.
Boynton, Peter F. & Eliza Jane Cadot. 10 Jan. 1848. MA, R, B-115.
Boynton, Sumner & Elisabeth Flanders. 12 Sep. 1855. D-21.
Boynton, William & Ann Vandervort. 24 Feb. 1856. R, D-26.
Boynton, William L. & Nancy Feurt. Benjamin Locke att. his age.
   Her father Peter Feurtt cons. 1 Jan. 1822. MA, R, A-63.
Bozer (Boyer), Thomas D. & Hannah Bliss. 4 Aug. 1855. R, D-19.
Bracy, James W. & Mary A. Field. 22 Mar. 1855. R, D-16.
Bracy, N.P. & Phebe C. Fields. 27 Mar. 1855. R, D-16.
Bradburn, Ignatius & Catharine Degare. 11 July 1838. MA, R, A-256.
Bradburn, Michael & Elizabeth Alexander. Mark Bradburn att. ages.
   21 Aug. 1844. MA.
Bradburn, Notingham & Rebecca Basham. 4 Mar. 1841. R, B-16.
Bradford, Abel & Rachel Sylva. 22 Apr. 1824. R, A-81.
Bradford, C.F. & Ann Thompson. 27 Aug. 1857. R, D-59.
Bradford, Cornelius F. & Emily Moore. 11 Dec. 1839. R, A-277.
Bradford, Littleton & Abbe Sampson. 13 Nov. 1817. R, A-31.
Bradford, Samuel C. & Louise Wilcoxan. 6 Oct. 1831. MA, R, A-156.
Bradford, Wesley & Rosanna P. Dewey. 3 Apr. 1851. B-217.
Bradley, William & Sarah Brown. 15 Jan. 1857. R, D-46.
Bradshaw, George & Jane Gilkison. 21 Mar. 1805. R, A-4, A-278.
Bradshaw, George Washington & Malinda Miller. Her father Thomas
   T. Miller cons. 19 Apr. 1853. (D-14 shows 1854.) MA, R, D-14.
Bradshaw, Harvey & Frances Salter. 18 Mar. 1841. R, B-18.
Bradshaw, Henderson & Anna C. Brock. 14 Oct. 1834. R, A-192.
Bradshaw, Henderson & Permina Minard. 11 Dec. 1838. MA, R, A-274.
Bradshaw, Hiram & Elizabeth Cunningham. His father Isaac Brad-
   shaw, and her mother Nancy Bradshaw cons., witn. Thomas Katon,
   Robert Bradshaw. 27 June 1843. MA, R, B-47.
Bradshaw, Isaac & Nancy Cunningham. 27 Dec. 1840. MA, R, B-15.
Bradshaw, Isaac & Nancy Saladay. 1 Mar. 1812. R, A-316.
Bradshaw, Isaac & Anna Windle. William Munyan att. ages. 16 Mar.
   1848. MA, R, B-120.
Bradshaw, James & Cecelia Huffman. 3 Jan. 1860. MA, R, D-103.
Bradshaw, James & Sally Babcock. 18 Oct. 1827. MA, R, A-113.
Bradshaw, Levi & Hannah Wishon. 12 May 1859. MA, R, D-92.
Bradshaw, Robert & Susannah Baccus. 5 Sep. 1811. MA, R, A-314.
Bradshaw, William & Elliner Rardon. 18 Mar. 1809. R, A-293.
Brady, David & Sarah Ann Bebee. 2 Oct. 1850. MA, R, B-189.
Brady, Levi & Emily Enslow. Her father David Enslow cons., witn.
   Samuel J. McCloud. 14 July 1825. MA, R, A-90.
Brady, Levi & Adeline Scofield. 29 Sep. 1853. B-269.
Brady, Samuel & Mariah Watterhouse. 10 Apr. 1817. MA, R, A-28.
Brady, William P. & Nancy Grinder. 22 Sep. 1851. MA, B-223.
Brafford, William & Mary Ann Mallen. 14 Feb. 1837. MA.
Brainard, H.W. & Marintha Chatfield. 11 Dec. 1844. MA, R, B-66.
Brainard, H.W. & Mahala Sharp. 12 Nov. 1848. MA, R, B-135.
Brainard, John & Elizabeth Downing. 25 Nov. 1850. MA.
Brainard, John & Sarah Steece. 15 Oct. 1854. R, D-11.
Bramble, William & Mary Kregg. 3 Oct. 1860. MA, R, D-125.
Brame, John & Harriet Baker. 4 Oct. 1860. MA, R, D-127.
Brammer (Brown), Corbley M. & Elizabeth Robinson. 3 Feb. 1853.
   MA, B-279.
Branch, A.G. & Abigail McCown. 21 Sep. 1849. MA, R, B-157.
Branch, Orange & Mary Myers. 13 Sep. 1846. MA, R, B-91.

Branch, William & Mary White. 18 Apr. 1844. MA, R, B-58.
Brand, Adam & Mary Maseh (Marsh). 2 Apr. 1856. R, D-28.
Brand, Harman & Eliza Gehouht. 10 July 1856. R, D-33.
Branham, Isom & Emeline McCleary. 22 Sep. 1858. MA.
Brannin (Bramen), John A. & Elizabeth Allen. 8 Oct. 1840. MA, R,
    B-12.
Brant, Christian & Ellen Crull. 29 May 1846. MA.
Brant, Daniel & Rachel Roberts. 28 Feb. 1845. MA, R, B-69.
Brant, John & Elizabeth Adwell. 27 Dec. 1841. R, B-13.
Brant, Joseph & Susanah Willson. 14 July 1842. MA, R, B-33.
Brant, Joseph & Mary Vannort. 25 Dec. 1835. MA, R, A-212, A-227.
Bratt, James & Harriet Hunter. He is 28, born France, res. Ports-
    mouth, son of John & Harriet. She is 28, born France, res.
    Portsmouth, second marriage, dau. of Morris & Phoebe Bratt.
    4 Oct. 1857. C-8.
Brayman, Jared & Margaret Wayley. 23 Nov. 1839. MA.
Breier, Charles & Hannah T. Merker. 24 Sep. 1857. R, D-62.
Brewer, Amaziah & Any Winneford Smith. Of Washington Tp. 23 Dec.
    1824, by Reuben Wait, J.P. MA, R.
Brewer, Jacob & Mary Rinely. 29 Oct. 1807. R, A-287.
Brewer (Bruer), Stephen & Lucinda Boyer (Bowyer). 2 Aug. 1807.
    R, A-286.
Brewer, William & Malvina Burt. 23 Jan. 1847. MA, R, B-98.
Brian, John & Adaline Edwards. 25 Aug. 1836. MA, R, A-225.
Briarfield (Penfield), John & Carline Baldridg. 21 Mar. 1856.
    R, D-26.
Bridges, James & Sarah Tyson. 10 Apr. 1819. MA, R, A-46.
Bridwell, David & Sarah Hamilton. 5 Apr. 1845. MA, R, B-71.
Bridwell (Breadwell), William & Easter Ann Harmon. 17 Oct. 1858.
    MA, R, D-92.
Briggs, Albert & Mary Roberts. 10 May 1849. MA, R, B-151.
Briggs, Anthony & Cynthia Turner. 2 Jan. 1834. R, A-184.
Briggs, Henry & Ann E. Noel. He is son of Samuel, she is dau. of
    Aman (?). Both born & res. Scioto Co. 24 Feb. 1857. R, C-1,
    D-52.
Briggs, Horace & Sally Wood. 4 Aug. 1825. MA, R, A-91.
Briggs, John K. & Mary Miller. 2 Jan. 1850. R, B-171.
Briggs, John Y. & Sarah Ann Eliza Quintner. 25 Oct. 1835. MA, R,
    A-206.
Briggs, Orrin & Elizabeth Squires. 24 Jan. 1827. R, A-103.
Briggs, Samuel C. & Rebecca Timbrook. 29 Dec. 1825. R, A-94.
Briggs, Samuel C. & Elizabeth Smith. 1 July 1824. R, A-83.
Briggs, Samuel C. & Sarah Barber. 27 Oct. 1842. R, B-45.
Briggs, Samuel C. & Marinda Barber. 20 Dec. 1843. R, B-51.
Briggs, Thomas G. & Adaline Spalding. 28 Nov. 1830. R, A-149.
Briggs, William & Mary M. Orms. She is within 2 months of 18,
    and her guardian has no objections. 25 Dec. 1851. MA, B-232.
Bright, Bazzel P. & Louisa Priest. 1 Aug. 1822. MA, R, A-68.
Brine (Brince?), H. & Phillipine Ranshaw. 13 Aug. 1856. MA.
Bring, John & Catharine Doonsberger. 20 Dec. 1856. R, D-47.
Bringham, Levi & Mandana Burton. Her father James Burton cons.
    5 Aug. 1858. MA, R, D-94.
Brisendine, John & Bula Grubb. 9 June 1833, by Benjamin Feurt,
    J.P. MA, R.
Brock, George & Sarah Graves (Grover?). 29 Dec. 1829. R, A-140.
Brock, James & Elizabeth Caster. His father Thomas Brock cons.,
    att. Aaron Hollingshead. 2 Sep. 1852. MA, B-250.
Brock, Sheridan & Sally Shoemaker. His father George Brock cons.,
    witn. Joseph Faverty, Allin Brock. 19 Feb. 1826. MA, R, A-95.
Brock, Sylvester G. & Sarah Pool. 6 Nov. 1845. MA, R, B-79.
Brock, Thomas & Abigail Mead. Ezra Mead att. her age over 18.
    12 June 1849. MA, R, B-151.

Brock, Wilkison & Margaret Sutterfield. George Brock cons., witn.
Reuben Bonner, Emline Saladay, Aaron Honel. 4 July 1837. MA,
R, A-245.
Brockman, Asa & Mary Jane Cushing. 24 Nov. 1841. MA, R, B-20.
Brodbeck, Peter & Eleonora Legler. 10 Oct. 1842. MA, R, B-35.
Brodbeck, Stephen & Rosa Legler. 21 Jan. 1840. R, A-278.
Brodbeck, Vincent & Matilda Maze (Mus, Mews). 29 Nov. 1838. MA,
R, A-263.
Brom, John & Elizabeth Mentel. 16 Sep. 1844. MA, R, B-62.
Brooker, Ambrose & Mary Rider. 9 Nov. 1856. R, D-57.
Brooker, Charles & Emily Dulcina Shoemaker. Her pars. (not named)
cons., att. Abigail Shoemaker. 12 Apr. 1852. MA, B-238.
Brooker, Frederick & Hannah Wills. His father Jacob Brooker cons.
22 Oct. 1853. MA.
Brooker, Jacob & Jane H. Crull. 3 Jan. 1850. R, B-166.
Brooks, James & Susan Powell. 2 Dec. 1841. MA, R, B-26.
Brooks, Jancy & Mary Hall. James Brooks cons. 11 Feb. 1850. MA.
Brooks, John & Liza Jane Scurvin. His father James Brooks cons.
24 Aug. 1852. MA.
Brooks, Samuel & Elizabeth Simonton. 30 Apr. 1842. MA.
Brooks, Samuel & Elizabeth Payton. 20 May 1845. MA, R, B-74.
Brooks, W.C. & Eliza A. Hutton. 31 Dec. 1857. R, D-66.
Broom, Edward & Susannah Baker. Of Upper Tp. 19 Mar. 1809. R,
A-296.
Brophy, Daniel & Lidia Leduke. 31 Dec. 1852. MA, B-254.
Brouse, Andrew & Angeline Parr. He is 30, born & res. Scioto Co.,
son of Andrew & Hannah. She is 22, born Washington Co., Oh.,
res. Scioto Co., dau. of Isaac & Ruth. 24 Feb. 1858. R, C-9,
C-13, D-71.
Brouse, Samuel & Louisa McCall. 13 Jan. 1848. R, B-113, B-118.
Brown, Aaron & Catherine Yingling. 29 Mar. 1808. R, A-288.
Brown, Benjamin Y. & Rebecca Turner. 8 July 1852. MA, B-240.
Brown, Charlton & Rhody Bonser. 15 Nov. 1840. R, B-18.
Brown, Christopher & Betsy Blind. 16 Jan. 1854. D-7.
Brown, Daniel & Nancy Smith. 2 Jan. 1848. MA, R, B-115, B-120.
Brown, David & Jerusha Gifford. 18 Apr. 1846. MA.
Brown, David & Martha Mark. 29 Dec. 1845. MA.
Brown, David & Lavina Pool. 1 Jan. 1834. MA, R, A-187 (says 1839).
Brown, David & Eleanor LeForge. 1 May 1817. MA, R, A-27.
Brown, David A. & Lucinda D. Cockrell. 16 Dec. 1830. R, A-150.
Brown, David J. & Catherine Ray. He is 20, born & res. Pike Co.,
son of John H. She is 15, born Pike Co., res. Madison Tp.,
dau. of Thomas. His father J. H. Brown cons., att. to cons.
of her guardian (not named). 4 Mar. 1858. MA, R, C-11, D-74.
Brown, Eli & Rachel Howard. 30 May 1822. MA, R, A-67.
Brown, Franklin & Rebecca Rickey, both of Madison Tp. Her father
cons. 30 Jan. 1838. MA, R, A-248.
Brown, George & Anna Higgins. 14 June 1808. R, A-291.
Brown, George W. & Narrissa L. Wheeler. 24 Nov. 1853. MA, D-3.
Brown, Hiram P. & Harriet Dewey. 15 May 1848. MA, R, B-123.
Brown, Hugh & Nancy Shope. 3 Jan. 1850. R, B-167.
Brown, James & Catherine Sidnor. 24 Aug. 1837. MA, R, A-237.
Brown, James & Patsey Cross (McIntire). Sally McIntire att. her
age over 18. 10 Dec. 1818. MA, R, A-43.
Brown, James & Elizabeth Smith. 3 Sep. 1853. MA, B-271.
Brown, James & Mary Tindall. 8 June 1834. MA, R, A-189.
Brown, John & Rebecca Corray (Carney). 1 July 1828. R, A-121.
Brown, John & Susannah Melson. 27 Aug. 1820. MA, R, A-54.
Brown, John & Catharine Bradburn. 11 Sep. 1843. MA, R, B-48.
Brown, John & Mary Caster. 9 Jan. 1857. D-46.
Brown, John & Nancy Montgomery. 21 Sep. 1858. MA, R, D-79.
Brown, John F. & Mary Belote. 28 July 1831. MA, R, A-157.

Brown, John J. & Amelia Nurse. His father John Brown, of Portsmouth, cons. 1 May 1838. MA, R, A-254.

Brown, Joseph & Elizabeth Smith. 1 Mar. 1849. MA, R, B-146.

Brown, Joseph & Phebe McKinney. 4 Nov. 1846. MA.

Brown, Joseph & Eda Riley. 20 Jan. 1848. MA, R, B-115, B-119.

Brown, Joseph & Louisa Wadkins. 3 Mar. 1858. MA, R, D-70.

Brown, Lewis & Mary Magden Roseborne (Rosehome). 5 Dec. 1854. MA, R, D-12.

Brown, Malen & Mary D. Feurt. Gabriel Feurt cons. 1 May 1838. MA, R, A-254.

Brown, Milton W. & Sarah Wood. He is 21, born Pike Co., res. Pike Co., son of Royal. She is 19, born Adams Co., res. Scioto Co., dau. of Simeon. Royal Brown cons. 21 Aug. 1856. MA, R, C-5, D-32.

Brown, Nathaniel & Diana Wilson. Benjamin Rockwell att. ages. 31 Dec. 1851, by H. Mead, J.P. MA, R.

Brown, Peter & Sarah (Sally) Cole. 18 June 1817. MA, R, A-28.

Brown, Peter H. & Lydia Beloat. 30 Apr. 1843. R, B-44.

Brown, Ransom & Sarah Richards. 24 Dec. 1829. R, A-141.

Brown, Ransom S. & Martha Kirk. 16 Oct. 1855. MA.

Brown, Samuel S. & Fanny Walls (Watts). Her father Levi Walls cons., witn. Thomas Walls, Lemuel Walls. 21 Dec. 1825. MA, R, A-87.

Brown, Samuel T. & Sally Young. 26 Mar. 1845. MA, R, B-71.

Brown, Sardine & Harriet M. Gibbons. 18 Jan. 1854. D-7.

Brown, Stephen & Malissa Holmes. 5 July 1857. R, D-55.

Brown, Thomas & Rhody Howard. 9 Apr. 1818. R, A-38.

Brown, Thomas & Mary Daniels. 28 Mar. 1837. MA, R, A-239.

Brown, Thomas H. & Mary Webber. 25 July 1822. R, A-69.

Brown, Thornton & Scioto Shoush. 23 Aug. 1849. MA, R, B-155.

Brown, William & Ann Melson. Her father Jesse Melson cons., witn. Samuel Brown, Joseph Melson. His mother Nancy Brown cons., witn. John Brown. 7 Oct. 1824. MA, R, A-84.

Brown, William & Sarah Ann Sidney. 1 Nov. 1843. MA.

Brown, William & Frances Coriell. 13 Sep. 1840. MA, R, B-13.

Brownlee, Walter & Harriet Elizabeth Guy. 7 Sep. 1855. B-286.

Bruce (Brice? Bruer?), John & Margey Ferguson. John Ferguson att. her age over 18. 19 Mar. 1811. MA, R, A-309.

Bruce, Samuel M. & Cynthia Ann Hatfield. 29 Jan. 1848. MA, R, B-121.

Bruck, John & Mary Ann Huebner. His father Lewis Bruck (Brouck) cons., witn. Elijah Dubbard. Her father Moritz Huebner, of Meigs Co., cons., witn. George W. Gallup & David Dullenfoher (?). 6 June 1851. MA.

Bruffey, John & Maria Lawson. 6 Aug. 1835. A-204.

Bruner, Abram & Eliza Deaver (Devers). 26 Oct. 1843. MA, R, B-50.

Bruner, Owen & Udocius Brown. 3 Dec. 1845. R, B-83.

Bruner, Owen & Mary Overt. 10 July 1844. R, B-61.

Bruner, Rudolf & Barbara Bender. He is 28, born Switzerland, res. Portsmouth, son of Samuel & Mary Brunner. She is 17, born Germany, res. Portsmouth, dau. of Jacob & E. Bender. 15 Apr. 1856. C-1.

Bruner, William P. & Angelina Grubb. Abram Bruner att. ages. 8 Feb. 1846. MA, R, B-85.

Brunner, Frederick & Elizabeth Bruner (Lizzie Burns). He is 28, born Switzerland, son of H. She is 23, born Switzerland, dau. of S. Burns. 20 Feb. 1858. R, C-13, D-71.

Brunton, John & Rebecca Brown. 29 Dec. 1853. MA, D-4.

Brunton, Joseph & Margaret Bonser. 8 Oct. 1851. MA, B-224.

Brush, Benjamin & Ellen Butterfield. 14 Dec. 1846. MA, R, B-96.

Brush, Joseph & Mary Story. 21 Nov. 1844. MA, R, B-65.

Brust, William & Elizabeth Steinhour. 2 Mar. 1859. MA, R, D-90.

Bryan, Daniel & Nancy Winkler. 10 Mar. 1836. R, A-251.

17

Bryan, Moses & Elizabeth Roberts. 3 Mar. 1833. MA, R, A-174.
Bryan, Robert A. & Sarah E. Givens. William Givens Jr. att.
    ages. 23 Dec. 1860. MA, R, D-139.
Bryant, Harris & Matilda Iman. 5 Aug. 1846. MA, B-242.
Bryant, Jackson & Elizabeth Turner. 4 Oct. 1853. MA.
Bryson, Noah & Eleanor Vanbibber. Jacob Vanbibber, of Greenup,
    Ky. cons., witn. Jacob Vanbibber Jr. 25 Aug. 1830. MA, R,
    A-146.
Buchameyer, Enrich & Catherine Swable. 12 Aug. 1860. MA, R,
    D-128.
Buck, Elisha & Frances Kelly. 8 May 1838. MA, R, A-254.
Buck, Massie (?) & Mary Ann Beauchamp. His father John Buck
    cons., witn. Daniel Gooden. 1 Dec. 1824. MA.
Buckels, William & Nancy Collins. 25 Dec. 1817. R, A-32.
Buckles, John & Nancy Clark. 3 Mar. 1821. MA.
Buckley, Samuel & Cyntha Hall. 22 Dec. 1853. MA, D-4.
Buel, A.J. & Susan A. Davy. 2 Jan. 1851. MA, B-200.
Buk, George & Filina Locey. 10 Oct. 1854. R, D-10.
Bumgardner, Joseph & Sophia Dewit. 25 May 1854. D-1.
Bumgarner, Henry & Mary Cutlip. 15 Nov. 1858. MA, R, D-133.
Bunch, Joseph & Abigail Hood (Hoor). 20 Aug. 1853. MA, B-268.
Bunch, Joseph & Polly Wolf. 2 Nov. 1848. MA, R, B-140.
Bunzo, John & Nancy Swaim. 15 Mar. 1860. MA, R, D-117.
Bunzo, Peter L. & Mary A. Knowles. 22 Nov. 1860. MA, R, D-125.
Burch, Samuel & Rebecca Cooper. 8 Oct. 1845. MA, R, B-80.
Burch, Squier S. & Sarah Hall. 8 Jan. 1832. MA, R, A-160.
Burch, Thomas & Louiza Wilson. Smith Wilson att. ages. 12 Nov.
    1857. MA, R, D-65.
Burdick, Barney & Caroline Ashten. 4 July 1856. R, D-33.
Burgan, Charles & Peggy Morgan. 30 July 1840. R, B-10.
Buris (Burns?), Solomon & ___ Johnson. 2 June 1858, by D. W.
    Murphy, J.P. R.
Buriss, Mathew & Mary Bradford. 23 Mar. 1840. R, B-3.
Burk, Jacob & Rhoda Sheldon. 29 July 1843. MA.
Burk, John & Dorothy Songer. 26 July 1845. MA, R, B-78.
Burk, John & Catherine Stewart. 17 July 1815. MA, R, A-282.
Burk, John C. & Elizabeth E. Bennett. 18 Sep. 1854. B-284.
Burk, Lewis & Caroline Gibben. 17 July 1834. R, A-190.
Burk, Samuel & Mary Ann Griffith. Her father Frederick Griffith
    cons., witn. George W. Gardner, J.H. Chaffin. 3 Jan. 1833.
    MA, R, A-173.
Burk (Buck?), Thomas & Nancy Hunter. Her father's cons. is
    written in pencil, very faint, appears to be Andrew Hunter.
    28 Nov. 1822. MA, R, A-70.
Burk, Thomas & Mary Colbit. 2 Dec. 1859. MA, R, D-118.
Burk, William & Elizabeth Brooks. 24 Mar. 1860. MA, R, D-120.
Burke, Hugh & Margaret Livingston. 31 Aug. 1852. MA, B-277.
Burke, John S. & Lovina Barrett. 7 Aug. 1831. R, A-156.
Burke, O.H.P. & Elizabeth Ann Thompson. 11 June 1843. MA, R,
    B-46.
Burke, Patrick & Anne Coyne. 16 Aug. 1853. MA.
Burke, William & Jane Mead. 21 May 1853. MA, B-263.
Burkel, Valentin & Susanna Schlichter. 21 Jan. 1857. R, D-61.
Burkhard, Charles & Barbary Ilch. 8 May 1841. MA, R, B-26.
Burkhiver, Hanly (Bockhoofer, E. Henry) & Mary Duvendack. Adam
    Duvendack att. ages. 11 June 1853. MA, B-267.
Burner, David & Nancy Tyree (Lyra?). 15 Oct. 1846. MA, R, B-95.
Burner, George & Margaret Sheldon. 25 Aug. 1837. MA, R, A-237.
Burnett, Andrew H. & Hulda Rowley. 7 Feb. 1860. MA, R, D-128.
Burnett, Joel & Rachel Lucetta Taylor. He was born Scioto Co.
    She is 17, born Scioto Co., dau. of Jeremiah. J. Taylor
    cons. 21 Sep. 1856. MA, C-5, D-50.
Burnfield, George W. & Lucinda Storer. 19 June 1853. B-264.

Burns, Thomas & Polly Robison (Robinson). His father Andrew
Burns cons., witn. Jeremiah Armstrong. 14 May 1818. MA, R,
A-38.
Burns, William & Catharine Runhan. Paul Sutton att. ages. 7 Feb.
1852. MA.
Burress, Henry R. & Scienda Daniels. 18 July 1850. MA, R, B-185.
Burress, James Q. & Calphurnia Williams. 23 Nov. 1854. MA, R,
D-12.
Burriss, Joseph & Matilda Collier. 9 July 1860. MA, R, D-131.
Burriss, Nathan & Julia Right. 18 Aug. 1859. MA, R, D-100.
Burriss, William B. & Latitia Moore. 3 Mar. 1831. R, A-151.
Burroughs, Horatio & Nancy Worley. 25 Dec. 1828. R, A-125.
Burrows, Horatio & Lucy Murse. 23 Aug. 1860. MA, R, D-122.
Burt, Benjamin Jnr. & Elizabeth Swaar. Of Porter Tp. Her father
Jacob Swaar cons., att. her brother George Swaar. 29 May 1817.
MA, R, A-29.
Burt, Benjamin & Adeline Owens. 6 Nov. 1828. R, A-124.
Burt, Benjamin & Polly Crull. 2 Apr. 1840. R, B-9.
Burt, Benjamin W. & Sarah Jane Rice. 11 Aug. 1847. MA, R, B-105.
Burt, Brewer & Rachel Rockwell. Her father James Rockwell cons.,
witn. Ezra Rockwell. 26 Dec. 1822. MA, R, A-71.
Burt, Charles E. & Louisa Cook. 22 Apr. 1858. MA, R, D-73.
Burt, Christopher & Elizabeth Brittenham. 28 July 1810. R, A-302.
Burt, Eleaza & Catharine E. Loofborough. His third marriage, her
second marriage. 29 July 1856. R, C-3, D-35.
Burt, Erastus & Margaret McCuffrey. 1 Aug. 1857. R, D-64.
Burt, Isaac & Margaret Barber. 24 May 1827. MA, R, A-106.
Burt, James W. & Mary (Polly) Brady. 9 Aug. 1823. MA, R, A-76.
Burt, Joseph & Peggy Munn, of Madison Tp. 16 Jan. 1812. MA, R,
A-316.
Burt, Lemuel & Philosse Wait. 12 July 1822. R, A-69.
Burt, Munsell & Hannah Munn. His father Benjamin Burt cons.
James Munn Senr. cons., witn. Solomon Munn. 19 May 1818. MA.
Burt, Peter & Margaret Woodring. His mother Margaret Burt cons.,
said they are both 19 years old, the 19th of March next. 30
Dec. 1829. MA, R, A-141.
Burt, Samuel & Mary Jane Briggs. 21 Oct. 1847. MA, R, B-109.
Burt, Thomas & Cornelia Ann Bufington. 23 Apr. 1826. R, A-96.
Burt, Thomas J. & Esther Ratcliff (Ridiliff). 7 July 1848. MA,
B-244.
Burt, William & Rebecca Davis. 10 Mar. 1851. MA, B-203, B-204.
(B-204 shows her name Rebecca Burt, the date 18 Mar. 1851.)
Burt, William & Mary Boen. 15 July 1810. R, A-302.
Burton, John & Nancy Murphy. 15 Aug. 1816. MA, R, A-24.
Burton, John & Anna Boydston (Boilston). He res. Adams Co. Her
mother Sarah Cross cons., witn. Rezin Wilcoxon. 9 Jan. 1820.
MA, R, A-61.
Burton, Turpin R. & Catharine Ann Pollock. 3 July 1850. MA, R,
B-186.
Burwell, James & Mary Williamson. 6 Jan. 1840. MA, R, A-276.
Bush, George & Amanda Cooper. 8 July 1847. MA, R, B-103.
Bush, John & Amanda Howe. 8 Aug. 1850. MA, R, B-185.
Bush, Seth R. & Melissa Wait. 21 Mar. 1844. MA, R, B-58.
Busker, William & Maria Raynor. 14 Sep. 1859. MA, R, D-110.
Busly, Amas (Rusley, James) & Nansay Seth. 22 Oct. 1814. R,
A-343.
Bussey, Peter Jun. & Sarah Jane Louderback. His father cons.
8 June 1853. MA.
Bussey, Valentine & Elsy Munyan. His father John Bussey cons.,
att. William Munyan, Joseph Littlejohn. 15 Feb. 1855. MA, R,
D-15.
Bussy, John & Margaret Littlejohn. 18 Mar. 1830. R, A-140.
Butcher, Adam J. & Nancy Adams. 13 Mar. 1851. MA, B-204.

Butler, B.M. & Drusilla Crabtree. 5 Mar. 1848. MA, R, B-111.
Butler, Beder M. & Sarah Jane Shoemaker. 8 Oct. 1846. R, B-95.
Butler, Beder M. & Christena Plumb. Christena Plumb cons., att.
  John Plumb, Nancy Plumb. 27 Apr. 1848. MA, R, B-117.
Butler, Frances W. & Elcey Thomas. 4 Feb. 1834. MA, R, A-186.
Butler, Nathan & Mirenda Dawson. 26 May 1841. MA, R, B-20.
Butt, John & Eliza White. His father William Butt cons., witn.
  John H. Shepherd, Charles F. Campbell. 18 Sep. 1827. MA, R,
  A-109.
Butt, John W. & Margaret Morgan. 31 Jan. 1835. MA, R, A-196.
Butterfield, Benjamin & Mary E. Powells. 14 Jan. 1819. MA, R,
  A-42.
Butterfield, John & Ellen J. Rankin. 15 Dec. 1859. MA, R, D-103.
Button, Tillman & Amanda McConkle. 16 Sep. 1855. D-21.
Byers, Adam & Mary E. Daniels. 30 Sep. 1860. MA, R, D-128.
Byers, Isaac & Margaret Sayres. 6 Aug. 1851. MA, B-214.
Byers, Samuel & Mary Plummer. His father William Byers Sr. cons.,
  witn. Joseph Horner. __ Apr. 1815. MA.
Byers, William Junr. & Margaret Tucker. 4 Jan. 1811. R, A-308.
Byers, William Sr. & Hannah Burwick (Burniel). 25 May 1815, by
  William Byers Sr., J.P. R, A-281.
Byers, William Sr. & Hannah Bunnel. 25 Aug. 1815, by Robert
  Lucas, J.P. MA, R, A-282.
Cabel (Caleb), Jacob & Elizabeth Hornes (Homes?). 22 Oct. 1829.
  R, A-137.
Cable, Adam & Sally Shope. 10 Oct. 1816. MA, A-23.
Cable, Jacob & Abigail A. Faverty. 17 Mar. 1853. MA, B-262.
Cable, Jacob W. & Orlenda Debar (Bebar). 23 Jan. 1848. MA, R,
  B-121.
Cable, John G. & Susanna Charlotte Lane. 18 Feb. 1844. MA, R,
  B-55.
Cable, Jonathan & Harriet Lindsey. 26 May 1839. MA, R, B-6.
Cable, Jonathan & Rebecca Price. 17 Dec. 1850. MA, R, B-196.
Cable, Michael & Betsy Rawlins. 9 July 1821. R, A-59.
Cable, Michael & Catharine Cross. 20 June 1830. MA, R, A-143.
Cable, Philip & Asia S. Aldrich. 1 Jan. 1839. MA, R, A-265.
Cable, Philip S. & Mary Smith. 2 Nov. 1832. MA, R, A-168, A-171.
Caddo, Cladius & Nancy Ball. 1 Dec. 1819. R, A-49.
Cade, Isaac & Eliza Ann Oard. 24 Dec. 1846. MA, R, B-96.
Cadot, Claudius & Cynthia Ann Stockham. 3 Oct. 1838. R, B-5.
Cadot, Lemuel & Katherine Bacus. 29 Jan. 1828. R, A-116.
Cady, David K. & Ann Eliza Kinney. 11 May 1824. R, A-83.
Cady, John M. & Emily West. He is 32, born Ashtabula Co., res.
  Portsmouth, son of Silas & Martha. She is 18, born Lewis Co.,
  Ky., res. Portsmouth, dau. of B.G. & Amy. 2 June 1856. R,
  C-2, D-32.
Cahail, Edward & Sophia Noel. 25 Jan. 1816. MA, R, A-19.
Cahill, Sylvester & Mary French. Her father Jeremiah French
  cons. 9 Oct. 1852. MA.
Cain, Patrick & Elizabeth Ann Stephens. 29 Nov. 1840. MA.
Calder, Alexander & Rachel Kittle. John Campbell att. ages.
  7 Sep. 1852. MA, B-249.
Calder, George & Martha D. Boyer. 6 Aug. 1854. R, D-9.
Caldwell, James G. & Sarah Leonard. MA is dated 11 Oct. 1830;
  A-174 shows their marriage recorded in 1833. MA, R, A-174.
Calkins, Ephraim & Amelia A. Clark. 7 Apr. 1844. MA, R, B-57.
Call (Cable), Hugh & Nancy Jenkins. 5 June 1845. MA, R, B-72.
Call (Cable), Jeremiah & Nancy Lewis. 20 June 1847. MA, R, B-107.
Call, Mathew & T.M. Dunlap. 1 Feb. 1854. D-6.
Call, Thomas & Susan Jenkins. 16 July 1846. MA, R, B-91.
Call, William & Elizabeth Kneff (Kniff). 13 Apr. 1824. MA, R,
  A-87.

SCIOTO COUNTY MARRIAGES

Call, William R. & America Copen. 1 Oct. 1857. R, D-63.
Calvert, Charles & Anna Murfin. His mother Elizabeth Calvert
    cons. 12 Sep. 1823. MA, R, A-77.
Calvert, Elijah & Elizabeth Smith. 15 June 1843. MA, R, B-46.
Calvert, Elijah & Sarah Vigus (Vigers). 7 Mar. 1838. MA, R,
    A-251.
Calvert, Francis & Mary J. Knap. 27 June 1847. MA, R, B-103.
Calvert, George & Jane E. Reed. 2 Feb. 1859. MA, R, D-87.
Calvert, George & Mary Emma Dent Hoskinson. Her father Josiah
    Hoskinson cons. 15 Sep. 1833. MA, R, A-179.
Calvert, Hezekiah & Sally Ann Bennet. Her stepfather John Knapp
    said she is over 14 and has the consent of her mother. 11
    Jan. 1834. MA, R, A-185.
Calvert, Jacob & Mary Ann McKinney. 31 Oct. 1853. B-281.
Calvert, Jacob & Cynthia Moore. 7 Nov. 1826. R, A-101.
Calvin (Colvin), John & Margaret Davisson, of Upper Tp. 27 May
    1807. R, A-284.
Camden, William P. & Margaret Brunn. 3 June 1848. R, B-125.
Camp, John & Martha Wilson. 26 Oct. 1845. MA, R, B-79.
Campbell, Andrew & Elizabeth Dickey, of Bloom Tp. 3 Oct. 1834.
    MA, R, A-192.
Campbell, Andrew J. & Anna Noel. 4 Apr. 1841. MA, R, B-17.
Campbell, Edward & Mary Lewis. 13 Feb. 1823. R, A-72.
Campbell, George & Celia Chandler. 21 Mar. 1844. MA, R, B-56.
Campbell, Thomas J. & Cynthia M. Brown. Her par. Lou (?) Brown
    cons. 18 Mar. 1854. MA, D-2, D-5.
Campbell, William & Eliza Maltimore. 9 Oct. 1833. MA.
Campbell, William & Jane Martin. 2 Dec. 1846. MA.
Campbell, Willis & Catharine Thompson. 18 Apr. 1833. R, A-175.
Canaday, Thomas & Nancy Stout. 27 Nov. 1814. MA, R, A-342.
Canaday, Xanthus & Celia Scott. John Brown att. her age over 18.
    11 Apr. 1823. MA, R, A-74.
Canady (Kennedy), Josiah & Mary Melson. 16 Aug. 1838. MA, R,
    A-261.
Canary, Adison & Margaret Arthur. 16 Mar. 1854. D-6.
Canary, Simeon & Almira Louisa Dillon. 20 Dec. 1848. MA, R,
    B-144.
Canfield, Orcemis & Mary Kent (Trent?). 28 Oct. 1824. R, A-83.
Canles (Canter?), Isaac & Catharine Kier. 30 Oct. 1854. R, D-11.
Cann, John M. & Ellen D. Norman. 18 Dec. 1831. MA.
Canter, Amos & Rosanna George. John George att. ages. 13 Oct.
    1855. MA, D-22.
Canter, Elijah & Electa S. Woodruff. Her father Picket Woodruff
    cons. 6 Jan. 1859. MA, R, D-93.
Canter, Harrison & Hannah Keller. Her father John Keller cons.
    3 Feb. 1859. MA, R, D-80.
Canter (Canley?), Hennery & Mary Miler. 6 Mar. 1823. R, A-73.
Canter, Henry & Mary Halermun. 11 June 1854. R, D-14.
Canter, James & Emeline Chaffin. Michael Toppins att. ages.
    7 May 1848. MA, R, B-127.
Canter, John & Sarah Ann Umphreys. Her pars. cons., att. William
    Clark. 15 Apr. 1852. MA, B-257.
Canter, Madison & Emily Jane Miler. Her father William Miler
    cons., att. Nelson Marshall. 18 Mar. 1852. MA, B-236.
Canter, Milton & Mary Jane Woodruff. He is 21, born & res.
    Madison Tp., son of William. She is 18, born Jackson Co.,
    res. Madison Tp., dau. of Picket. 1 Jan. 1857. R, C-4, D-47.
Caps, Casper & Catherine Coffman (Koughman). 9 Feb. 1847. MA, R,
    B-99.
Caraway, Henry & Nancy Jane Penn. 10 July 1851. MA, B-215.
Caraway, Thomas L. Hamer & Ruth Ann Ralston. Return is not
    dated, MA is dated 16 Mar. 1860. MA, R, D-129.

21

SCIOTO COUNTY MARRIAGES

Carel, Virgil & Eliza B. White. He res. Gallipolis. Her father
  Matthew White, of Green Tp., cons., witn. Edward White. 26
  May 1833. MA, R, A-175.
Carey (Cacy?), James & Melinda Baker (Barker). 12 Apr. 1818. MA,
  R, A-38.
Carey, William & Viene Harrison. Philip Moore att. ages. 16 Jan.
  1818. MA, R, A-32.
Carl (Carroll), Lexis & Catherine Poyls (Piles). 9 Nov. 1840.
  MA, R, B-13.
Carl, Joseph & Magdeline Winter. 5 Nov. 1852. MA.
Carl, Laurence (Karl, Lorens) & Eva Houbert. 7 Apr. 1845. MA, R,
  B-70.
Carlan, James & Susan Jane Greenslate. 5 Oct. 1854. B-285.
Carlen, James & Margaret Jane Hall. 6 Feb. 1843. MA, R, B-41.
Carly, Simeon & Mary Jane Miller. 19 Jan. 1860. MA, R, D-113.
Carmine, John & Emma (Emelia) Smith. 6 Sep. 1837. MA, R, A-249.
Carnahan, James & Mary Johnson. 1 Sep. 1825. R, A-90.
Carner (Comer), A.W. & Henrietta B. Kittle. 10 Aug. 1854. R, D-9.
Carner, John & Amanda Smith. 16 Dec. 1845. MA, R, B-81.
Carney, J.E. & Elizabeth E. Grant (Trout? Front?). 20 Oct. 1851.
  MA, B-243.
Carns, John & Sarah Chestnut, of Washington Tp. 31 Dec. 1843.
  MA, R, B-52.
Carpenter, Jefferson & Liza Lewis. 11 Aug. 1853. B-280.
Carpenter, Philip & Katharine Arnold. 18 July 1853. B-270.
Carpenter, Reason & Maria Bennet. 10 Feb. 1838. MA.
Carpenter, William & Hannah Clark. 22 Dec. 1814. R, A-347.
Carpenter, William H. & Catharine Young. Her mother Hannah
  Elliott cons., witn. J.M.G. Trutt (?), Hambleton Willis.
  15 Mar. 1843. MA, R, B-43.
Carr, Hamilton J. & Ziar Lucas. 5 Oct. 1859. MA, R, D-108.
Carr, James & Nancy Carr. 21 Jan. 1855. MA, R, D-14.
Carraway, Henry & Sarah McCollister. 10 Feb. 1859. MA, R, D-77.
Carrell, Michael & Ellen Kelly. He is 26, born Ireland, res.
  Portland, Duckson Co. She is 24, born Ireland, res. Ports-
  mouth. 29 Aug. 1856. R, C-2, D-49.
Carrell (Connell? Councle? Counid?), Samuel & Sally Triggs.
  Peter Chabot att. her age over 18. 5 Feb. 1811. MA.
Carriger (Craighead), James A. & Elizabeth (Betsy) Smith. 21
  July 1848. MA, R, B-128.
Carriway, John & Nancy Newman. 10 Jan. 1856. D-24.
Carroll, Charles & Susannah Bacom. 4 Mar. 1823. R, A-73.
Carroll, Electious & Eliza Burk. 10 Feb. 1844. R, B-53.
Carroll, John & Keziah Strutt (Street?). His father James
  Carroll cons., witn. W. Gharky, Berry Hicks. 19 Mar. 1835.
  MA, R, A-198.
Carroll, John B. Jr. & Fanny Cutler. 29 Jan. 1829. R, A-126.
Carroll, Richard & Mary Degear. 10 Nov. 1825. R, A-93.
Carroll, Thomas & Bridget Liden. 20 Nov. 1851. MA, R, B-228.
Carson, William & Elizabeth Mann. 1 Jan. 1856. R, D-26.
Carson, William G. & Mary E. Goodrich. 12 Oct. 1859. MA, R, D-108.
Carter, Alexander & Susanna Miller. 23 Nov. 1844. MA, R, B-66.
Carter, David (Daniel) & Lucy Ann Morgan. 2 Nov. 1853. MA, B-281.
Carter, Henry & Whelthy Ann Wheeler. She is over 14. John
  Ruckman signed MA. 29 Oct. 1846. MA, R, B-93.
Carter, Jacob & Francis E. Harris. Her mother Francis Harris
  Senr. cons. His father Alexander Carter cons. 20 Nov. 1845.
  MA, R, B-82.
Carter, James & Mary Ann Coleman. 14 Sep. 1842. MA, R, B-34.
Carter, John & Amazilla Walls. 24 Sep. 1847. MA, R, B-109.
Carter, Peter & Loreta Walker. 31 July 1855. MA, R, D-25.
Carter, Philip & Mary Ann Walls. 18 Aug. 1849. MA, R, B-156.
Carter, William S. & A.A. Boyd. 26 Sep. 1855. R, D-20.

22

Cartney, Vincent M. & Susanah Ingles. 24 Mar. 1831. R, A-152.
Cartron, Frances & Mary Saro. 13 Jan. 1806. R, A-9, A-280.
Cartwright, Syrus & Sarah Ann Pierpoint. Her father Larken
    Pierpoint cons. 9 Sep. 1860. MA, R, D-132.
Cartwright, William & Mary Brown. Washington Partlow att. ages.
    11 May 1851. MA, B-207.
Casey, James McConners & Jemima Grounds. 7 Aug. 1845. MA, R, B-75.
Casey, Michael & Mary Ellen Burcaw. Her mother Melissa Ann Willis
    cons., witn. Henry H.A. Evans, William Mullen. 18 July 1859.
    MA, R, D-99.
Casky, John F. & Elizabeth Hill. Jacob Hill cons., att. Israel H.
    Howell. 6 June 1852. MA, B-241.
Cassett, John W. & Rebecca T. Moore. 10 May 1853. B-263.
Cassiday, Michael & Catharine McGeene. 19 Dec. 1842. MA, R, B-39.
Cassidy, Michael & Catherine Gordy. 9 Oct. 1852. MA.
Caster, William & Nancy Graham. 25 May 1845. MA, R, B-73.
Caswell, Horatio & Lucy Vincent. 9 Mar. 1826. R, A-96.
Cathey, William & Eunice Squires. 28 Jan. 1841. MA, R, B-20.
Caton, Edward & Cath (Ann) Reynolds. He is 26, born Ireland, res.
    Portsmouth. She is 28, born Ireland, res. Portsmouth. 27 July
    1856. MA, R, C-2, D-49.
Caudil, Silas & Phoebe Crain. 11 Jan. 1856. D-24.
Caughern (Cochran), Andrew J. & Melvira Ann Funk. 20 Feb. 1838.
    R, A-250.
Caul, Charles & Margaret Ashley. 18 Feb. 1816. MA, R, A-19.
Caul, James & Lucinda Ball. 30 Sep. 1838. R, A-260.
Cauley, George & Margaret Stratten. Cauley's affidavit says "I
    am unable from bodily infirmity to either walk or ride to
    town." N. Smith att. Cauley is a res. of Vernon Tp. and "a
    very clever man." 9 Aug. 1841. MA, R, B-22.
Cauley, James & Amanda Secrist. 26 Jan. 1847. MA, R, B-98.
Caulfield, Alexander & Mary Ann Gay. Thomas Gay att. ages.
    14 Jan. 1845. MA, R, B-70.
Cave, Aquila & Sarah Ann Dunlap. His mother Eliza Williams cons.,
    att. Isaac Hough, J.P. 3 Nov. 1854. MA, R, D-11.
Cerrens, Jasper & Lucinda Boggs. MA not completed, or dated. 1860.
Cessner, Charles & Julia Ann Phillips. 23 Mar. 1840. MA, R, B-4.
Chabot, Uriah & Lavina Hudson. 29 Sep. 1841. R, B-24.
Chaffin, D. S. & Mariah Thompson. 25 Nov. 1853. B-271.
Chaffin, Daniel & Polly Gillis. 1 Jan. 1829. MA, R, A-126.
Chaffin, Francis M. & Susannah Perry. 5 Aug. 1855. D-21.
Chaffin, John & Rebecca A. Patten. 9 Jan. 1851. MA, B-200.
Chaffin, Phineas & Almyra Wheeler. His mother Nancy Chaffin cons.,
    and her mother Abigail Wheeler cons., att. Franklin Wheeler.
    15 Mar. 1821. MA, R, A-59.
Chaffin, Phineas & Persis L. Lamb. 19 Dec. 1848. MA, R, B-138.
Chaffin, Reuben & Sarah Smith. 22 Oct. 1820. R, A-55.
Chaffin, Shadrach & Sally Salladay. 13 May 1819. MA, R, A-46.
Chaffin, Shadrack & Julia Hayward. 3 Nov. 1840. R, A-273 (gives
    year 1839).
Chain, William & Eliza Moore. 16 Nov. 1831. MA.
Chalfan (Chaffin), John & Susan Catharine Lee. 26 Nov. 1853.
    MA, D-1.
Chamberlain, Anson & Mary Montgomery. Her father William Mont-
    gomery cons. 4 Apr. 1814. MA, R, A-335.
Chamberlain, Dorvill & Sarah Baccus. 20 Feb. 1840. R, B-6.
Chamberlain, Oliver & Clarissa Baccus. 2 Jan. 1838. MA, R, B-5.
Chamberlain, Wyatt & Polly White. Daniel White att. her age over
    18. 14 Oct. 1813. MA, R, A-327.
Chambers, James & Peggy Taylor. 23 Mar. 1816. MA, R, A-21.
Chance, Benjamin & Rosanna Slavens. His mother, res. Pa., cons.
    Her pars. James & Elisabeth Slavens cons., witn. Robert Lynch,
    Jonathan Wolfe, res. Bloom Tp. 22 July 1845. MA.

SCIOTO COUNTY MARRIAGES

Chance, Thomas H. & Julia (Julina) Park. 14 Aug. 1842. MA, R,
   B-34.
Chandler, Clark & Ann Combs. 16 Dec. 1860. MA, R, D-125.
Chandler, Milton & Sarah E. Skidmore. 22 Apr. 1860. MA, R, D-117.
Chandler, Stephen & Mary Lamb. 3 Mar. 1819. R, A-43.
Chandler, Stephen & Levisa Lucas. 8 Sep. 1825. R, A-92.
Chaney, Abijah & Minerva Angel. Mathies Angel cons., witn.
   Delila Benson, John Gilmore. 22 June 1845. MA, R, B-78.
Chaney, David & Jane Pickerel. 16 July 1851. MA, B-245.
Chany, Jacob & Mary Burtwell. 18 Mar. 1819. R, A-45.
Chapman (Chaffin), C. P. & Eliza Weaks. 4 Apr. 1848. MA, B-245.
Chapman, Greenup & Minerva Lawson. Her father John Lawson cons.
   17 Oct. 1833. MA, R, A-182.
Chapman, Jacob N. & Mary J. Bonso. 1 Mar. 1860. MA, R, D-113.
Chapman, James & Mary Powell. 6 Apr. 1837. MA, R, A-245.
Chapman, James William & Betsey Ann Brooks. 6 Aug. 1853. MA,
   B-267.
Chapman, John & Polly Reeves. 13 Aug. 1815. MA, R, A-283.
Chapman, Josiah & Isibel Hitchcock. 26 Nov. 1815. R, A-18.
Chapman, Obediah & Amanda Burt. 31 Dec. 1856. R, D-45.
Chapman, Reubin & Nancy Ferqua. 2 Aug. 1809. R, A-296.
Chapman, William & Joanna B. Hitchcock. Her father Jesse Hitch-
   cock cons. 16 Oct. 1825. MA, R, A-92, A-93.
Charlesworth, H. R. & A. M. Whitney. 4 July 1853. D-1.
Charlesworth, Henry & Orrissa W. Lindsey. 14 Sep. 1844. MA.
Chase, Abishai & Lettica Shelpman. 25 June 1817. MA, R, A-40.
Chase (Case), John L. & Marilda Halstead. 11 Sep. 1828. MA, R,
   A-122.
Chase, Philip W. & Rhoda Collis. 15 Nov. 1849. MA, R, B-167.
Chatfield, Reuben & Elizabeth Minard. 27 Aug. 1840. MA, R, B-11.
Chatfield, Reuben & Catherine Konklin. 23 Feb. 1857. R, D-48.
Chatman, James W. & Lydia Digers. 5 Feb. 1857. R, D-45.
Chenoweth, Joel & Harriett McNutten (McNott). 29 Dec. 1836. MA,
   R, A-222.
Chenoweth, Joseph F. & Mary Jane Glaze. 1 Mar. 1849. R, B-147.
Chenoweth, Reason S. & Mary Vincent. 22 Dec. 1837. MA.
Chenowith, Francis & Mary Meister (Muster). He signs aff. Frans
   Schenwit. 5 Feb. 1850. MA, R, B-173.
Chesney, David A. & Elizabeth J. Orrs (Oris). 4 Aug. 1851. MA,
   B-243.
Chestnut, Presley & Emaline Eulit. He is 24, born & res. Scioto
   Co., son of A. & M. She is 19, dau. of Isaac & Mary. 9 July
   1857. R, C-10, D-58.
Chestnutwood, Samuel & Sirena Slimp. 2 Dec. 1846. MA, R, B-95.
Cheuvront, James E. & Cynthia A. Huls. 1 Jan. 1852. MA, B-228.
Chick, Charles & Sarah Lawson. 5 June 1854. B-284.
Chick, Franklin & Flora Stuart. 21 May 1852. MA.
Chick, William P. & Mary Ann Shope. Her father James Shope cons.
   MA is dated 11 Dec. 1851. Part of return is missing, filed
   20 July 1852. MA, R.
Chopein, Jacob & Margaretta Catsmyer. 2 Jan. 1853. MA, B-255.
Chopple, William & Hannah Write. 27 July 1831. R, A-158.
Chorpenning, Henry & Rachel Walton. 31 Oct. 1840. MA.
Christ, Nicholaus & Kunegunda Hartman. 4 June 1857. R, D-54.
Church, Joel & Nancy Cook. 23 Jan. 1811. MA, R, A-309.
Churchill, John L. & Mary Kellogg. 11 Apr. 1842. MA.
Cissna, Evans & Elizabeth Dunham. 12 Mar. 1822. R, A-67.
Clapper, Henry & Anna Maria Relles (Rose). 12 Sep. 1847. MA, R,
   B-107.
Clark, Aaron & Elizabeth Orm. 14 Apr. 1836. R, A-218.
Clark, Amos B. & Sarah Ellison. 11 Oct. 1848. MA.
Clark, Andrew & Eliza Ann Craig. 20 Sep. 1847. MA, R, B-108.
Clark, Charles & Pertrina Taylor. 14 Dec. 1856. R, D-43.

24

Clark, Daniel & Sidney Griffith. 10 May 1847. R, B-102.
Clark, Franklin F. & Abigail Rickey. 14 Sep. 1844. MA, R, B-65.
Clark, George W. & Nancy S. Adams. 11 June 1851. MA, B-215.
Clark (Clerk), Hiram & Elizabeth Balena. 14 Dec. 1848. MA, R, B-138.
Clark, Isaac W. & Nancy McKean. 22 Apr. 1858. MA, R, D-74.
Clark, Isaiah & Martha Sheflin. 5 Feb. 1854. D-1.
Clark, J. W. & Sarah Ellen Morford. 2 Dec. 1856. R, D-42.
Clark, James & Elizabeth Buckels. 18 Aug. 1830. R, A-145.
Clark, John & Abigail Lucas. 15 Mar. 1810. R, A-298.
Clark, John & Hester Coal. 28 June 1814. R, A-336.
Clark, John & Mary Ann Brown. 8 June 1840. MA, R, B-9.
Clark, Jonas & Eliza L. Hitchcock. 16 July 1843. MA, R, B-47.
Clark, Joseph M. & Mary E. Huston. 11 Oct. 1835. MA, R, A-211.
Clark, Josiah D. & Esther Tracy. 23 June 1822. MA, R, A-68.
Clark, Mill H. & Mary Ann Edgington. 21 Jan. 1846. MA, R, B-84.
Clark, Richard & Katharine Albert. 24 Mar. 1814. R, A-333.
Clark, Richard & Mary Ann Sprinkle. 14 Sep. 1859. MA, R, D-101.
Clark, Samuel & Mary Utt. 6 Jan. 1821. MA.
Clark, Silas & Eveline Ophelia Calvert. His father Aaron Clark
  cons. 17 Mar. 1858. MA, R, D-72.
Clark, Silas H. & Elizabeth F. George. 22 Aug. 1860. MA.
Clark, William H. & Mary Moore. 11 June 1826. MA, R, A-98.
Clary, John D. & Elizabeth Ross. 6 Oct. 1836. MA, R, A-220.
Clary (Cleary) Thorndike & Sarah Woodring (Wotring). 25 July
  1844. MA, R, B-61.
Clausmann, Martin & Frances Krae. 12 Jan. 1855. MA, R, D-13.
Clay, John & Maria Reynold. 11 Feb. 1852. MA.
Clemens, Daniel & Mary Brunner. 21 Aug. 1851. MA, B-215.
Clemmer, Jacob & Ann Hardin. 6 Dec. 1854. MA, R, D-12.
Clemmons, Jarvis & Cynthia Ann Huddleston. 5 Jan. 1854. D-4.
Clemmons, William T. & Lavina Chaffin. Her father Shadrach
  Chaffin cons. 19 Dec. 1839. MA, R, B-6.
Clemons, Andrew & Ann E. Adams. Her mother Eveline Farmer cons.
  23 May 1855. MA, R, D-18.
Cleveland, Francis & Margaret Waller. 6 Nov. 1834. R, A-192.
Clifford, Andrew Jackson & Lydia Alliway. 20 Aug. 1844. MA, R,
  B-62.
Clifford, Henry & Martha Bowman. Names are written in margin
  only. Not dated, probably 1853 or 1854. D-5.
Clifford, John & Belinda (Melinda) Hodges. His father Anthony
  Clifford cons., witn. Henry Clifford. 13 Jan. 1829. MA, R,
  A-127.
Clifford, John & Delitha Lockart. 21 Nov. 1855. D-23.
Cliffords, Elisha & Susey Hodges. Her mother Sally Hodges cons.,
  witn. Robart D. Hodges, Washington McK'ney. 16 Aug. 1832.
  MA, R, A-166.
Cline (Kline), Christian & Sarah Rouse. 16 Apr. 1856. MA, R, D-28.
Cline, Daniel & Mary Ann White. He is 22, born Scioto Co., res.
  Adams Co., son of Daniel & E. Cline. She is 18, born & res.
  Scioto Co., dau. of John & E. White. 2 Oct. 1856. MA, R, C-5.
Cline, Michael & Elizabeth Elick. 9 Aug. 1838. MA, R, A-258.
Cline, Peter & Rosina Loth. 13 Aug. 1844. MA.
Cline, Samuel & Rosanna Russel. 10 July 1850. MA, R, B-182.
Cline, William H. & Eliza Dewitt. 7 Mar. 1850. MA, R, B-174.
Cline, William H.L. & Elizabeth Johnson. 13 Nov. 1851. MA, B-221.
Cline, William M. & Charlotte Jackson. Evan & Elisabeth Jackson
  cons., of Bloom Furnace, witn. Warren D. Murfin, George Danels.
  22 Feb. 1844. MA, R, B-55.
Clinesmith, Laurenz (Lawrence C. Smith) & Mary Ann Barr. 1 Sep.
  1849. MA, R, B-155.
Clingman, Abner B. & Sarah Woolever. 16 May 1822. R, A-66.
Clingman, Cyrus & Polley Richart. 10 Feb. 1825. R, A-86.

SCIOTO COUNTY MARRIAGES

Clingman, Jacob & Jane Bacom. 7 Dec. 1818. R, A-41.
Clingman, John B. & Sarah P. Turner. 1 May 1828. R, A-117.
Clingman, John M. & Margaret Lewis, both of Bloom Tp. 30 May
    1826. R, A-96.
Clingman, Josiah & Mariah Simpson. 25 Nov. 1830. R, A-149.
Clopper, Martin & Minerva Wheeler. 14 Mar. 1850. R, B-174.
Clure, Julius & Mary Monin. 8 Mar. 1857. R, D-52.
Coale, Daniel W. & Mary J. Burroughs. 25 Sep. 1833. R, A-178.
Coale, John P. & Sarah Veach. 23 Aug. 1827. R, A-102.
Coburn, Jonathan G. & Elizabeth Cooper. Her father (not named)
    present and cons. 31 Mar. 1848. MA, R, B-121.
Coburn, William T. & Sophia F. Murphy. 20 Oct. 1859. MA, R,
    D-102.
Cochran, A. J. & Ellen Robinson. Jackson Robinson att. ages.
    13 June 1850. MA, R, B-183.
Cochran, John & Elizabeth Jaynes (James). 2 Oct. 1849. MA, R,
    B-158.
Cochran, John & Mary Nichols. 20 Feb. 1859. MA, R, D-77.
Cochran, William & Nancy Cochran. Her father James Cohrine (?)
    cons., says she was born July the __ (rest is illegible).
    25 Oct. 1821. MA, R, A-60.
Cockerel, Elijah & Polly McAuley. 31 Mar. 1816. R, A-20.
Cockrel, Asa (Jesse) & Mary Glaze. 11 Aug. 1839. R, A-276.
Cockrell, Charles H. & Margaret Slavens. 2 Feb. 1851. MA, B-201.
Cockrell, George C. & Minerva Darlington. 28 Sep. 1839. MA, R,
    A-273.
Cockrell, George W. & Rebecca Williams. 10 Jan. 1850. R, B-168.
Cockrell, Jesse Jr. & Anne Marsh. 30 Oct. 1819. R, A-48.
Cockrell, Paton & Harriet Cockrell. 14 Feb. 1830. R, A-139.
Coe, Milbourn & Sarah Jane Brown Auld. 9 Jan. 1855. MA, R, D-14.
Coffee, Patrick & Adaline Davisson. 29 Sep. 1850. R, B-189.
Coffman, Benjamin & Mary White. 28 July 1830. MA.
Coffman, Daniel & Celia A. Edwards. 24 Apr. 1856. R, D-29.
Coffrin, Constantine & Rachel Ellis. 13 Dec. 1852. MA, B-255.
Coffrin, George M. & Barbary Ann Willcoxonson. 27 Mar. 1841. R,
    B-18.
Coil (Cail), John & Margaret Feurt. 1 Nov. 1837. R, A-235.
Coil, Ludson & Suzan Muas (Lozina Moor). The return is illegible.
    26 Sep. 1857. R, D-65.
Coke, James & Phebellim Williams. 5 Dec. 1849. R, B-164.
Cole, Alexander & Esther A. Hall. He is 21 (19), born Fleming Co.
    Ky., res. Nile Tp., son of Thomas & Mary. She is 19, born
    Scioto Co., res. Nile Tp., dau. of Aaron & Harriet. 31 Oct.
    1857. R, C-9, C-13, D-69.
Cole, Alonzo & Ann Bennett. William Curry att. his age over 21.
    1 Jan. 1843. MA, R, B-40.
Cole (Call), Amos & Nancy Watts. 19 June 1831. R, A-153.
Cole, Amos B. & Martha E. Orm. 2 Jan. 1851. B-198. The record
    incorrectly reported Amos B. Cole married to Rebecca Price.
    Martha E. Cole, widow of Amos B. Cole, petitioned to have
    the record corrected on 12 Dec. 1898 (See Complete Record 9,
    p. 42.) Her petition says she is the daughter of John Orm
    Jr., who was the son of John Orm Sr., both deceased, her
    father dying on 28 July 1851. She gives her age as 18 on
    20 Aug. 1850. She states Amos B. Cole was 23 on 13 Dec. 1850,
    and the son of Silas W. Cole. Amos Cole died 3 Oct. 1897,
    the father of seven children, according to her petition.
Cole, Charles O. & Sarah A. Orm. 12 Feb. 1852. B-231.
Cole, Daniel M. & Lydia Worley. 7 June 1832. R, A-164.
Cole, David & Polly Flemings. 30 Dec. 1847. R, B-112, B-117.
Cole, George W. & Prudence Sabina Alfred. 18 Sep. 1845. R, B-80.
Cole, Harry & Sarah Bradford. 23 Aug. 1832. R, A-166.

26

SCIOTO COUNTY MARRIAGES

Cole, James M. & Mary Jane Paul. 29 Aug. 1836. R, A-224.
Cole, Lucius & Alma Pool. 5 Oct. 1822. R, A-70.
Cole, Marcus & Maria Higgins. 3 Apr. 1819. MA, R, A-45.
Cole, Orson & Katharine A. Grier. 16 Sep. 1847. MA, R, B-110.
Cole, Samuel & Nancy Ellen Peebles. 6 Oct. 1836. R, A-223.
Cole, Silas W. & Elizabeth Huston. 21 Nov. 1822. R, A-71.
Cole (Coale), Thomas & Mary Wallingford. 12 Apr. 1827. MA, R,
   A-106.
Cole, William & Eliza Lindsey. 13 Mar. 1860. MA, R, D-121.
Cole, William C. & Rhoda Elizabeth Orm. 27 Dec. 1848. R, B-136.
Colegrove, Benjamin & Laura Cole. 15 Nov. 1829. R, A-136.
Colegrove, Benjamin F. & Catherine Hartman. 29 Aug. 1859. MA, R,
   D-109.
Colegrove, Henry S. & Mary McNaly. 16 Nov. 1856. R, D-39.
Colegrove, Peleg & Anna Johnston. Her father Levi Johnston
   cons. 23 May 1811. MA, R, A-313.
Colegrove, Peleg & Susan Bennett. 15 Mar. 1840. MA, R, B-4.
Colegrove, Peleg & Hanah Benner. 12 Mar. 1856. R, D-27.
Colegrove, William & Elizabeth Calvert. 13 Nov. 1827. R, A-110.
Colegrove, William H. & Abigail Burt. 18 Dec. 1839. MA, R, A-277.
Coleman, Thomas & Harriet Strait. 5 Apr. 1855. R, D-17.
Coley, Allen & Catherine Gifford. 19 Aug. 1859. MA, R, D-99.
Colin (Colvin), William & Martha Monroe. 27 Nov. 1851. MA, B-243.
Colisson, William, of Pike Co. & Mary Adams. 24 Dec. 1835. R,
   A-210, A-218.
Collar, Sidney & Elizabeth McCloud. He is 28, born New York, res.
   Portsmouth, son of Enos & Elizabeth. She is 24, born Medina
   Co., Oh., res. Portsmouth, dau. of David & Margaret. 3 Nov.
   1856. R, C-1, D-43.
Coller, Enos & Jane Carr. 6 Oct. 1852. MA, B-247.
Coller, Enos & Elizabeth Lee. 21 May 1858. MA, R, D-84.
Collett, A. M. & Sarah Howell. 27 July 1853. B-265.
Colley, William & Hester Fortress. 14 Mar. 1846. MA, R, B-86.
Collier (Collis), Ambrose & Matilda McCleary. 20 July 1836. MA,
   R, A-216.
Collier, Ambrose & Nancy Hall. 23 Apr. 1856. R, D-29.
Collier, Thomas & Adeline Eliza Orcut. 14 May 1840. R, B-5.
Collings, Thomas & Susy Carey. 14 Dec. 1812. R, A-323.
Collins, Ennos & Margaret Groniger. 15 Aug. 1822. R, A-69.
Collins, George H. & Sophia Watts. 8 June 1831. MA, R, A-153.
Collins, Gillen H. & Cecilia A. Huston. He is 20, born Clermont
   Co., res. Portsmouth, son of E.A. & N. She is 21, born
   Scioto Co., res. Portsmouth, dau. Samuel & Elizabeth.
   26 Mar. 1857. R, C-8, D-51.
Collins, James R. & Eunice B. Saladay. 20 May 1858. MA, R, D-96.
Collins, John & Casander Moore. 1 Jan. 1817. R, A-25.
Collins, Joseph & Rosana Ervin (Evins). 1 Oct. 1828. R, A-123.
Collins, Martin & Elizabeth Shonkwiler. MA dated 5 Aug. 1815.
   MA, R, A-282.
Collins, William & Margaret Worley. 20 Jan. 1830. R, A-139.
Collins, William & Fanny Patterson. 22 Jan. 1847. MA, R, B-97.
Collis, James T. & Elizabeth Titus. His guardian James Titus
   cons., witn. R. T. Collis. 4 July 1838. MA, R, A-258.
Collis, Orason & Hannah Murfin. 19 July 1827. MA, R, A-109.
Collis, Osemus & Emeline Howell. 2 Mar. 1823. R, A-73.
Collis, R. T. & Julia Crull. He is 49, born Massachusetts, res.
   Scioto Co., son of James & Louisa, third marriage. She is
   44, born & res. Scioto Co., dau. S. & Jane, third marriage.
   1 July 1856. R, C-4, D-31.
Collis, Royal & Roxey Smith. 25 Oct. 1827. R, A-111, A-118.
Collis, Royal T. & Nancy Telen. 30 Sep. 1830. R, A-148.
Collis, Thomas & Lucy Hood. 26 Apr. 1858. MA, R, D-75.
Colly, Edward M. & Sophia Smith. 18 Nov. 1847. MA, R, B-115.

27

Colvin, George & Elizabeth Faverty. 16 Mar. 1851 (1850), by
Samuel Gould, J.P. MA, R.
Colvin, George N. (W?) & Mary Ann Smith. 6 Sep. 1838. MA, R,
A-257.
Colvin, Harrison & Sarah Jane Bingham. 14 Oct. 1858. MA, R,
D-85.
Colvin, Jefferson & Louisa Porter. 27 July 1856. MA, R, D-33.
Colvin, John & Mille Caloway. 29 Oct. 1854. R, D-11.
Comer, Adam & Sarah Ann Blakeman. 6 Jan. 1842. MA, R, B-40.
Comer, Henry & Delila Bennett. 23 Feb. 1840. MA, R, B-3.
Complement (Kampelman), Barney & Apolonia Kuhnel. 30 Sep. 1856.
MA, R, D-38.
Compton, Joseph W. & Martha Jane McLoud (McLain). 18 Apr. 1840.
MA, R, B-11.
Conal, William & Elizabeth Snedicor. Joseph Davisson att. ages.
20 Oct. 1850. MA, B-192.
Congrove, John G. & Harriet Bennet. 10 Jan. 1828. R, A-116.
Conklin, Gideon & Rachel Patton. Thomas Patton cons., witn.
Thomas Patten, Jeremiah Patten, all of Green Tp. 9 July 1807.
MA, R, A-286.
Conklin, Joseph & Catherine Smith. Her father John Smith cons.,
witn. John Smith Junr., Washington Morison. 28 June 1838. MA,
R, B-5.
Conklin, William & Mary Conklin. 15 Aug. 1808. R, A-291.
Conly, William & Susan Roberts. 5 Dec. 1850. MA.
Conn, Aaron (Cann, Arthur) & Mary Jones, both of Covington, Ky.
9 Dec. 1854. MA, R, D-12, D-14.
Connaway, Simon & Rachel McAuley. 25 Feb. 1808. R, A-288.
Connell, Alexander & Aidy Martin, widow. 16 Mar. 1810. R, A-301.
Connell (Campbell), Thomas M. & Martha Robinson. 20 Nov. 1846.
MA.
Connelly, John & Martha Roberts. 31 Dec. 1846. MA, R, B-96.
Conner, Calvin & Mary Jane Hart. 16 Oct. 1855. D-22.
Connolly, Carter & Margaret P. Field (Pearsfield). 10 Nov. 1855.
MA, D-22.
Conrow, John & Lucretia Graham. 21 July 1850. MA, R, B-185.
Conroy, Dennis & Mary Mulligan. He is 25 (26), born Ireland,
res. Portsmouth, son of Thomas. She is 19, born Ireland,
Portsmouth, dau. of Edward. 21 Sep. 1856 (19 Oct. 1856).
R, C-2, C-7, D-48.
Conroy, Timothy & Margaret Kelly. He is 28, born Ireland, res.
Portsmouth. 18 May 1856. MA, R, C-1, D-49.
Constance, Isaac & Drusilla Highly. 7 July 1816. MA, R, A-21.
Cook, Coonrod & Betsy Ridenour. 5 Feb. 1835. MA, R, A-195.
Cook, Edward & Rhoda Leadbetter. 14 July 1856. R, D-33.
Cook, George W. & Sintha Evridge. 6 Sep. 1855. R, D-20.
Cook, Henry & Lucy Neil. 23 Sep. 1852. MA, B-249.
Cook, Hugh & Mercy (Mary?) Smith. 8 Oct. 1822. R, A-70.
Cook, James L. & Lucinda Littlejohn. 20 June 1839. MA, R, B-6.
Cook, James L. & Mary Allard. 28 Nov. 1854. MA, R, D-12.
Cook, John & Julian Roush (Raushe). 8 Feb. 1838. MA, R, A-252.
Cook, John & Lydia A. Critzer. 21 Nov. 1841. R, B-20.
Cook, John & Sarah U. McCoy. 7 Nov. 1848. R, B-134.
Cook, Joseph & Rosena Clobine. 26 Nov. 1858. MA, R, D-133.
Cook, Joseph & Sarah J. Hannahs. 20 Nov. 1848. R, B-136.
Cook, Robert H. & Sarah H. Clemons (Martha A. Clemmins). 25
July 1849. MA, R, B-155.
Cook, Uriah T. & Jane Craig. 1 Dec. 1841. MA.
Cook, William & Hannah Taylor. 5 Feb. 1843. MA, R, B-41.
Cook, William H. & Jane Gaines. 30 Sep. 1852. MA, B-277.
Cook, William L. & Califurnia McCall. 31 Jan. 1856. R, D-27.
Cook, William S. & Malinda J. Earley. 7 Feb. 1856. D-24.
Cook, William T. & Anna Gunn. 11 Sep. 1853. MA, B-270.

Cookes, William G. & Caroline Krutz. 14 July 1840. MA, R, B-10.
Cooley (Conely), James & Mehealy Yates. 25 May 1848. MA, R,
   B-123.
Cooley, John & Mary Montgomery. 27 Apr. 1853. MA, B-262.
Cooley, O. U. P. & Mary F. Cropper. 24 Apr. 1856, by E. P. Pratt.
   R.
Cooley, Richard & Rachel Brown. 18 May 1859. MA, R, D-91.
Coon (Corn), John & Betsy Chadd. 15 Apr. 1819. MA, R, A-45.
Coon, Joseph & Ann Elizabeth Morgan. 23 Jan. 1845. MA, R, B-67.
Cooper, Abner & Lucinda Loveland. 4 July 1844. MA, R, B-62.
Cooper, Amaziah & Rebecca Hodges. 3 Sep. 1847. MA, R, B-107.
Cooper, Clay & Lucinda Mathews. George Bush att. her pars. cons.
   16 Oct. 1856. MA, R, D-38.
Cooper, George & Caroline Billen (Dillen). 25 Aug. 1858. MA, R,
   D-84.
Cooper, Hiram & Nancy Evans. 6 Jan. 1848. MA, R, B-114, B-119.
Cooper, Jacob & Rachel Boyer. 5 June 1845. MA, R, B-74.
Cooper, James & Virginia Duduit. 10 Apr. 1817. MA, R, A-40.
Cooper, James & Viny (Ciny) Burt. 4 Mar. 1838. MA, R, A-252.
Cooper, Jeremiah & Phebe McCoy. 17 Sep. 1848. MA, R, B-132.
Cooper, John & Isabell (Elizabeth) Cooper. 26 June 1823. MA, R,
   A-75.
Cooper, Samuel & Parmelia Flanders. 27 Mar. 1825. MA, R, A-87.
Cooper, Solomon & Louisa A. Vastine. 30 Mar. 1859. MA, R, D-109.
Cooper, Thomas & Rebecca Hodges. 15 July 1830. R, A-145.
Cooper, Washington & Ada M. Sear. 24 Apr. 1849. MA, R, B-147.
Cooper, William & Sarah Cowen, of Nile Tp. 30 Mar. 1837. MA, R,
   A-241.
Cooper, William Jr. & Minerva Piatt. His father Jeremiah Cooper
   cons. 28 Nov. 1839. MA, R, B-1.
Cooper, William D. & Lany Applegate. 10 May 1855. R, D-18.
Cooper, Zachariah & Levina Haines. 15 May 1851. MA, B-207.
Cooper, Zachariah & Amanda Welsh. 2 Mar. 1853. MA, B-266.
Copen, William & Ermina Huddleston. 17 Mar. 1857. R, D-51.
Copes, Parker & Letha Ann Seisel (Lixsal). 12 Dec. 1830. MA, R,
   A-149.
Copes (Copen), Samuel W. & Avis Amelia Orcutt. 14 Sep. 1829. MA,
   R, A-134.
Copes, Southy & Ruth Hutton. 28 Oct. 1819. R, A-47.
Copley, Robert & Nancy Jones. 5 Oct. 1859. MA, R, D-109.
Cordier, Charles & Margaret Luther. 30 Aug. 1849. MA.
Coriell, Abraham & Mary White. Her father Daniel White cons.,
   witn. Ira Coriell. 1 Aug. 1841. MA, R, B22.
Coriell, Daniel & Sarah Welch. Her father James Welsh cons.,
   witn. Solomon Welch, Peter Coriell. 28 Mar. 1833. MA, R, A-174.
Coriell, Ira & Syrena White. 7 Jan. 1836. MA, R, A-211.
Coriell, Peter & Mary Colvin. 26 Dec. 1837. MA, R, A-248.
Coriell, Thomas & Maria Yeley. 3 June 1858. MA.
Corn, Edward & Nancy Scott. His mother Phoebe Corn cons., att.
   Joshua Bailey. 6 May 1813. MA, R, A-324.
Cornes, Wesley D. & Hannah A. Enslow. 3 July 1854. R, D-8.
Corns, David & Levina Thomas. 17 Nov. 1853. MA, B-282.
Corns, Jonathan & Elizabeth Welch. 3 Apr. 1831. MA, R, A-152.
Corns, Samuel & Caroline Brown. 13 Feb. 1854. D-5.
Cornstalk, Leander & Mary Y. Hurd. 23 May 1845. MA, R, B-78.
Cornstock (Comstock), George G. & Caroline H. Fuller (Glidden).
   Wallace M. Finch att. ages. 10 Nov. 1846. MA, R, B-93.
Cornwell, Moses & Ruth Fitzmorris. 9 Nov. 1839. MA, R, B-12.
Correll, Hiram & Amanda Colegrove. 3 Dec. 1829. R, A-140.
Correll, Levi & Nancy McCollister. Job Pettit att. ages. 21 Sep.
   1859. MA, R, D-101.
Corriell, Sele & Mary Welch. Her father James Welch cons., witn.
   Daniel V. Coriell. 6 May 1838. MA, R, A-254.

SCIOTO COUNTY MARRIAGES

Cortney, Richard & Jane Price. 17 Feb. 1848. R, B-122.
Corwin, Calvin H. & Elmanda Boyer. He is 31, res. Bloom Tp., son
   of Elbinzer Corwine. She is 18, res. Bloom Tp., born Scioto
   Co., dau. of John. 1 Nov. 1857. R, C-12, D-63.
Corwin, Daniel & Eliza Dorrell. 1 July 1820. R, A-53.
Corwin, Ebenezer & Alice Hatch. 16 Mar. 1826, by Dan Young. R.
Corwin, James & Lucinda Myers. 31 Mar. 1836. R, A-213, A-230.
Corwin, William & Beaulah Lindsey. 16 June 1853. MA, B-262.
Coryell, Dewitt & Mary H. Stebbins. 2 Sep. 1843. MA, R, B-48.
Coryell, George & Mary Deitrich. He is 23 (33), born Ohio (Pa.),
   res. Harrison Tp., son of Lydia. She is 22 (33), born Ohio,
   res. Bloom Tp., dau. of John & Elizabeth. 2 May 1857. R, C-12,
   C-14, D-66.
Coryell, Peter D. & Sarah Jane Coriell. 16 Jan. 1846. MA, R, B-85.
Coryell, Samuel & Esther Scofield. 24 (28) Apr. 1850. MA, R, B-181.
Coss (Cass), John & Calista Ring. Samuel Ring att. her age over
   18. 6 June 1842. MA, R, B-31.
Cottel, Daniel & Sally Fleming. 4 May 1819. MA, R, A-45.
Cottle, Daniel & Sarah Hartley. 20 Mar. 1859. MA, R, D-95.
Cottle, William & Margaret Jones. 22 Mar. 1855. R, D-16.
Counce, Philip & Elizabeth Short. 7 Dec. 1809. R, A-300.
Courtney, Henry & Rebecc Waw. 19 Dec. 1848. MA, R, B-136.
Cousins, Fleming & Laura Young. 12 Sep. 1838. R, A-258.
Cousins, Jonathan & Henrietta Roberts. 23 May 1855. R, D-18.
Coverlid (Koblenz), Martin & Carenia Hoster (Clarinda Harter).
   5 May 1848. MA, B-244.
Cowan, Samuel & Polly Hodges. Aaron D. Hodges att. ages. 26 Aug.
   1826. MA, R, A-99.
Cowen, Samuel & Susan Reeves. 13 May 1851. MA, B-209.
Cowles, Lewis D. & Selina Dole. Samuel Dole cons. 15 May 1848.
   MA, R, B-123.
Cowling, John & Mary Ann Wilson. 25 Sep. 1844. MA.
Cox, Henry & Vicy Utt. Her father Henry Utt cons., witn. George
   Beloat, Henry Utt Junr. 21 Oct. 1823. MA, R, A-77.
Cox, John T. & Lurania Tipton. 5 July 1840. MA, R, B-10.
Cox, Samuel Smith & Thersene Crabtree. Her pars. James & Ailcy
   Crabtree cons. His pars. Jacob & Sinthey Cox cons. 4 Oct.
   1858. MA, R, D-79.
Cox, William & Lucinda Porter, of Porter Tp. His father Thomas
   Cox cons., witn Edward Cranston, Thomas Porter. 17 July
   1834. MA.
Cox, William H. & Susannah Holtness. 17 Oct. 1858. MA, R, D-80.
Coyl, Jesse & Mercy Feurt. Her father Peter Feurt cons., witn.
   Benjamin Feurt, Giles McNeal. 19 Feb. 1829. MA, R, A-128.
Crabtre, James & Emily Jenkins. 1 Jan. 1850. R, B-169.
Crabtree, Elisah & Margaret McIntyre. Her father Joseph McIntyre
   cons., witn. Isaac Yates, Job Crabtree. 27 Oct. 1860. MA, R,
   D-124.
Crabtree, Stephen & Elizabeth Perry. 29 Dec. 1853. D-6.
Crabtree, Stephen & Eliza J. McNally. He is 22, born Jackson Co.,
   res. Bloom Tp., son of W., second marriage. She is 23, born
   & res. Harrison Tp., dau. Hannah McNelly (McNetty). 24 Dec.
   1857. R, C-14, D-75.
Crabtree, Stephen & Lydia J. Robnet. Her mother Rachel Robnet
   cons., att. Foster Throckmorton. 24 Mar. 1859. MA, R, D-95.
Crabtree, Thomas & Phebe Graham. Joseph Graham att. her age over
   18. 16 Dec. 1813. MA, R, A-328.
Crabtree, Thomas & Margaret Roark. 5 Dec. 1850. MA, B-197.
Crabtree, Thomas M. & Elizabeth Crabtree. 11 Feb. 1855. MA, R,
   D-15.
Crabtree, Thomas S. & Bula Perry. 17 June 1854. R, D-8.
Crabtree, Vinton & Suzana Throckmarten. He is 18, born Jackson
   Co., son of William & Jane. She is 20, born Jackson Co., dau.

30

SCIOTO COUNTY MARRIAGES

of James & M. 1 Apr. 1856. R, C-5, D-29.
Crabtree, William & Elizabeth Clemmons. His father Lewis Crab-
tree cons., att. John Cuykendall. 5 Nov. 1823. MA, R, A-77.
Crabtree, William & Eliza Gilliam. His father Thomas Crabtree
cons., witn. John Pewtheren, Thomas Bowen. 25 Dec. 1823. MA,
R, A-80.
Cracraft, Charles & Sarah Stephenson. 20 Dec. 1809. R, A-298.
Cracraft, George W. & Mary Jane Campbell. J.E. Campbell att.
her age. 29 Dec. 1842. MA, R, B-39.
Cracraft, Jonathan S. & Emily Hunt. 15 Mar. 1843. MA, R, B-42.
Craft, Frederick (Friedrick Kraft) & Catherine Keadauk. 31 Aug.
1858. MA, R, D-80.
Craig, Jacob & Margaret Tippon. 4 Dec. 1841. MA, R, B-25.
Craig (Crage), John & Katherine Campbell. 15 Jan. 1835. MA, R,
A-196.
Craig, John & Nancy Powell. 2 Apr. 1842. MA.
Craig, Thomas & Mary Glaze. 12 Sep. 1850. MA, R, B-189.
Craig, Thomas & Elizabeth N. Short. 23 Sep. 1852. MA, B-247.
Craig, William & Mary Bennett. 12 Jan. 1815. R, A-345.
Craig, William S. & Anna G. Parks. 7 July 1856, by E. P. Pratt.
R.
Craigmiles, James & Ellen Cragmiles. 29 Mar. 1855. MA, R, D-16.
Crain, Adonijah & Mary Morgan. Jan. 17, 1832. R, A-158.
Crain, Horace & Juliett Miller. 4 July 1850. MA, R, B-182.
Crain, Horace M. & Sarah Jane Farrington. 24 Feb. 1841. MA, R,
B-18.
Crain, Martin & Ellen Gibbs.. 1 May 1854. D-5.
Crain, Martin & Maria Hall. He is 30, born Scioto Co., res.
Portsmouth, second marriage, son of Martin & Abigail. She is
17, born & res. Portsmouth, dau. of Rebecca. 4 Jan. 1857. R,
C-1, D-52.
Craine, Leonard & Nancy Smith. Orin H. Abbott att. ages. 25 Nov.
1844. MA, R, B-65.
Craine, Leonard H. & Dorcas Ann Hennis. 10 Apr. 1842. MA, R,
B-31.
Cramer (Cremer), Henry & Abigail Clarke. 24 Mar. 1818. MA, R,
A-37.
Cramer (Creamer), John & Mary Abigail Jones. Her father David
Jones cons. 17 June 1827. MA, R, A-110, A-117.
Cramer, John & Mary Myer. 13 Apr. 1854. B-283.
Crandall, Joseph T. & Rebecca Powell. 1 Aug. 1839, by Samuel
Barbery. MA, R.
Crandall, Wesley & Nancy A. Glidden. 4 Nov. 1852. MA, B-251.
Crandel, Elias & Nancy F. Forsythe. 1 Jan. 1857. R, D-48.
Crane, George B. & N. M. Young. 3 Nov. 1833, by Dan Young. R.
Crank, Enoch & Nancy Welsh. 15 Nov. 1838. MA.
Cranson, B.E. & Margaret J. Henderson. 8 Nov. 1855. D-22.
Cranston, Caleb G. & Alzina Cole. 19 May 1836. MA, R, A-215.
Cranston, Edward & Nabby Cole. 18 Feb. 1821. MA, R, A-56.
Cranston, Jeremiah & Abigel Dutremont. 30 Jan. 1850. R, B-170.
Craton, John H. & Angeline Stapleton. 20 Dec. 1860. MA, R, D-130.
Craton, William & Phebe Woolry. 4 Mar. 1860. MA, R, D-118.
Crause, Jacob & Lucretia Ann Jones. 15 June 1854. B-284.
Crawford, George & Mary G. Glidden. 26 Dec. 1849. R, B-167.
Crawford, George & Lucy Hartley. 28 Oct. 1854. R, D-11.
Crawford, John & Letitia McClury (McClung). 6 Feb. 1851. MA,
B-202.
Crawford, John & Mary Kibby. 15 Nov. 1855. D-22.
Crawford, Robert & Lilly A. Brown. Alex Foster att. ages. 30
Sep. 1860. MA, R, D-130.
Creamer, William B. & Mary Thomas. 26 Mar. 1839. R, A-267.
Creamer, William H. & Caroline Beloat. 11 Sep. 1845. R, B-80.
Creighton, James & Ruby R. Whitcomb. 13 Mar. 1845. R, B-72.

31

Cresmer (Crasmer), Henry & Sophia Radh. 13 Apr. 1847. MA, R, B-101.
Crichton, Andrew C. & Mrs. H. M. Scott. 13 May 1852, by E. P. Pratt. MA, R.
Criswell, Daniel & Sophronia Church. Her father Joel Church cons., att. she is over 18, witn. Philip Blake. 29 Aug. 1833. MA, R, A-179.
Crites, Jacob & Maria Heath. 14 Nov. 1837. R, A-234.
Crits, John & Cecilli Heath. 20 Nov. 1838. MA, R, A-262.
Crmin, John M. & Eliza Reed. 25 June 1859. MA, R, D-100.
Crockston (Crookston), Thomas & Barbary Moore. 24 Mar. 1847. MA, B-242.
Cromly, Thomas & Mary Jane Campbell. 7 Sep. 1857. R, D-58.
Cropland (Crossland?), A. D. & Sarah E. Barnett. 2 Aug. 1856. R, D-33.
Cropper, Dyas P. & Elizabeth Malcolm. 13 May 1857, by E. P. Pratt. R.
Cropper, Major V. & Mary C. Johnston. 18 June 1855, by Rev. E. P. Pratt. R.
Cross, George & Sarah Vilet. 29 Oct. 1821. MA, R, A-61.
Cross (Corn? Com? Ghrams?), Jesse G. & Sarah A. Canterbury. He is 24, born Gallia Co. She is 19, born Lawrence Co., res. Clinton Furnace, dau. of Hugh Canterbury & M. Wara (?). 16 Aug. 1857. R, C-13, D-59.
Cross, Joseph & Elizabeth Helmer. 9 Dec. 1815. MA, R, A-17.
Cross, N. B. & Caroline Rollins. 9 Oct. 1845. MA, R, B-77.
Cross, N. B. & Elizabeth Berry. 14 June 1846. MA, R, B-89.
Cross, Thomas & Eve Lewis. 7 Nov. 1816. MA, R, A-25.
Cross, Washington & Cynthia Givens. 12 Sep. 1860. MA, R, D-129.
Crouse, Christian Frederick & Mary Elizabeth Cool. 2 Dec. 1852. MA, B-255.
Crow, Abraham & Elizabeth Harris. 15 Feb. 1814. MA, R, A-330.
Crozier, Robert & Nancy Ward. His mother Elizabeth Crozier cons., att. John Crozier. 25 Sep. 1848. MA, R, B-131.
Crugare, Proverbs & Catharine Blackburn. 23 Mar. 1854. D-4.
Crull, Andrew B. & Amanda Bennett. He is 27, born Scioto Co., res. Jefferson Tp., son of John & Abigail Crull. She is 21, born & res. Madison Tp., dau. of Caleb & Eliza Bennett. 21 Jan. 1858. R, C-8, C-12, D-68.
Crull, Caleb B. & Rebecca Jones. 9 Dec. 1841. R, B-26.
Crull, Caleb B. & Jane Crull. 20 Feb. 1845. R, B-71.
Crull, Charles & Elizabeth Cramer. 26 Sep. 1809. R, A-297.
Crull, David & Rhoda Pool. __ June 1843. R, B-50.
Crull, Henry & Martha McDowell. 6 Apr. 1818. R, A-35.
Crull, Jefferson & Levisa Noel. 28 Mar. 1839. R, A-267.
Crull, John H. & Sally Squires. 12 Mar. 1829. R, A-126.
Crull, Joshua J. & Maria Bennett. 1 Apr. 1847. MA, R, B-101.
Crull, Samuel Jr. & Sally Dodge. 22 Sep. 1836. R, A-223.
Crull, Samuel Jr. & Catherine S. Collis. He is 25, born & res. Harrison Tp., son of B. Crull. She is 25, res. Webster, dau. of Regal T. Collis. 4 Mar. 1858. MA, R, C-14, D-88.
Crull, Thomas J. & Juliann Slattery. 30 Oct. 1846. MA.
Crull, William & Ruth Stockham. 11 Apr. 1811. MA, R, A-308.
Crull, William & Polly Cathey. 15 Feb. 1827. MA, A-105.
Crull, William M. & Melinda Munn. 15 Dec. 1830. A-166.
Crumm, John & Martha E. Stiger. 1 Nov. 1860. MA, R, D-132.
Csunkelton, Samuel & Sarah Jones. Her father Hiram Jones cons. 16 Dec. 1852. MA, B-253.
Cuberly, William G. & Amy Wilson. 16 Sep. 1858. MA, R, D-82.
Cuddihy, Michael & Bridget Cashan. 12 Aug. 1855. MA, R, D-27.
Culbertson, Cambridge & Emily A. Rankin. 21 May 1857. R, D-55.
Culp, Jacob & Nancy Bowen. Her father George Bowen cons. 3 Feb. 1814. MA, R, A-332.

SCIOTO COUNTY MARRIAGES

Culp, Jacob & Sarah Millirons. Her father Michael Millirons
  cons., witn. Solomon Dever, Michael Millirons Jr., of
  Madison Tp. His father Cornelius Culp att. Jacob is over
  21, witn. Zenas Keller. 22 Nov. 1827. MA, R, A-113, A-119.
Culp, Jacob & Rebecca Turner. 22 Dec. 1846. MA.
Culp, John C. & Eliza M. McDowell. 15 July 1840. MA.
Culp, Samuel & Mary Dever. 4 Apr. 1847. MA, R, B-103.
Cumming, Hubbard S. & Eliza Jane Goudy. 15 Aug. 1848. R, B-129.
Cummins, Joseph L. & Elizabeth Dunahue. 7 Dec. 1830, by Luther
  Wheeler, J.P. R.
Cummins, Joseph L. & Mary Flanders. 4 July 1837. R, A-247.
Cummins, Thomas & Achse F. Hall. 28 Jan. 1829. MA, R, A-127.
Cumpston, Alfred & Lucina Stewart. 28 Sep. 1842. MA, R, B-35.
Cumpston, Alfred F. & Martha Jane Stevens. 16 Apr. 1857. R, D-55.
Cumpston, Isaac & Susanah Rawson. 1 Oct. 1846. R, B-94.
Cumpston, Newton & Elizabeth Jones. 14 July 1857. R, D-55.
Cumston, Enos & Eva Halterman. Samuel Rawson att. ages. 12 May
  1850. MA, R, B-180.
Cunning, Samuel W. & Mary A. Scott. 19 Dec. 1850. MA, B-197.
Cunningham, David & Mary Ellen Price. 16 Nov. 1851. B-226.
Cunningham, John D. & Malissa Burt. 2 Dec. 1847. MA, R, B-110.
Cunningham, Peter & Ann Kelly. 28 Aug. 1842. MA, R, B-33.
Cuppet, John & Sarah White. 8 Dec. 1853. MA, D-6.
Curey, Ezra & Elizabeth Leeth. 22 Nov. 1814. R, A-343.
Curran, Michael & Bridget Murphy. 24 Nov. 1857. R, D-69.
Currant (Corrett), Samuel & Mary Oritt (Trett). Her father (not
  named) cons. 2 Mar. 1854. MA, D-6.
Currey, Charles & Elizabeth White. 14 Oct. 1849. MA, R, B-160.
Currie, William & Naoma Carter. 31 July 1860. MA.
Curry, Henderson & Arcade Walls, of Seal Tp. 23 Nov. 1809. R,
  A-298.
Curtis (Cartis), Abijah & Minerva Whitney. Allen C. McArthur
  att. ages. 3 May 1838. MA, R, A-254.
Curtis, Wesley & Elizabeth Peral. 3 Apr. 1853. MA, B-261.
Custice, Thomas & Katharine Smith. 19 Oct. 1815. R, A-16.
Custice, William & Nancy Beloat. 29 June 1815. R, A-282.
Custis, John & Elizabeth Smith. 27 May 1827. R, A-129.
Cutler, Charles T. & Isabella Feurt. 7 Apr. 1835. R, A-198.
Cutler, Charles T. & Maria Bliss. 24 Feb. 1839. R, A-265.
Cutler, Demas H. & Hannah M. Scott. 2 Mar. 1843. R, B-47.
Cutler, Joshua & Laura Howard. 23 Nov. 1820. R, A-57.
Cutler, Lucius & Sarah Mustard. 31 Jan. 1842. R, B-27.
Cutler, Pliney & Murdwell Lamb. 22 June 1843. R, B-46.
Cutler, Pliny Jr. & Nancy Rankins. 24 Oct. 1844. R, B-63.
Cutler, Samuel & Rusinah Hadley. 31 Aug. 1848. MA, R, B-130.
Cutler, William S. & Mary F. Fuller. 20 Sep. 1858, by E. P.
  Pratt. MA, R.
Cutlip, Daniel B. & Michal Spriggs. 16 Jan. 1851. MA, B-201.
Cutlip, George & Pamelia Wilson. 3 Mar. 1853. MA, B-260.
Cutlip, John S. & Margaret Wilson. 28 June 1849. MA, R, B-152.
Cutright, John & Ruth Wolf. 8 May 1812. MA.
Cutshall, Jno.(?) & Ann Dougherty. 28 May 1853. B-264.
Cutter, Harvey & Rhoda Whitmore. 2 Nov. 1848. MA, R, B-137.
Cutter, Henry & Maria Shelpman. 26 Feb. 1835. R, A-197.
Cutter, Henry (Heinrich Kotter) & Mary Harmire. 24 Mar. 1852.
  MA, B-237.
Cutter, Nahum H. & Lidia Andrews. 4 June 1837. R, A-245.
Cutterjohn, Henry & Hannah Sollman. 15 Jan. 1852. MA, B-240.
Dabl, Daniel & Mary Emlet. His German signature on the MA looks
  like Daupel. 28 June 1860. MA, R, D-119.
Dace, Philip F. & Ruth A. McCollister. 24 May 1860. MA, R, D-124.
Dagaul (Dugan?), Thomas & Mary Rankins. 22 Sep. 1839. R, A-273.
Dages, Peter & Anne Hubbart. 2 July 1844. MA, R, B-62.

33

Dahler, Charles & Ann M. Lichner. 10 Apr. 1859. MA, R, D-99.
Dahler, Peter & Catherine Chetz. 10 Feb. 1859. MA, R, D-90.
Dailey, Owen & Emeline Owens. 11 Jan. 1830. MA.
Dailey, Ralph & Emily Cross. 28 Mar. 1839. R, A-267.
Dailey, Thomas & Mary Connroy. 12 Nov. 1853. MA.
Dalton, Daniel & Sophia Ross. 17 Nov. 1860. MA, R, D-125.
Damarin, Lewis C. & Mary C. Peck. 27 Dec. 1852. MA, B-254.
Damerin, Charles A. M. & Hariet C. Offnere. 10 Sep. 1835. R,
    A-205.
Dane (Dare), Enoch & Matilda Miller. 31 Dec. 1836. MA, R, A-233.
Daniel, George & Theressa Coonel. His father cons. German script
    sign. looks like Gabel or Sabol Daniel. 29 Aug. 1852. MA,
    B-251.
Daniel, James & Nancy Cockrell. 26 Dec. 1819. MA, R, A-51.
Daniel, John & Elizabeth Riggerish (Richard). 16 Aug. 1843. MA,
    R, B-50.
Daniels, John & Electa Conklin. 16 Aug. 1849. R, B-156.
Daniels, John L. & Camilla Stull. Harris Dodge att. her age over
    18. 15 Apr. 1838. MA, R, A-254.
Daniels, Joseph & Mary Mitchell. 25 Aug. 1829. R, A-133.
Daniels, Naham L. & Phebe Brady. 23 May 1819. R, A-46.
Daniels, S. W. (S.H.) & Anastatia Dawson. Pulaski Dawson att.
    ages. 14 Jan. 1853. MA, B-255.
Dannis (?), Jacob & Sabacthina Stumbaugh. His father Michael
    Dannis (?) cons., att. William F. Boyer. 9 Aug. 1836. MA.
Darby, Hugh & Ursula Shope. 18 June 1839. MA, R, A-271.
Darling, Samuel & Sarah M. (Hannah) Pratt. 21 Apr. 1843. MA, R,
    B-44.
Darlington, Abisha & Eve Creamer. 4 Mar. 1813. R, A-324.
Darlington, Robert & Margaret Snook. 3 Dec. 1821. MA.
Darlington, Robert & Belinda Howel. 3 Oct. 1822. R, A-73.
Darlington, Robert & Melinda McCanley (Mahala McCaulay). Her
    father James McCanley cons. 9 May 1833. MA, R, A-176.
Darlington, William & Taxy McKee. 1 Mar. 1852. MA, B-275.
Darlington, William M. & Rebecca Emmons. 25 Sep. 1838. MA, R,
    A-260.
Darlington, William M. & Mary B. Moulton. 8 Jan. 1851. MA, B-201.
Dauber, John & Cunnyander Kulb. 28 Mar. 1841. MA, R, B-17.
Daum, George & Lizzy Benter (Elizabeth Bender). 16 Sep. 1852.
    MA, B-247.
Dautremont, James P. & Ellen Murphy. 27 Mar. 1859. MA, R, D-89.
Davenport, Whitte & Elizabeth Brown. 19 Sep. 1852. MA, B-247.
Davey, P. & Mary Jane Varner. 12 May 1853. MA, B-270.
Davies (Davis), David & Mary Jenkins. 21 May 1840. MA, R, B-5.
Davies (Davis), Jenkin & Nancy Jane Dear. 21 Nov. 1853. MA,
    B-281.
Davies (Davis), Owen & Margaret Hughs. 8 Mar. 1844. MA, R, B-55.
Davis, Alexander W. & Cynthia A. Graves. Her father Thadeus
    Graves cons. 4 Apr. 1858. MA, R, D-72.
Davis, Arthur & Margaret Leonard. 11 June 1828. R, A-129.
Davis, Arthur W. & Susannah Leonard. 30 Apr. 1837. R, A-241.
Davis, Benjamin & Jane Woolsey. 27 Mar. 1811. MA, R, A-311.
Davis, David M. & Catherine Lewis. 1 Apr. 1852. MA, B-235.
Davis, Elnathan & Mary Kniff. 4 Nov. 1810. A-306.
Davis, Freeman & Lucy Chamberlain. 6 Nov. 1817. MA, R, A-30.
Davis, Henry & Anna M. Stout. 27 Sep. 1860. MA, R, D-121.
Davis, Jacob W. & Roseanna M. Smith. 22 May 1853. B-263.
Davis, James & Margaret Lewis. 9 Sep. 1853. MA, B-268.
Davis, James & Vashti Chick. Jobe Kittle att. ages. 22 Apr. 1860.
    MA, R, D-116.
Davis, James R. & Elizabeth J. Emory. 14 Mar. 1860. MA, R, D-114.
Davis, John & Elizabeth Russell. 4 Feb. 1855. MA, R, D-15.

34

SCIOTO COUNTY MARRIAGES

Davis, John & Ellen Marshall. Elisabeth Marshall cons. 1 Sep.
1860. MA, R, D-127.
Davis, John S. & Anne Maria Tracy. 4 July 1854. R, D-8.
Davis, Thomas & Martha E. Wymer. 16 Oct. 1857. R, D-63.
Davis, William & Rachel Poss. 7 Jan. 1810. R, A-301.
Davis, William & Emeline Harvey. D. Young of Young's Furnace
att. she is of age and willing to marry. 15 Oct. 1833. MA, R,
A-178.
Davis, William & Winneford Hughes. 11 Aug. 1851. MA, B-213.
Davison, Alfred D. & Harriet Stevenson. 28 Feb. 1843. MA, R,
B-42.
Davison, Reuben S. & Hannah Guthrie. 14 Feb. 1816. MA, R, A-18.
Davison, Thomas & Eliva (Elvin) White. 20 Oct. 1846. MA, R, B-96.
Davisson, Andrew & Sarah Thompson. Her father James Thompson
cons., witn. Rees Thompson, Joseph L. Thompson. 28 Sep. 1820.
MA, R, A-55.
Davisson, Isaac & Mary Lionbarger. Her father Peter Lionbarger
cons., witn. Peter Lionbarger Jr., John Davisson. 16 July
1816, by John Lee. MA, R.
Davisson, J. Hamilton & Adeline Hard. Her mother Sophronia Hard
cons., witn. Syrenia Slimp, Edwin Hard, of French Grant.
18 Nov. 1846. MA, R, B-94.
Davisson, John & Nancy Lawson. 6 Feb. 1832. MA, R, A-159.
Davisson, Thomas & Eliza Chapman. 11 Apr. 1850. R, B-176.
Dawsin, George A. & Mary F. McNelly. 30 Jan. 1851. MA, B-205.
Dawson, Abijah & Anna Shoemaker. 26 Aug. 1810. R, A-303.
Dawson, James & Anna White. 28 Apr. 1812. R, A-321.
Dawson, James & Hannah Goble. 18 Apr. 1823. MA, R, A-75.
Dawson, John & Lydia Margaret Bloomer. 13 Jan. 1831. R, A-151.
Dawson, John & Mary Mahala Milam. 11 Oct. 1851. MA, B-230.
Dawson, John & Nancy Songer. 18 Apr. 1852. MA, B-237.
Day, Alfred C. & Hester Eisman. 2 Jan. 1854. D-4.
Day, Allen & Emily McFan. His father John Day cons., att. Josiah
Hayns. Kimber McFan att. ages. 21 Dec. 1845. MA, R, B-82.
Day, Christopher & Jane McJunkin. 2 Jan. 1849. MA, R, B-137.
Day, Daniel & Martha West. 15 May 1833. MA, R, A-176, A-177.
Day, David & Mary Jones. 24 Mar. 1859. MA, R, D-95.
Day, Dudley & Patience T. Jones, both of French Grant. 16 Dec.
1830, by Dan Young. R.
Day, E. C. & Eliza Jane Wheeler. 14 June 1852. MA, B-240.
Day, Ezekiel & Rebecca Bowen. He res. Upper Tp. She res. Bloom
Tp. 30 Dec. 1813. R, A-331.
Day, James R. & Margaret Bishop. 22 Mar. 1846. MA, R, B-85.
Day, Kimber B. & Lucy J. Hard. 11 Dec. 1842. R, B-38.
Day, Lewis B. & Cintha Chandler. Her father Ellis Chandler cons.,
witn. Stephen Chandler. 21 Feb. 1822. MA, R, A-66.
Day, Lewis B. & Nancy Jane Noel. 20 Dec. 1853. D-4.
Day, Willis & Lanah Feurt. Her father Peter Feurt, of Green Tp.
cons., witn. Benjamin Feurt. 9 Jan. 1826. MA, R, A-94.
Days, Godlob & Mary Jane Petit. 28 Oct. 1858. MA, R, D-87.
Dean, Isaiah & Elizabeth Buckley. 30 July 1846. MA, R, B-89.
Dean, James & Mary Susan Stokes. 4 Jan. 1847. MA, R, B-96.
Dear, Lewis & Sarah Jackson. 20 Dec. 1860. MA, R, D-136.
Deaver, John & Gracey Monroe (Munrow). 1 May 1817. MA, R, A-28.
Deaver, Michael & Elizabeth Walker. 26 Dec. 1854. MA.
Deaver, Michael & Minerva Nail. 24 Aug. 1856. R, D-34.
Debo, Augustus & Emily Warren. Originally entered as Augustus
DeBlau and Emily Varner, this record was corrected in 1900.
2 Aug. 1857. D-58.
Debow, Elias & Elizabeth Cable. 8 Sep. 1850. MA, R, B-188.
Debow, George & Seny Sargent. Her pars. John & Fanny Sargent
cons., witn. Wm. Salter, Branson Miles, of Scioto Furnace.
25 Dec. 1833. MA, R, A-176.

35

Deegin (Diggin), John & Lydia Verbeck. His father B. B. Deegins
  cons., witn. Willis Bumnt (?), Alva Virback. 31 Dec. 1831.
  MA, R, A-162.
Deen, William & Hannah Peyton. 19 July 1808. R, A-289.
Degare, Peter & Katherine Hipsher. 4 Nov. 1817. R, A-32, A-33.
Degear, Abraham & Harriet Dain. 27 Jan. 1852. MA.
Deger, John Jr. & Eunice Heath. 30 Oct. 1828. R, A-123.
Degroat, Henry & Adrian Adams. 13 Oct. 1842. MA, R, B-36.
Degrummand, William J. & Arabell B. Gessenger. 13 Aug. 1854. R,
  D-9.
Deill (Dill), John & Elizabeth Rolfes. 12 Feb. 1850. R, B-172.
Delabar, Michael & Sena Virbeck. MA says she has a former
  husband living. 26 Sep. 1850. MA, R, B-188.
Delaney, Patrick & Sarah Renchenhouse. 29 Dec. 1859. MA, R, D-103.
Delaney, William & Sarah Barklow. 8 Feb. 1849. MA, R, B-140.
Delany, Elijah & Elizabeth Halterman. 10 Nov. 1844. MA, R, B-64.
Delany, Milton & Sarah Sumantha Hesler. 3 June 1858. MA, R, D-76.
Delay, Jerry & Amanda Colwell. 21 July 1835. R, A-204.
Delhotal, Francois & Mary Bowman. 15 Sep. 1851. MA.
Delhotal, Xavier & Adeline Hucher. 7 Dec. 1851. MA, B-225.
Delong, Jesse & Mary Ann Bowen. 6 Dec. 1841. MA, R, B-26.
Delong, Simon & Catherine Moore. 25 Dec. 1827. R, A-114, A-120.
Delrymple, E. W. & Margaret Ann Gifford. 5 Nov. 1845. MA, R,
  B-81.
Demarest, Samuel & Elizabeth Corwine. 6 July 1846. MA, R, B-88.
Dener, Ambrose & Caroline Hilz. 14 July 1857. R, D-58.
Dennewitz, Charles & Doretz Lell (Dauherty Lill). 6 Mar. 1855.
  MA, R, D-16.
Denney (Denning), Newton B. & Mary Adaline Williams. 19 June
  1853. MA, B-263.
Dennis, David & Lucy Hammett. 16 Nov. 1818. MA.
Dennis, J. W. & Joanna Noel. 2 Nov. 1852. B-278.
Dennison, George W. & Harriet Werts (Wortz). 6 Dec. 1860. MA, R,
  D-127.
Denny, Lewis & Charity Dunn. Nancy Dunn cons., witn. S. S.
  Glidden. 14 Apr. 1851. MA, B-205, B-210 (shows her name
  Charity Denny, dated 26 June 1851).
Detricks, Henry & Mary Woolford. 8 Nov. 1857. R, D-63.
Dever, Branson & Julia Ann Eppeheimer. 22 May 1845. MA, R, B-79.
Dever, Caleb & Catharine Shoemaker. 4 Oct. 1855. R, D-25.
Dever, David & Nancy Shonkwiler. 19 May 1822. MA, R, A-66.
Dever, Dempsey & Sarah Helen Gifford. 28 Dec. 1856. R, D-44.
Dever, George & Mahala White. 19 Aug. 1849. MA, R, B-157.
Dever, Jackson & Elizabeth Matheny. 26 Nov. 1849. MA, R, B-164.
Dever, Jackson & Abysina P. Daniels. 2 Jan. 1851. MA, B-205.
Dever, James & Mary Barns. 6 Mar. 1817. R, A-26.
Dever, Jefferson & Evaline Crull. He is 26, born & res. Jackson
  Co., son of Solomon. She is 20, born & res. Scioto Co., dau.
  of William M. 20 May 1856. R, C-5, D-30.
Dever, Joseph M. & Rebecca F. Wheeler. He is 29, born & res.
  Morgan Tp., son of William & A. She is 19, born Virginia,
  res. Morgan Tp. 14 Sep. 1856. R, C-3, C-6, D-36.
Dever, Martin J. & Elizabeth Bennett. 7 Dec. 1843. MA, R, B-54.
Dever, Noah & Emaline Bean. 31 Mar. 1831. MA, R, A-153.
Dever, William & Aseaneth McDougall. 16 May 1816. R, A-22.
Dever, William & Louisa McDowell. Her father (not named) present
  and cons. 26 Mar. 1848. MA, R, B-124.
Devil, Daniel & Katharine Humbolt. 25 Oct. 1857. R, D-68.
Devor (Devers), James & Julianna Finney. 22 Aug. 1853. MA, B-268.
Devore, Hiram & Betsy Vantine. 19 Oct. 1825. R, A-92.
Dew, John & Nancy Ann Field. 30 Jan. 1859. MA, R, D-80.
Dewey, Israel J. & Elizabeth M. Kirkpatrick. 30 Mar. 1851. B-218.

Dewey, Israel J. & Elizabeth Ann Samson. Her father William
Samson, of Madison Tp. cons. 1 Jan. 1855. MA, R, D-14.
Dewey, Joseph W. & Louise Ann Slattery. 16 Dec. 1853. B-273.
Dewey, Walter & Nancy Ketcham. 8 Mar. 1843. MA.
Dewey, Walter & Charlotte Kretzer. 27 Sep. 1846. MA, R, B-92.
Dewey, William T. & Melinda Bradford. 3 Mar. 1852. MA, B-232.
Dewit, George & Hannah Williams. 2 May 1832. MA.
Dewitt, Andrew J. & Mary Hanson. 23 May 1860. MA, R, D-131.
Dewitt, Washington & Mary Ann Swager. 6 July 1854. R, D-8.
Dewitt, William & Rebeccah Monrow. Her father Solomon Monrow
cons., witn. William Baker. 7 Jan. 1821. MA, R, A-56.
Didwit, John & Levina Colegrove. 20 Nov. 1836. MA, R, A-234.
Dieckman, Henry (Heinrich) & Rebecca Orse. 19 Sep. 1852. MA,
B-250.
Dilley, Washington & Mary Ann Biggarstaff. 25 Dec. 1849. R,
B-165.
Dillman, E. C. & Lucy Jane Loomis. 7 Apr. 1852. MA, B-236.
Dillon, Bishop & Malissa (Josephine) Williams. 10 Mar. 1858.
R, D-71.
Dillon, Isaac E. & Clarinda McManagale. 5 May 1848. MA, R, B-123.
Dillon, James & Elizabeth Bush. Her guardian Fielden H. Dillon
cons. 24 Nov. 1859. MA, R, D-106.
Dillon, James T. & Ann B. Thompson. 16 Nov. 1827. MA, R, A-112.
Dills, Francis N. & Eliza Jane Nail. 31 Aug. 1856. MA, R, D-41.
Dilly, William H. & Elizabeth Walburn. Thomas J. Baccus att.
ages. 29 Aug. 1847. MA, R, B-107.
Diveley, Isaac & Elvira Groves. 25 Mar. 1830. MA, R, A-142.
Dixon, Eli & Elizabeth Graham. Her mother Mary Graham cons.,
att. John Graham. Henry Dixon att. Eli's age. 18 June 1814.
MA, R, A-337.
Dixon, George V. & Rebecca Mead. 1 June 1860. MA, R, D-114.
Doan, Seth & Joanna Waddle. 3 Aug. 1832. R, A-165.
Dobbins, William N. & Jane Arena Willis. Her pars. John &
Rebecca Willis cons. 15 July 1841. MA, R, B-22.
Dod, Isaac & Nancey Hannaman, both of Seal Tp. 18 Feb. 1808.
R, A-290.
Dodds, David T. & Berthena R. Dunn. William T. Dodds att. ages.
25 Jan. 1855. MA, R, D-17.
Dodds, John & Ann Tucker. Her father John Tucker att. ages.
29 May 1823. MA, R, A-75.
Dodds, John B. & Nancy A. Lucas. 29 Feb. 1852. B-233.
Dodds, Owen C. & Nancy McMurry. 15 Nov. 1860. MA, R, D-134.
Dodds, William B. & Eliza McMasters. 17 May 1834. R, A-189.
Dodge, Daniel & Emaline A. Fields. 1 Apr. 1855. MA, R, D-16.
Dodge, Daniel H. & Abigail Mead. 28 Jan. 1841. MA, R, B-20.
Dodge, Frances & Mary Ann Wood. 5 Apr. 1838. MA, R, A-253, B-5.
Dodge, Francis & Sally Kottle. 28 Dec. 1840. MA.
Dodge, Harris & Susannah Cummings. 9 Sep. 1846. MA, R, B-92.
Dodge, John C. & Margaret Irwin. 12 Dec. 1852. MA, B-262.
Dodge, Jonathan Jr. & Delitha Snook. 2 July 1846. MA, R, B-89.
Dodge, Jonathan & Rebecca Bennett. 11 Apr. 1852. MA, B-239.
Dodge, Oliver W. & Hester Fleming. 6 Jan. 1839. MA, R, B-6.
Dodge, Rufus & Ellen Patterson (Helen Batterson). 31 Dec. 1848.
MA, R, B-140.
Dodge, William M. & Rebecca Clark. 11 Aug. 1854. R, D-9.
Dodson, John R. & Rachel Kinney. 15 Sep. 1833. MA, R, A-181.
Doerres (Derris), John K. & Mary Fagel. 10 Jan. 1840. MA, R,
A-277.
Dole, Eben & Elizabeth Carrol. 25 Apr. 1824. R, A-81.
Dole, Edward P. & Mary Ellen Lusk. 26 Jan. 1854. D-5.
Dole, John & Hanna Herman. 15 Jan. 1856. D-24.
Dole, Joshua & Eliza A. Dunkin. 6 May 1855. B-286.
Dole, Samuel & Elizabeth Jane Tucker. 25 Mar. 1860. MA, R, D-121.

Doll (Dole), John J. & Margaret Graham. Her father Seth Graham
of Pond Creek cons. 25 June 1834. MA, R, A-189.
Doll, Peter & Ellen Eulitt. He was born Scioto Co., res. Morgan
Tp. She was born Scioto Co., res. Morgan Tp., the dau. of
Isaac & Mary. 21 Jan. 1858. R, C-13, D-76.
Dollarhide, Thomas & Elizabeth Victor. John Leniger att. ages.
24 Sep. 1848. MA, R, B-136.
Donalson, Seth & Margaret S. Mills. 4 Sep. 1855. D-21.
Donalson, William & Druzilla Patterson. 29 July 1824. R, A-83.
Donavan, Jeremiah & Margaret D. Nolta. 19 June 1848. MA, R, B-123.
Donley, Isaiah (Josiah) & Sophia Colvin. Her stepfather Samuel
Slater cons. 29 Sep. 1853. MA, B-272.
Donnally, Gilfoil & Sarah Ann Wild. 29 June 1831. MA.
Donoho, Danial & Rosa Callen (Cahler). 26 June 1850, by Eml.
Thienpont, M.G. MA, R.
Donohoo, Peter & Miranda Jeffords. 26 Aug. 1850. MA, R, B-186.
Doolittle, James & Martha Elizabeth Musser. Her mother Barbary
Ann Musser cons. 18 Aug. 1840. MA, R, B-11.
Dorch, Jno. & Susanna Greensby. 2 Aug. 1853. B-268.
Dories, Frederick & Charlotte Errot. 25 Oct. 1853. MA.
Dorn, Henry & Gertrude Yost. 1 June 1859. MA, R, D-99.
Dornan, Charles & Catharine Lindsey (Limley?). 17 Oct. 1854. R,
D-11.
Dornsbeck, Philip & Mary Slupf. 2 Apr. 1856. R, D-28.
Dortch (Dolch), George & Catharine Nagle (Nogle). 31 Oct. 1850.
MA, B-194.
Dortch, John & Susannah Stockham. His father William Dortch
cons., witn. Claibourn Roberts, John Stockham. 22 July 1824.
MA, R, A-82.
Dortch, John & Sarah Stockham. 8 Mar. 1834. MA, R, A-191.
Dotson, John & Rebeck Day. 14 Aug. 1831. MA, R, A-155.
Doty, Abner & Linnea Burrows. 27 July 1830. MA, R, A-144.
Doty, Daniel & Sarah Ann Swaar. 1 July 1832. MA, R, A-168.
Doty, William & Emeline Swaar. 13 Nov. 1834. MA, R, A-194.
Double, William & Margaret Carter. 17 July 1851. B-212.
Dougherty, Peter & Elizabeth Renolds. 11 Nov. 1848. MA.
Douglas, James T. & Margaret Noland. 24 Feb. 1860. MA, R, D-116.
Douglas, John & Adaline McLaughlin. He is 23, born Columbiana
Co., res. Madison Tp., son of James. She is res. Madison
Tp., born Columbiana Co., dau. of Samuel. 11 Mar. 1856. R,
C-4, D-27.
Douglass, Henry J. & Mary Grose. 4 July 1860. MA, R, D-132.
Dowes (Dawes? Dower?), William & Delilah Dawson. 6 Aug. 1816.
MA, R, A-23.
Dowley, James & Olivia Goudy. 18 July 1850. R, B-184.
Downey (Downing), Jefferson A. & Mary Jane Cottle (Carter).
8 Mar. 1846. MA, R, B-86.
Downey, Nathaniel & Eliza Dewey. 26 Nov. 1855. D-22.
Downey, Paul D. & Prudence Garey. Alexander I. Stanford att.
ages. 3 Dec. 1841. MA, R, B-24.
Doyal, Samuel, of Butler Co. & Julia Hoskinson. 21 Aug. 1831.
MA, R, A-155.
Doyal, Simon & Louisa M. Wilson. 13 June 1831. MA.
Doyle, William & Catherine Currens. 2 Oct. 1859. MA, R, D-110.
Drake, Austin & Sarah Wells. 3 Mar. 1847. MA, R, B-99.
Drake, Ephraim & Emeline Bennet. 22 Dec. 1853. B-282.
Drake, James H. & Caroline Marshall. 3 July 1839. MA, R, A-273.
Drake, John & Fanny Phillips. John Phillips att. her age over
18. 4 Jan. 1838. MA, R, A-248.
Drake, William & Sarah Jane Richarts. Her father William Richart
cons. 13 Mar. 1848. MA.
Dray, Elias & Hannah Mustard. He is son of Daniel; she is dau.
of William & Sarah. 3 ___ 1857. R, C-6, D-52.

Drennan, David (Daniel) & Matilda Wykoff. 7 June 1846. R, B-88.
Drennen, C. Wesley & Margaret Shupe. 6 July 1859. MA, R, D-98.
Dresler, William & Hulda Rowley. 4 July 1860, by M. D. Wilcox,
   J.P. R.
Dressler, William & Zire Huddleston. Her father Joseph Huddleson
   cons. 4 July 1860. MA.
Driggs, Daniel & Eliza Hawk. 15 Nov. 1838. MA, R, A-262.
Driver, William & Melinda Odle. 23 Aug. 1839. MA, R, A-272.
Dudley, David & Elizabeth Boynton. 30 Sep. 1818. MA, R, A-40.
Duduit, F. E. & Mary C. Oakes. 31 May 1855. R, D-18.
Duduit, Frederick & Helen H. Gilruth. Her father James Gilruth
   cons. 22 Sep. 1833. MA, R, A-183.
Duduit, William & Zier Lacroix. 3 July 1817. MA, R, A-29.
Duduit, William & Lucy Flanders, both of Green Tp. 26 Feb. 1826.
   MA, R, A-100.
Duffy, Ebenezer & Martha Hughs. Her father James Hughs cons.,
   att. Job Hughs. 8 Jan. 1834. MA, R, A-187.
Duffy, Ebenezer & Mary Wilson. 25 Oct. 1838. MA, R, A-261.
Duffy, Edward & Ann Melane (McLane). 4 Dec. 1856. R, D-44.
Duffy, John & Samartha A. Ellison. Her pars. Felix & Mary A.
   Ellison cons., witn. Jacob Webb. 10 Sep. 1859. MA, R, D-102.
Duflegny, Christopher G. & Peggy Tims (Gims). 19 Apr. 1832. MA,
   R, A-162.
Dulail, Samuel & Augusta Bowman. 29 May 1855. B-286.
Dulan, Thomas & Jane Stout. 13 Mar. 1859. MA, R, D-87.
Dulany, Samuel & Mary Halterman. Elijah Dulany cons., witn.
   Benjamin Dulany, Elijah Dulany. Her brother Gabriel Halter-
   man att. her age over 18, att. she has no father, no mother.
   15 Sep. 1844. MA, R, B-63.
Dunahoo, Thomas & Welthy A. J. Cooly. 13 Dec. 1840. R, B-15.
Duncan, Andrew J. & Anne Henry. John Hanna att. ages. 13 Sep.
   1859. MA, R, D-117.
Duncan, John & Sarah Ann Shandricks (Handricks). 3 Aug. 1832.
   MA, R, A-166.
Duncan, Joseph & Polly Barnhart. 1 May 1817. MA, R, A-28.
Duncan, Thomas & Mary Chesnutt. Benjamin Chestnut att. her age
   over 18. 29 Aug. 1830. MA, R, A-146.
Duniway, Isaac & Belinda Darlington. 24 Feb. 1838. MA, R, A-251.
Dunkin, Alexander & Elizabeth Gammon. 10 Oct. 1854. B-285.
Dunlap, James & Mary E. Brooker. 15 Aug. 1860. MA, R, D-122.
Dunlap, Robert & Mary Janes. Her pars. A. & Polly Crawford cons.,
   witn. Richard Malone. 7 Jan. 1836. MA, R, A-212, A-227, A-243.
Dunlap, Robert of Pittsburgh & Harriett Riggs. 20 Oct. 1847.
   R, B-110.
Dunn, Lewis C. & Maria McCall. 28 June 1849. MA, R, B-156.
Dunning, Palmer & Emily Bliss. 26 May 1832. MA, R, A-164.
Dunsmore (Densmore), Henry & Rebecca J. Watkins. He is 25, born
   Ireland, res. Portsmouth, son of Samuel & Martha. She is 23,
   born Scioto Co., res. Portsmouth, dau. of Thomas & Judah
   Watkins. 11 Apr. 1856. R, C-2, D-30.
Dupuy, William & Peggy Littlejohn. 5 Oct. 1817. R, A-30.
Dutiel, Francis & Polly Snedicor. 30 Oct. 1823. MA, R, A-79.
Dutiel, Francis Charles & Ann Eliza Perry. 31 Jan. 1855. MA.
Dutiel, John & Sary Ann Lewis. 4 Dec. 1855 (1853). R, D-14.
Dutiel, John & Mary M. Gifford. 11 Sep. 1856. R, D-35.
Dutiel, John & Jane Ann ___. 18 Mar. 1830. A-146.
Dutiel, Lewis & Katharine Snedigar. 10 Sep. 1833. R, A-177.
Dutiel, Lewis & Martha Jane Gifford. He is 27, born & res.
   Scioto Co., son of Frances. She is 17, born & res. Scioto
   Co., dau. of John Clifford. 28 May 1857. R, C-14, D-56.
Dutiel, Peter & Nancy Black. 1 Apr. 1824. MA, R, A-82.
Dutiel, Peter & Nancy Lewis. 27 Nov. 1856. R, D-43.

Duvendack, John Adam & Mary E. March (Masch). 19 June 1850. MA,
R, B-181.
Dyke, Charles & Harriet Masters. 14 Mar. 1848. MA, R, B-116.
Dyke, John & Jane Kilpatrick. 6 Mar. 1838. MA, R, A-250.
Dysart, Stephen & Susannah Hannaman. 23 Nov. 1809. R, A-298.
Dysert, Solomon & Margaret Doll. 14 Dec. 1834. R, A-199.
Ealey, Isaac & Ellen Tipton. 4 July 1850. MA, R, B-187.
Earharte, Jacob T. & Eliza McQuality. 13 Oct. 1852. MA, B-250.
Earl, Abram B. & Nany Pelhank. J. Pelhank cons. 2 May 1859. MA,
R, D-96.
Early, Anthony & Catherine Mackeltree. 2 Apr. 1818. MA, R, A-38.
Early, William & Mary Dent Oard. 26 Dec. 1837. A-246.
Eastman (Eastburn), Philip & Mary A. Aldridge, both of Alexan-
dria. 21 May 1812. MA, R, A-319.
Easton, Thomas & Martha Berryman. 8 Feb. 1839. MA, R, A-266.
Eatinger, George & Catherine Brown. 23 Sep. 1849. MA, R, B-158.
Eaton (Easton), Turner & Elizabeth Glaze. 1 Jan. 1854. D-7.
Eblin, William & Nancy Terry. 26 June 1854. R, D-14.
Echart, Absolom & Nancy Farmer. 2 Apr. 1857. R, D-54.
Edgar, Joseph & Nancy (Mary) White. 13 Aug. 1836. MA, R, A-224.
Edgington, Henry C. & Laura A. Clark. 25 Oct. 1845. MA, R, B-78.
Edgington, Jeremiah V. & Lucretia Bonser. Thomas Edgington att.
their ages. 12 May 1844. MA, R, B-59.
Edgington, Jeremiah V. & Margaret Worley. 9 Aug. 1848. R, B-129.
Edgington, Nathan & Mary Ann Storer. 17 Sep. 1848. R, B-132.
Edgington, Peter T. & Rachel Smedley. 24 Dec. 1846. MA, B-229.
Edgington, Thomas & Rhoda Bonser. 27 Aug. 1838. R, A-258.
Edmisten, John & Mary Ann Fowler. 19 Sep. 1850. MA, R, B-191.
Edward, Thomas & Nancy Sanford. Her mother Jane Williams cons.
29 Dec. 1836. MA, R, A-233.
Edwards, Abraham & Zabra Skinner. Norval Biggs att. ages. 21 May
1859. MA, R, D-93.
Edwards, Andrew & Mary Darlington. 23 Dec. 1835. MA.
Edwards, Charles & Margaret Buffington. His mother, Katharine
Edwards, widow of David Edwards, cons., att. Charles Mill-
holland. 18 Feb. 1827. MA, R, A-108.
Edwards, Edward A. & Ann Evans. He is 45. She is 30. Both res.
Scioto Co., second marriage for both. 16 Sep. 1857. R, C-9,
D-59.
Edwards, Jesse B. & Angeline Freeman. 15 Sep. 1850. MA, R, B-188.
Edwards, John & Mahala Davis. 6 Dec. 1832. MA, R, A-170.
Edwards, John Francis & Betsy Cottermole (Cattamole). 10 May
1833. MA, R, A-176.
Edwards, Samuel & Sarah Jane Dodds. 5 Mar. 1846. R, B-84.
Edwards, William & Jemima McCleland. 5 Jan. 1854. D-2.
Eggleston, Joseph & Nancy Lindsey. 14 Sep. 1823. R, A-78.
Egleston, Jonathan & Lavina Martin. 30 Dec. 1827. R, A-115, A-120.
Ehret, Adam & Christina Koch. 13 May 1854. R, D-8.
Eichels, Joseph & Charlotte Ghar. 24 Sep. 1853. MA.
Eicher, Abraham & Miriam McCoy. 24 Dec. 1846. MA, R, B-96.
Eifert, John & Mary Williams. 11 May 1848. MA, R, B-127.
Eifort, Henry & Sarah F. Cook. 23 Mar. 1854. D-6.
Eifort, Sebastian & Rachel Jackson. Her father William Jackson
cons., of Bloom Tp., says she is of full age. 17 Mar. 1842.
MA, R, B-29.
Eifort, William & Mary Evans. John Evans att. ages. 18 July
1851. MA.
Eisenhardt, Joseph & Barbary Will. 30 Nov. 1850. MA, B-195.
Elarton (Eliton), James & Elizabeth Cooper. John J. Cooper att.
her age over 18. 31 Jan. 1839. MA, R, A-265.
Elbert, Conrad & Barbara Barr (Ban?). 8 July 1855. MA, R, D-25.
Elden, William & Jerusha M. Morrell. 1 Aug. 1844. R, B-61.

Eldred, Samuel & Mary Walker. G.H. Smith att. her age over 18.
16 Sep. 1813. MA, R, A-326.
Eliton, Plesant & Mary Holland, of Upper Tp. 5 Oct. 1809. R,
A-300.
Ellcesser, Fred (Franz) & Mary Jane Dever (Jones). 25 Sep. 1853.
MA, D-6.
Elliot, R.W. & Elizabeth J. Storer. 26 Oct. 1854. R, D-11.
Elliott, Alexander & Hester Ann Worley. 2 Feb. 1845. R, B-68.
Elliott, Benjamin & Hannah Brouce. 15 Feb. 1838. R, A-254.
Elliott, Leroy & Rachel Hutton. 27 Sep. 1859. MA, R, D-101.
Elliott, Robert & Martha Bennet. 29 Sep. 1859. MA, R, D-104.
Ellis, James & Margaret Ann Garvin. 12 Feb. 1845. R, B-68.
Ellis, James & Sivilla Jane Starling (Sterling). 19 Mar. 1860.
MA, R, D-115.
Ellis, Lorenzo D. & Mary Hoffman. 18 Jan. 1846. MA, R, B-82.
Ellis, Mark & Mary Shepman. 27 Sep. 1854, by S.M. Donohoe, M.G.
(This is on a Pike Co. form.)
Ellis (Liles, Silas), Thomas & Mary Tomlison. 6 Jan. 1833. MA,
R, A-171.
Ellison, Elijah & Mary Ann Nichols. 18 Jan. 1827. MA, R, A-102.
Ellison, James W. & Mary Santey (Lauty). 3 Nov. 1856. R, D-40.
Ellison, Joseph & Eliza Huddleston. 8 Oct. 1839. MA, R, A-274.
Ellmore, George W. & Mary Jane Oard. 10 Dec. 1853. B-282.
Elmore, Charles Nelson & Mary Jane Hunt. 3 Dec. 1842. MA.
Elsiser, Martin & Waldburk Elsiser. 7 July 1857. R, D-65.
Ely, Peter & Polly Wood. Her father Jacob Wood cons. 18 Feb.
1833. MA, R, A-172.
Emerson, Taylor & Harriet Gale. 12 Dec. 1841. MA, R, B-23.
Emery, Dearborn & Juliet Chamberlain, of Vernon Tp. 11 Aug.
1842. R, B-34.
Emling, George & Catrina (Catherine) Wall. 19 June 1848. MA, R,
B-125.
Emmens, John & Sally Jane Jaynes. 14 May 1850. R, B-179.
Emmet, Peter & Catharine Wurth. 29 July 1850. R, B-184.
Emory, Israel James & Elizabeth Brock. 30 Jan. 1823. MA, R, A-72.
Emory, Oliver & Delila Hoppis. 9 July 1846. MA, R, B-90.
Emricks, Joseph & Joanna Carl. 12 Mar. 1840. R, B-3.
Engelbrecht, William & Remina Witmer (Jemine Wittick). 28 Sep.
1852. MA, B-248.
Engels, James & Ruth Cutright. Her father John Cutright cons.
11 June 1830. MA.
Englebreck, Frederick & Charlotte Brodbeck. Her father Anthony
Brodbeck cons., witn. Paul Brodbeck. 29 Nov. 1838. MA, R,
A-263.
Enkle, August & Charlote Varnager. 9 Sep. 1859. MA.
Enslow, Andrew J. & Nancy M. Bliss. 3 Dec. 1846. MA, R, B-95.
Enslow, Revilo & Sophia Andre. 23 Dec. 1852. MA, B-255.
Enslow, Rezin & Mary Sebring. Her father Thompson Sebring cons.,
witn. David Enslow, Abraham Enslow. 12 Mar. 1820. MA, R, A-52.
Enslow, Thomas J. & Eve James. 23 Nov. 1834. R, A-194, A-243.
Enslow, Thompson S. & Louisa Nurse. 29 Mar. 1842. R, B-45.
Enslow, Worthington & Filora Ann Weaver. 21 Nov. 1847. MA, R,
B-113, B-118.
Enyard, William & Mahala Cracraft. 21 July 1852. MA, B-276.
Erak, Andrew & Sophia Huffin. 26 Aug. 1851. B-218.
Erb, Hieronymus & Rosina Hoffman. 1 June 1841. MA, R, B-21.
Erlenwien (Allenwine), John & Mary Noland. 1 Apr. 1851. MA.
Ervin (Irwin), William & Mariah Stockham. 31 Dec. 1854. MA, R,
D-13.
Erwin (Irwin), Samuel W. & Nancy Stockham. 5 Nov. 1849. MA, R,
B-161.
Esker, Benjamin & Barbara Stetzinger. 5 Dec. 1855. D-24.
Estill, William & Mary Smith. 28 July 1851. B-245.

Etrick, Franklin & Flora Shirt. 22 May 1852. B-247.
Eulitt, Isaac & Mary B. Lemison. 21 July 1836. MA, R, A-219.
Euth, Martin & Louise Freund. 3 Oct. 1857. R, D-62.
Evans, Andrew J. & Marther J. Redman. 2 Oct. 1856. R, D-43.
Evans, Anthony & Francis Carver. 1 Apr. 1851. MA, B-205.
Evans, David & Hannah Salsbury. 20 Aug. 1856. R, D-34.
Evans, Elisha & Eve Halterman. 1 July 1819. R, A-46.
Evans, Evan & Martha Jane Lawhun. Her father John B. Lawhun cons.,
    witn. W.L. Evans, William F. McDowell. 3 Nov. 1845. MA, R,
    B-80.
Evans, Evan & Eliza Jane Cutright. 4 Oct. 1855. MA, D-21.
Evans, Evan D. & Elizabeth Phillips. 4 July 1853. MA, B-280.
Evans, H. A. & Salony Estophy. 15 Oct. 1855. D-22.
Evans, Harrison & Charity Grimes. 30 Aug. 1853. MA, B-280.
Evans, Isaac & Elizabeth Welch. 12 Nov. 1816. MA, R, A-25.
Evans, Isom & Eliza J. Holsinger. 28 June 1860. MA.
Evans, James & Elizabeth Lawhorne. 4 Nov. 1849. MA, R, B-161.
Evans, John & Eliza J. McGiddis. 10 Apr. 1860. MA, R, D-120.
Evans, John G. & Rebecca Storer. 9 July 1843. MA, R, B-48.
Evans, Levi & Elizabeth Shultz. Her father Henry Shultz att. her
    age over 18. 8 Feb. 1821. MA, R, A-56.
Evans, M. & Maria H. Bradford. 9 Nov. 1854. MA, B-285.
Evans, Stephen & Maria Hibbard. 2 Apr. 1859. MA, R, D-96.
Evans, Thomas W. & Mary Williams. 3 May 1858. MA, R, D-87.
Evans, William & Sarah Hardin. 1 May 1852. MA, B-238.
Everet, Septer & Louisa Louderback. His stepfather Owen Bruner
    att. ages. 10 Dec. 1852. MA, B-257.
Everett, John & Mary Snook. 31 Mar. 1831. R, A-152.
Everly, James & Catherine Compliment. 28 Nov. 1856. R, D-41.
Exlinn, Daniel M. & Sarah Mills. 22 Feb. 1857. R, D-48.
Eyates, John H. & Mary Butler. 28 Oct. 1819. R, A-47.
Fagans, Henry & Belinda Harrst (Harrison). 28 Aug. 1851. MA,
    B-215.
Fairfield, George M. & Sybil A. Gerwood. 1 Oct. 1848. R, B-131.
Fairington, James W. & Sarah Norris. 12 Mar. 1854. D-1.
Fairmann, Bernhard & Marie Lehman. 30 Sep. 1857. R, D-66.
Fairtrace, Jacob & Lovina Price. 31 Aug. 1857. R, D-57.
Fairtrace, John & Catherine Connolly. 19 Mar. 1859. MA, R, D-89.
Fairtress, Jacob & Anna Maria Jones. Her mother Sarah Ann
    Rickey cons., "Her father is dead," att. Joseph Edwards,
    Daniel Parshley. 15 Mar. 1860. MA, R, D-119.
Fallon, Michael & Mary Frawly. He is 21, born Ireland, res.
    Buena Vista. She is 18, born Ireland, res. Buena Vista.
    27 Jan. 1857. R, C-2, D-49.
Fann, John & Jane Lewis. 15 Mar. 1858. R, D-72.
Farington, Nathaniel & Elizabeth Lynch. Her mother cons., att.
    Robert Lynch; her father is in California. 4 Aug. 1853. MA,
    B-267.
Fark, Frederic & Rhoda Stewart. 14 Aug. 1842. R, B-36.
Farley, Claiborne & Jane Grant. 4 Jan. 1834. MA, R, A-185.
Farley, Henry & Sarah Bennett. 26 June 1845. MA, R, B-73.
Farley, John & Mary Grogan. 4 Jan. 1848. MA, R, B-114.
Farley, John & Eliza Robinson. 18 Oct. 1860. MA, R, D-124.
Farmer, Abner C. & Frances Applegate. His mother Mary Farmer
    cons., att. William S. Farmer. Her mother Mary Applegate
    cons., att. Robert Sowwash. 8 Apr. 1852. MA, B-275.
Farmer, Benjamin & Rhoda Ann Richardson. 21 Jan. 1856. R, D-26.
Farmer, Benjamin J. & Virginia C. Ellison. 5 Aug. 1846. R, B-90.
Farmer, Daniel & Mary Farmer. 21 Feb. 1856. R, D-26.
Farmer, Jacob & Evaline Adams. 18 Dec. 1853. MA, D-4.
Farmer, James Wesley & Mary Catherine Carlile. William Farmer
    att. his age over 21. 4 Mar. 1858. MA, R, D-72.

Farmer, John & Margaret Goolsbery. 26 July 1840. R, B-13.
Farmer, William & Susan Green. He is 23 (25), born Columbiana
   Co., res. Scioto Co., son of Blackson & Anna (Maria) Farmer.
   She is 24 (25), born Columbiana Co., res. Jefferson Tp., dau.
   of John & Lavina Green. 26 Mar. 1857. R, C-8, C-10.
Farmer, William S. & Susan Ann Degear. 22 Mar. 1838. MA.
Farney, James & Susannah Foster. David R. Farney att. ages.
   23 July 1841. MA, R, B-21.
Farney, Van B. & Minerva Coriell. 30 Sep. 1860. MA, R, D-133.
Farrington, James & Lucy Ellen Carter. 18 Aug. 1850. R, B-186.
Fasler, Michael & Mary Waller (Walker). 31 Aug. 1851. MA, B-217.
Faucet, Benjamin & Catharine Gaines. 8 May 1856. MA, R, D-30.
Faucot (Forcett), Isaac & Martha Edar. 28 Mar. 1847. MA, R,
   B-101.
Faukett (Pawkett), Joseph & Helen M. Veach. 3 Nov. 1853. MA,
   B-269.
Faulkner, Absalom M., of Jackson, Ohio & Eunace Melcher, of
   Portsmouth. 13 June 1822. R, A-69.
Faverty, Gallentine A. & Rebecca Powell. 27 May 1849. MA, R,
   B-154.
Faverty, John & Abigal Ann Sheldon. 31 Jan. 1830. R, A-141.
Faverty, John S. & Katharine Remy. Her father Thomas Remy cons.,
   witn. Gallentine A. Faverty. His father Joseph Faverty cons.,
   witn. Reason Faverty. 29 Aug. 1845. MA, R, B-76.
Faverty, Joseph & Leah Mosure (Mosier). 30 Mar. 1852. MA, B-236.
Faverty, Reason & Frances Cisson. 1 July 1850. MA, R, B-182.
Faverty, Resin & Caroline Hood. 9 Apr. 1854. D-1.
Faverty, Rezin S. & Cynthia Barnett. 4 Oct. 1849. R, B-159.
Favorty, Joseph Jr. & Sarah Brock. 1 Dec. 1822. MA, R, A-72.
Fawcet, Benjamin & Catharine Allen. 5 Mar. 1849. MA, R, B-142.
Fawcett, Edward & Sarah Jane Wilson. 24 Oct. 1847. R, B-109.
Fei (Fae), Philipp & Cecilia Garring. 16 Jan. 1849. MA, R, B-139.
Feist (Fist), John & Rosater Slaughler. 7 Jan. 1860. MA, R, D-111.
Fellows, David Jr. & Abigal Ingals. 1 Jan. 1840. R, A-276.
Felver, Lyman & Eliza J. Shepherd. 13 Aug. 1850. R, B-186.
Fennell, James & Sarah Ann Casey. 19 Apr. 1860. MA, R, D-114.
Feque (Fuqua), James & Francis Chapman. 26 Oct. 1823. R, A-77.
Ferguson, Joseph & Dianna Jones. Joseph & Mary Duncan cons., att.
   Abraham McConnel. 23 June 1822. MA, R, A-69.
Ferguson, S. S. & Josephine Clemens. 27 Mar. 1856. R, D-27.
Ferguson, Samuel & Jane Bonser. 7 June 1809. R, A-295.
Ferree, John & Rachael Moore. 3 Sep. 1831. R, A-155.
Ferrin (Ferres), John & Elizabeth Ann Moore. 9 June 1831. MA, R,
   A-154.
Ferron, Alpheus & Elizabeth Hammett. 16 May 1838. MA, R, A-254.
Feser, Johann & Louise Schmidt. 5 Nov. 1857. R, D-68.
Feurt, Benjamin & Mary Deavers. 26 Jan. 1812. R, A-317.
Feurt, Denton & Catherine Critzer. Henry Fourt att. ages.
   12 Aug. 1839. MA, R, A-272.
Feurt, Gabriel & Lydia Hitchcock. 13 Feb. 1812. MA, R, A-317.
Feurt, George & Catharine Smith. 20 Nov. 1817. R, A-32.
Feurt, James H. & Nancy Johnson. 2 Sep. 1855. D-21.
Feurt, John B. & Nancy Mead. 3 Apr. 1840. R, B-4.
Feurt, John D. & Maria Jane Oldfield. 2 July 1839. R, A-275.
Feurt, Joseph D. & Rachel Walls. 7 July 1842. MA, R, B-32.
Feurt, Thomas & Polly Bower. Mary Feurt cons., witn. Peter Noel.
   9 Mar. 1815. MA, R, A-348.
Field, Abner & Ruth A. Morgan. 27 Feb. 1852. MA, B-231.
Field, Acil & Sarah Jane McKinney (McKindall). 15 Dec. 1844.
   MA, R, B-65.
Field, Benjamin & Mary J. Ralphsnider (Snyder). He is 25, born &
   res. Madison Tp., son of James & Mary Field. She is 18, born

Columbiana Co. (Columbus), Oh., res. Jefferson Tp., dau. of
Andrew & Rachel Ralphsnider (Snyder). 24 Dec. 1857. R, C-8,
C-9, C-12, D-66.
Field, John & Olive Laferty. 7 Sep. 1839 (1838). R, A-264,
B-12.
Fields, James & Alas (Else) Parks. 2 Jan. 1844. MA, R, B-54.
Fields, James C. & Winnie Wooting (Uooting). 28 June 1849. MA,
R, B-170.
Fields, Jesse H. & Nancy Davis. He res. Green Tp. 6 Mar. 1856.
R, C-11, D-27.
Fields, Nathan & Mary Boothe. 5 Dec. 1847. MA, R, B-115.
Fields, Thomas & Susan Knapp. 28 Dec. 1838. MA, R, A-264.
Fields, William & Sally Cockran. 25 Dec. 1823. R, A-79.
Fife, John & Rebecca Chesnut. 10 Aug. 1859. MA.
Finch, Cyrus M. & Mary E. Bruner. 18 June 1857. R, D-54.
Finch, Morton R. & Mary E. Parker (Barker). 29 Dec. 1853. D-3.
Finey, Jeptha & Susan Branham. 25 Aug. 1860. MA, R, D-123.
Finley, A. W. & Susannah Lawson. 2 Oct. 1856, by E. P. Pratt. R.
Finney, George & Adaline Fullerton. 19 Dec. 1847. MA, R, B-112.
Finney, George K. & Eliza Fullerton. Her father James Fullerton
cons., witn. Horace Hall. 17 Nov. 1839. MA, R, A-278.
Finney, John & Ruth Spencer. 22 Nov. 1837. R, B-43.
Finney, John & Rhoda Allrige. 24 Apr. 1854. D-1.
Finney, Julius & Maria Perry. 1 Mar. 1834. R, A-201.
Finney, William & Mary Degrot. 2 July 1847. MA, R, B-103.
Finton, Elijah & Oret Valodin. 9 July 1829. R, A-133.
Finton, John J. & Emily A. Orm. 11 Dec. 1859. MA, R, D-103.
Finton, Thadeous B. & Nancy Bennett. 5 Sep. 1833. R, A-188.
Finton (Hinton), William & Mary Wees. 25 Nov. 1848. MA, R, B-134.
Finton, William J. & Susannah Baccus. 8 June 1837. MA, R, A-243,
A-247.
Firmstone, Joseph G. & Mary James March. 11 Nov. 1844. R, B-65.
Firrell, Daniel & Clarissa Slocumb. His mother Sarah Curey (?)
cons., of Bloom Tp., witn. John J. Holmes, Moses Murphy.
20 Jan. 1844. MA, R, B-53.
Fischer, Joseph & Anna Rosina Wiehle. 1 Jan. 1857. R, D-60.
Fishburn, William A. & Susan Stewart. 24 Feb. 1853. MA, B-260.
Fisher, Alfred & Sarah McKinley. 2 Mar. 1858. MA, R, D-72.
Fisher, Andrew & Mary Rockwell. His mother Lucretia Fisher cons.,
witn. Lewis Rockwell, Jonathan Rockwell. Her father Lewis
Rockwell cons. 31 July 1858. MA.
Fisher, Bartholamew (signs Barthelomaus Fischer) & Elizabeth
Wheeler. 3 Apr. 1860. MA, R, D-114.
Fisher, George & Louisa Welch. 29 Oct. 1850. MA, B-193.
Fisher, Jacob & Jane Ann Gebhardt. 6 Mar. 1856. R, D-28.
Fisher, John & Margaretta Fisher. 24 Feb. 1853. MA.
Fisher, John & Barbara Daum. 11 Sep. 1860. MA, R, D-122.
Fisher, Michael & Catharine Daniel. 31 Aug. 1847. MA, R, B-106.
Fisher, Peter & Lucretia Dodge. 8 Mar. 1837. R, A-244.
Fisselmeran, William & Whilemena Havenor. 25 Feb. 1853. MA.
Fitch, Elias Jr. & Margaret Finney. Bridget Finney cons., witn.
Thomas Finney, Elias Fitch. 6 Dec. 1843. MA, R, B-51.
Fitch, Elias & Elizabeth Cutshaw. 27 Sep. 1851. MA, B-216.
Fitch, Jeremiah & Lois Brown. Her brother and guardian Joshua
Brown cons., witn. William Swords. 28 Mar. 1817. MA, R, A-27.
Fitspatrick, Watson & Nancy McConnell. 2 Sep. 1834. R, A-199.
Fitzer, William & Drusilla Moler (Moulder). 24 Dec. 1844. MA, R,
B-67.
Fitzmorris, Ezekiel & Eliza Marshel. John Fitzmorris cons., witn.
John Dawson. 19 Jan. 1828. MA.
Fitzpatrick, Michael & Nora Kinney. 30 Aug. 1857. R, D-58.
Fixley, Daniel & Martha Bennett. 27 June 1837. MA, R, A-246.

44

Flack, William & Tobitha Martin. 6 Apr. 1843. MA, R, B-45.
Flagg, Laomi & Mary Perry. 17 Mar. 1854. D-6.
Flaherty, Richard & Martha Wilson. 7 Apr. 1831. MA, R, A-153.
Flanders, George W. & Hennrietta Welch. 2 May 1841. R, B-19.
Flanders, John M. & Jane Sebring. 1 Nov. 1831. R, A-167.
Flanders, William M. & Eliza Sebering. 9 Feb. 1837. R, A-238.
Flanigan, Patrick & Susan Call. Andrew Highland att. ages.
    23 Nov. 1860. MA.
Flannigen, George & Lucy Ann Davis. 5 Feb. 1841. MA, R, B-14.
Fleming, David & Katherine Yates. 30 Mar. 1834. MA, R, A-188.
Fleming, David & Sarah Saddler. 8 Aug. 1848. MA, R, B-132.
Fleming, Isaac & Jane Ritchie. William Grimes att. ages. 9 May
    1840. MA.
Fleming, Richard & Jane Johnson. 2 Dec. 1845. MA.
Flemming, Isaac Jr. & Sina Winkler. 23 June 1828. R, A-121.
Flesh, John & Mary Legler. 27 May 1856. R, D-31.
Flinn, Andrew J. & Eliza Kilpatrick. Brice Kilpatrick cons.,
    witn. Thomas White, John Wilfong (?). 6 July 1837. MA, R,
    A-237.
Flint, John G. & Levenia H. Feurt. 9 Mar. 1854. D-5.
Flower, Z. P. & Myle Wood. Her father Jacob Wood, of Bloom Tp.,
    cons. 24 Feb. 1833. MA, R, A-172.
Flowers, George W. & Laura C. Adams. 4 July 1844. R, B-60.
Fodge (Hodge), Adam & Mary Rose. 5 Nov. 1833. MA, R, A-177.
Fogleman, George & Margaret Cornish. 26 Oct. 1841. MA, R, B-24.
Folin, Ovid F. & Mary L. Dole. 20 May 1845. R, B-72.
Follmer, Joseph & Margaret Kennedy. (not dated) 1853. MA.
Folsom, James Smith & Sarah Bennett, both of Green Tp. 26 Apr.
    1827. R, A-105.
Folsom, Samuel & Abigail Barrett. 7 Apr. 1835. MA, R, A-200.
Folter, Anthony & Theresa Polis. 30 Nov. 1854. MA, R, D-12.
Forbush, Christopher & Elizabeth Ann Ellis. 31 Dec. 1859. MA, R,
    D-103.
Ford, Arthur & Catherine Lenan. 19 June 1859. MA, R, D-108.
Ford, Claudius W. & Rosanna Graft. 29 July 1860. MA, R, D-131.
Ford, John A. & Sarah Jane Osborn. 4 Aug. 1848. MA, R, B-131.
Forinash, Nathan & Eliza Ann Steen. 15 Feb. 1844. MA, R, B-53.
Fort (Feurt), Bartholmew & Mary Bean. 6 Dec. 1840. MA, R, B-16.
Fort, Daniel & Caroline W. McNeal. 24 Sep. 1857. R, D-60.
Foster, Archibald H. & Ellefair Green. 8 July 1849. MA, R, B-155.
Foster, J. A. & Mary Jane McCan. 1 Feb. 1854. D-3.
Foster, James & Rhode McClung. 30 Dec. 1856. R, D-44.
Foster, John C. & Alasanna Jones. His father Job Foster cons.,
    att. Benjamin Barklow, Moses Dupuy. Job Foster res. Greenup
    Co., Ky. Alasanna Jones res. Green Tp. 7 Oct. 1819. MA, R,
    A-48.
Foster, John J. & Ethalinda Ramsey. 4 Jan. 1855. MA, R, D-13.
Foster, Joseph & Margaret Hamilton. 21 Dec. 1852. MA, B-257.
Foster, Luke & Sarah Reed. 9 Dec. 1805. A-9, A-280.
Foster, Mathew & Lucinda Emmons. 2 Apr. 1843. MA, R, B-43.
Foster, Otho D. & Lucinda Shaw. 9 Sep. 1860. MA, R, D-127.
Foster, Robert & Mary McCann. 26 June 1850. MA, R, B-185.
Foster, W. Scott & Sarah Bradshaw. W. F. Smith att. ages. 8 Jan.
    1860. MA, R, D-104.
Foulk, James & Julia Ann Huddleston. 24 Dec. 1840. MA, R, B-7.
Foulks, James & Catharine Burt. 21 July 1842. MA, R, B-33.
Fout, Henry T. & Elizabeth Gelson. 5 Jan. 1859. MA.
Foutt, William & Mary Jackson, of Bloom Tp. 16 Feb. 1832. R,
    A-161.
Fowler, John & Amanda Ingrum. 4 July 1860. MA, R, D-120.
Fox, Benjamin & Nancy Smith. 25 July 1850. R, B-184.
Fox, Daniel & Jane Barnett. James Barnett att. ages. __ Apr.
    1853. MA.

Fox, Jacob & Lucretia Hinton. 6 Nov. 1846. MA, R, B-93.
Fox, Ludwig & Lina Arna. 15 June 1852. MA, B-276.
Fox, Ml. & Margret Flaherty. 9 Aug. 1857. R, D-58.
Fox, Theodore & Mary Dautstral. 18 Apr. 1859. MA.
Foy, R.C.W. (Fog, R.E.W.) & Mary Ellen Slack. 11 Nov. 1853. MA,
    B-271.
Frailer (Failer), Alfred & Milly Hawkins. 28 Oct. 1841. MA, R,
    B-24.
Frank, Charles & Catharine Rapp. 27 Oct. 1849. MA, R, B-160.
Frank, Michael & Barbara Daner. 28 June 1848. MA, R, B-124.
Franklin, John (John F. Rankley) & Mary McCann. L. Perry att.
    ages. 18 Feb. 1850. MA, R, B-177.
Franklin, William & Clarinda Slocumb. 26 June 1845. MA, R, B-74.
Franks, William & Polly Russell. 26 Jan. 1817. MA, R, A-26.
Frasier, John & Eliza Burk. Her guardian Nancy Burk cons., att.
    Alexander Green. 11 May 1854. MA, D-2.
Frazee (Frazer), William C. & Nancy E. Woodruff. 13 June 1852.
    MA, B-242.
Frazer, William & Hester A. Gappan. 11 July 1850. MA, R, B-183.
Frazier, John R. & Laurah A.W. Blyfe. 10 Mar. 1849. MA, R, B-142.
Frazier, William A. & Hester Snyder. He is 22, res. Harrison
    Tp. She is 16, born Harrison Tp. John S. Snyder cons., att.
    Mary Snyder, Ezra Snyder. 24 Mar. 1858. MA, C-14.
Frederick, Christian & Elizabeth Bower (Lower). 11 Jan. 1848.
    MA, B-243.
Frederick, Medard & Susana Canter. 26 Nov. 1853. MA.
Freeland, James & Lucinda Canter. 28 Oct. 1855. D-22.
Freeland, Middleton & Delilah Carder. 21 Oct. 1853. MA, B-272.
Freelich, Jacob & Margaret Bey. Casper Wirtz att. ages. 13 Jan.
    1853. MA, B-256.
Freeman, David & Martha Caraway. 27 Jan. 1848. R, B-116.
Freeman, Isaac & Jemima Moore. His father Michael Freeman cons.,
    says Isaac is 20 on the 25th of the month. Witn. L. Feurt (?)
    MA shows her name Jemima Noel. 26 Dec. 1822. MA, R, A-71.
Freeman, Isme & Martha Thompson. 8 Jan. 1850. R, B-167.
Freeman, James & Mary Wheeler. 12 Apr. 1851. MA.
Freeman, James G. & Millie E. Tracy. 11 Sep. 1856. R, D-36.
Freeman, John & Angeline McLaughlin. 27 Apr. 1843. MA, R, B-44.
Freeman, John P. & Elizabeth Jones. 9 Jan. 1851. MA, B-199.
Freeman, Laurens & Susan B. Gale. He res. Cuyahoga Co., Oh.
    29 Oct. 1844. MA, R, B-63.
Freeman, Michael & Amanda Thompson. 26 Jan. 1843. MA, R, B-42.
Freeman, William & Margaret Thompson. Her pars. George & Mar-
    garet Thompson cons., witn. Isme Freeman, Michael Freeman,
    of Brush Creek Tp. 6 Aug. 1846. MA, R, B-93.
Freeman, William & Adaline Spencer. 29 Nov. 1849. R, B-163.
Freenote, Nicholas & Caroline Batram. 30 Apr. 1854. R, D-7.
Freschel, George & Josephine Bumment. 15 Aug. 1851. B-213.
Freye, John & Elizabeth Hornung. 12 Dec. 1856. R, D-43.
Friday, Henry & Magie Schaffer. 6 Jan. 1849. R, B-141.
Friedli, Jacob & Barbara Schramm. 31 Mar. 1857. R, D-61.
Friedmann, Joseph & Mary Rohn. 14 Aug. 1860. MA, R, D-123.
Fritz, Thomas J. & Ellenora Simpson. James Simpson att. ages.
    23 Oct. 1860. MA, R, D-128.
Frizzle, Mathias & Sarah Ann Townsend. 5 Nov. 1832. MA, R, A-170.
Frock (Trask?), John & Hannah Helms. 7 Oct. 1830. MA, R, A-147.
Frost, John & Lucinda Wildburn. 3 Dec. 1849. MA, R, B-163.
Frost, John & Mary (Nancy) Jane Vickers. 10 Dec. 1853. MA, D-4.
Frost, Samuel & Liza Cochenane. 12 June 1854. B-283.
Frost, Welty & Elizabeth Squires. 1 June 1854. D-1.
Fry, Daniel & Polly Hall. 27 Nov. 1815. MA, R, A-16.
Fry, Henry & Mary Shaafer. 24 Mar. 1848. MA, R, B-120.

Fryer, Benjamin L. & Matilda Workman. 13 Sep. 1848. R, B-131.
Fryer, John H. J. & Nancy A. Glover. 17 Nov. 1842. R, B-37.
Fryley, William & Elizabeth McKeever. 17 Nov. 1856. R, D-171.
Fuget, Benjamin & Catharine Clingman. He is 42, born Ky., res.
    Portsmouth, son of C. & Cloe Fuget. She is 29, born Pa.,
    res. Portsmouth, dau. of Samuel & C. Clingman. 6 May 1856.
    C-5.
Fuller, Alphonse & Mary Swain. 11 Sep. 1814. R, A-339.
Fuller, John & Louisa Haubert. 25 July 1857. R, D-58.
Fuller, Maxmillan & Calfornia Patten. 16 Feb. 1851. MA, B-202.
Fuller, Orange & Mary Catherine Diduit. Her father William
    Diduit cons., att. John Diduit. 6 Dec. 1835. MA, R, A-209.
Fuller, Samuel L. & Sarah Hennis. 19 Oct. 1848. MA, R, B-134.
Fullerton, Adam & Mary Beloat. 18 June 1837. R, A-244.
Fullerton, Andrew & Lucy Dean. 12 May 1843. MA, R, B-47.
Fullerton, H. H. & Mary Jane Cadot. 10 Sep. 1846. R, B-94.
Fullerton, Isaac & Elizabeth Mead. Her father Judah Mead cons.
    His father John Fullerton cons. 19 Nov. 1829. MA, R, A-136.
Fullerton, John M. & Lydia Kettles. 17 Dec. 1833. R, A-186.
Fullerton, Smith & Nancy Graham. 13 Jan. 1859. MA, R, D-77.
Fulmer, August & Catherine Star. 18 June 1855. MA.
Funk, A. G. & Mary A. Flowers. He is 24, born Wayne Tp., res.
    Portsmouth (Wayne Tp.), son of John & Margaret Funk. She is
    18, born England, res. Portsmouth, dau. of John & Mary Flowers.
    18 Dec. 1856. R, C-1, C-7, D-52.
Funk, Jacob C. & Hester Purnell. 27 Aug. 1850. R, B-189.
Funk, John & Margaret Glover. 1 June 1815. R, A-348.
Funk, Samuel & Julia Anna Moore. He is 24, born & res. Portsmouth,
    son of John & Margaret Funk. She is 24, born Scioto Co., res.
    Portsmouth, dau. of Julianna Moore. 18 Nov. 1856. R, C-3, D-43.
Funk (Ferrell), William S. & Mary Gillenwaters. Leonard Gillen-
    water att. ages. 17 Mar. 1853. MA, B-261.
Furguson, William & Ellen Noel. 19 Dec. 1849. R, B-171.
Fusset, Edmond & Maria Herron. 15 Oct. 1854. R, D-11.
Gable, Nicholas & Mary Degere (Degar). 7 Aug. 1845. MA, R, B-75.
Gabler, John & Julia Lellich (Lelix). 17 Oct. 1837. MA, R, A-236.
Gabouda, Louis (or Louis Gaboudel) & Bibica Stica. 17 Sep. 1859.
    MA.
Gaddis, John & Catherine Dasher. 2 July 1855. B-286.
Gaddis, Robert F. & Margaret H. Carnes. 24 Jan. 1859. MA, R, D-78.
Gaddis, William E. & Harriet M. Burke. 4 May 1859. MA, R, D-91.
Gaffy, George H. & Isabella Jones. 11 Apr. 1853. B-258.
Gage, Andrew E. & Mary Loomis. 29 Apr. 1849 (1848). MA, B-245.
Gahm, John & Catherine Eckhart. 17 Apr. 1860. MA, R, D-117.
Gahr, Philip & Caroline Schuh. He is 20, born Strasburg, France,
    res. Portsmouth, son of Valentine & Charlotte Gahr. She is
    18, born Strasburg, France, res. Portsmouth, dau. of George
    & Caroline Schuch. 7 Apr. 1857. R, C-8, D-53.
Gaines, William & Catherine Clingman. 24 Aug. 1843. R, B-47.
Gale, William D. & Sarah Ann Russell. 9 Oct. 1842. MA, R, B-35.
Galford, John & Roxe (Bacey) Ann Fullerton. 11 Aug. 1836. MA,
    A-225.
Galford, William J. & Eliza Ann Vincent. 21 Dec. 1840. MA, R,
    B-16.
Gallaghar, Hugh & Ruth Marsh. 17 Mar. 1849. MA, R, B-143.
Gallagher, Clark & Mary Houchins. 5 Mar. 1848. MA, R, B-123.
Gallagher, Thomas & Sarah McMahon (McMan). He is 30, born Ire-
    land, res. Portsmouth. She is 25, born Ireland, res. Ports-
    mouth. 21 Oct. 1856. MA, R, C-2, D-49.
Gallaher, Maxfield & Hannah Ullem. John Dayley att. her age
    over 18. 29 Nov. 1812. MA, R, A-322, A-324.

47

Gallant, John & Sarah Travis. Her mother Mary Travis and his
father Patrick Gallant cons., witn. William Gallant & Scure-
man (?) Travis. 29 Oct. 1807. MA, R, A-286.
Galligher, Cornelius & Rachel Mead. 22 Feb. 1855. MA, R, D-15.
Galliher, Samuel & Mary Creely (Curly). 2 Oct. 1851. MA, B-218.
Gallop, Austin P. & Elizabeth Ann Bennett. 30 Aug. 1846. R, B-94.
Gallop, John P. & Nancy Sullivan. 8 Dec. 1846 (1847?). MA, R,
B-97.
Gallup, Jerry & Jane Angeline Carter. 19 Jan. 1848. MA, R, B-102.
Gallup, Reuben W. & Sarah Lair. 4 Nov. 1849. MA, R, B-169.
Gamby, Isaac & Jane Horne. 1 Dec. 1838. MA, R, A-262.
Gampp, Johan & Margaret Thomas. 27 Mar. 1849. MA, B-244.
Gang, John & Adel Haning. 11 Nov. 1858. MA, R, D-86.
Gapin, Eli & Susan McNeal. Her mother Margaret McNeal cons.,
says Susan was 17 the 7th of March 1858. Witn. George
Deaver. 27 May 1858. MA, R, D-79.
Gappen, Charles & Sarah Feurt. Benjamin Feurt cons. 1 Dec.
1832. A-170.
Garaghty, Eugene & Louisiana Burk. 24 Apr. 1834, by Edward
Cranston, J.P. MA, R.
Garlach, Conrad & Catherine Bower. 8 Nov. 1851. MA, B-222.
Garld (Todd), Benjamin & Mary Bishup. 27 Aug. 1857. R, D-57.
Garner, Peter & Sarah Price. 2 Jan. 1840. MA, R, A-276.
Garret, Barton & Susan G. M. O'Brien. 14 Mar. 1846. MA, R, B-85.
Garrett, Benjamin & Melvina Vangorder. J.Q. Shumway att. ages.
1 June 1860. MA.
Garrett (Everett), Edward & Martha White. 25 June 1851. MA,
B-210.
Garrett, Jacob & Francis Suitor. 7 June 1837. MA, R, A-244.
Garrett, Jacob & Mary McClene (McClure). 26 Nov. 1844. MA, R,
B-65.
Garrett, Russell & Elizabeth Randall. 6 Jan. 1814. MA, R, A-329.
Garrison, Mitchel & Hariet Graves (Groves). 12 Apr. 1832. MA, R,
A-165.
Garvin, Thomas & Mary Allison. 18 Jan. 1844. MA, R, B-54.
Garvin, William & Amanda Dear. 4 Sep. 1857. R, D-59.
Gaston, J.L. & Matilda Turner. 2 Aug. 1860. MA, R, D-131.
Gaston, Joseph & Rhuhamah Allen. 15 July 1849. MA, R, B-190.
Gaston, Joseph S. & Abigail J. Dewey. 6 Mar. 1843. MA, R, B-45.
Gaston, Lorren T. & Mary Jane Henson. His father E. L. Gaston
cons., witn. Joseph L. Gaston, Jackson Henson. Her mother
Mary Henson cons., witn. Samuel Henson, Jackson Henson.
11 July 1844. MA, R, B-61.
Gasway, Nicholas & Mary Lewis. 6 Jan. 1848. MA, R, B-114, B-119.
Gates, Charles V. & Mercie Cook. He is 24, born Gallia Co., Oh.,
res. Portsmouth, son of Samuel P. & Bethia Gates. She is 26,
born Scioto Co., res. Portsmouth, dau. of Hugh & Mercy Cook.
7 May 1857. R, C-8, D-53.
Gates, Dewitt Clinton & Annie L. Wilkins (Williams). He is res.
Cincinnati, born Portsmouth, son of Wilson & E. Gates.
25 June 1856. R, C-4, D-31.
Gates, Erastus & Maria L. Thompson. 16 Mar. 1854. D-2.
Gates, Wilson & Elizabeth Kinney. 30 Nov. 1820. MA, R, A-56.
Gates, Wilson & Julianna Dodson. 19 Sep. 1855. R, D-20.
Gavin, Patrick & Margaret Kelly. 14 Sep. 1859. MA, R, D-116.
Gay, William & Mary A. Ross. 4 June 1848. MA, R, B-130.
Gay, Zebulon & Phebee Putnam. 11 Apr. 1816. R, A-21.
Gaylord, Benjamin B. & Margaret Jane Hempstead. 23 Oct. 1845.
R, B-78.
Gearon, Patrick & Maery Enyar (Duyer). 29 Oct. 1850. MA, B-192.
Gebel (Gable), Augustus & Mary Ann Bruner. 7 Sep. 1847. MA, R,
B-108.

Gebhardt, Lewis & Temperance Wishon. 7 Sep. 1832. MA.
Gee, Aaron & Catharine Fields. 13 Sep. 1841. MA, R, B-35.
Gee, Joseph & Sally Kilpatrick. 27 Nov. 1816. MA, R, A-25, A-31.
Geiger, Michael & Sally Heev (Sleev? Hew?). 27 May 1854. R, D-8.
Geiss (Christ, Geist), Adam & Elizabeth Wolf. 28 Apr. 1856. MA, R, D-30.
Genat (Ginatt), John B. & Barbary Smith. Her father Godfrey Smith cons., witn. Jonithan Smith, Peter Bacus. 29 Aug. 1806. MA, R, A-282.
George, James & Martha Jane Angel. Her stepfather William Monk cons. 27 Oct. 1858. MA, R, D-85.
George, Jesse & Eliza Swords. 1 Jan. 1856. D-24.
Geppert, William & Hanna Hillbrecht. 21 Feb. 1850. R, B-172.
Geraghty, Thomas & Katherine Philbin. 24 May 1852. MA.
Gerlach, Conrad & Lesetta Willka. 3 Apr. 1859. MA, R, D-92.
Gess, John & Catharine Linz. 12 July 1857. R, D-58.
Gessert, Jacob & Lissette Fortride. 22 Jan. 1857. R, D-47.
Gharky, George Henry & Martha E. Oldfield. 20 Sep. 1852. MA, B-249.
Gharky, John & Susan Francis. 19 Mar. 1838. MA, A-251.
Gharky, John C. & Eliza McDowell. 15 Oct. 1846. MA, R, B-92.
Gibbens, George & Cordelia Savage. 2 Dec. 1849. MA, R, B-165.
Gibbens, Jefferson & Ann Coil. 20 Sep. 1857. R, D-59.
Gibbs, Barna & Nancy (Anna) Smith. 27 Aug. 1818. MA, R, A-39.
Gibbs, G. W. & Susan Gilbert. 6 May 1851. B-208.
Gibler, Morgan & Mary Graham. Her father Seth Graham, of Pond Creek, cons. 30 (31) May 1838. MA, R, A-255.
Gibson, David & Elizabeth Allison. 28 Mar. 1847. MA, R, B-101.
Gibson, Mark & Ann Marie Moore. 30 Sep. 1830. MA, R, A-146.
Gibson, Norman & Sophia McKeever. His father Samuel Gibson, of Clinton Furnace, and her father James McKeever cons. 19 Oct. 1856. MA, R, D-38.
Gickler (Giekler), John & Christina Seal (Siel). 2 Sep. 1851. MA, B-217.
Gies, George & Sibilla Brust. 10 Oct. 1842. MA, R, B-35.
Giesser, Henry & Regina Worth. 22 Sep. 1853. MA.
Gifford, George W. R. & Mariah Triggs. 2 Oct. 1856. R, D-40.
Gifford, James & Molissia Newman. Peter Randall att. her age over 18. 23 Apr. 1841. MA, R, B-19.
Gifford, Joseph & Susan Butlar. 18 Dec. 1855. R, D-25.
Gifford, Levi T. & Nancy Jane Wait. 19 June 1856. R, D-32.
Giggis, John & Constantina Fuller. 25 Sep. 1851. MA.
Gilbert, Giles & Levina Long. 12 Jan. 1843. R, B-41.
Gilbert, Giles & Mary E. Currie. He is 34, born Marietta, Oh., res. Portsmouth, son of Giles & Effie Ann Gilbert, second marriage. She is 19, born & res. Portsmouth, dau. of T.S. & Hannah Currie, first marriage. 27 May 1857. R, C-8, D-56.
Gilbert, Joseph C. & Sarah C. Varner. George H. Gharky att. ages. 25 Mar. 1852. MA, B-265.
Gilbert, Martin B. & Laura T. Hancock. 12 May 1840. R, A-270.
Giles, John & Jane Atkinson. 13 Aug. 1841. MA, R, B-23.
Giles, Thomas C. & Nancy Brown. 4 Dec. 1860. MA, R, D-126.
Gilland, Hugh & Mary Wayne. 19 Oct. 1854. B-285.
Gillen, Samuel & Eliza Jane Coyl. 1 Jan. 1846. MA, R, B-83.
Gillenwaters, Leonard & Lucetta White. 15 June 1854. D-1.
Gillespie, William & Margaret Williams. 1 Dec. 1859. MA.
Gillet, Robert & Sarah J. Giles. 5 Aug. 1855. R, D-20.
Gilley (Pilley), Henry & Mary Solomon. 20 Feb. 1851. MA, B-202.
Gillilan, Preston & Agnes (Agaliha) Duduit. 6 Dec. 1810. MA, R, A-306.
Gilliland, Jacob & Mary Welch. 31 Aug. 1856. R, D-35.
Gilliland, Nathan & Catharine Adams. 10 (12?) Jan. 1844. MA, R, B-58.

Gillinwater, John & Nancy Woten. Her father cons. 8 Dec. 1847. MA, R, B-115.
Gillis (McGillis), Daniel H. & Aveline Bradshaw. Daniel Chaffin att. ages. 21 Apr. 1836. MA, R, A-213, A-230.
Gillis, George & Lucinda Chatfield. 2 Feb. 1842. MA, R, B-29.
Gillis, William & Biddy Perry. 19 Jan. 1847. MA.
Gillispie, John & Mary Smith. 24 July 1818. MA.
Gilmore, Abraham C. & Bethania Adams. 11 Nov. 1830. MA.
Gilmore, Conrad & Catherine Scott. 22 Aug. 1841. MA, R, B-23.
Gilroy, Hugh & Barbara Shearer. 10 Jan. 1849. MA, R, B-139.
Gilroy, James & Mary Donohoe. 2 Apr. 1857. R, D-54.
Gilsdorf, Jacob & Mary Elizabeth Martin. Her brother James J. Martin att. her father's cons. 4 Mar. 1858. MA, R, D-73.
Gilson (Gibson), James B. & Sarah A. Williams. He is 23, born Columbiana Co., res. Madison Tp., son of Rich Gibson. She is 17, born Columbiana Co., res. Madison Tp., dau. of William Williams. 17 Apr. 1857. R, C-12.
Givens, James Harvy & Margaret Burris (Bauch). 4 May 1847. MA, R, B-102.
Givens, John & Eliza Jane Collier. Her father Thomas Collier cons., witn. Thomas Collier Jr., Mary A. Collier. 29 Dec. 1835. MA, R, A-210, A-218.
Givens, Thomas J. & Elizabeth Laten. 6 Apr. 1852. MA, B-239.
Givens, William & Susana Anderson. 13 July 1809. R, A-295.
Givens, William & Rachal Stockham. 24 Oct. 1810. MA, R, A-305.
Givens, William Jr. & Elizabeth Elliott. 10 Oct. 1834. R, A-192.
Glaize, Airhart & Ruth Marret. 16 June 1811. MA, R, A-312.
Glaize, John & Elizabeth Merret. 12 Feb. 1807. R, A-283.
Glass (Gloss), John & Mary Anna Louder. 14 Aug. 1856. MA, R, D-37.
Glass, Robert & Phebe Johnson. 19 May 1836. MA.
Glatz, Theodore & Mary A. Hugar. 9 June 1852. MA.
Glaze, Abraham & Sarah Owens. 24 June 1815. MA, R, A-281.
Glaze, Abraham & Mary Kirkendol. 17 Sep. 1840. MA, R, B-13.
Glaze, Anderson & Mary Shelpman. 25 Oct. 1853. MA.
Glaze, Andrew Jr. & Susannah Cockrell. 19 Mar. 1812. MA, R, A-319.
Glaze, Andrew Jr. & Rebecca Weaver. Her father John Weaver cons. 31 Jan. 1819. MA, R, A-43.
Glaze, David & Seeley Shelpman. 17 Mar. 1842. MA, R, B-28.
Glaze, George & Rachel (Glaze). (The original return does not show her last name.) 22 Feb. 1848. R, B-116.
Glaze, George W. & Sarah Morgan. 19 Dec. 1858. MA, R, D-92.
Glaze, Henry & Lydia A. Shook. 25 July 1848. MA, R, B-129.
Glaze, Henry & Fanny Witherup. 29 Jan. 1851. MA, B-205.
Glaze, Isaac & Mitelday Connor. Her father William Connor cons. 3 Feb. 1824. MA.
Glaze, Jacob & Rachel Rardin. 20 Jan. 1825. R, A-87.
Glaze, Jonathan & Eve Glaze. 16 Aug. 1838. MA, R, A-257.
Glaze, Martin L. & Mary Ann Cockrel. 14 Dec. 1845. MA, R, B-84.
Glaze, Socrates & Irene Dean. Her former husband had been absent 14 years, no word received for 13 years, when it was said he was returning home, very ill, now presumed dead. 7 Aug. 1845. MA, R, B-76.
Glaze, William W. & Rhoda Glaze. 7 June 1849. MA, R, B-153.
Glaze, William Wilkinson & Elizabeth Coleman. 7 Sep. 1853. MA.
Gleim, Adam & Ellen Mender (Mindle). 4 Oct. 1849. MA, R, B-158.
Gleim, John & Caroline Nagel. 10 Feb. 1853. MA, B-261.
Glenn, John & Caroline Davis. 13 Jan. 1842. MA, R, B-27.
Glidden, Charles & Mary Colvin. 27 Dec. 1856. R, D-43.
Glidden, Daniel A. & Mary Ellen Robinson. 16 Aug. 1848. R, B-130.
Glidden, Jefferson W. & Catherine W. Young. 7 Apr. 1831. R, A-152.

Glidden, Obadiah H. & Linchy Blair. 28 Feb. 1841. R, B-18.
Glotz, John & Constina Fowler. 1 Nov. 1856. MA, R, D-47.
Glover, Azel & Elizabeth B. Dearing. 30 Dec. 1824. R, A-85.
Glover, Elijah B. & Sarah Jane Offner. 17 Jan. 1833. R, A-172.
Glover, John & Eliza Nurse. 22 Sep. 1836. R, A-224.
Glover, Nathan & Polly Jones. 11 July 1808. R, A-288.
Glover, Samuel G. & Sarah M. Fuqua. Thomas B. King att. ages.
    2 Mar. 1836. MA, R, A-208, A-229.
Gobler, Frederick & Christina Messerer. 25 Nov. 1847. MA, R,
    B-111.
Godare (Godderd), James & Mary Godare (Godderd). 25 Oct. 1815.
    MA, R, A-16.
Gohun, James & Rosana Johnson. 2 Nov. 1859. MA, R, D-107.
Golden, Fletcher & Maria Scott. 20 May 1852. MA, B-239, B-240.
Goldsberry, Jacob & Mary Martin. 1 June 1851. MA, B-210.
Goldsberry, Peter & Cynthia Pearl. 13 Oct. 1854. R, D-10.
Goldsbery, Isaac & Maria Barber. 7 Dec. 1856. R, D-42.
Gooden, Alexander & Mary McCollister. 14 July 1853. MA, B-280.
Gooden, Daniel & Sarah Buck. 9 Sep. 1810. R, A-304.
Goodman, Michael & Theresia Amberg. 27 Dec. 1849. R, B-170.
Goodnough, Charles E. & Margaret Stapleton. 1 Dec. 1857. R, D-65.
Goodrich, Richard & Jane Bonser. 3 Nov. 1840. R, B-7.
Goodwin, Commodore P. & Nancy Ann Zorns. 6 Nov. 1847. MA.
Goodwin, Wesly & Jane Atherton. 20 Dec. 1821. R, A-63.
Gordon, James Y. & Cornelia Wetherbee. 9 Apr. 1855. R, D-17.
Gordy, George M. & Georgiana Baeoch. 15 Apr. 1857, by E. P.
    Pratt. R.
Gore, Walker & Charlotte Grey. 30 July 1838. MA, R, A-256.
Gow, William P. & Mary A. Brown. 1 Apr. 1857. R, D-85.
Grabhorn, Antony & Sophia Brunken. 7 July 1850. MA, R, B-183.
Grable, Joseph & Hester Hesler. 18 Dec. 1853. D-4.
Gracy, David D. & Mary M. Fields. 3 Oct. 1852. MA, B-247.
Graf, Conrod & Augustin Schuster (Huester). 13 Jan. 1849. MA, R,
    B-141.
Graf, Herman & Margaret Wirth. His stepfather T. J. Kunz (?)
    cons. 16 Mar. 1858. MA, R, D-84.
Graff, Eli & Harriet Winkler. C. W. Ford att. ages. 9 Dec.
    1860. MA, R, D-125.
Graham, Cyrus & Elizabeth Duncan. 16 Oct. 1851. MA.
Graham, Elijah & Nancy Hardin. 18 Feb. 1844. R, B-53.
Graham, H. V. & Mariah Jane Long. 31 Dec. 1858. MA, R, D-94.
Graham, James & Polly Louderback. 15 Nov. 1807. R, A-289.
Graham, James & Margrate Helmer. 12 June 1831. MA, R, A-157.
Graham, James & Matilda Bonser. 2 Nov. 1851. MA (dated 1850),
    R, B-231.
Graham, James Jr. & Angeline McLaughlin. 25 Mar. 1858. R, D-73.
Graham, James C. & Caroline Ely. 7 June 1855. R, D-18.
Graham, John & Caty Richaback. 2 Feb. 1810. R, A-299.
Graham, Jonathan & Mimy Duncan. 15 May 1851. MA, B-213.
Graham, Joseph & Barsheba Crabtree. William Crabtree att. she
    is over 18, and that Joseph's father (not named) cons.
    11 Dec. 1812. MA.
Graham, Lewis B. & Rebecca Hoover. Both pars. cons. (not named).
    9 Oct. 1852. MA, B-277.
Graham, Peter N. & Minerva Coppage. 1 Apr. 1849. MA, R, B-145.
Graham, Peter N. & Margaret Utt. 12 Feb. 1855. MA, R, D-15.
Graham, Seth & Susannah Noel. John Graham att. his age over 21.
    10 Oct. 1811. MA, R, A-314.
Graham, Troilus J. & Eliza Mary Tobins. 10 June 1855. R, D-18.
Graham, Wesley & Susan Fullerton. 1 Mar. 1860. MA, R, D-119.
Grant, Frank & Sarah C. Goudy. He was born Buffalo, N.Y., son of
    Peter & Mary Grant. She is dau. of Edward. 12 Oct. 1856. C-3.

SCIOTO COUNTY MARRIAGES

Grant, George W. & Rebecca Windgate (Mudgate). 27 Oct. 1853.
    MA, B-269.
Grant, John & Phebe Osborne. 26 Nov. 1850. MA, B-195.
Grant, William & Bethia Pliment (Plymole). 12 Apr. 1838. R, A-252.
Grant, William J. & Ann Eliza Mathews (Mathers). 25 July 1860.
    MA, R, D-120.
Graves, George & Sally Hunt. 27 Mar. 1834. R, A-191.
Graves, George W. & Sarah Shelpman. 30 Jan. 1840. R, B-8.
Graves, Hubbard & Cynthia Robey. 16 May 1830. R, A-142.
Graves, John N. & Mary Rankin. 8 May 1833. MA, R, A-175.
Graves, William M. & Lydia Dugan. Thomas Duggan of Seal Tp.
    cons., witn. Lewis Graves, David Baoltinghar (Daniel Boulten-
    hous?). 18 Mar. 1806. MA, R, A-11, A-280.
Gray, George & Susan Warren. 12 Nov. 1853. D-3.
Gray, Robert & Louisa Irvin. 9 Dec. 1829. MA.
Gray, William P. & Thankful E. Graves. 28 June 1842. R, B-33.
Grayson, John F. & Mary A. Filsley. 30 Oct. 1851. MA, B-220.
Green, Alexander & Eliza Wilds. Her mother Mary Wilds cons.,
    witn. James Hammon. 4 Nov. 1841. MA, R, B-24.
Green, Andrew & Lydia Lewis. 3 Jan. 1828. MA, R, A-114, A-120.
Green, Clarke & Eliza Logan. 8 Sep. 1810. R, A-303.
Green, Francis & Isora Bennett. 17 Feb. 1853. MA, B-260.
Green, George W. & Sarah Nail. 21 Dec. 1856. R, D-46.
Green, Henry Ellis & Mary Evelina Gardner. 29 Aug. 1816. R, A-24.
Green, James & Polly Ritchie. His father Patrick Green cons.,
    att. Capt. Wm. N. Burk. 16 May 1815. MA, R, A-281.
Green, James & Effie Marie Gentry. 3 Mar. 1838. MA, R, A-249.
Green, Jesse & Fanny Sears. Her father Samuel Sears cons., att.
    Emanuel Sears. 4 Aug. 1837. MA.
Green, John & Levina McManaghiel. 7 Mar. 1849. MA, R, B-143.
Green, Samuel & Catherine Machmanagel (McManighel). Her father
    James McManighel cons., witn. Alexander Green. 30 Dec. 1841.
    MA, R, B-27.
Green, William H. & Mary Elizabeth Oolery (Whachrery). He is
    22, born Adams Co., son of W. & Eliza Green. She is 19, born
    Fayette, Penn., dau. of John & S. (Whachrery). 15 Apr. 1858
    (1857). MA, R, C-10, D-76.
Greenslate, John & Sarah Oliver. 8 June 1826. MA, R, A-97.
Gregory, David & Mary J. White. Jeremiah White att. ages.
    14 Oct. 1849. MA, R, B-160.
Gregory, Moses & Eliza Belli (Balli). Philip & Sintha Moore
    cons. for her. 22 Oct. 1826. MA, R, A-101.
Gregory, Moses & Mary Tilton. 14 Nov. 1833. R, A-178.
Gregory, Nabthaliam & Harriet Sharpe. 26 June 1836. MA, R,
    A-226.
Gregory, Nathan & Lydia Jane Smith. 8 Apr. 1841. MA, R, B-17.
Griffith, Squire M. & Caroline Hall. 12 Oct. 1840. MA.
Grimes, Carroll (Campbell) & Lucinda Hodges. Her mother Eliza-
    beth Hodges cons., att. Ransom Hodges, Abner Anderson.
    4 Apr. 1837. MA, R, A-241.
Grimes, Christopher & Jemima Elon Evans. 26 Mar. 1856. R, D-30.
Grimes, Daniel & Margaret Rankin. 17 Apr. 1856. R, D-30.
Grimes, James & Avirtha Rankins. 23 Oct. 1848. R, B-135.
Grimes, Samuel & Elizabeth Cottle. 18 Mar. 1843. MA, R, B-43.
Grimes, Samuel & Martha Cottel. 31 Mar. 1846. R, B-86.
Grispum, Christian & Magdalena Sepolt. 30 Aug. 1857. R, D-62.
Grizzley (Griggley), John & Elizabeth Hoothday (Hootsley).
    Gabriel Grouse att. ages. 18 Nov. 1845. MA, R, B-82.
Groce, Jacob & Polly Golson. 9 May 1838. R, A-253.
Groce, Job & Betsy Monday. 17 Oct. 1848. R, B-133.
Grogin, Thomas & Keziah Carter. 21 May 1846. MA, R, B-89.
Groker, John & Sophia Rolfer. 31 Oct. 1854. R, D-11.

SCIOTO COUNTY MARRIAGES

Groninger, John & Elenor Munn. 8 Jan. 1818. R, A-32.
Groninger, Leonard & Susanna Clark. 10 Nov. 1831. R, A-158.
Groninger, Leonard & Mary B. Darlington. 27 Dec. 1855. R, D-25.
Gross (Groce), Elijah & Roseann Cook. 17 Dec. 1836. MA, R, A-220.
Grounds, Uriah & Martha Anderson. 25 Aug. 1858. MA.
Grove, Charles & Mary A. Jeffords. 13 Apr. 1850. R, B-177.
Grover, Isaiah & Sarah Dodge. 10 May 1846. MA, R, B-86.
Grover, Isaiah & Lucretia Call. Eli Smith att. ages. 4 Oct.
   1851. MA.
Grover, Isaiah & Hannah Malone. 19 July 1853. MA, B-263.
Groves, Jacob & Margaret Gregans. He is 23, born Germany, res.
   Portsmouth, son of Jacob & C. Groves. She is 19, born Ger-
   many, res. Beaver, Jackson Co., dau. of Martin & A. Gregans.
   10 Nov. 1856. C-1.
Groves, Thomas & Eliza Autls. 28 Mar. 1831. MA.
Grubb, John & Sarah Ann Alderman. Her father E. H. Alderman
   cons. 14 Mar. 1844. MA, R, B-57.
Guillauime, Victor & Mary Pack. 9 Aug. 1847. MA, R, B-104.
Guillaume, Xavier & Mary Minego. 10 July 1848. MA, R, B-128.
Guis (Grin?), Henry & Catherine Powell. 9 Sep. 1850. MA, R,
   B-188.
Guiss, Sebastian & Mary Smith or Shoe (sic). 12 Mar. 1843. MA,
   R, B-42.
Gunn, Bela & Almia Andrews. 4 Sep. 1828. R, A-121.
Gunn, Enos & Nancy McDonald. Her father John McDonald cons.
   20 Sep. 1827. MA, R, A-109.
Gunn, Henry C. & Harriet E. Calvert. Her father H. B. Calvert
   cons. 7 Mar. 1859. MA, R, D-95.
Gunn, Leverett H. & Almeda E. Cassidy. 3 Aug. 1854. R, D-9.
Gunn, Samuel W. & Margaret Moran. 30 Aug. 1853. MA.
Gunn, William & Nancy Jane Cary. 16 Dec. 1851. MA, B-227.
Gunn, Zina & Clarrisa Harrisson. 25 Nov. 1821. R, A-64.
Gurney, Henry & Mahala Boyd. 10 July 1860. MA, R, D-132.
Gustin, Bennaja & Ann B. Isaminger. 14 Oct. 1847. MA, R, B-110.
Guth, Francis & Barbara Baum. 24 May 1841. MA.
Guthery, Joseph & Hannah Dever. 2 Mar. 1815. MA, R, A-348.
Guthgesell, Francis Joseph & Atelaiunta Glockner. 28 Oct. 1853.
   MA.
Guthrie, Alfred C. & Julia Houtchins. 25 June 1848. MA, R,
   B-124.
Guthrie, Martin & Rosan Hogan. 23 Oct. 1860. MA, R, D-123.
Guthrie, William & Elizabeth Nelson. 22 Oct. 1849. R, B-160.
Gwathney, George & Ann Pollock. 12 Feb. 1836. MA, R, A-212, A-228.
Hackney, Thomas & America Brown. 8 Jan. 1834. R, A-185.
Hackward, Eugene & Fanny Foulner (Fullmer? Faedner? - illegible).
   9 Feb. 1858. R, D-70.
Hacquard, Charles & Roselle Ducate. 19 Jan. 1854. D-6.
Hacquard, Francis & Mary Ann Mathew. C. Hacquard signed MA.
   9 Apr. 1860. MA, R, D-118.
Hacquard, Horrace & Caroline Richart. 7 ___ 1854. R, D-14.
Hacquard, Louis & Mary F. Corns. 25 Sep. 1860. MA, R, D-123.
Hacquard, Victor & Josephine Jondebow. Xavier Guillieme att.
   ages. 19 Apr. 1855. MA, B-285.
Hadley, Frederic B. & Hannah Eaton. 30 June 1850. MA, R, B-186.
Hadley, James H. & Jane Cutler. 6 Oct. 1847. MA.
Hadlock, Benjamin & Almena White. 31 Oct. 1827. MA, R, A-111.
Hadlock, Samuel & Eliza Owens. 18 Jan. 1824. R, A-80.
Hafener, William (Wilhelm Hensener) & Suranna Eifort. 8 Dec. 1852.
   MA. B-241 shows his name Charles Haffner, marriage date 25
   July 1852.
Hafflinger, Martin & Mary Minech. 18 Apr. 1839. MA, R, A-268.
Hagendarn, Charles & Mary Seifert. 5 Aug. 1859. MA, R, D-107.

53

Hahn, David & Mary Free. 14 Apr. 1839. MA, R, A-269.
Hailey, Andrew B. & Lucina Church. 3 Apr. 1840. MA, R, B-5.
Hailey, Carter & Elizabeth Drury. 6 June 1822. R, A-68.
Hailey, Horrace & Mary Critser. 28 Nov. 1835. MA, R, A-209.
Haines, Josiah & Elizabeth Crichton. 11 Nov. 1846. MA, R, B-95.
Hains, John & Mary Roberts. 13 Sep. 1858. MA.
Hale, Daniel & Pheobe Adams. Her mother Abigail Adams cons., of
    Porter Tp., witn. James Mead, David Parker. 8 Sep. 1817. MA.
Hale, Daniel & Adah Pool. 2 Jan. 1831, by William Jackson, J.P.
    R.
Hale, Harvy & Elizabeth Dean. 5 Aug. 1841. MA, R, B-23.
Hale, Octave V. & Rebeccah Sappington. 2 Feb. 1832. R, A-159.
Haley, Carter & Hana Gililan, of Upper Tp. 5 Oct. 1810. R, A-306.
Hall, Aaron & Margaret Edison. Her father Jas. Edison cons.
    15 Feb. 1815. MA, R, A-346.
Hall, Aaron & Harriet McKinney. 24 Dec. 1835. R, A-213, A-228.
Hall, Anthony & Charlotta Lawson. 29 Apr. 1857. R, D-51.
Hall, Daniel & Nancy Bolen. 21 May 1841. MA, R, B-20.
Hall, David B. & Sophia Vanduzen. Her mother Charlotte Lair
    cons. 16 Jan. 1838. MA, R, A-249.
Hall, Eli & Laura Slocumb. 5 Apr. 1856. R, D-29.
Hall, H. T. & Lucy Fullerton. 24 Feb. 1853. MA, B-258.
Hall, Henry & Caroline C. Thompson. 19 Feb. 1852. B-232.
Hall, Horace J. & Vilena Chaffin. 17 Dec. 1840. R, B-14.
Hall, James & Mary Ball. 3 Jan. 1859. MA, R, D-79.
Hall, James E. & Louise F. Worley. 9 Mar. 1843. R, B-42.
Hall, Moses S. & Lidia Worley. 25 June 1852. MA, B-242.
Hall, Nimrod & Susannah Freeland. 26 July 1840. MA, R, A-270.
Hall, Robert & Elizabeth Dillon. 3 Aug. 1829. R, A-132.
Hall, Thomas F. S. & Sallie Rigdon. 24 May 1859. MA, R, D-97.
Hall, William & Margaret Kinney. 29 Apr. 1833. R, A-174.
Hall, William T. & Malinda Shaw. Her father Alexander Shaw
    cons., att. Charles Shaw. 30 Oct. 1859. MA, R, D-104.
Hall, Zechariah & Juliana Ball. Her father David Ball cons.
    7 Mar. 1822. MA, R, A-65.
Haller, Benjamin L. & Angelina E. Brewer. 17 Sep. 1853. MA, B-281.
Haller, William A. & Sarah J. Powers. 17 May 1853. MA, B-264.
Halterman, Henry & Catharine Habble (Hoble). 3 May 1847. MA, R,
    B-104.
Halterman, Jacob & Elizabeth Thompson. Her father John Thompson
    cons., witn. James Thompson, Jos. L. Thompson. 19 Apr. 1838.
    MA, R, A-255.
Halterman, Jacob & Nancy Roadarmour. John Roadarmour att. her
    age. 14 Apr. 1842. MA, R, B-30.
Halterman, John & Katherine Mock. 10 Jan. 1820. MA, R, A-50.
Halterman, Joseph & Abigail Barnet. 2 Jan. 1848. MA, R, B-113.
Halterman, William & Sally Munyan. 19 Nov. 1856. R, D-43.
Hamilton, Aaron & Cassey J. Wishon (Mershon). 21 Dec. 1850. MA,
    B-200.
Hamilton, Henry & Lovina Early. 6 Aug. 1831. MA, R, A-154.
Hamilton, James & Phebe Horner. 11 Apr. 1839. MA, R, A-266.
Hamilton, John & Elizabeth Kinney. 28 Mar. 1843. MA, R, B-43.
Hamilton, Reubin & Elizabeth Kahal. His father John Hamilton
    cons. Her brother Edward Kahal att. her age over 18. 9 Jan.
    1812. MA, R, A-315.
Hamilton, Robert & Rachel R. Peebles. 20 Feb. 1839. R, A-265.
Hamilton, Wesley & Mary Byers (Meyers). Reuben Hamilton att.
    ages. 26 Aug. 1847. MA, R, B-107, B-113.
Hamilton, William & Mary McLaughlin. 18 Mar. 1838. R, A-251.
Hamilton, William & Jane Byers. 27 Dec. 1842. R, B-39.
Hamlin, Hanabal G. & Mary Whitney. 1 Feb. 1825. R, A-88.
Hamm, Adam & Mary Emerich. 4 Nov. 1858. MA, R, D-79.

Hammerstein, George & Clementa McFadden. 11 Apr. 1839, by Wm. Timmons, Minister. MA, R.

Hammon, James & Elizabeth Sears. His mother Rebecca Green cons., witn. John Canterbury, John Sears. 7 Dec. 1834. MA, R, A-194.

Hammond, Benjamin & Theresa Estel. 12 Aug. 1854. R, D-9.

Hampton, Cary & Mary C. Nye. 24 July 1859. MA, R, D-100.

Hampton, Morgan & Mary Smith. 23 July 1845. R, B-74.

Handel, George & Barbara Russ. 4 Feb. 1856. R, D-30.

Hanes, Abraham & Eliza Rebecca Grant. 9 Dec. 1860. MA, R, D-125.

Hanes, Nelson & Janes (?) Betts. 24 May 1857. R, D-55.

Haning, Jacob & Harriet Stropes. 11 Nov. 1860. MA, R, D-130.

Hankins, Rollins & Mary (Polly) Knox (Nox). 30 July 1816, by John Lee. MA, R.

Hanlin, Patrick & Mary Burns. 31 Oct. 1851. MA, B-221.

Hanna, Charles & Martha J. Gratton. Thomas Gratton att. ages. 10 Dec. 1850. MA.

Hannah, Alexander & Nancy Fuqua. 13 Dec. 1832. R, A-172.

Hannahs, James & Elvira (Eliza?) Sheflin. 12 Apr. 1848. MA.

Hannell, Christopher & Mary Jane Holbert. 7 Jan. 1854. D-7.

Hanour, Peter & Eunice Rickey. 25 Oct. 1854. R, D-11.

Hanour, Philip & Louisa Baker. 1 Nov. 1860. MA, R, D-126.

Hans, Georg & Julia Browns. 29 July 1856. R, D-37.

Hans (Haas), Henry & Elizabeth Heflinger. 9 Jan. 1840. MA, R, A-277.

Hansgen (Henchen), John & Mary Polena Mossman. Her father John Mossman cons., att. Hartley Mossman, Augusten Mossman. 28 Mar. 1859. MA, R, D-92.

Hansicker, Daniel & Hannah Watkins. 17 Feb. 1831. MA, R, A-150.

Har, Michael & Bridget Kelly. 24 May 1860. MA, R, D-122.

Harbet, William & Anna Nickels. 28 Aug. 1834. R, A-191.

Hard, B. W. & M. A. Burk. 1 Nov. 1855. D-22.

Hard, Barton & Frances Copenhaver. 27 Nov. 1856. R, D-45.

Hard, Chester P. & Sarah Kimball. 3 Jan. 1826. MA, R, A-94.

Hard, Edwin & Mary Hammack. 1 Feb. 1849. MA, R, B-143.

Hard, Jonathan B. & Sophronia White. 22 Feb. 1816. MA, R, A-18.

Hard, Phillip E. & Melissa Lawhorn. C. S. Guilkey att. "I have raised Melissa Lawhorn by the dying request of her mother... have neither adopted her nor...appointed her guardian," witn. W. W. Ferguson, M. Hard. 22 Feb. 1860. MA, R, D-113.

Hardin, Andrew & Sarah Whitney. 13 Dec. 1828. MA, R, A-125.

Harding, Alfred J. & Francis J. Sidney. 15 Apr. 1846. R, B-85.

Hardy, John C. & Julia Hunt. 24 June 1834. MA, R, A-190.

Harmon, Henry C. & Rachel A. Hamon. 23 Sep. 1860. MA, R, D-127.

Harmon, James & Margaret Anne Cunningham. 28 Aug. 1856. R, D-34.

Harmon, Middleton & Mary Evans. Ester Evens att. her age over 18, witn. A. S. Woodruff. 24 Nov. 1830. MA.

Harness, Aaron (Adam) & Deniza Bennett. 12 July 1849. MA, R, B-153.

Harness, George B. & Sarah Rankins. 28 Apr. 1831. R, A-153.

Harness, James & Susan E. Wheeler. 21 Mar. 1853. MA, B-279.

Harper, Cyrus L. & Harriet Starling. 16 Aug. 1831. MA.

Harper, Henderson & Elizabeth Thompson. 20 Apr. 1837. MA, R, A-242.

Harper, John J. & Emily Jones. 6 Feb. 1856. D-24.

Harris, Benjamin & Winfred (Gweny) Jones. 12 Dec. 1857. R, D-67.

Harris, Jordan & Barbary Hice (Hail). 24 July 1836. MA, R, A-226.

Harris, William & Ann Lewis, both of Portsmouth. 25 Nov. 1856. R, D-39.

Harris, William D. & Jane Clark. Clark Green Jr. att. her age over 18. 25 Mar. 1811. MA, R, A-309.

Harrison, Thomas & Mary Baker. 27 May 1844. MA.

Harrison, William & Levina Swearingen. 17 Oct. 1833. MA, R, A-182.

Harrison, William H. & Margaret Graft. 26 July 1857. R, D-63.
Harrs (Starr or Stans), John & Eliza Burns. He was born Ire-
    land, res. Berlin, Oh., age 28. She is 23, born Ireland,
    res. Berlin, Oh. 24 Feb. 1857. R, C-2, D-50.
Hart (Hard), Erastus & Adelia Andrews. 2 Nov. 1836. R, A-221.
Hart, Samuel J. & Sarah E. Eckley. Her pars. Eli & Mary Eckley
    cons. 15 Apr. 1860. MA, R, D-117.
Hart, William & Mary Adeline Howard. 14 Aug. 1856. MA, R, D-42.
Hartley, John & Nancy Lemon. Her father Lemuel Lemon cons.
    29 May 1859. MA, R, D-97.
Hartley, Thomas & Sarah Johnson. 23 Dec. 1852. MA.
Hartley, William & Mary Ann Patton. 4 Nov. 1849. R, B-161.
Hartman, Daniel & Jane Street. 11 June 1846. R, B-87.
Hartman, William & Emily Heath. 8 Feb. 1849. MA, R, B-140.
Hartmann, Adam & Louise Rollers. 19 Feb. 1852, by John Voelkel. R.
Hartmann, Friedrich & Maria Brugger. 1 Oct. 1857. R, D-62.
Harwood, Benjamin F. & Adi C. Graham. John Conroe att. ages.
    24 Feb. 1850. MA, R, B-174.
Harwood, Daniel & Hannah Darlington. 24 Jan. 1850. R, B-173.
Haskins, Asa & Hillenah Canary. 23 Feb. 1843. MA, R, B-42.
Haskins, Squire & Rebecca Saxton. 8 Mar. 1856. R, D-27.
Hasson, Michael & Ann Bagley. 24 July 1851. B-212.
Hatch, John & Emily Jones. 9 Mar. 1826, by Dan Young. R.
Hathorn, William & Elizabeth Miller. Her father Cornelius Miller
    cons., witn. Dan'l. Bumgarner. 13 Sep. 1838. MA, R, A-259.
Hatmaker, Frederick & Margaret Swartz. 1 Aug. 1859. MA, R,
    D-110.
Hatton, John & Elenor Colgan. Her brother William Colgan att.
    her age over 21, and att. William Hatton's cons. 24 Feb.
    1814. MA, R, A-334.
Haubert (Harbet), John & Elizabeth Minnego. 17 Nov. 1851. MA,
    B-220.
Haubert, Peter & Elizabeth Davis. 6 Aug. 1857. R, D-62.
Hauser, John & Elizabeth Motz. 28 Feb. 1857. R, D-48.
Hausleutner, Ernst & Seraphine Vern. 12 May 1860. MA, R, D-115.
Havens, Howard & Sarah Briant. Nancy Pendall cons., witn. Hugh
    Woods, David Bayse. 27 May 1853. MA, B-264.
Havens, Joel & Cynthia Ann Bivins. Her pars. Joseph & Cynthia
    Bivins cons., witn. William F. Bivins. 8 June 1839. MA, R,
    A-273.
Havens, Lewis K. & Katherine White. 14 Feb. 1841. MA, R, B-16.
Hawke, Ferdinand W. & Mary J. Shipman. 9 May 1849. R, B-149.
Hawkins, Aaron & Jemimah Wood. 11 Apr. 1818. MA, A-38.
Hawkins, Edmond & Sarah Ann Bennett. Samuel Boggs att. ages.
    27 May 1847. MA, R, B-102.
Hawkins, John & Polly Vantine. MA states he is part Indian, not
    black or mulatto. 12 Jan. 1826. MA, R, A-104.
Hawkins, Moses Jr. & Frances Anna Gaston. 14 Feb. 1843. MA, R,
    B-42.
Hawkins, Wesley & Sydney H. Stephens. 1 Jan. 1860. MA, R, D-111.
Hay (Hey), George & Agathe Seifried. 21 Mar. 1850. MA, R, B-174.
Hay (Hey), Jacob & Catherine Busker. 14 Nov. 1853. MA.
Hay, John & Friederika Brickdeschler. 14 Nov. 1857. R, D-67.
Haynes, Archibald S. & Elizabeth Titus. 5 Nov. 1854. R, D-14.
Haynes, Joseph & Eleanor A.Cyrus (Smith). George Carter att.
    ages. 16 Sep. 1851. MA, R, B-223.
Hayward, Eliphus & Mary Cadot. 24 Aug. 1837. R, A-247, B-5.
Hayward, Hesekiah & Olive A. Wait. 22 Mar. 1855. R, D-16.
Hayward, Leonard & Mary Ann Musgrove. 14 Dec. 1826. R, A-103.
Hayward, Moses & Julinn Reynolds. 10 Aug. 1826. R, A-100.
Hayward, Philip S. & Elizabeth Reys. 8 Sep. 1825. R, A-91.

SCIOTO COUNTY MARRIAGES

Hayward, Philip S. & Henrietta Reynold. Her father Joshua
    Reynold cons. 4 May 1828. MA, R, A-129.
Hayward, Zenas & Sally Hiner. (not dated, prob. 1833) A-174.
Hazelbake, William R. & Sarah J. Holt. 24 Dec. 1849. R, B-166.
Hazelbaker, John & Sophia Thompson. His pars. Abraham & Juliann
    Hazelbaker cons., witn. George Thompson, George Cable. 8 Jan.
    1844. MA.
Hazelbaker, Peter & Cynthia Ann Holt. 24 Dec. 1847. R, B-114.
Hazelbaker, Reason & Sarah Boldman. He is 18. 17 Apr. 1856.
    R, C-5, D-29.
Headen, John & Polly Cole. 16 Sep. 1856. R, D-35.
Headley, George & Rebecca Hitchcock. 11 Dec. 1850. MA, B-225.
Heahl, C. & Margaretta Cilley. 2 Jan. 1853. B-255.
Hearn, Thomas C. & Frances H. Fuller. 23 Dec. 1858. MA, R, D-94.
Heath (Heuth), J. B. & S. J. Gray. He is 25, son of J. B. Heuth.
    She is 18 (20), born Gallia Co., dau. of John Gray. 7 Jan.
    1858. R, C-9, D-67.
Heath, James & Mary Conn. 16 Dec. 1819. MA, R, A-53.
Hechinger, Anthony & Mary Nugent. 19 Oct. 1851. MA, B-218.
Hedding, Isaac & Lydia (Julia) Graham. Her pars. Samuel &
    Elizabeth Graham cons., witn. Pearson McCoy, Daniel Townson.
    19 Jan. 1840. MA, R, B-2.
Hedger, Thomas & Emily Smith. 13 Mar. 1856. R, D-28.
Hedges, David & Cumfort Stumbaugh. 15 July 1830. MA, R, A-145.
Hedges, William & Lavina Louderback. 14 Nov. 1848. MA, R, B-139.
Hedicor, Modest & Mary Bennett. Mathaus Hetlinger signed MA.
    12 June 1849. MA, R, B-152.
Heffren, Anthony & Ellen Flinn. 5 July 1843. MA.
Heid, Conrad & Mary Jane Foster. His father George Heid cons.
    22 July 1858. MA, R, D-84.
Heid, George & Margaret Mile. (Myer is pencilled over Mile in
    the book.) 1 Sep. 1849. R, B-156.
Helt, Frederick & Christena Crauser. 14 Aug. 1855. MA.
Hempstead, Dr. Giles S. B. & Elizabeth Peebles. 11 Apr. 1821.
    R, A-59.
Henchen, Nicholas & Mary E. Daniel. 12 May 1856. MA, R, D-31.
Henderson, John & Sarah Conrow. 3 Aug. 1854. R, D-9.
Henderson, John & Lucretia Veach. 17 July 1859. MA, R, D-98.
Henderson, Thomas & Emely Squires. 26 July 1838. R, A-256.
Henderson, Thomas & Elizabeth Moore. 18 Nov. 1855. D-23.
Henderson, W. H. & Lydia Neucun. 26 Feb. 1855. R, D-15.
Hendricks, William & Hulda Sanford. 10 Mar. 1841. MA, R, B-17.
Henry, Alexander & Margt. Jeaugenot. 9 Feb. 1858. R, D-69.
Henry, Daniel & Hester Ann Queen. 2 May 1835. MA, R, A-203.
Henry, Francis & Maria L. (T.) Morgan. 14 Oct. 1852. MA, B-250.
Henry, John & Mary Millirons. 6 Feb. 1850. MA, R, B-177.
Henry, Joseph & Martha Ann Culp. 13 Feb. 1842. MA, R, B-31.
Henry, Louis August & Mary Vernier. He is 21, born France, res.
    Pond Creek. She is 18, born France, res. Pond Creek. 1 Mar.
    1857. R, C-2, D-49.
Henry, Robert & Julia Ann Merriman. 21 Aug. 1843. MA, R, B-47.
Henson, John & Mary Ann Benner. Alexander Urquhart att. ages.
    4 Nov. 1858. MA, R, D-85.
Henson, Joseph & Jane Cline. 8 Dec. 1841. MA, R, B-25.
Henson, Stephen & Ann Mar. 23 Mar. 1845. R, B-70.
Henthorne, Henry & Caroline Giffords. 14 Nov. 1850. MA, R,
    B-193.
Hepburn (Hibborn), John & Harriet Welsher. 29 July 1847. MA,
    R, B-104.
Hepler, Elza & Mary Rollins. 13 June 1859. MA, R, D-97.
Herder, John & Catharine Baghe (Leryfa). 5 Dec. 1854. MA, R,
    D-12.

Herder, John M. & Christina Byer. 16 Sep. 1858. MA, R, D-77.
Herdman, James & Nancy Moore. 2 Mar. 1852. MA, B-238.
Herman (Sterman?), Benjamin & Margaret Butz. 3 June 1850. R,
  B-187.
Hermon (Harmon), Henry & Delilah Reaves. 16 Oct. 1818. MA, R,
  A-61.
Herms, F. C. & Catherine Martin. H. P. Yeager att. ages. 3 Oct.
  1860. MA, R, D-130.
Hernandez, Louis A. & Ellen Lodwick. 14 Nov. 1859. MA, R,
  D-107.
Herr, Abraham & Catherine Wilhelm. 10 Mar. 1859. MA, R, D-90.
Herr, Jacob K. & Delilah Hickman. 6 Nov. 1846. MA, R, B-93.
Herrel (Heorald), William & Sarah Pierce. 27 Feb. 1848. MA, R,
  B-122.
Herrell, Nimrod & Amanda Pierce. His mother Elizabeth Herell
  cons., att. Green Titus. 26 Oct. 1853. MA, B-270.
Herron, John & Mary Stokeley. 6 Aug. 1855. R, D-20.
Herron (Hirron), Stephen M. & Fanny Murphy. 29 Dec. 1825. MA,
  R, A-139.
Heskitt, James & Margaret Sutherland. She is 23, born Germany,
  dau. of James & Jane Sutherland, 2nd marriage. 13 June 1856.
  R, C-6, D-32.
Hesler, Andrew & Nancy Winkler. 29 May 1831. MA, R, A-154.
Hesler, Moses & Elizabeth Louderback. 20 Feb. 1825. R, A-86.
Hesler, Moses & Sophia Lewis. 17 Oct. 1859. MA, R, D-103.
Hethe, Hiram & Phebe Wilson. 21 Dec. 1834. R, A-194.
Heuth, Andreas & Marianne Minrups. 9 Jan. 1856. R, D-26.
Hewes, Edward & Harriett A. Robinson. 20 Apr. 1854, by E. P.
  Pratt. R.
Hewitt, James T. & Catherine Reynolds. He is 26, born Ireland,
  res. X Roads, Jackson Co. She is 21, born Ireland, res.
  Portsmouth. 21 Sep. 1856. MA, R, C-2, D-49.
Hey, Frederick & Adaline Adam. 10 July 1859. MA, R, D-110.
Hibbard, William & Maria Kirkendall. 25 Feb. 1847. MA.
Hibbs, Jacob & Rebeccah Lucas. His father Aaron Hibbs, of Meigs
  Tp., Adams Co., Oh. cons., witn. Henry Rinely, Curtis Cammon.
  25 Feb. 1814. MA.
Hibbs, Jacob C. & Barbara Ann Williamson. 13 Apr. 1857. R, D-50.
Hice, Aaron & Anne Turner. 23 Mar. 1820. R, A-58.
Hickenbottom, James & Susanah Chaffin. 27 July 1814. R, A-336.
Hickey, John W. & Elizabeth Rankin. 1 Jan. 1843. MA, R, B-40.
Hickman, Dolphin & Mary Hesler. 18 Sep. 1856. R, D-35.
Hickman, Dolphin & Mary Jane Hesler. 7 Mar. 1859. R, D-91.
Hickman, Francis M. & Martha Graham. 27 Oct. 1859. R, MA, D-105.
Hickman, James & Anna Tobins. 9 Sep. 1846. R, B-91.
Hickok, H. C. & Katharine Usher. 6 July 1832. MA, R, A-164.
Hicks, Berry & Polly Carroll. 25 Apr. 1835. MA, R, A-200.
Hicks, William & Elizabeth Smart. 31 Mar. 1846. MA, R, B-85.
Hicks, William & Maria Minard. John W. Hicks att. ages. 9 Mar.
  1848. MA, R, B-116.
Hicks, William & Lucinda Mault. 9 Dec. 1855 (?). D-23.
Hicks, William & Mary Jane Strasbach. He is 22, son of James
  Hicks. She is 20, born Penn., both res. Scioto Co. 4 Nov.
  1857. R, C-9, D-65.
Higgins, John & Patsy Bennett. 22 Feb. 1806. R, A-11, A-279.
  (Return is totally illegible. This interpretation is from
  Volume A.)
Higgins, Robert Burns & Matilda Simonton. 7 Apr. 1853. MA,
  B-259.
Higher, Jesse & Elizabeth Skidmore. 13 Dec. 1836. MA.
Highland, Philip & Bridget Conley. 10 June 1857. R, D-58.

Highly, Simon & Lucy Newton. His mother Susannah McCormick cons. 14 Aug. 1820. MA.

Hiles, John & Lavina Kirkindell. 17 May 1846. MA, R, B-86.

Hill, A. J. (Andre) & Mary J. Longwith. He is 26, born Scioto Co., res. Jefferson Tp., son of Nathan & Jane. She is 16, born & res. Jefferson Tp., dau. of Henry & Susan Longworth. 29 Dec. 1857. R, C-10, D-70.

Hill, Adam & Catharine Johnston. 5 Apr. 1837. MA, R, A-243.

Hill, Anthony & Nancy Patton.(Volume A shows Barber.) 10 Nov. 1839. MA, R, A-275.

Hill, Hiram & Matilda Goodwin. 2 Aug. 1835. MA, R, A-206.

Hill, John P. B. & Ruby Seelye. Her pars. Samuel & Electa Seelye cons., witn. John Fuller, Amos Seelye. 5 Nov. 1835. MA, R, A-207.

Hill, Perry & Catherine Hill. John Hill att. ages. 28 Oct. 1852. MA, B-248.

Hill, Samuel & Patience Moore. 6 Mar. 1834. R, A-191.

Hill, William & Martha Benson. 16 June 1860. MA.

Hilt, John & Margaret Rife. 18 Nov. 1845. MA, R, B-82.

Hiltz, Phillip & Josephine Mesmer. 30 Apr. 1856. MA, R, D-28.

Hinckley, Jonathan & Hannah Wilson. 18 Jan. 1844. MA, R, B-52.

Hinkel, John & Barbara Heutzman. 19 Nov. 1855. D-23.

Hipshar, Andrew & Susannah Slack. 21 Nov. 1817. MA, R, A-31.

Hirrmand (Harmon? Nirrmand?), Henry & Eliza Jane Stewart. 24 Sep. 1843. MA, R, B-51.

Hise, Andrew & Hannah Hoppis. He is about 24, she is in her 18th year. 17 June 1821. MA, R, A-60.

Hise (Heiss), John & Fanny Simpkins. 21 Feb. 1850. MA, R, B-178.

Hise (Hice), Philip & Hannah Louderback. 11 Sep. 1814. MA, R, A-341.

Hise, Philip & Nancy McCleary. 26 Oct. 1853. MA, B-273.

Hitchcock, Caleb & Sarah Ann Rice. 19 May 1853. MA, B-266.

Hitchcock, Elias F. & Mary Chapman. Her father James Chapman cons. 16 Jan. 1831, by John Lawson, J.P. MA, R.

Hitchcock, Ira & Mary Canfield. 13 Sep. 1839. R, A-272.

Hitchcock, James & Sarah F. Clarke. 26 Dec. 1847. R, B-112.

Hitchcock, John F. & Esther Valodin. 20 Nov. 1839. R, A-273½.

Hitchcock, John P. & Emily Adams. 22 Sep. 1841. R, B-24.

Hitchcock, Smith F. & Rebecca Stockham. Hannah Stockham cons., witn. Aaron Stockham, Maria Stockham. 19 Dec. 1833. MA, R, A-187.

Hitchcox, Thomas & Ann Butler. 24 Jan. 1833. MA.

Hoach (Hoeh? Hock?), Phillip & Mary Staub. Her father Kasper Staub cons., witn. Michael Heied. 21 Apr. 1842. MA, R, B-30.

Hobart, Jacob & Elisabeth Eck. 30 Dec. 1851. B-227.

Hobart (Hubbard), Nicholas & Mary Smith. 11 Jan. 1849. MA, R, B-139.

Hock, John & Mary Anson. 24 Jan. 1856. D-24.

Hock, Joseph & Barbara Luther. 1 Aug. 1854. R, D-9.

Hodges, Aaron D. & Martha Queen. 3 Jan. 1828. MA, R, A-116.

Hodges, Hiram & Elizabeth Nichols. His father Robert Hodges cons., att. John Clifford. 3 Aug. 1834. MA, R, A-191.

Hodges, Jeremiah & Nancy Nichols. 9 Aug. 1838. MA, R, A-261.

Hodges, Moses & Elizabeth Cowen. Her father Samuel Cowen cons., says her mother is dead. She is 16, att. A. D. Hodges. Ransom Hodges att. Moses' age over 21. 29 Sep. 1831. MA, R, A-156.

Hodges, Robert & Polly Hawkins. 12 July 1830. MA, R, A-145.

Hodges, Stephen & Sarah Cooper. 26 Jan. 1854. D-4.

Hodges, Thompson & Margaret Welb. 13 May 1840. R, B-5.

Hodges, William & Phebe Cooper. 13 Feb. 1823. R, A-79.

Hodges, William & Eliza Grimes. 24 Oct. 1837. MA.

Hodges, William & Minerva Jane Cooper. 6 July 1852. MA, B-248.
Hodges, William & Keziah Grogan. 29 Dec. 1855. R, D-25.
Hoffman, George Lucas & Sarah Littleton. 26 Nov. 1833. MA, R, A-177.
Hoffman, Jacob & Elizabeth Bush. 19 Aug. 1859. MA.
Hoffman, John & Magdalene Derstence (Dernlerin?). 24 Apr. 1846. MA, R, B-86.
Hofman, Peter & Francis Mail. 24 Jan. 1857. R, D-58.
Hogan, Loyd S. & Eliza Ann Smith, both of Washington Tp. 14 Apr. 1832. MA, R, A-161.
Hogan, William Granville & Martha Ann Reynolds. 23 Nov. 1854. MA, R, D-12.
Holbert, Harrison & Cyanthian Curby (Kirby). He is 24, born Louis Co., Va., res. Green Tp., son of John & Maria Holbert. She is 22, res. Green Tp. 18 Jan. 1857. R, C-3, D-45.
Holcum, Amos & Louisa Griffeth. 9 May 1854. R, D-14.
Holes, Tingley & Ann Holliday. 11 Dec. 1850. MA, B-226.
Holland, Frances & Margaret Buck. 29 Oct. 1804. R, A-3.
Holland, William & Susannah Buck. 16 June 1808. R, A-291.
Hollemback, Adam & Wilhelmina Obruk. 23 Sep. 1858. MA, R, D-83.
Holler, John H. & Eliza Jane Jeffords. 20 Mar. 1843. R, B-43.
Holley, Daniel S. & Sarah Jayne Ballenger. 30 July 1836. MA, R, A-224.
Hollingshead, Aaron & Cordelia M. Castor. Her father Hezekiah Castor cons. 16 Mar. 1848. MA, R, B-117.
Hollister, Lyman & Margaret Flick. 30 Mar. 1841. MA, R, B-16.
Hollowswell, James & Rebeckah Culler (Cutter). 31 July 1816. MA, R, A-22.
Holman, John & Laura E. Curtis. 20 Dec. 1846. R, B-96.
Holmes, Isaac B. & Ann Eliza Bennet. 28 Aug. 1833. R, A-182.
Holmes, Isaac B. & Eliza Hanen. 10 Oct. 1836. MA, R, A-222.
Holmes, John J. & Harriet Stover (Stephen). Elizabeth Ball, of Upper Tp., Lawrence Co., cons., witn. Joel Stover, Walter Whitten. Says guardian Judge John Davidson is dead. 4 Aug. 1831. MA, R, A-160.
Holmes, Sidney S. & Harriet Watkins. 27 June 1849. R, B-154.
Holmes, Warren & Filoura Harper. He is 23, son of J. & Harriet Holmes. She is 18, born Lawrence Co., dau. of H. E. Harper. 16 Nov. 1856. R, C-4, D-42.
Holmes, William & Candace Hides. 15 Apr. 1826. MA.
Holmes, William & Mary E. Morgan. 18 Feb. 1858, by William Allgood, M.G. R.
Holstead, Amos & Nancy Anderson. 12 May 1849. MA, R, B-151.
Holsted, Amos & Elizabeth Chapman. He is 36, born & res. Va., son of Benjamin & Catharine Holstead, second marriage. She is 26, dau. of William & Mary Payton, second marriage. 11 Mar. 1857. R, C-8, D-54.
Holsted, Ira & Sally Cheney. 19 Feb. 1824. R, A-80.
Holt, Charles & Mary Jane Shurtz. 3 Feb. 1859. MA, R, D-82.
Holt, David & Sophia Noel. 25 Dec. 1835. MA, R, A-210, A-218.
Holt, David & Jerusha Mershon. 24 Mar. 1841. R, B-18.
Holt, David & Susan Brannum. 24 Dec. 1855. MA, D-23.
Holt, Elias & Ritter Hall. She is between 16 and 17. Her mother Susanah Hall cons., att. her uncle Isam Morgan. 18 May 1858. MA.
Holt, Ezirah & Virginia Pullum. 3 Mar. 1853. MA, B-265.
Holt, Henry & Catharine Boldman. 5 Dec. 1844. MA, R, B-65.
Holt, James & Mary Ann Wilson. 9 Nov. 1848. MA, R, B-137.
Holt, John & Sally Lewis. Her brother Frederick Lewis att. her age over 18. 14 Aug. 1821. MA.
Holt, John & Lidia Jane Smith. His father Henry Holt cons. 11 May 1852. MA, B-276.

Holt, Levi W. & Harriet Tims. 28 Apr. 1831. MA.
Holt, Nathan & Catherine Wallace. 23 Dec. 1845. MA, R, B-83.
Holt, William & Isabel Nickols. 22 Jan. 1846. MA, R, B-82.
Holten, Nicolas & Lucy Dupey. 29 Apr. 1833 (?) R, A-174.
Honaker, Peter & Electa A. Coriell. Her father A. Coriell cons.
    24 Jan. 1859. MA, R, D-87.
Hoobler, Daniel & Frances Dortch. 28 Oct. 1847. MA, R, B-109.
Hoobler, Jacob & Sarah Hutton. 7 Oct. 1845. MA, R, B-77.
Hood, Ebenezer K. & Else Monroe. 30 May 1845. MA.
Hood, Edward W. & Elizabeth Myres. 3 Mar. 1840. MA, R, B-4.
Hood, Francis & Lucinda Jane Rice. 28 Mar. 1858. MA, R, D-74.
Hood, George & Nancy Lord. 21 Mar. 1844. R, B-59.
Hood, George W. & Nancy Sophronia Henson. Her mother Mary Henson
    cons., witn. W. J. Henson, Zaida Copen, Andrew J. Henson.
    6 Nov. 1845. MA, R, B-81.
Hood, George W. & Amanda Jane Williams. 11 Apr. 1852. MA,
    B-238.
Hood, Waitman & Percilla Sheldon. Henry P. Westbrook att. ages.
    21 Aug. 1827. MA.
Hopkins, Charles & Sophronia Head. 25 Aug. 1821. MA, R, A-60.
Hopkins, Charles (Carls) & Sarah Dillon. 22 Dec. 1833. MA, R,
    A-186.
Hopkins, Joseph & Sarah Montgomery. 25 Sep. 1856. MA, R, D-36.
Hopkins, Thomas & Mary Weaver. Her father John Weaver cons.,
    witn. Andrew Glaze, Elijah Weaver. 13 Aug. 1820. MA, R,
    A-55.
Hopkins, Thomas & Matilda Jane Colegrove. 5 Nov. 1858. MA, R,
    D-93.
Hopkins, William & Hester Funk. 8 Mar. 1853. MA, B-268.
Hoppis, Michael & Rachel Reynolds. 4 Oct. 1833. R, A-188.
Hoppis, Michael & Ruth Hubbard. 17 Aug. 1851. MA, B-215.
Hore, Philip H. & Matilda C. Wilhelm. 25 Sep. 1856. R, D-36.
Horn (Hour), George A. & Minerva Bankin (Bank). 27 Jan. 1852.
    MA, B-236.
Hornbuckel, Joseph & Mary Jane Purdy. N. B. Cross att. ages.
    16 Oct. 1845. MA, R, B-77.
Horner, Frances W. & Joanna Burriss. 6 Apr. 1843. MA, R, B-44.
Horner, Joseph C. & Emeline Steward (Stuart). He is 27, born
    Belphrey (or Delphi), Oh., res. Nile Tp., son of Richard &
    Catherine, second marriage. She is 18, born Adams Co., res.
    Nile Tp., dau. of Samuel & Mary Stewart (Stuart), first marr.
    28 Feb. 1858. R, C-9, C-13, D-72, MA.
Horre (Horn), George & Mary Apple. 17 July 1854. R, D-9.
Horton, Joseph & Mary Jenkins. 4 July 1824. R, A-82.
Hosch, Frederich & Katharine Helmreich. 2 Oct. 1857. R, D-62.
Hoskins, Samuel T. & Elizabeth Rees. 22 Sep. 1831. MA, R, A-156.
Hoskinson, Josiah & Margaret Liston. 12 Sep. 1822. R, A-70.
Hosley, Wat Andrews & Margaret Fuget. 2 Apr. 1860. MA, R, D-116.
Hossman, Christian & Mary Thomas. 8 Apr. 1858. MA, R, D-73.
Houch, Peter & Margaret Carr. 17 Feb. 1851. MA.
Houchin, William M. & Margaret Sheward. 13 Feb. 1851. MA, B-202.
Houchins, David W. & Ellen R. Basten. 3 Nov. 1860. MA, R,
    D-124.
House, John & Eliza Pry (Try). George Masters att. her age over
    18. 29 July 1838. MA, R, A-256.
Hoves, A. J. L. & Caroline Tucker. 10 Oct. 1854. R, D-10.
How, John & Sarah Bower (Bowen). Her pars. George & Lettitia
    Bower cons., witn. James McFann, Wm. Charol. 27 Aug. 1834.
    MA, R, A-192.
Howard, Enoch & Jemima Lewis. 9 May 1851. MA, B-206.
Howard, Gabriel & Abigal Ferguson. 17 June 1819. MA, R, A-46.

Howard, Michael & Emeline Hood. Her father Robert Hood cons., witn. A. Clough, Nancy Hood. Nancy Hood of Franklin Furnace cons., att. William Davis. 13 Oct. 1833. MA, R, A-179.

Howard, Nathan (Amos?) & Nancy McDougal. Richard McDougal att. ages. 9 Nov. 1813. MA, R, A-330.

Howe, George W. & Mary McKee. Her father Arthur McKee cons. 18 Mar. 1847. MA, R, B-100.

Howe (Hall), Henry & Susan Stockham. 17 Nov. 1847. MA, R, B-114.

Howe, Henry & Ella Avery. 22 Aug. 1856. MA, B-287.

Howe, Joseph & Orriett Finton. 30 Oct. 1842. MA, R, B-36.

Howe, Samuel E. & Rebece Taylor. 25 Jan. 1850. R, B-170.

Howel, William & Sally Bliss, of Washington Tp. 12 Feb. 1823. R, A-75.

Howell, Israel H. & Melinda Darlington. 21 Nov. 1851. MA, B-226.

Howell, Jeremiah & Elizabeth Shaw. 11 May 1860. MA.

Howell, Jonathan Jr. & Drusilla Castor. Jonathan Howell Sr. att. ages. 20 Feb. 1846. MA.

Howell, Linley & Harriet McDowell. Her father Samuel McDowell cons. 26 Aug. 1859. MA, R, D-100.

Howell, Samuel C. & Mary Andre. 18 Mar. 1852. MA, B-239.

Howell, Samuel C. & Josephine Andre. 10 Apr. 1856. R, D-28.

Howell, Thomas N. & Lucretia Munn. 24 July 1836. MA, R, A-225.

Howener, Gotlieb & Charlotte Lampe. Sabastian Eifort att. ages. 19 Oct. 1852. MA, B-250.

Hoxworth, J. M. & Isabella Bamey (Barney?). 20 May 1847. MA, R, B-102.

Hoyt, Alanson & Anne Bonser. 27 Dec. 1846. MA, R, B-97.

Hoyt, Benjamin & Elizabeth Rowley. 23 Feb. 1844. MA, R, B-54.

Hoyt, Henry & Amanda Combs. 22 Feb. 1827. R, A-105.

Hoyt, Henry & Sophronia Holley. 23 May 1833. MA, R, A-175.

Hoyt, William & Charity Pray. 17 July 1845. MA, R, B-74.

Hubball, Jonathan & Rozisa Dunlap. 19 Oct. 1840. MA.

Hubbard, Edmond & Elizabeth Munion (Bunion). Charles Price att. ages. 12 Sep. 1858. MA, R, D-83.

Hubbard, Edmond Crockit & Phoeba Allen. Her father Stephen Allen, of Wheelersburg, cons. 24 Oct. 1858. MA, R, D-83.

Hubbard, James & Charlotte Kinnison (Rinneson). 14 Nov. 1848. MA, R, B-139.

Hubbard, John C. & Catherine Bower. Cons. of Sylvanus T. Shumway, of Madison Tp. says "He has No Father living and his mother gave him in to my char befor i came in the State and he has done for himself this year past," witn. John Bower. 24 Mar. 1824. MA, R, A-81.

Hubbard, John T. & Jane Skidmore. 30 May 1854. B-283.

Hubbard, Stephen & Francis McGlone. 10 Oct. 1850. MA, R, B-189.

Hubertus, Peter & Margaret Coopper (Cropper). 14 Apr. 1858. MA, R, D-75.

Huddleson, Abraham & Rosina Hubble. 20 Aug. 1842. MA, R, B-34.

Huddleson, Abraham & Charlotta Saxton. 16 Aug. 1854. R, D-9.

Huddleston, Abraham & Abigail Gallup. 11 July 1847. MA, R, B-104.

Huddleston, John, of Porter Tp. & Fanny Wood, of Harrison Tp. 16 Feb. 1837. MA, R, A-239.

Huddleston, Joseph & Frances Marshel. 11 Mar. 1832. R, A-161.

Huddleston, Powell & Eliza Moore. 11 May 1837. MA, R, A-247.

Huddleston, Thaddeus & Martha Hughes. 16 Aug. 1851. B-214.

Hudson, A. J. & Malissa Patten. Thomas J. & Julian Baccus, of Green Tp. cons., witn. __ler Hudson, __cis M. Patten. 27 Dec. 1854. MA, R, D-13.

Hudson, Armstead & Frances Andrews. 10 July 1839. MA, R, A-270.

Hudson, Elijah & Susannah Swaar. 22 May 1825. R, A-89.

Hudson, Francis M. & Charlotte Pierce. Charles T. Hudson att. ages. 1 Jan. 1859. MA, R, D-95.
Hudson, Joseph & Elizabeth Mathew (Mayhue). 20 Jan. 1842. MA, R, B-27.
Hudson, William & Matilda Sullivan. 29 Dec. 1859. MA, R, D-112.
Hues, Ephraim & Lucinda Hungerford. 3 Sep. 1837. R, A-236.
Huffman, Peter & Frances Spitznogle. He is 28, born Germany, son of John & Mary Huffman. She is 22, born Germany, dau. of J. & M. A. Spitznogle. 4 Feb. 1857. C-5.
Hughes, Abijah & Abigail Roberts. 21 Oct. 1850. MA, B-192.
Hughes, E. B. & Elizabeth Wigham. 31 Jan. 1856. D-24.
Hughes, Eli & Mary Huddleston. 11 Aug. 1848. MA, R, B-132.
Hughes, Enoch & Annie Phillips. Her father Asa (?) Phillips cons. 16 Feb. 1859. MA, R, D-90.
Hughes, Henry & Sarah Simmons. 24 Feb. 1836. MA, R, A-213.
Hughes, Milton & Eunice Jaynes. 5 Feb. 1834. R, A-188.
Hughes, Nathan & Polly Leach. 3 Feb. 1833. MA, R, A-172.
Hughes, Owen & Lois Webber. 25 Dec. 1844. MA, R, B-66.
Hughes, Samuel & Martha A. Sturgeon. 17 Aug. 1848. MA, R, B-130.
Hughes, Samuel & Martha A. Roberts. 29 Nov. 1850. MA, B-195.
Hughes, Silvester & Nancy Dawson (Dawnor). 19 Jan. 1847. MA, B-229.
Hughes, William & Elizabeth Young. 13 July 1811. R, A-311.
Hughes, William E. & Mary Skouter (Mary L. Konts). 3 Dec. 1856. R, D-47.
Hulch (Nolon?), Michael & Therisa Weber (Weaver). 6 Oct. 1856, by John Joseph Reboa, Cath. priest, Aetna Furnace, Lawrence Co. MA, R.
Hull, Isaac & Anna Burt. 21 Mar. 1809. R, A-295.
Hull, Isaac & Sarah Lewis. 21 Nov. 1820. R, A-57.
Hull, Julius & Jane M. Fuller. 12 July 1854. R, D-8.
Huls, Ezekiel & Elizabeth Piles. 9 June 1822. R, A-68.
Humble, Bentley & Cyenda Byers. 4 Mar. 1849. MA, R, B-142.
Humble, R. B. (Elias Umble) & Susan Worley. Joseph Worley cons. 29 Sep. 1853. MA, B-273.
Humble, S. J. & Melissa F. Mott. 30 June 1856. R, D-32.
Hummel, Philip & Dorothy Dortch (Doli). 4 Oct. 1852. MA, B-248.
Humphreys, Samuel & Elizabeth Tipton. 6 July 1842. MA.
Humphries, Allen & Rachel Nail. 17 June 1854. R, D-8.
Humphries, Charles & Mary Jane Fitz Randolph. Robert F. Randolph cons., says she is over 14. 18 Aug. 1842. MA, R, B-34.
Humphries, James & Francis Lair. 2 Mar. 1844. MA, R, B-55.
Humphries, John & Hannah Perry. 1 Dec. 1841. MA, R, B-26.
Hungerford, Horace & Jane Coryell. 4 Mar. 1819. R, A-43.
Hungerford, James C. & Samantha Lair. 8 Jan. 1843. R, B-41.
Hungerford, James C. & Amanda Wilson. 15 Feb. 1849. MA, R, B-141.
Hungerford, James Harvey & Susan Coryell. 4 Mar. 1819. R, A-44.
Hunnell (Honel), Aaron & Mary Hoppis. Her mother Catherine Hoppis cons., att. William Hoppis, Henderson Bradshaw. 24 May 1836. MA, R, A-216, A-232.
Hunsinger, Samuel & Frances Lesler. 16 Oct. 1860. MA, R, D-132.
Hunsucker, Nathan & Mary A. Brown. 1 Jan. 1851. MA, B-197.
Hunt, Bazil & Sally Acheson. 9 Apr. 1839. R, A-267.
Hunt, Charles & Mary Jane Oard. 27 Mar. 1834. MA, R, A-191.
Hunt, Harvey H. & Sarah Clifford. 5 Jan. 1848. MA, R, B-114.
Hunt, Jackson & Emely Pugh (Pew). 25 Mar. 1843. MA, R, B-46.
Hunt, Michael & Louisa Sloat. 28 Aug. 1851. MA, B-215.
Hunter, Archable & Hester Triggs (Higgs). 29 Aug. 1825. R, A-92.
Hunter, Franklin S. & Susannah Bowen. 10 Jan. 1854. D-4.
Hunter, Grant & Maria E. Witherow. 18 Jan. 1848. R, B-113.
Hunter, Horace & Jane Knapp. 15 Nov. 1838. MA.
Hunter, James & Sally Plowman (Rowman). 24 Apr. 1817. MA, R, A-27.

Hunter, John & Elizabeth Wilson. 12 June 1834. MA, R, A-190.
Hunter, R. B. & Sarah A. McCann (Mary McCama). 7 Feb. 1858.
    R, C-16, D-69.
Hunter, Spencer & Mary Johnson. 25 Apr. 1856. R, D-29.
Hunter, Squire & Mary Jane Middaugh. 12 Dec. 1845. MA, R, B-80.
Huntley, Charles P. & Celinde Clemmons. 29 Mar. 1832. R, A-161.
Hurd, Jesse Y. & Catherine Ann Rogers. 1 Nov. 1842. R, B-36.
Hurd, Jonathan B. & Theresa Reeves. 23 July 1846, in Leeburg,
    Highland Co., Ohio. R, B-92.
Hurd (Hard), Moses & Mary Osborn. 22 June 1837. MA, R, A-244.
Hurd, Travis & Rosanna Bertrand. 3 Sep. 1851. MA.
Huse, Hugh & Mary Spangle. His mother Keziah Huse cons. 21 Mar.
    1816. MA, R, A-20.
Hush, Peter & Sarah M. Thomas. Joseph Thomas att. ages. 23 Feb.
    1852. MA.
Huston, James & Isabel Vannort. 22 Apr. 1824. MA, R, A-81.
Huston (Hinton?), James M. & Mary E. Andrews. 26 July 1827. R,
    A-107.
Huston, James P. & Rebecca Murphy. 4 July 1853. B-265.
Huston (Hutton), John & Ann McNeal. 31 Oct. 1827. R, A-110.
Huston, Joseph & Matilda Vannort. 6 Jan. 1831. MA, R, A-150.
Huston, Joseph Sr. & Mary Ann Price. 12 Sep. 1847. R, B-107.
Huston, Joseph & Eliza Long. 11 Nov. 1857. R, D-66.
Huston, Marcus & Mary Signor. 18 Feb. 1837. MA, R, A-238.
Huston, Samuel J. & Elizabeth Leonard. 28 May 1823. R, A-75.
Huston, Thomas J. & Carrie Albertson. 1 Dec. 1859. MA, R, D-107.
Huston, William & Martha Murphy. 31 May 1849. MA, R, B-150.
Hutchins, Wells A. & Cornelia Robinson. 23 Feb. 1843. R, B-42.
Hutton, George & Marey Nicholas. 6 Aug. 1830. R, A-145.
Hutton, George & Mary Arnold. 20 Sep. 1832. R, A-168.
Hutton, James Jr. & Nancy Brous. 2 Aug. 1832. R, A-165.
Hutton, James & Anna Hamilton. 23 Apr. 1840. R, B-10.
Hutton, James & Abigail Clark. 5 May 1841. MA, R, B-18.
Hutton, James P. & Catharine E. Worley. 20 Mar. 1849. MA,
    B-144.
Hutton, James T. & Hariot Hamilton. 10 Nov. 1826. MA.
Hutton, John & Franky Burriss. 31 Jan. 1828. R, A-115, A-119.
Hutton, William & Elizabeth Stoner (Storer?). 31 Dec. 1818. R,
    A-42.
Hyatt, Charles P. & Mary D. Thoroman. 18 Nov. 1841. R, B-20.
Hyatt, E. & Prudence Goodrich. 11 Aug. 1840. R, B-10.
Hyatt, James & Mary Wilhelm. 6 Dec. 1844. MA.
Iams, Percival I. & Maimette Oldfield. 17 Apr. 1849. R, B-150.
Iams, Soloman & Mary Ann Gappen. 3 Jan. 1851. MA, B-191, B-198.
Ileffe, James & Alice Smith. 7 Feb. 1859. MA, R, D-77.
Ilich, Jacob & Pauline Spring. 6 Oct. 1842. MA, R, B-35.
Imler, James & Rebecca Ely. 17 July 1851. MA, B-212.
Ingals, James H. & Laura Boynton. 28 Mar. 1850. MA, R, B-178.
Ingerson, Benjamin F. & Mary Rickards. H. Taylor, of Harrison
    att. ages. 4 Apr. 1835, by James Sampson, J.P., Madison Tp.
    MA, R.
Ingles, Harrison & Elizabeth Hardin. 14 Sep. 1848. MA, R, B-131.
Inman, William & Charilla Dixon. 12 Dec. 1850. MA, B-196.
Irwin, James & Melessa Finney. 19 Jan. 1860. MA, R, D-110.
Irwin, Jeremiah & Barbary Morgan. 29 Dec. 1836. MA, A-238.
Irwin, John & Sarah A. Wood. 16 Dec. 1846. MA, R, B-98.
Irwin, Robert & Huldy Rockwell. Jonathan Rockwell att. ages.
    13 Jan. 1855. MA, R, D-14.
Irwin, Thomas & Mary Smith. 14 Apr. 1849. MA, R, B-147.
Isanhour, Martin & Rebecca Allen. 30 Nov. 1838. MA.
Ivert, Thomas & Maria Hodge. William Finney att. her age. 29
    Mar. 1848. MA, B-245.

SCIOTO COUNTY MARRIAGES

Jackson, A. J. & Mary A. Journey. Her father William Journey
cons. "..for my eldest daughter..", witn. W. S. Foster,
Joshua Foster. 25 May 1858. MA, R, D-81.
Jackson, Alfred & Zillah Halstead. 2 Apr. 1837. MA, R, A-247.
Jackson, Arthur F. & Sarah Hunsucker. Her father cons. 4 July
1848. MA, R, B-127.
Jackson, George W. & Flora A. Holmes. He is son of Joseph
Jackson, born & res. Bloom Tp. She is dau. of W. C. Holmes,
born & res. Bloom Tp. 4 Apr. 1858. MA, R, C-12, D-74.
Jackson, James & Marther Harmon. 13 Sep. 1804. R, A-1.
Jackson, James & Jane Patten, both of Porter Tp. 16 Sep. 1836.
MA, R, A-238.
Jackson, Joseph & Elizabeth Fout. 28 Mar. 1833. MA, R, A-175.
Jackson, Joseph & Lavinia Bardwell. 18 Apr. 1849. MA, R, B-146.
Jackson, Roswell & Elizabeth Bibby. 9 May 1841. MA, R, B-19.
Jackson, Solomon & Mary Johnson. Her father George Johnson cons.
Vol. A describes him as "colored", her as "black as the ace of
spades". 6 Jan. 1831. MA, R, A-150.
Jackson, Solomon & Ellen Johnston. 28 Nov. 1836. MA, R, A-222.
Jackson, William Jr. & Melissa Jane (Lizzie T.) Smith. 27 Feb.
1853. MA, B-261.
Jackson, William Jr. & Elizabeth Jane Bennett. He is 38, son of
William & R. Jackson, second marriage. She is dau. of Cias
Bennet, first marriage. 15 June 1856. R, C-5, D-31.
Jacob, Godfrey & Margaret Brust. 15 May 1848. MA.
Jacobs, Jacob & Hannah Utt. 18 Oct. 1810. R, A-305.
Jacobs, John & Susanna Trexler. 25 Apr. 1809. R, A-295.
Jacobs, Wilson & Esther Blodget. 12 Dec. 1835. MA, R, A-210.
Jacques, Lewis & Clotilda Magnet. He is 27, born France, res.
Dearborn Co., IA., son of Peter & Elizabeth Jacquese. She
is 17, born Hamilton Co., res. Scioto Co., dau. of J.N. &
C. E. Magnet. 3 Sep. 1857. R, C-8, D-64. [This marriage
is also recorded on C-12 as Lewis J. CADOT & Clotilda Magnet.]
Jager, Jacob & Catharina Miller. 24 June 1855. R, D-19.
James, Daniel & Ruth Nicoles. 20 July 1829. MA, R, A-132.
James, Henry T. & Catharine Miller. 2 Feb. 1850. MA, R, B-170.
James, Jacob & Jemima Hodges. Thomas Cooper att. she is over
14, has no pars. living. Her mother left her in his care
for more than 2 years prior to her death, and that before the
death of Sally Hodges (Jemima's mother), he has acted as her
guardian. 13 July 1837. MA, R, A-237.
James, Joseph & Susan Warren. His father Josiah James cons.,
witn. Thompson N. Stratton, W. T. McAtee, Jonathan James.
She att. she is over 21, witn. Thompson N. Stratton. 3 Oct.
1828. MA, R, A-124.
James, Josiah & Olivina James. 7 May 1848. R, B-126.
James, Levi & Sarah Allaways. 26 May 1853. B-264.
James, Perry & Elizabeth Halterman. 6 Mar. 1845. MA, R, B-69.
James, Perry & Maria Wales. 4 Mar. 1841. R, B-26.
James, William & Maria Donason. 20 Dec. 1849. R, B-169.
Jamison, David & Mary Logan. 7 Jan. 1816. MA, R, A-17.
Jamison, William W. & Nancy Miller. 25 Jan. 1850. R, B-168.
Jaquay, Anthony & Marrietta Hall. 3 Jan. 1836. MA, R, A-210.
Jatho, Charles Henry Frederick (Carl) & Caroline Benner. 4 Dec.
1833. MA, R, A-177.
Jaugnot, Eugene & Lovina Knapp. 11 June 1857. R, D-55.
Jayne, Isaac & Polly Melone. 20 Dec. 1808. R, A-295.
Jaynes, Stephen & Sally Everett. 30 Jan. 1816. MA, R, A-19.
Jeandeson (Jeandesboz), Charles Francis & Ann Louisa Huchey.
21 June 1848. MA, R, B-124.
Jefferson, Benjamin L. & Mariah Moore. 8 Oct. 1839. R, A-275.
Jeffords, Elza & Nancy P. Turner. 8 Nov. 1849. R, B-170.

65

SCIOTO COUNTY MARRIAGES

Jeffords, Ezra & Phebe Willey. 1 Jan. 1854. D-6.
Jeffords, Ezra & Ann Pray. 15 Apr. 1850. R, B-177.
Jeffords, Henry & Sally A. Craig. 29 July 1854. B-284.
Jeffords, Henry C. & Mary Bradshaw. 27 June 1852. MA, B-276.
Jeffords, John & Emily Rhodes. 15 Oct. 1851. B-219.
Jeffords, Joseph & Ann A. Crain. 31 Aug. 1858. R, D-81.
Jeffords, Josiah & Mary C. Craig. 15 Apr. 1857. R, D-173.
Jemes, John (James James) & Lodicy Rockwell. John Scott att.
   ages. 4 Feb. 1851. MA, B-200.
Jenkins, Joseph & Lucinda Call. Her father Charles Call cons.,
   witn. Thomas Call. 8 Jan. 1846. MA, R, B-84.
Jenkins, Joseph & Semantha A. Davis. J. W. Hicks att. ages.
   13 Jan. 1852. MA.
Jenkins, Squire (also known as Squire Laire) & Peggy Caster.
   Her father Hezekiah Caster cons., witn. Aaron Hollingshead.
   16 Sep. 1852. MA, B-250.
Jenkins, Walter & Mary Piggott. He is 20, born New York, son of
   Colvin & Sarah Jenkins. William Dodds att. their cons. She
   is 19, born Ohio, dau. of John & Electa Piggott. 28 Aug.
   1857. MA, R, C-9, D-59.
Jenkins, William & Eliza Locke. 27 May 1830. MA, A-146.
Jenkins, William (divorced) & Polly Vangorder. 16 Jan. 1849.
   MA, R, B-140.
Jenkins, William & Jane Lewis. 14 Feb. 1851. MA, B-206.
Jenks, Liberty & Margaret Ames. 23 June 1832. R, A-163.
Jewett, David & Mahala A. Boldman. 10 Sep. 1857. R, D-59.
Jewett, John & Loisa Markum. 19 Oct. 1843. MA, R, B-50.
Jewett, Nathan & Julia Ann Santa. 23 Dec. 1849. R, B-166.
Jewett (Jowete), William & Nancy Wilson. 20 Jan. 1818. MA, R,
   A-34.
Jewett, William & Sarah Farmer. 8 Nov. 1840. R, B-14.
Jewitt, Jeremiah & Emma F. Hayden. 24 Nov. 1859. MA, R, D-105.
Jinkens, Azariah & Susannah Potters. 7 Aug. 1845. MA.
Jobes, Abraham & Ann E. Miller. 18 Feb. 1851. MA, B-245.
Jobling (Jopland), Charley & Margaret Morten. 4 Sep. 1857. R,
   D-59.
Jochem, John & Fredrica Ickenberg. 26 June 1852. MA.
John, Jacob & Christina Hied. 21 Jan. 1859. MA, R, D-95.
John, Nicholas & Barbary Will. 19 Sep. 1853. MA.
Johnson, Charles & Sally Batchellor. His father John Johnson
   cons., witn. Thomas & Andrew Thoroman, att. Henry Dieterick.
   Her pars. Parin & Sarah Batchellor cons., witn. Joseph Batch-
   ellor. 14 July 1830. MA.
Johnson, Cyrus & Luruhama Harris. 11 Feb. 1830. MA, R, A-138.
Johnson (Jonsin), Daniel L. & Margaret T. Jones (Johnson).
   2 Nov. 1853. MA, B-271.
Johnson, David J. & Kaziah Dalson. 24 June 1817. R, A-30.
Johnson, George & Mary R. Tracy. 24 Aug. 1847. R, B-106.
Johnson, George W. & Jane White. 20 Dec. 1860, by John Wallace,
   J.P. MA, R.
Johnson, Isaac N. & Sarah Ann Cockrell. 23 Oct. 1845. R, B-78.
Johnson, James & Elizabeth Parker. 24 Nov. 1818, by John Carney,
   Elder of Baptist Church. MA, R.
Johnson, James & Mary C. Melcher. 1 Dec. 1842. R, B-38.
Johnson, James & Lydia Ann Butler. 5 Mar. 1846. MA, R, B-84.
Johnson, James A. & Betty F. Payne. 29 Mar. 1854. D-5.
Johnson, James E. & Rebecca Maltimore. 22 June 1830. MA, R,
   A-145.
Johnson, James O. & Pheby Jeffords. 10 Mar. 1833. R, A-174.
Johnson, Jesse & Ann Simpson. 26 Feb. 1829. R, A-128.
Johnson, Joel C. & Malinda (Belinda) Voorhees. 23 Jan. 1831.
   MA, R, A-150.

Johnson, John & Sarah Ann Snediger. 22 Jan. 1843. MA, R, B-41.
Johnson, John & Elizabeth McDowell. 15 Jan. 1847. MA, R, B-97.
Johnson, John Henry & Mary Jane Davis. 11 Apr. 1859. MA, R, D-98.
Johnson, John L. & Nancy Cockrell. 4 June 1840. R, B-13.
Johnson, John W. & Elizabeth Bennett. 28 Sep. 1854. MA, R, D-10.
Johnson, Joseph & Lucretia Call. 25 Dec. 1851. MA, B-228.
Johnson, Lewis H. & Rachael Crain. 11 Aug. 1850. R, B-186.
Johnson, Moses & Susannah Weaver. 24 Aug. 1837. MA, R, A-237.
Johnson, Moses & Christiana Biggs. 30 June 1842. R, B-32.
Johnson, Moses & Ann Wilson. 12 Oct. 1845. R, B-77.
Johnson, Moses & Hannah Hill. 15 May 1850. R, B-184.
Johnson, Richard W. & Lavina Johnson. 23 Oct. 1845. MA.
Johnson, Roswell W. & Mary Burt. 9 Sep. 1819. MA, R, A-48.
Johnson, Samuel & Amanda Miler. 3 July 1859. MA, R, D-98.
Johnson, Solomon & Hester F. Smith. 28 May 1849. MA, R, B-150.
Johnson, Thomas & Ellen Snedicour. 9 Jan. 1845. MA, R, B-68.
Johnson, Thomas H. & Josephine Montgomery. 13 June 1860. MA, R, D-120.
Johnson, Timothy & Lucinda Hulce. 10 Feb. 1842. MA, R, B-27.
Johnson, Warren & Mary Fortner. 18 May 1830. MA, R, A-142.
Johnson, William & Ellen Gardner. 12 Feb. 1838. R, A-249.
Johnson, William & Mary Jane Wilson. 19 Aug. 1841. MA.
Johnson, William & Matilda Jayne Holt. Jonathan James (Jones?) att. ages. 16 Aug. 1847. MA, R, B-105.
Johnson, William & Melinda Arthur. 17 Sep. 1851. MA.
Johnson, William & Catherine Mathews. A. Mathews cons. 12 Feb. 1853. MA, B-258.
Johnson, William & Catherine Farley. His father Adam Johnson cons. 3 July 1859. MA, R, D-99.
Johnson (Janson), William H. & Eliza Ellen Berry. 19 Apr. 1860. MA, R, D-116.
Johnson, William S. & Louisa Jane Wilson. 5 July 1853. MA, B-280.
Johnson, William W. & Sarah C. Johnson. 8 Oct. 1860. MA.
Johnston, James & Rebecca Pyles. 30 Dec. 1849. R, B-168.
Johnston, Oliver P. & Margaret Downey. He res. Madison Tp. She res. Madison Tp., dau. of Sarah Downey. 9 Oct. 1856. MA, R, C-4, D-40.
Jones, Allen & Mary Ann McClovis. 18 Dec. 1849. R, B-164.
Jones, Andes (Andrew) & Lucinda Hailey (Haley). John R. Chitwood att. his age over 21. 18 July 1815. MA, R, A-282.
Jones, Andrew B. & Margaret Riley. 7 Dec. 1852. MA, B-251.
Jones, Barnett & Betsey Smith. 25 May 1853. MA, B-261.
Jones, Benjamin & Lydia Headlock. 7 Jan. 1819. MA, R, A-42.
Jones, Charles & Mary Ann Hanford (Hairford). 10 Nov. 1838. MA, R, A-260.
Jones, Cyrus & Katharine Ghalliher. 11 July 1816. MA, R, A-21.
Jones (James), D. L. & Margaret E. Evans. 22 Oct. 1853. MA, B-272.
Jones, Daniel & Ann Hopkins. 4 __ 1857. R, D-55.
Jones, Daniel James & Ruhama McClese. His father John Jones Sr., of Greenup Co., Ky. cons. 31 Mar. 1859. MA, R, D-90.
Jones, David & Catherine Timberlake. He is 55, born & res. Ky., son of David J. Jones, second marriage. She is 30, born & res. Ky., second marriage. 1 Dec. 1857. R, C-9, D-67.
Jones, Edward & Sarah Shaw (Cose, Case?). 17 June 1852. MA, B-240.
Jones, Edward J. & Elizabeth Farney. 9 Feb. 1859. MA, R, D-133.
Jones, Francis M. & Ellen Reineger. 24 June 1851. B-209.
Jones, George O. & Marjory J. Crull. 9 Jan. 1845. R, B-71.
Jones, Hiram & Rebecca Everett. 6 Nov. 1832. MA.

Jones, Hiram & Ellen Riley. 22 Mar. 1849. MA, R, B-145.
Jones, J. B. & Eliza A. Hogan. 4 Dec. 1855. D-24.
Jones, J. F. & Mary Ann Price. 30 Mar. 1857. R, D-54.
Jones, James & Margaret Osborn. 12 June 1851. MA, B-209.
Jones (James), James & Rachel Hartley. 5 Oct. 1851. MA, B-225.
Jones, James C. & Amelia Scott. 15 Mar. 1860. MA, R, D-119.
Jones, John & Esther Jones. 1 Mar. 1838. MA, R, A-250.
Jones, John & Nancy Stiles. 11 Nov. 1849. MA, R, B-162.
Jones, John & Elsy Powers. 20 Mar. 1851. MA.
Jones, John & Rebecca Archabold. 2 Apr. 1854. D-1.
Jones, John C. & Susannah Baird. 15 Jan. 1852. MA, B-228.
Jones, John I. & Ann Evans. 2 Jan. 1860. MA, R, D-103.
Jones, John L. & Mary J. Crull. 19 June 1843. R, B-71.
Jones, John L. & Martha J. Dunaway. 15 Oct. 1840. MA, R, B-12.
Jones, Levi & S. C. Thomas. 25 Mar. 1855. R, D-16.
Jones, Louis & Ellen Coriell. His father S. G. Jones of Harri-
    son Tp. cons., att. D. V. Coriell, Thomas M. Coriell.
    29 July 1858. MA, R, D-84.
Jones, Nathan Jr. & Eliza Clare. 13 Feb. 1856. R, D-27.
Jones, Robert & Mary Jane Ellison. 28 Mar. 1844. MA, R, B-57.
Jones, Robert W. & Laura Fitch. 13 Feb. 1860. MA, R, D-113.
Jones, Samuel G. & Anne Holybee. 3 Oct. 1847. MA, R, B-111.
Jones, Samuel G. & Clarrissa Ferrill. 25 May 1858. MA, R, D-75.
Jones, Samuel Griffith & Elizabeth Shane. His father S.G. Jones
    cons., witn. William Jones, John Wallis. 15 Nov. 1835. MA, A-207.
Jones, Thomas & Teresa Finton. 9 May 1849. MA, R, B-148.
Jones, Thomas C. & Patsy D. Cockrell. 4 Aug. 1835. R, A-204.
Jones, Thomas K. & Charity Ruby. N. L. Jones, of Portsmouth,
    cons. 8 Sep. 1859. MA, R, D-101.
Jones, Thomas W. & Letitia Morton. 29 Sep. 1853. B-281.
Jones, W. W. & Susannah Yemens. 1 Oct. 1850. B-194.
Jones, William & Elizabeth Howel. 16 Nov. 1821. R, A-62.
Jones, William & Ruhama Adams. 13 May 1832. MA, R, A-162.
Jones, William & Amanda Williams. 28 Dec. 1849. R, B-165.
Jones, William C. & Nancy Cole. Her father D. W. Coale cons.
    5 May 1852. MA, B-275.
Jones, William K. & Rachel Morgan. 17 Oct. 1852. MA, R, B-268.
Jones, William K. & Jane Whitney. 29 Sep. 1849. MA, R, B-158.
Jones, William P. & Margaret Waters. 2 July 1853. MA.
Jones, William R. & Elizabeth Walles (Walls). 29 Oct. 1831.
    R, A-157.
Jordan, E. W. & Augusta W. Ricker. 27 Oct. 1852. MA, B-248.
Jugenot, Peter & Rosalie Rose. 6 Nov. 1857. R, D-69.
Junkin, John M. & Mary Carter. David W. M. Junkin att. his age
    over 21. 30 Sep. 1845. MA, R, B-80.
Justes, Hiram & Anny Martin. 29 Nov. 1842. R, B-37.
Justice, Henry J. & Mary Leadenham. 12 June 1860. MA, R, D-121.
Justice, James & Jane McConnell. 2 Dec. 1842. MA, R, B-27.
Kah (Kough), Mathias & Catharine Clise (Cline). He is 25, born
    Germany, res. Portsmouth, son of Jacob & S. Kah. She is 18,
    born Germany, res. Portsmouth, dau. of Phillip & Louisa
    Clairy. 24 Apr. 1856. MA, R, C-1, D-28.
Kahal, Edward & Sophia Noel. Samuel Nicols att. she is over 18.
    9 Nov. 1812. MA.
Kain (Kean), William & Phebe Vanhorn. 15 Oct. 1835. MA, R,
    A-206.
Kaltenback, John & Bena Haukenheimer. 4 Apr. 1859. MA, R, D-99.
Kanzler, Christian & Catarine Ruf. 22 Aug. 1849. R, B-155.
Karstens, Henry & Elisabeth Hoffner. 11 Sep. 1857. R, D-59.
Kast, Andrew & Barbara Shiebler. 6 Feb. 1855. MA.
Katon, Thomas & Lydia Halterman. 25 Dec. 1836. MA, A-238.
Katon, Thomas & Malissa Smith. 5 Mar. 1848. MA, R, B-116.

Kaufman, Michael & Juliana Kah (Rap). 16 May 1846. MA, B-242.
Kays, Major Jr. & Harriet Ballard. Her stepfather & guardian
   Conrad Taylor, of Union Tp., cons., says she is 17, witn.
   John Auld, Thomas Kirk. 25 May 1848. MA, R, B-123.
Kazer, Peter & Emily Duwit (Dewitt). 1 May 1850. R, B-179.
Keairns, Alexander & Tobitha Smith. 23 Feb. 1843. MA, R, B-43.
Keairns (Cornes), John & Mary Toland. Augustus Keairns att. his
   age. 28 July 1840. MA, R, B-10.
Keans (McKean), James M. & Jane Elizabeth Lodwick. 4 June 1846.
   R, B-87.
Keeny, John & Mary Ann Arthur. Stephen S. Price att. ages.
   7 Aug. 1853. MA, B-268.
Kegle, Jacob & Katharine Ging. 12 Dec. 1857. R, D-67.
Kehone, Jesy & Ellen Sullivan. 27 Jan. 1856. R, D-25.
Kehrer, Charles & Louisa Cook. 23 Apr. 1848. MA, R, B-122.
Keinke (Kienker, Hauka), John & Barbara Luther. He is 25, born
   Germany, res. Portsmouth. She is 21, born England, res.
   Portsmouth. 27 Jan. (Feb.) 1858. R, C-13, D-68.
Keiser, Jacob & Elizabeth Ingles. 1 Apr. 1842. MA.
Keitler (?), Turnes (James?) & Jully (Sally) Lawder. 11 Oct.
   1854. R, D-10.
Keitly, George W. & Sarah Ann Basham. 4 June 1837. R, A-243.
Kellander, William & Nancy Holbert. He is 23, res. Green Tp.
   She is 22, res. Scioto Co. Both born Scioto Co. 6 July
   1856. R, C-3, D-33.
Kellar, John J. & Sarah (Nancy) Woten. 7 Nov. 1852. MA, B-249.
Keller, Conrad N. & Marilda Holmes. Her father William Holmes
   cons., att. Charles Norten. 9 Feb. 1852. MA, B-233.
Keller, Cornelius S. & Lydia J. Rickey. Her father Joseph
   Rickey cons. 24 Feb. 1859. MA, R, D-92.
Keller, Enoch & Mary E. Warren. 31 May 1860. MA, R, D-118.
Keller, Jacob & Ruth Culp. 28 June 1860. MA, R, D-17.
Keller, John & Mary Hofstedter. Martin Koblenz att. ages.
   5 Oct. 1850. MA, R, B-189.
Keller, Joseph & Phebe Ann Culp, both of Madison Tp. 4 July
   1839. MA, R, A-270.
Keller, Kenady & Mary Snyder. 28 Sep. 1836. MA, R, A-222.
Keller, Martin & Mena Mila (Maria Wind). 12 Apr. 1847. MA,
   B-242.
Kelley, Anthony & Nancy Amanda Russel. Levi Kelly att. his age.
   Her pars. Nathan & Elizabeth Russel cons., witn. Samuel Ross.
   23 Nov. 1854. MA, R, D-14.
Kelley, George Ross & Ann Cooper. 13 June 1830. MA, R, A-144.
Kelley, James M. & Sarah Ann Baccus. Her father James Baccus
   cons. 25 Oct. 1838. MA, R, A-262.
Kelley, Joseph & Ritty Dollarhide. 7 Apr. 1808. R, A-290.
Kelley, William H. & Maria Lawson. 8 June 1837. R, A-237.
Kellogg, Alfred & Cynthia Hard. 25 Dec. 1844. MA, R, B-66.
Kellogg, Hiram & Luna Jones. 4 Feb. 1841. MA, R, B-14.
Kellogg, Julius & Mary Winet. 17 Nov. 1845. MA, R, B-79.
Kellogg, Warren & Levina Hard. 15 Apr. 1838. MA, R, A-253.
Kellogg, William & Thursa Story. 28 Oct. 1852. MA, B-255.
Kellum, William & Sarah Payton. 31 Dec. 1840. MA, R, B-16.
Kelly, Henry & Harriet E. Call. 6 Dec. 1854. MA, R, D-12.
Kelly, Hugh S. & Jemima Moore. 7 Aug. 1834. MA, R, A-183.
Kelly, J. H. & E. A. Hill. 21 Feb. 1854. D-5.
Kelly, Jacob & Susan Halstead. 9 Jan. 1831. MA, R, A-151.
Kelly, John & Abegail Lambert. 11 Sep. 1804. R, A-3.
Kelly, Joseph & Levina Stewart. 20 Feb. 1848. MA, R, B-122.
Kelly, Joshua & Mary Lee. 6 May 1816. MA, R, A-21.
Kelly, Michael & Margaret McKleroy. John Kelly att. ages. 27
   Aug. 1852. MA, B-251.

Kelly, Michel & Ann Connally. He is 25, born Ireland, res.
Chillicothe. She is 23, born Ireland, res. Chillicothe, dau.
of Peter Connally. 15 Apr. 1856. C-7.
Kelly, Thomas D. & Minerva Gelruth. 1 Jan. 1856. D-24.
Kemp, George N. & Rebecca M. Mastin. 15 Dec. 1829. R, A-137.
Kenady, Hezekiah & Martha Melson. 2 July 1829. MA.
Kendall, Frank & Mariette Hall. 21 Nov. 1859. MA, R, D-106.
Kendall, George & Levina Turner. 9 Dec. 1841. MA, R, B-27.
Kendall, Jeferson & Elizabeth Finton. 9 Dec. 1832. R, A-171.
Kendall, John & Francis A. Reeve. 18 Oct. 1834. R, A-192.
Kendall, Smith & Nancy Freeman. 23 Apr. 1844. MA, R, B-60.
Kendall, Stephen & Rebecca Ann Riggs. 6 Aug. 1839. R, A-271.
Kendall, Thomas & Ann M. Glover. 16 Nov. 1836. R, A-221.
Kendall, Thornton & Rachel Rardon. 12 Mar. 1818. MA, R, A-34.
Kendall, William & Rachel Brown. 29 May 1806 "by personal
request of the parents of the female." R, A-10, A-280.
Kendall, Gen. William & Christina Lawson. 11 Oct. 1821. R,
A-60.
Kenneda, Hezekiah & Elizabeth White. 10 Jan. 1830. R, A-139.
Kennedy, Hezekiah & Urch Tumbleson. 4 Dec. 1850. MA, B-198.
Kennedy, John H. & Dilly Welch. 7 Jan. 1849. MA, R, B-140.
Kennedy, Milton & Josephine B. Hutchinson. 20 Oct. 1850. MA,
R, B-191.
Kennedy, Peter & Sarah Timmons. 28 Dec. 1851. MA, B-227.
Kennedy, Rezin & Rebecca Trumbo. 1 Apr. 1847. MA, R, B-100.
Kennedy, Rezin & Elizabeth White. 8 Mar. 1855. R, D-17.
Kennedy, Robert & Hannah Enslow. 22 Mar. 1818. MA, R, A-37.
Kennedy, Warren & Levina Turner. 16 Jan. 1856. D-24.
Kennedy, William & Keziah Moore. 17 Mar. 1829. R, A-130.
Kennedy, Zanthus M. & Mary A. Walker. 7 July 1859. MA, R, D-98.
Kenney, Adam & Susan Collins. 11 Nov. 1855. D-23.
Kenney, Godfred & Ann Keys. 1 Oct. 1854. R, D-10.
Kent, Nathan W. & Rosetta A. Rickey. His father John Kent cons.
Her father E. W. Rickey cons. 1 Jan. 1859. MA, R, D-93.
Kent, Stephen & Ruby Whitcomb, both of Porter Tp. 12 Dec. 1822.
R, A-73.
Kent, V. L. & Selina D. Bondurant. He is 22, res. Madison Tp.,
born Ohio, son of John Kent. She is 22, born Jackson, Oh.,
res. Madison Tp., dau. of Thomas Bondurant. 18 (11) April
1857. R, C-11, D-50.
Kepler, Ernst Frederic & Karoline Meyers. 5 Jan. 1850. R, B-166.
Kepner, Bernard & Willhelmina Jefferson. 17 Mar. 1845. R, B-56.
Kerr, Adam & Lucinda Rollins. 26 Dec. 1837. R, A-235.
Kerr, Jacob & Sarah Combs. David Combs cons. 18 Sep. 1851. MA.
Kesler, Joseph & Louisa Ludwig. 7 Apr. 1842. MA, R, B-29.
Kessler, Leopold & Elizabeth Kaps. 17 July 1859. MA, R, D-110.
Ketcham, John & Sally Tomlinson. 4 Jan. 1818. MA, R, A-32.
Kettle, Jesse & Lucy Nurse. 31 Oct. 1837. R, A-234.
Kettle, Job & Lucinda Pool. 28 Feb. 1833. R, A-175.
Kettre (Kettle), Coonrod & Elizabeth Brandy. 9 July 1846. MA,
R, B-92.
Keys, Major & Elizabeth Taylor. 29 Apr. 1857. R, D-53.
Kibble, James W. & Temperance Bonser. 22 June 1851. MA, B-212.
Kiger, Nathaniel & Martha Hawkins. 11 Nov. 1838. MA, R, A-262.
Kikendall (Kirkendale), Daniel & Sarah (Sally) Campbell. 7 Oct.
1813. MA, R, A-326.
Kikendall, Levi & Minerva Beloat. Her mother Mary Brown cons.,
witn. Daniel Kikendall. 15 Mar. 1838. MA, R, A-253.
Kikendall, William & Sarah Culp. 30 Nov. 1841. MA, R, B-25.
Kikendall, William & Renda Peyton. 31 Mar. 1835. R, A-198.
Kilborn, Marcus & Mary Price. 11 June 1818. R, A-39.
Kilbourn, Osmen M. & Annis E. Taylor. 9 Jan. 1848. R, B-113.

Kilburn, Osmer M. & Dulina Lindsey. 14 Apr. 1842. R, B-30.
Kilian, John & Anna Hagan. 30 May 1859. MA, R, D-99.
Kilpatrick, William & Esther Mead. Her father Judah Mead cons.,
  witn. Isaac Mead. 31 Jan. 1822. MA, R, A-63.
Kimball, Augustine & Amazetta Jones. 22 July 1845. MA, R, B-75.
Kimball, Ira & Polly Skinner. Charles C. Boynton att. her age
  over 18. His mother Elizabeth Kimball cons. 15 Mar. 1818.
  MA, R, A-37.
Kimball, Moody & Anna Adkin. 28 Jan. 1816. MA, R, A-18.
Kimball, William & Elizabeth Stewart. Benjamin Butterfield att.
  his age. 16 Oct. 1817. MA, R, A-30.
Kimble, Joseph & Elizabeth McDowell. John Culp att. ages.
  1 Dec. 1850. MA, B-195.
Kimmle, Frank & Mary Hedhen. 1 July 1859. MA, R, D-100.
Kindle (Kendall), Milton & Ruth Lawson. 23 Jan. 1833. R, A-171.
Kinear, Alexander & Elizabeth Harvey. 17 Oct. 1849. R, B-159.
King, Eli & Elizabeth Jones. 20 May 1858. MA, R, D-92.
King, John (Johann) & Nancy Dugan. 19 Sep. 1813. MA, R, A-328.
King, John & Lucinda Haney (Harvey). 3 Dec. 1840. MA, R, B-7.
King, Lawrence & Nancy Fitch. 17 Sep. 1859. MA, R, D-101.
King, William & Esther Manly. 6 Mar. 1851. MA, B-204.
King, William & Mary Pounds. 7 Mar. 1857. R, D-48.
King, William A. & Malinda Dusan. 27 Sep. 1854. R, D-10.
Kinkleton, John & Eutheba Concklin. 20 May 1839. MA.
Kinney, Alfred & Mary L. Sill. 26 Jan. 1853. MA, B-259.
Kinney, Eli & Martha Lodwick. 10 Oct. 1837. R, A-273.
Kinney, Franklin & Mary J. Young. 29 July 1859. MA, R, D-100.
Kinney, Henry R. & Mary McNairn. 7 Nov. 1843. R, B-50.
Kinney, John & Mary Brittingham (Britenham). 21 Aug. 1822. MA,
  R, A-68.
Kinney, John & Margaret Hay. 28 Jan. 1850. R, B-168.
Kinney, John & Cerena (Celina) Wright. Her father William
  Wright cons. 11 Aug. 1853. MA, B-267.
Kinney, P. C. & Maria Clark. 4 June 1850. R, B-183.
Kinney, Peter & Elizabeth Readhead. 29 Apr. 1833 (?), by
  Eleazer Brainard. Their marriage is in a list of twelve
  marriages, not individually dated. R.
Kinney, Washington & Mary Waller. 14 Dec. 1820. R, A-56.
Kinnison, James & Catherine Louderback. 11 Nov. 1831. MA, R,
  A-159.
Kinnison, James & Jane Rabourn. 5 Sep. 1848. MA, R, B-134.
Kinnzler (Keensler), Christian & Lena (Sina) Mye. 19 Aug. 1848.
  MA, B-244.
Kinslla, John & Eliza Blake. 24 Apr. 1860. MA, R, D-117.
Kirby, Isaac & Rhozinna (Rosina) C. Dole. Her father E. Dole
  cons. 14 Dec. 1841. MA, R, B-27.
Kirby, John M. & Amanda Berkley. 5 Nov. 1851. MA.
Kirchheus, George & Martha Mary Ross. 8 Nov. 1859. MA, R, D-107.
Kirk, Thomas & Mary E. Auld. 18 Oct. 1849. MA, R, B-159.
Kirk, Thomas & Nancy Biggs. 26 July 1852. B-246.
Kirkendall, Daniel & Elizabeth McLary. His mother Mary E.
  McClary cons. 23 June 1850. MA, R, B-182.
Kirkendall, John & Mary Martin. Derrick Allensworth att. ages.
  29 Sep. 1848. MA, R, B-134.
Kirkendall, Stephen & Margaret Walk. 2 Mar. 1854. D-6.
Kirkendall, William & Margaret Cramer. 17 Nov. 1825. R, A-93.
Kirkhause, George & Ellen Smith. 25 Dec. 1852. MA, B-254.
Kirkpatrick, John & Sarah Wilson. 21 Sep. 1848. MA, R, B-133.
Kirkpatrick, Madison & Eleanor Bennet. 28 Mar. 1820 (1819). MA,
  R, A-57.
Kirkpatrick, Milton & Judah Strought. 18 Oct. 1849. MA, R, B-161.
Kirkpatrick, Milton A. & Sarah Samson. 25 Aug. 1855. R, D-20.

Kirkpatrick, Thomas & Sarah Musgrave. 5 Dec. 1850. MA, B-197.
Kirkpatrick, William & Martha Bennet. 16 Sep. 1847. R, B-110.
Kirkpatrick, William & Cynthia A. Minard. 3 May 1851. MA, B-206.
Kischoff, William & Phillipina Klaus. 26 Nov. 1840. R, B-8.
Kittle, David & Sophia Powell. 9 Aug. 1842. R, B-36.
Kittle, Jesse W. & Sarah Burk. William M. Burk cons., witn.
Seymour Pixley, John D. Miller. 10 May 1827. MA, R, A-109.
Kittle, Job & Rachel Stockham. 7 Dec. 1831. R, A-160.
Kizer, Benjamin & Mariah (Emmenah) Snow. 10 June 1848. MA, R,
B-125.
Kizer, Jackson & Jane Carpenter. Richard Kizer cons. "Uncle
present..all willing..father is deceased." 31 Dec. 1848.
MA, R, B-152.
Kizer, Jacob & Sally Brooks. James Brooks att. her age. 2 Mar.
1853. MA.
Kizer, William & Maria Gist (Giess). 25 May 1848. MA, R, B-126.
Klain (Klean), Adam & Catherine Singer. 16 Feb. 1860. MA, R,
D-113.
Kline, Henry & Nancy Hodge. 29 June 1854. D-2.
Kline, John & Susan Wheeler. 16 Aug. 1854. R, D-9.
Klingman, Philipp & Catharine Kugleman. 20 Mar. 1858. MA, R,
D-84.
Klumpp, Christian & Jane Sturgeon. 9 Aug. 1859. MA, R, D-28.
Knap, Riley & Catharine Wilson. 1 Dec. 1831. R, A-158.
Knapp, Cary & Nancy Monroe. 2 Sep. 1834. MA, R, A-183.
Knapp, Frederick & Elizabeth Smith. 4 Dec. 1860. MA, R, D-126.
Knapp, Hiram & Cynthia J. Richards. Her father Christopher
Richards cons. 29 Apr. 1858. MA.
Kneff, Christopher & Elizabeth Lewis. 14 May 1828. MA.
Kneff, Henry & Amanda A. Aldrich. Tho. Aldrich, of Bloom Tp.,
att. her age "..and if you want more witness, you may call on
John Clingman at your office for he went to School with her."
Henry Kneff att. his pars. are dead, he has no guardian, and
is over 18. 3 Aug. 1826. MA, R, A-99.
Kneff, Jacob & Louise Wallbright. 10 Oct. 1816. MA, R, A-25.
Kneff, John & Emily Smith. 30 Nov. 1834. MA.
Kneff, Jonathan & Martha Miler. 14 Apr. 1839. MA, R, A-268.
Kneff, Joseph & Barbara Stover. 20 July 1848. MA, R, B-130.
Kniff (Kneff), George & Eleanor Bigham McCreary. James Bishong
att. her age. 22 Dec. 1814. MA, R, A-343.
Knight, George & Orinda P. Simmons. 8 Sep. 1810. R, A-304.
Knitles, Jacob & Sarah Snider. 11 May 1849. MA, R, B-148.
Knochel, August & Elisabeth Brandow. Return says "..August
Knochel, only son of Matheus and Elisabeta Knochel from
Kaiserslauter Rhein Cr. Bawarya, with Barbara Elisbeta
Brandau, third daughter of John and Anna Catarina Brandau."
14 Feb. 1858. R, D-7, D-89.
Koch, Henry (Heinrich) & Hannah Besko. 12 Nov. 1851. MA, B-221.
Koch, John & Nancy Wilson. Her guardian Jacob Lair cons., witn.
Hiram Heath, Margaret Humphreys. 4 Dec. 1849. MA, R, B-166.
Koenig, Casper & Anna Mary Tise. 25 Oct. 1860. MA, R, D-129.
Kolb, Johann & Theodora Wolf. 12 Dec. 1845. MA.
Korb, Adam & Gertrude Oeffinger. 20 May 1857. R, D-53.
Kost (Nost), Frederick & Louisa Engallage. Henry Spellman att.
ages. 5 Sep. 1852. MA, B-251.
Kowlans (Howlans), John & Nancy Price. 8 Oct. 1857. R, D-63.
Krauser, John & Katharina Schedele. 18 Jan. 1858. R, D-71.
Krauser, Joseph G. & Mary Jane Lordier. He is 22, born Germany,
res. An Canal. She is 18, born France, res. Pond Creek.
24 Feb. 1857. R, C-2, D-50.
Kreitzer, John M. & Sarah Draine. 1 Dec. 1853. MA, B-272.
Kremer, Andrew & Sophia Klap. 17 Mar. 1845. MA.

72

SCIOTO COUNTY MARRIAGES

Kricker, Mathias & Margaret Myers. 23 Nov. 1844. MA, R, B-66.
Krincle, Jacob & Mary Jane Meddough. 31 May 1855. R, D-18.
Krites, Martin & Katherine Blake. (not dated, between returns
    that are dated 4 July and 12 July, 1854) B-284.
Kromer, William & Elizabeth Watkins. 30 Nov. 1839. MA.
Krumholtz, Gottlieb & Corinna Lintz. 30 Dec. 1851. MA, B-227.
Kruse, Gerhard & Mary Frische. 28 May 1848. MA, R, B-125.
Kubler, Martin & Sophia Miller. 17 Nov. 1859. MA, R, D-111.
Kuhn (Coon), Peter & Elizabeth Ann Sweet. 8 Feb. 1844. MA, R,
    B-55.
Kulman (Coolman), Edward & Margaret Bernn. 8 Apr. 1853. MA,
    B-259.
Kulmer, Gottlieb & Sophia Keener. 14 Oct. 1849. MA, R, B-162.
Kummer, Jacob & Marthy Jane Monroe. 20 May 1860. MA, R, D-131.
Kuntz, Martin & Catharine Beck. 8 July 1855. D-21.
Kunz, Casper & Amelia Stautsman. 27 Sep. 1851. MA.
Kyser, Abraham & Elizabeth Washeo. 10 Feb. 1852. MA.
Laber, Blasy & Rosina Messman. 29 Sep. 1856. R, D-38.
Lachemeyer, Gottlob & Melinde Dolch. 1 Nov. 1857. R, D-68.
Lacroix, Alexander & Rebecca Power. 12 Apr. 1832. R, A-161.
Lacy, Isaac & Mahulda Lowry. 24 Nov. 1847. R, B-111.
Lafferty, William & Olive Paul. Her bro. Perris Paul att. his
    mother cons. & that Olive's father is dead. 8 July 1830.
    MA, R, A-144.
Laforge, Joseph & Margaret McQuerry. 13 Feb. 1850. MA.
Laforge, Joseph & Matilda Brown. 4 Apr. 1850. MA, R, B-175.
Laininger, Michael & Mary Hubbard. 11 Sep. 1848. MA.
Lair, George & Jane Martin. 18 Nov. 1860. MA, R, D-124.
Lair, Jacob & Sarry Finney. 18 Mar. 1822. MA.
Lair, Jacob & Susannah Sheward. 16 Nov. 1844. R, B-65.
Laird, Robert McD. & Nancy McCleary. 9 Feb. 1851. MA, B-201.
Laire, Francis Marion & Harriet Welch. Richard M. Laire cons.
    16 Feb. 1853. MA, B-258.
Laire, Jacob C. & Elizabeth Craigh. 4 June 1845. MA, R, B-74.
Laire, Richard H. & Elizabeth Humphreys. 10 Oct. 1847. MA, R,
    B-111.
Laire, Washington & Mary Kettle. 17 Aug. 1854. R, D-9.
Lake, Henry & Maria Scott. 31 Dec. 1855. R, D-25.
Lake, John A. & Mary (Nancy) Crull. 23 Dec. 1852. MA, B-268.
Lakin, William & Abigail Murphin. 13 Sep. 1819. MA.
Laman, John & Serilda Davis. Her guardian A. C. Davis cons.,
    witn. David Laman, L. E. Addis. 7 Sep. 1851. MA, B-218.
Lamaster (Lancaster?), Ransom & Lucy Hard. 8 May 1845. R, B-77.
Lamb, Abijah & Mary Ann Campbell. Her father Sevrekan (?)
    Campbell cons., att. Josiah James. 27 Mar. 1834. MA, R,
    A-189.
Lamb, Benona & Mary Ann Raburn. 5 Nov. 1844. R, B-67.
Lamb, Benoni & Clarissa Ann Manges. 1 Feb. 1855. MA, R, D-15.
Lamb, Reuben Jr. & Levina Chaffin. 5 May 1842. R, B-31.
Lambart, Richart & Nancy Carpenter. 11 Oct. 1804. R, A-3.
Lambert, James & Jemima Wilson. 10 July 1839. R, A-270.
Lambert, James & Jane Russell. 10 Dec. 1858. MA, R, D-77.
Lambert, James H. & Elizabeth Hunt. 29 Apr. 1841. MA, R, B-17.
Lambert, Richard & Barbary Heslar, of Upper Tp. 13 Aug. 1811.
    R, A-312.
Lambert, Samuel & Eveline Harper. Her father Henderson Harper
    cons. 17 Mar. 1859. MA, R, D-98.
Lambion, Nickolas & Margaret Haubert. 16 May 1856. R, D-31.
Lamp, John & Mary Bone. 7 Mar. 1855. R, D-16.
Lampman, John V. & Marilla Hyatt. 3 Dec. 1843. MA, R, B-50.
Lancaster, John & Anna Copes. 17 June 1821. R, A-59.
Landlord, Dieterick & Elizabeth Amslinger (Amberger). 3 Nov.
    1852. MA, R, B-273.

73

Landon, Charles C. & Mary C. Row. 13 Sep. 1858. MA, R, D-78.
Landwehr, John Henry & Julia Anna Alert. 19 Sep. 1858. MA, R, D-81.
Lane, William & Eliza Haskins. 23 May 1844. MA.
Lane, William & Sarah E. Potts. 29 Nov. 1858. MA.
Lane, Wilson M. & Rhoda Watson. 4 Feb. 1854. D-3.
Lang, Jacob & Sybille Gies. 26 Aug. 1857. R, D-62.
Lang, John & Irene Dean. 13 Feb. 1831. MA, R, A-151.
Lang, John & Catherine Sherer. 25 Sep. 1859. MA, R, D-106.
Langhorn (Laughlin), James & Sarah Farmer. 16 Sep. 1853. MA, D-5.
Langshore, Thomas J. & Emily Moore. 19 Apr. 1840. MA, R, B-10.
Lanin, Freak & Catherine Kankan. 13 July 1855. MA.
Lansing, Obediah G. & Ann Witherwax. 4 Aug. 1846. MA, R, B-90.
Lantz (Lance), Henry & Levina Bennett. Edwin Knapp att. ages. 21 Dec. 1852. MA, B-259.
Lare, Henry & Mary Batchelor. MA dated 4 May 1835. R not dated. MA, R, A-225.
Larimer, John & Emily Pierson. 25 Dec. 1827. MA, R, A-113.
Larimer, John V. & Mary McLean. 4 June 1840. R, B-9.
Lasker, Raphael & Ernstine Karger. 9 Nov. 1858. MA, R, D-94.
Laubaugh, Ephraim & Julia White. 22 Sep. 1833. R, A-179.
Lauble (Laable), John & Mary Lauble. 2 (8) Nov. 1856. R, D-40.
Lauderback, Peter & Lavina Vanbibber. 16 Apr. 1843. MA, R, B-44.
Lauderback, Thomas & Jane Bussey. 6 Mar. 1846. MA, R, B-85.
Lauderback, William & Nancy Hesler. 12 July 1852. MA, B-241.
Laufferer, John Adam & Christiana Bender. 21 July 1848. MA, B-243.
Lawrence, Archibal & Arey Graves. 15 Sep. 1829. R, A-134.
Lawrence, David & Marcella Cunningham. E. Seip att. ages. 13 Aug. 1857. MA, R, D-56.
Lawrence, James & Louisa Craycraft. 19 May 1836. MA, R, A-208.
Lawrence, Solomon Jr. & Lucinda Sampson. 9 Sep. 1847. MA, R, B-110.
Lawson, Abraham W. & Nancy Barber. 10 Nov. 1842. R, B-45.
Lawson, Abraham W. & Mary J. Monroe. 4 July 1847. R, B-103.
Lawson, James & Phebe Metz. 17 Nov. 1831. R, A-159.
Lawson, James Madison & Julia Ann Spalding. 29 July 1829. R, A-132.
Lawson, John & Hannah M. Quillen (Guillen). 10 Sep. 1829. R, A-133.
Lawson, Manasse & Argate Valadin. 4 Sep. 1822. R, A-70.
Lawson, Silas & Matilda Hitchcock. 24 Sep. 1835. R, A-205.
Lawson, Thomas S. & Sarah Ann Crank. 31 Sep. 1849 (sic). MA, R, B-158.
Lawson, Thomas S. & Susan E. Crank. 10 Aug. 1848. MA, R, B-129.
Lawson, William & Lavina Hitchcock. 29 Oct. 1835. R, A-207.
Lawson, William & Margaret Stilwell. 10 Jan. 1849. MA, R, B-143.
Lawson, William F. & Abigail Barker. 21 Sep. 1853. B-281.
Lawton, Thomas J. & Angeline E. Wilcox. 16 May 1840. MA, R, B-5.
Leard, James & Catharine Fox. 9 July 1850. MA, R, B-191.
Leastley, Joseph (Leighty, John) & Elizabeth Humphreys. 4 May 1837. MA, R, A-242.
Leclere, Francis & Mary Louise Cadot. 21 Oct. 1809. R, A-298.
Ledbetter, Edward & Mary A. Lewis. 29 Oct. 1857. R, D-65.
Ledend (Liden? Linder?), John & Cornelia Ransome. 3 May 1849. MA, R, B-152.
Lee, Charles & Mary Hibshear. 25 June 1823. R, A-76.
Lee, Daniel & Eleanor Melson. Her mother Martha Melson cons., witn. Willing D. Wilson. 6 Mar. 1834. MA, R, A-187.
Lee, Daniel & Juliann Green. 31 Aug. 1837. MA.

SCIOTO COUNTY MARRIAGES

Lee, Denius & Mitilday Jones. 20 Feb. 1831. R, A-150.
Lee, John & Adelaine Bayless. 21 Apr. 1837. MA, R, A-240.
Lee, John H. & Sarah M. Dunaway. 13 Aug. 1851. B-214.
Lee, Oliver & Eleanor Welch. 2 Apr. 1812. MA, R, A-320.
Lee, Richard C. & Rebecca Richards. 21 Sep. 1852. MA, B-277.
Lee, Wesley & Sarah Jane Morrison. 3 Nov. 1847. MA.
Lee, William & Venia Anderson. 24 Oct. 1860. MA, R, D-124.
Leffler, Henry & Johanna Berkheimer. 1 Nov. 1860. MA, R, D-127.
Leforgey, John & Allennor More (Moore). 18 June 1807. R, A-286.
Leforgey, William & Rosita Ann Lemison. 8 Feb. 1844. MA, R,
   B-55.
Leger, John Adam & Regana Stump. 16 Dec. 1854. MA, R, D-13.
Leglar, Augustin & Catharine Hock. 12 Mar. 1843. MA, R, B-42.
Legler, Ferdinand & Eva Eck. 8 Jan. 1857. R, D-47.
Legrand, Philipp J. & Anna Margaretha Weber. 4 Jan. 1857. R,
   D-60.
Lehmen, William & Mary Martain. Her father Friedrich Martten
   cons. 20 Aug. 1859. MA, R, D-109.
Leiby, John & Margaret Serat. 2 Oct. 1852. B-248.
Leichner, William & Caroline Seifert. 29 Oct. 1857. R, D-68.
Leigler (Lögler, Legler), Joseph & Catharine Adeer (Adair).
   8 June 1848. MA, B-245.
Leininger, Christian & Elizabeth Miller. 21 Jan. 1845. MA, R,
   B-67.
Leitz, Veit (Fiate Leetes) & Mary Rubery. 5 Jan. 1853. MA.
Lelich, John & Margaret Messer. 7 Mar. 1841. R, B-26.
Lellick, Andrew & Christena Stauf. 25 Apr. 1840. MA.
Lemison, Teamon & Nancy Eliza Alford. Her pars. Chauncey &
   Harriet J. Alford cons. 7 Sep. 1845. MA, R, B-94.
Lenley, James S. & Martha Ann Sly. 27 Dec. 1853. D-3.
Lennin, Patrick & Ann Riley. 19 Aug. 1859. MA, R, D-107.
Leonard, B. C. & Nancy McLean. 19 Oct. 1851. B-224.
Leonard, David & Elizabeth Wood. W. D. Murfin att. ages.
   16 Dec. 1849. MA, R, B-164.
Leonard, George & Ann Prescott. 24 Dec. 1855. R, D-25.
Leonard, John & Hester Cunningham. 2 June 1850. MA, R, B-184.
Leonord, Jacob & Sintha Simpson. Her father John Simpson cons.,
   witn. David Noel, Seymour Pixley. 9 Apr. 1823. MA, R, A-74.
Leroy, William & Rebeckah Beatty. 7 Apr. 1810. R, A-299.
Lesley, Allen & Elisabeth Bennet. Thomas Bennet cons., witn.
   Edward Milam, Margery Bennet. 15 Dec. 1820. MA.
Levering, Jacob & Mary Collard. Washington Debow att. ages.
   21 Mar. 1843. MA, R, B-44.
Levi, Ambrose & Electa Konklin. 30 Mar. 1855. R, D-16.
Levi, Ambrose & Mary Slack. 11 Nov. 1859. MA.
Levisay (Livesay), Moses & Delilah C. Frazure. 18 Nov. 1858.
   MA, R, D-133.
Lewis, Amaziah & Margaret Teters. His father David Lewis cons.
   21 May 1860. MA, R, D-131.
Lewis, Andrew & Mary Thomas. Jesse L. Thomas cons., att. B. J.
   Farmer. 2 May 1852. MA, B-238.
Lewis, David & Rebeccah Throne. 19 Oct. 1815. MA, R, A-16.
Lewis, David & Sarah McGraw. His mother Isabella Cooper and
   stepfather John Cooper cons., witn. William McGraw, Martin
   M. Keller, says he is over 18. Nile Tp. 16 Feb. 1837. MA,
   R, A-238.
Lewis, Elexander & Melissa Cable. 4 Oct. 1855. R, D-21.
Lewis, Eli & Susan Sweet. 21 Apr. 1853. MA, B-261.
Lewis, Henry & Lydia Melone. 28 Feb. 1828. R, A-116.
Lewis, James & Prudy Casaway. 5 Oct. 1844. MA.
Lewis, John & Jane Bennett. Her father Samuel Bennett cons.,
   witn. Gilbert Bennet, Candas Holms. 27 June 1826. MA, R, A-98.

75

Lewis, John & Lucinda Evans. Anthony Evans att. her age.
27 Aug. 1846. MA, R, B-91.
Lewis, John & Martha Jane Brock. George Brock cons., att.
Isaiah Grover. 23 Oct. 1852. MA, B-248.
Lewis, John & Marilda Baccus. 21 Jan. 1858. R, D-69.
Lewis, Joseph & Barbary Skelton. 4 Oct. 1838. MA, R, A-261.
Lewis, Josiah & Eliza Sweet. 12 Sep. 1844. MA, R, B-63.
Lewis, Josiah W. & Maria E. Hitchcock. 18 Mar. 1852. MA, B-234.
Lewis, Philip Senr. & Elizabeth Mcbride, widow. 19 Feb. 1805.
R, A-5, A-278.
Lewis, Rodman & Mary A. Alderman. 1 Apr. 1841. R, B-26.
Lewis, Stephen & Anna Morgan. 26 Mar. 1834. MA, R, A-187.
Lewis, Thomas C. & Sophia Rice Malcom. 15 July 1848. MA, R,
B-129.
Lewis, William & Jane Pennington. 5 June 1855. R, D-18.
Liles, Henry & Civilia Ann Morgan. 13 May 1852. MA, B-276.
Lillick, Jacob & Elizabeth Brediger. 27 Nov. 1839. MA, R,
A-274.
Lind, Johan (John Linn) & Sarah Wilson. 1 Nov. 1840. MA, R,
B-12.
Lindsey, Johnson & Mitty Wheeler. 28 Feb. 1843. MA, R, B-46.
Lindsey, Lemuel & Maria Price. 11 Feb. 1819. MA, R, A-43.
Lindsey, Levi & Elizabeth Bennett. 27 June 1839. MA, R, A-271.
Lindsey, Oliver & Orissa Whitney. 24 Oct. 1839. R, A-273½.
Lindsey, Peter T. & Abigail Wheeler. 14 May 1820. MA, R, A-51.
Lindsey, William & Rhoda Wilson. 21 June 1814. MA, R, A-340.
Lindsey, William & Currence Ann Hamilton. 17 Aug. 1853. B-269.
Ling, John W. & Sarah Belle Flanders. 17 Oct. 1855. D-22.
Lingenfalter, Cristopher & Feby Strouse. 4 Mar. 1855. R, D-16.
Link, Joseph & Rosena Shuler. 27 Feb. 1855. MA, R, D-15.
Linn, James & Rachel Jones. 16 July 1818. R, A-39.
Linn, John H. & Mary Ann Dickson. 25 Apr. 1854. B-283.
Lionbarger, Peter & Sarah Lambert. 24 Feb. 1812. R, A-335.
Lionbarger, Peter & Mary Ann Skelton. 6 Mar. 1845. MA, R, B-89.
Liston, George & Elizabeth Nottingham. 20 July 1816. R, A-23.
Liston, John & Priscilla Robinson. Joshua Robinson cons., att.
Perry Liston. 5 Mar. 1818. MA, R, A-34.
Liston, Perry & Victoria Gilliume. 2 Dec. 1849. MA, R, B-114.
Liston, William & Nancy Thompson. 13 May 1851. MA, B-210.
Liston, William & E. J. Cox. 17 Jan. 1856. R, D-26.
Little, William W. & M. A. J. Timmonds. 29 Jan. 1854. D-6.
Little, William W. & H. Amanda Timmonds. 9 Sep. 1856, by E. P.
Pratt. R.
Littlejohn, Henry & Margaret Bradshaw. 28 May 1837, by Edward
Cranston, J.P. MA, R.
Littlejohn, Henry & Caroline Smith. 2 Jan. 1853. MA, B-262.
Littlejohn, James & Cynthia Smith. 12 Oct. 1843. MA, R, B-49.
Littlejohn, John & Francis Henry. 26 July 1836. MA, R, A-226.
Littlejohn, Joseph & Mary Ann Perry. 29 Sep. 1856. R, D-37.
Littlejohn, Valentine & Margaret Griffin (Griffiths). 13 Oct.
1850. MA, R, B-190.
Littlejohn, Vallentine & Polly Foster. 14 Dec. 1809. R, A-301.
Littlejohn, William & Louisa Debow. 16 Dec. 1860. MA, R, D-125.
Lloyd, Henry & Susannah White. 21 Nov. 1841. R, B-20.
Lloyd, Joseph T. & Martha A. Meakley. 27 June 1855. R, D-19.
Lloyd, Richard & Anna Camfield. 18 Oct. 1829. R, A-135.
Lloyd, William & Levinia E. Price. 26 Feb. 1854. D-1.
Lober, John Charles & Phillipian Ricerich. 13 Nov. 1846. MA,
R, B-93.
Locher, Thomas & Matilda Crank. 25 May 1851. MA, B-209.
Lock, Frederick J. & Sarah Jane Glover. Her father Azel Glover
cons. 13 May 1852. MA, B-240.

Locke, Benjamin & Cynthia Boynton. Her father Asa Boynton cons.
22 Dec. 1814. MA, R, A-343.
Lockhart, David W. & Elizabeth Schoonover. 24 Mar. 1850. MA,
R, B-179.
Lockhart, John & Mary F. Webb. 16 Feb. 1860. MA, R, D-113.
Lockhart, Thomas & Emma Oakley. 10 Dec. 1840. MA, R, B-7.
Locy, Daniel & Elisabeth Boyd. 20 Dec. 1855. D-23.
Locy, Elijah & Rachel McLaughlin. 9 Apr. 1854. D-3.
Lodge, John B. & Martha Jones. 16 Sep. 1820. R, A-61.
Lodwick, James & Jane Hempstead. 14 Oct. 1819. R, A-48.
Lodwick, Kenady & Caroline Wood. 12 Jan. 1825. R, A-94.
Lodwick, Michael L. & Amanda M. Anderson. 4 Mar. 1830. A-140.
Lodwick, Oliver A. & Margaret R. Hall. 24 June 1853. B-262.
Lodwick, William & Eliza Boyd. Joseph Jackson att. her age
over 18. 20 Aug. 1835. MA, R, A-209.
Logan, Adam & Hannah Buddick. 13 Jan. 1820. MA, R, A-50.
Logan, James W. C. & Phebe Moore. 5 Jan. 1835. MA, R, A-195.
Lohrberg, Augustus & Anna Schaffer. 4 Dec. 1848. MA, R, B-135.
Long, Benjamin & Eliza Richards. 22 July 1846. MA, R, B-89.
Long, George M. & Sarah J. Nogle (Nangle?). He is 24, res.
Harrison Tp., son of Valentine Long. She is 19, res. Madison
Tp., dau. of Isaac Nangle. 1 Jan. 1857. R, C-4, D-47.
Long, Henry & Christina Otter. 7 June 1841. MA, R, B-20.
Long, Isaac & Mary Carroll. 18 May 1831. R, A-154.
Long, Isaiah & Jane McJunkin (M. Junkin). He res. Morgan Tp.
She res. Morgan Tp., dau. of William & Mary Junkin. 23 Sep.
1856. R, C-6, D-39.
Long, James & Mary Jane Lawson. 28 Mar. 1849. R, B-150.
Long, James & Emma Morrison. 23 Nov. 1858. MA, R, D-86.
Long, James W. & Rachel S. Noel. 10 Oct. 1850, by D. Vance,
G.M. MA, R.
Long, John & Miami Martin. 10 Sep. 1845. MA, R, B-76.
Long, Nuton & Margret Carroll. 18 Feb. 1835. R, A-197.
Long, Robert & Elizabeth Dunlap. James Luddick (Suddick?) att.
his age. 5 Aug. 1813. MA, R, A-327.
Long, William & Elizabeth Walduk (Waldrick). 11 Sep. 1815. MA,
R, A-283.
Long, William & Nancy Lawson. 9 Apr. 1851. MA, B-205.
Long, William & Mary A. W. Matson. 21 Jan. 1854. D-4.
Longhead, James & Eleanor Wallace. 15 July 1830. MA, R, A-146.
Longman, John Fredrick & Alzina Correll. 3 Aug. 1841. R, B-22.
Longshore, John & Martha A. Masters. 29 Apr. 1857. R, D-53.
Longwitt, William H. H. & Susan Cockerell. 14 Mar. 1841. MA,
R, B-19.
Loofbourron, Wade & Catharine Mytener. 23 Mar. 1849. MA, R,
B-143.
Loomis, Henry W. & Martha J. Richart. Her father W. C. Richart
of Bloom Tp. cons., witn. Perlina Richart. 27 Sep. 1859.
MA, R, D-101.
Loomis, Thomas D. & Caroline Metcalf. 13 Jan. 1853. MA, B-257.
Lorburger, Auther & Martha Crawford. He is 25, born Germany,
res. Portsmouth, son of Fred & Fredricka (Fosbrager). She is
19, born Columbus, res. Portsmouth, dau. of John & Margaret
Crawford. 22 Nov. 1856. R, C-3, D-45.
Lord, Alexander (Abner) & Susannah McMullan. 24 Apr. 1845. MA,
R, B-73.
Lord, Ezra F. & Eliza Lord. Elizabeth Lord cons., att. Abner
Lord. 22 Nov. 1845. MA.
Lord, John & Hannah Hesler. Ezra F. Lord att. ages. 11 Dec.
1852. MA, B-278.
Losee, Silas O. & Sarah E. Weatherwax. 30 June 1859. MA, R,
D-98.

SCIOTO COUNTY MARRIAGES

Losey, Isaac & Phebe Vessel. 9 June 1837. MA, R, A-244.
Losey, Stephen & Mary Liston. 21 May 1846. MA, R, B-87.
Lott, Jacob & Mary Wagerly. 5 Nov. 1856. R, D-39.
Louder, John A. & Charata Stapleton. 13 Oct. 1854. R, D-10.
Louderback, Perry & Eve Bussey. 4 Sep. 1856. R, D-36.
Louderback, Peter & Pegge Hise. 16 Mar. 1816. MA, R, A-20.
Louderback, Phillip & Ann Thompson. 25 Sep. 1855. D-21.
Louderback, Samuel & Elizabeth McCall. 1 Mar. 1838. R, A-250.
Louderbough, John & Rachel Burrows. 6 June 1830. MA, R, A-143.
Louis (Lewis), John C. & Margaret Ann Funk. Jacob P. Noel att.
  her age. 27 Dec. 1852. MA, B-256.
Louis, John C. & Margret Funk. 23 Mar. 1859. MA, R, D-88.
Loupner, Andrew & Catherine Stoupin. 21 Nov. 1854. MA.
Love, John & Lorene (Susan) Green. Bun Green att. his sister's
  age over 18. 4 Jan. 1814. MA, R, A-328.
Loveland, Aaron & Nancy Hodges. 27 Nov. 1844. MA.
Loveland, Samuel & Clarinda Blankenship. Her father cons.
  29 Nov. 1849. MA, R, B-164.
Loveland, William P. & Elizabeth Webb. 11 Apr. 1854. D-4.
Lovell, John & Mary McKinney. 7 Jan. 1813. MA, R, A-324.
Low, Ephraim & Jane Hungerford. 2 Jan. 1823. MA, R, A-71.
Low (Law?), James & Jane Rickey. 22 July 1827. MA, R, A-108.
Low, John & Caroline Wait. 22 Oct. 1826. MA, R, A-100.
Low (Row?), John & Margaret Low. 29 Aug. 1858. MA, R, D-88.
Lowderback, John Jr. & Elizabeth Short. 16 Oct. 1833. R, A-188.
Lowderback, Michael & Ellse Munyon. 14 Dec. 1813. R, A-327.
Lowe, Frederick & Mary Chaffin. 15 Feb. 1860. MA, R, D-112.
Lowery, George W. & Caroline Howe. 30 June 1859. MA, R, D-97.
Lowery, John W. & Hulda Vigus. 22 Apr. 1839. MA, R, A-267.
Lowry, George & Eliza O'Neal. 6 Oct. 1850. MA, R, B-191.
Lowry, James P. & Elizabeth Peatling. He is 23, born Penn., res.
  Portsmouth, son of Jacob & Mary Lowry. She is 18, born Eng-
  land, res. Portsmouth, dau. of William & M. Petting. 29 Jan.
  1857. R, C-1, D-47.
Loyd, Thomas G. & Lowly Adams. 8 May 1833. R, A-176.
Lozier, Campbell & Lucinda Arman. 19 Jan. 1851. MA, B-199.
Lucas, Adrian & Elizabeth Bains. 23 Oct. 1824. R, A-85.
Lucas, Benjamin & Saluta Baker. 26 Apr. 1860. MA, R, D-116.
Lucas, Edwin R. & Ziare Marshall. 18 Sep. 1849. MA, R, B-161.
Lucas, Harlow & Nancy Burriss. 19 Mar. 1835. MA, R, A-197.
Lucas, Horace M. & Mary Margaret Eldred. 26 Dec. 1833. MA, R,
  A-185.
Lucas, John W. & Mary Parter. 11 Apr. 1849. R, B-146.
Lucas, Napolien B. & Alyda Spangle. Her mother Susannah Spangle
  cons., of Jefferson Tp. 11 Oct. 1829. MA, R, A-135.
Lucas, Robert & Eliza Brown. 3 Apr. 1810. R, A-298.
Lucas, General Robert & Friendly A. Sumner. 7 Mar. 1816. R,
  A-19.
Lucas, Samuel & Nancy Keller Hitchcock. Her father Jesse Hitch-
  cock cons. 17 Oct. 1833. MA, R, A-181.
Lucas, William & Elizabeth Triggs. 20 Dec. 1821. R, A-62.
Lucas, William H. & Mary J. Farrer. 15 July 1860. MA, R, D-123.
Lucus, Daniel & Nancy Ann Lewis. 26 Oct. 1854. R, D-11.
Lumm (Lumins), Highland & Mariah Hughey. Her pars. Samuel &
  Charlotte Hughey cons., att. James Murfin, Solomon Skouton.
  10 July 1838. MA, R, A-257.
Lummis, John W. & Elizabeth Chaffin. 4 Feb. 1849. MA, R, B-145.
Lunbner, Andrew & Mary Wise. 6 Apr. 1858. MA, R, D-73.
Lusher (Lucher), Lewis W. & Cynthia Chapman. William E. Feazel
  att. ages. 12 Oct. 1855. MA, D-22.
Lust, Philip & Christina Winter. 19 July 1853. B-271.
Luster, Stephen & Elenor Blackford. Joseph Blackford att. ages,
  "her father present". 6 Apr. 1848. MA, R, B-126.

78

SCIOTO COUNTY MARRIAGES

Lute, Daniel & Elizabeth Arnold. Thomas Arnold cons., witn.
Joel Shively. 6 Jan. 1835. MA, R, A-199.
Lute, George & Druzilla Crabtree. 12 Apr. 1855. MA, R, D-17.
Lutes (Lutz), Abraham & Catharine Ruby. 25 Nov. 1856. R, D-42.
Luther, Andrew & Permelia J. Drake. 8 Feb. 1849. MA, R, B-144.
Luther, George & Mary Jane Smart. 13 Oct. 1851. MA, B-219.
Luther, Lawrence (Lorenz) & Effa McGee. 3 Mar. 1844. MA, R,
B-55.
Luther, Lawrence (Lorence) & Esther W. Cranson. 24 May 1849.
MA, R, B-152.
Lutz, Lawrence & Margaret Luther. 14 Apr. 1853. MA, B-260.
Lybrook, Henry & Mary Rapp. 19 Aug. 1852. MA, B-246.
Lydy, Benjamin & Elizabeth Salsbury. 15 June 1843. MA, R, B-46.
Lyerduce, David & Caroline Craig. 9 Feb. 1854. D-7.
Lynch, Edward & Elenora Moran. 14 Aug. 1855. MA, R, D-27.
Lynch, Robert & Susan Williams. 3 Sep. 1846. MA, R, B-92.
Lynn, James H. & Anne Elizabeth Westwood. 17 June 1845. R, B-75.
Lynn, John M. & Alice Richardson. 4 May 1854, by E. P. Pratt.
R.
Lynn, Trusty M. & Susan Cockrell. 14 June 1859. MA, R, D-97.
Lynnheart, George & Magdalene Layman. 5 May 1848. MA.
Lytle, Charles & Ellen Ferrel. 15 May 1835 (MA). MA, R, A-225.
Lytle, Robert & Esther Malone. 13 June 1840. MA, R, A-270.
Maack, Augusta & Matilda Hazelbaker. 10 Sep. 1840. MA, R, B-13.
Mace, William & Sarah Crabtree. 29 Apr. 1847. MA, R, B-101.
Mackey, Thomas R. & Martha Morrison. 2 June 1846. MA, R, D-162.
Maddock, William & Elizabeth Buffington. 17 Oct. 1833. MA, R,
A-178.
Madison, James & Louisa Minard. 21 Mar. 1836. MA, R, A-208.
Magaha, Jacob & Mary Ann Wolfe. 14 Feb. 1839. MA, R, A-165.
Magnet, John E. & Mary Aldrich. He is 19, born Hamilton Co.,
son of J.N. & C. E. Magnet. Cons. of his pars. att. by
Frederick Winter. She is 19, born & res. Scioto Co., dau. of
Eugene & Mahala Aldrich. 3 Sep. 1857. MA, R, C-8, C-12,
D-64.
Magrane, James & Rebecca Stonebarger. 6 June 1817. MA, R, A-28.
Majiony, Luis & Elizabeth Coleman. 25 Sep. 1804. R, A-2.
Malone, Henderson & Minerva Pile. 13 Oct. 1852. MA, B-250.
Malone, Isaac & Polly Perry. 13 Apr. 1826. R, A-97.
Malone, Isaac & Mary Ann Utt. 27 Feb. 1844, by James Andrews,
J.P., Seal Tp. MA, R.
Malone, Jackson & Emily Calver. 12 Jan. 1855. MA, R, D-13.
Malone, John & Mary Penrod (Penroot). 6 Nov. 1852 (1853). MA,
D-3.
Malone, John & Eunice Chaffin. 17 Aug. 1856. MA, R, D-35.
Malone, Samuel & Matilda Munk. Her father Dauswell Munk cons.
19 Sep. 1851. MA.
Malone, Thomas & Elizabeth A. Keogh. 26 Sep. 1860. MA, R,
D-123.
Malone, William & Mary Patten, of Vernon Tp. 8 Dec. 1842. MA,
R, B-38.
Malone, William & Elenor Piles. 7 Aug. 1854. R, D-9.
Malony, Isaiah & Margaret McCurdy. 23 Jan. 1856. D-24.
Maloy, Henry & Catharine Robertson. 4 July 1841. MA, R, B-22.
Manego, Augustus & Elizabeth Usua. 22 Aug. 1853. MA.
Manley, Isaac & Esther Colvin. 27 Nov. 1814. MA, R, A-342.
Manley, Isaac & Maryann Marteness. He is 63, born & res. Brush
Creek Tp., son of Jas. & M. A. Manly. She is 57, born Flem-
ing Co., Ky., dau. of H. & N. Boling. 27 Jan. 1858. R,
C-15, D-68.
Mann, Moritz & Elisabeth Halterman. Augustus Sadler att. ages.
4 Sep. 1850. MA, R, B-188.

Manning, Mark & Nancy Fox. 18 Nov. 1856. R, D-40.
Manring, Jordan & Margaret Shoemaker. Her father Peter Shoe-
maker cons., of Ohio Furnace, witn. Jacob Kerr, J. A. Womack.
17 Jan. 1849. MA, R, B-145.
Mapes, Nathaniel H. & Sarah Titus. 13 July 1837. MA, R, A-245.
Mapes, Thomas & Fanny Sullivan. Joseph M. Glidden att. ages.
18 May 1850. MA.
Mapes, Thomas & Amelia Ann Parker (Parks). 5 Jan. 1851. MA,
B-245.
Marchant (Mechant), Jacob & Maria Violet (Vilet). Her father
John Violet cons., att. Constance Vilet. 14 Apr. 1818. MA,
R, A-37.
Marcumroman, Stephen & Mary Ann Spence. 15 Sep. 1839. MA, R,
A-272.
Marford, James & Clssy Boil (Clary Coil). 5 Sep. 1857. R,
D-65.
Markle, John D. & Eliza Darling. 6 Feb. 1831. MA, R, A-150.
Markley, Joseph & Francis E. Sly. 27 Apr. 1851. MA, B-211.
Marks, Jacob & Catherine Munion. 22 Sep. 1852. MA, B-246.
Marquart, Henry & Charlotte Wilson. 16 Nov. 1848. MA, R,
B-134.
Marquett, H. & Christean Ledensmith. 14 Dec. 1849. B-245.
Marrett, Daniel & Anna Glaze. 24 Dec. 1818. R, A-43.
Marsh, Loyd & Rhoda Sanford. 30 Jan. 1820. MA, R, A-51.
Marsh (Marsid?), Thomas J. & Zerilda Thomas. 20 Dec. 1855. R,
D-25.
Marsh, W. & Mary Stinemyer. 12 Apr. 1857. R, D-51.
Marsh, William A. & Eleanor Morgan. 26 June 1850. R, B-183.
Marsh, William Absolam & Emily Frances Herodth. 25 Mar. 1847.
R, B-100.
Marshal, Francis & Martha White. 8 July 1831. MA, A-166.
Marshal, Jesse & Caroline M. Dean. 9 June 1856. R, D-32.
Marshall, Clinton & Julian Powell. 15 Dec. 1844. MA, R, B-66.
Marshall, Clinton & Orphy Moore. 12 Sep. 1858. MA, R, D-78.
Marshall, Elias & Ann Beloat. 11 Jan. 1842. R, B-28.
Marshall, Henry & Hester Morrow. 29 Sep. 1853. MA, B-270.
Marshall, Henry C. & Elizabeth Green. Her father George W.
Green cons. 11 Aug. 1858 (MA). R. says "Return given to
W. Smith, who returned it. Marriage performed one day after
license was issued- do not recall date..", apologizes for
being so late, William Holmes, M.G. 14 Sep. 1859. MA, R,
D-112.
Marshall, Jesse & Mary Carteron. 8 Jan. 1820. R, A-50.
Marshall, John & Eleanor Groinger. 21 Nov. 1839. MA, R, A-274.
Marshall, Luther & Phebe Dean. 3 Mar. 1844. R, B-176.
Marshall, Nelson & Elizabeth M. Bennet. 22 Aug. 1835. MA.
Marshall, Rodney & Nancy Scott. 28 June 1846. MA, R, B-91.
Marshell, Jesse & Hannah Kerkandoll. 2 Feb. 1809. R, A-292.
Marshon, George & Polly Shoe (M. Shaw). 3 Mar. 1847. MA, R,
B-99.
Marshon, Stephen & Mary Ann Hall. 13 July 1855. R, D-19.
Marten (Morton?), James & Mary Peterson. 11 Nov. 1816. R, A-24.
Marteness, Cornelious & Margaret Manley. 29 Nov. 1846. MA, R,
B-95.
Marteness, Samuel C. & Ruhama Dayton (Payton?). 5 July 1857.
R, D-55.
Marther (Mather), Ebenezer & Maria Bisset. 20 Jan. 1820. MA,
R, A-50.
Martin, Calvry & Mary Jane Shelton. 17 Oct. 1858. MA, R, D-77.
Martin, Daniel L. & Jane Snyder. 29 June 1845. MA, R, B-73.
Martin, Frederick & Louisa Shaffer. 23 Dec. 1852. MA, B-254.
Martin, Henry & Elmira Scofield. 17 Aug. 1854. R, D-9.

Martin, James & Persis D. Rankin. 6 May 1850. MA, R, B-180.
Martin, James J. & Harriet Swaim. 25 Feb. 1858. MA, R, D-76.
Martin, James T. & Mary Ann Pennington. 8 Dec. 1853. D-7.
Martin, Jesse & Mary Ann Bowers. 4 Nov. 1813. R, A-329.
Martin, John Clark & Sarah Ann Rogers. He res. Harrison Tp.,
    born Va. She res. Harrison Tp. 31 May 1857. R, C-14, D-56.
Martin (Morton), John G. & Hellen M. Huston. He is son of J.H.
    & Catharine Morton, born & res. Portsmouth. She is 16, res.
    Portsmouth, dau. of S. J. & Elizabeth Huston. 19 Nov. 1856.
    R, C-4, D-41.
Martin, John W. & Sarah Hall. John G. Baker att. ages. 14 Nov.
    1849. MA, R, B-162.
Martin, Joseph A. & Nancy Baker. Ervin Baker att. her age.
    15 Nov. 1843. MA, R, B-49.
Martin, Nathaniel & Mary McManegel. 2 Feb. 1845. MA, R, B-68.
Martin, Richard & Elizabeth Turner. 5 July 1852. MA, B-242.
Martin, Robert & Sarah Osborne. 16 Dec. 1852. MA, B-255.
Martin, Samuel & Anna Hues. 20 Feb. 1821. MA.
Martin, Thomas & Mary Mastin. 1 Oct. 1846. R, B-92.
Martin, William & Evangely Wells. 3 Mar. 1837. MA, R, A-240.
Martin, William & Charlotte Wadabrok (Willebreack). Henry
    Spellman att. ages. 11 Apr. 1852. MA, B-237.
Martin, William & Mary Halterman. 12 Feb. 1854. D-3.
Martin, William & Louisa Hubbard. He is 24, res. Ky., son of
    William Martin. She is 20, res. Ky., dau. of John Hubbard.
    11 Feb. 1858. R, C-10, D-71.
Martin, William & Susan Crosser. His father William H. Martin
    and her father (Johan?) Crosser cons. 22 Apr. 1860. MA, R,
    D-117.
Martin, William H. & Durfoilece Lemons. 25 July 1835. MA.
Martin, William H. H. & Elizabeth A. Hyder. 3 July 1851. MA,
    B-211.
Martin, William McIntosh & Isabella Urquhart. 23 Dec. 1842.
    MA, R, B-39.
Marzetti, John & Anna Maria Wingle. Her mother Louisa Wingle
    cons. 25 Oct. 1860. MA, R, D-126.
Mason, Asal G. & Ellen Bottenness. 6 Mar. 1847. MA.
Mason, Charles B. & Margaret Smith. 14 June 1853. MA, B-271.
Mason, James & __ Grant. 7 Jan. 1834. MA, R, A-135.
Masters, George & Anna Beauchamp (Hannah Baukamp). Enoch
    Spalding att. ages. 23 Dec. 1817. MA, R, A-31.
Masters, John & Susan Lawson. 26 Mar. 1846. R, B-85.
Masters, Lee & Sallie Stephens. 10 May 1860. MA, R, D-117.
Masters, Stephen & Malinda Martin. Her brother Jacob Martin
    att. she was 18 in January last, witn. Claudious Cadot,
    William M. Burk, of French Grant. 9 Oct. 1816. MA, R,
    A-24.
Masters, William & Nancy Moore. 30 Dec. 1847. R, B-112.
Masters (Morton?), William B. & Caroline J. Smith. 15 May
    1852. MA, B-276.
Masterson, James & Hannah Byers. 13 Apr. 1853. MA, B-260.
Maston, William B. & Catherine Stockham. 4 Sep. 1859. MA, R,
    D-105.
Mathena, Elisha & Maria Jane Kelly. 18 Aug. 1850. MA, R,
    B-188.
Matocks, Solomon S. & Mary Cregg. 8 Sep. 1829. R, A-134.
Matthews, Hugh H. & Mary (Sarah) Jane Freeland (Freeling).
    14 June 1846. MA, R, B-88.
Mattocks, Edward Oathy & Eliza Matthews. 5 June 1856. MA,
    B-287.
Mattucks, John D. & Julia A. Mathews. 22 Jan. 1852. MA, B-228.
Mattucks, Solomon S. & Margaret Randall. 22 Nov. 1853. MA,
    B-269.

Maule, Henry & Magdalene Stemshorne. 19 Jan. 1852. MA, B-229.
Maule, John & Otilda Wachco. 25 Sep. 1855. R, D-20.
Mault, Anderson & Lucina Searls. 7 Apr. 1850. MA, R, B-180.
Mault, James & Rachel Sweet. 7 June 1853. MA, B-279.
Mault, Moses & Melissa Darling. 27 Apr. 1843. MA, R, B-47.
Maury, Georg & Caroline Link. 14 Jan. 1856. R, D-26.
Mavilsher, John & Mary Sutherland. 23 Apr. 1856. R, D-28.
May, Hugh & Eliza Snobbeary (Swobbeary). 4 June 1858. MA, R,
   D-76.
May, Joseph & Mary Ann Roushman. 16 Jan. 1849. MA, R, B-139.
May, Joseph & Hockaday Schwander. Lukas Schwander cons.
   22 Oct. 1852. MA, B-278.
May, Mathias (Martin) & Sophia Aha (Och). George Aha cons.,
   att. W. W. Wilkins, Charles Moore. 29 Apr. 1852. MA, B-239.
Mayer, S. T. & Mary Braun (Brown). 5 June 1857. R, D-54.
Mayhue, Amos & Peggy Stumbough. 12 Jan. 1837. MA, R, A-227.
Mayse, John D. (L. D. Maze) & Jane Baker. 21 Mar. 1852. MA,
   B-235.
Mazurette, Joseph & Jane Bayless. 24 Sep. 1837. MA, R, A-236.
McAlister, James B. & Amanda Thomas. 26 Apr. (1855?). B-285.
MCall, Andrew B. & Mary Ann MJunkins. Her father William T.
   MJunkins cons. 26 Nov. 1858. MA, R, D-81.
McAllister, Jackson & Miriam Scott. Elijah Scott att. her age.
   25 Sep. 1851. MA, B-216.
McAllister, John & Catherine Bagby. 1 Dec. 1846. MA, R, B-94.
McAlly (McCally), Danil & Elizabeth Cockral. 14 Mar. 1816. R,
   A-21.
McArthur, Allen C. & Olive Whitney. 9 May 1838. MA, R, A-254.
McAtee, George & Nancy Storer. 8 Oct. 1829. R, A-136.
McAtee, Washington & Caroline Sullivan. P. Sullivan cons.
   28 Feb. 1854. MA, D-5.
McAuley, James & Anna Hughes. 11 Feb. 1808. R, A-287.
McAuley, Robert H. & Catharine Sturgeon. 23 Feb. 1847. MA, R,
   B-99.
McBride, Hugh & Martha A. Garliner. 29 Oct. 1860. MA, R,
   D-127.
McBride, John & Mary McKinney. 8 Feb. 1825. R, A-86.
McCabe, James & Mary Murphy. 27 Aug. 1854. R, D-10.
McCall, Alexander & Martha Daniels. 15 Dec. 1842. MA, R, B-39.
McCall, David & M. J. Banfield. 15 Apr. 1857. R, D-51.
McCall, David B. & Mary A. Anderson. 3 Mar. 1852. MA, B-233.
McCall, Henry & Frances Worley. Her mother Sarah A. McCall
   cons. 25 Mar. 1852. MA, B-234.
McCall, Henry & Sarah McDermit. 4 Dec. 1845. MA.
McCall, Hugh & Margaret Bennet. Her father Gilbert Bennet says
   she is of age, witn. Walter Whitten, Jacob Tyson. 15 Feb.
   1838. MA, R, A-250.
McCall, John & Sidney Niblick. 1 Feb. 1816. MA, R, A-20.
McCall, John & Anna Crull. Her father William Crull cons. His
   guardian Isaac Williams cons., att. William Givens Jr.
   24 Apr. 1834. MA, R, A-188.
McCall, Michael & Rebecca Daniels, of Bloom Tp. Her mother
   Rachel Morrison says she was 20, the 4th of Dec. last, witn.
   Jacob Steece. 8 Sep. 1835. MA, R, A-204, A-243.
McCall, S. B. & Maria Moore. 5 Nov. 1851. MA, B-230.
McCall, Solomon & Elizabeth Jane Dunn. 16 Oct. 1845. MA, R,
   B-79.
McCall, Solomon & Louisa Bradford. 14 Aug. 1846. MA, R, B-92.
McCall, Solomon B. & Sarah Clark. 16 Feb. 1831. R, A-163.
McCan, Benjamine & Elizabeth Early. 24 July 1838. R, A-257.
McCan, Daniel & Sally Fletcher. 30 Jan. 1812. MA, R, A-316.
McCan, John & Mary Hodges. 23 Aug. 1846. MA, R, B-91.

McCanley, Henry & Katharine Hues. 24 Mar. 1817. MA.
McCann, A. J. & Sarah A. Gunn. 10 June 1855. R, D-18.
McCann, Arthur & Barbary Smith. 12 Nov. 1810. MA.
McCann, Jennings & Nancy Vessell. 2 Aug. 1852. MA, B-247.
McCarthy, Charles & Mary Rady. 5 Mar. 1849. MA, R, B-142.
McCartney, Andrew & Polly Warren. Daniel Warren att. ages.
   29 Jan. 1822. MA.
McCarty, Charles & Margaret Carroll. 17 Sep. 1842. MA.
McCarty, Harvy & Rulaney Matthews. 26 Apr. 1839. MA, R, A-268.
McCarty, Henry & Susan Williams. 4 Apr. 1844. MA, R, B-59.
McCarty, James M. & Jane Sweet. 27 Jan. 1850. MA, R, B-173.
McCarty (M. Carts), John M. & Mary C. Cameron. Stephen Cameron
   att. her age. 20 Dec. 1838. MA, R, B-6.
McCarty, Michael & Julian Henry. 8 Aug. 1836. MA, R, A-220.
McCauley (McColey), James & Hanah Huse. 6 Apr. 1836. R, A-214.
McCauley, James M. & Mary Cockerell. 2 Sep. 1849. R, B-157.
McCauley, Josiah & Eliza Sheeley. 21 Nov. 1833. R, A-177.
McCauley, William & Comfort Largent. 9 Mar. 1848. MA, R,
   B-116.
McChesney (Mecheny), Samuel B. & Margaret Ann Urquhart. He is
   45 (46), born Penn., res. Madison Tp., son of Richard Mc-
   Chesney, second marr. She is 30 (32), born Columbiana Co.,
   Oh., res. Jefferson Tp., dau. of Robert & Isabella Urquhart,
   first marr. 9 June 1857. MA, R, C-10, C-12, D-57.
McClaine, Sylvanus & Elvira Campbell. 22 Apr. 1832. R, A-162.
McClary (McCrary), Alexander & Nancy Rolands (Rollins). 8 Aug.
   1849. MA, R, B-154.
McClary, James & Mrs. Metilda Smart. 27 Apr. 1832. MA, R,
   A-162.
McClary, Robert & Mary Ann Mershon. He res. Union Tp., son of
   Andrew & Mary McClary. 19 Mar. 1857. R, C-6, D-52.
McClary, Thomas & Elizabeth Jane Peterson. 5 Mar. 1840. MA,
   R, B-3.
McCleary, William & Margaret Ghornley. 25 Mar. 1841. R, B-17.
McCleery, William & Jane Buckner (Barker). 24 Nov. 1836. MA,
   R, A-222.
McCloud, David N. D. & Varina G. Fletcher. 21 Mar. 1859. MA,
   R, D-87.
McCloud, Robert & Eliza Degare. 4 July 1838. MA, R, A-256.
McCloud, Samuel T. & Anna Campbell. 19 Jan. 1826. R, A-95.
McCloud, Uriah & Sarah Gandy. 12 July 1849. R, B-153.
McCloud, William & Vienaes (Vienna) Brown. 15 Feb. 1844. R,
   B-55.
McClure, Emmet & Sarah Stevenson. 26 Jan. 1860. MA, R, D-112.
McCollister, Thomas & Margaret Shelleg. 13 Aug. 1860. MA, R,
   D-121.
McColm, William S. & Eliza Jane Orm. M. McColm cons., witn.
   L.H. Gunn, Naoma Sill. 1 Dec. 1853. MA, D-5.
McConild, William & Eary Armstrong. 18 Sep. 1825. R, A-91.
McConkey, Samuel & Electa Piggott. 5 Oct. 1859. MA, R, D-104.
McConnel, Abraham & Elizabeth Ferguson. 22 Feb. 1816. MA, R,
   A-19.
McConnel, Archibald & Huldah Sanford. 10 Dec. 1829. MA, R,
   A-140.
McConnel, John & Sophia Oard (Oad). 8 May 1825. R, A-89.
McConnel, Robert & Abiah P. Emery. Her father Samuel Emery
   cons. 6 Sep. 1832. MA, R, A-167.
McConnell (McDonald), David & Nancy Munn. 5 Jan. 1815. MA, R,
   A-345.
McConnell, John & Phebe Sallie Worley. 28 May 1855. D-21.
McConnell, Robert & Elizabeth Morford. 27 Mar. 1856. R, D-29.
McConnell, Samuel & Cassa Tipton. 3 Dec. 1846. MA, R, B-94.

McCormack (Cormack), Samuel & Elizabeth Chandler.   3 Nov. 1816.
   MA, R, A-25.
McCormick, James P. & Elizabeth Collier.   16 Oct. 1844.   R, B-64.
McCormick, William & Margaret Collier.   17 Feb. 1848.   MA, R,
   B-116.
McCowan, Nathan & Harriet Shumway.   9 Dec. 1842.   MA, R, B-50.
McCowan, Thomas J. & Hester Ann Jones.   24 Apr. 1856.   R, D-29.
McCowen, Nathan & Elanora Gow.   16 Mar. 1854.   D-2.
McCown, Nelson & Sarah Squires.   3 Dec. 1846.   MA, R, B-98.
McCown, Samuel & Anna Crain.   23 Dec. 1830.   MA, R, A-149.
McCoy, Cornelius & Elenor Patten.   19 Oct. 1819.   MA, R, A-48.
McCoy, Jackson & Eliza Skellenger.   8 Oct. 1856.   MA.
McCoy, John & Ann Martin.   11 Nov. 1838.   MA, R, A-262.
McCoy, Joseph & Isabella J. Eddenstone.   Her father cons.
   5 Oct. 1848.   MA, R, B-133.
McCoy, Joseph & Lucretia Zorn.   15 Sep. 1859.   MA, R, D-101.
McCoy, Oliver & Mary Butler.   19 Oct. 1820.   MA, R, A-55.
McCoy, Pearson & Cynthia Colegrove.   10 Sep. 1840.   MA, R, B-8.
McCrery, Nathan & Mary Dix, both of Bloom Tp.   10 Nov. 1814.
   MA, R, A-344.
McCurdy, Hugh & Margaret Perry.   15 June 1845.   MA, R, B-74.
McDade, Solomon & Elenor Mountjoy (Currie).   John Colvin att.
   her age.   11 Apr. 1849.   MA, R, B-151.
McDaniel, James & Sarah Darling.   James C. & Diana Darling of
   Clinton Furnace cons.   14 Feb. 1834, by Jacob Ward, M.G.
   MA, R.
McDaniel, Waitman & Eliza Shoemaker.   23 Dec. 1847.   MA, R,
   B-116.
McDaniel, William & Phebe Miller.   "Please issue license and
   send it by Adam Bowen."   18 May 1806.   MA.
McDare, Bazzle & Sarah O'Neal.   24 June 1858.   MA, R, D-85.
McDermet, Abraham J. & Eliza C. Allwise.   2 Dec. 1858.   MA, R,
   D-85.
McDermet, David & Mary Tucker.   3 Dec. 1814.   MA.
McDermet, John & Cynthia Ann Givens.   11 Dec. 1841.   MA, R, B-26.
McDermet, Joseph & Margaret Wilson.   8 Sep. 1847.   MA, R, B-108.
McDermit, David & Harriet Collier.   31 Oct. 1844.   MA, R, B-64.
McDermit, William & Mary Williams.   David McDermet att. ages.
   14 Nov. 1850.   MA, B-193.
McDonald, James & Olive Bennet.   Josiah Bennitt att. her age.
   15 Jan. 1821.   MA.
McDonald, Jonathan & Ann Rebecca Shroud.   29 Aug. 1841.   MA, R,
   B-33.
McDonald, W. D. & Sally Ann Moss.   22 Mar. 1853.   MA, B-265.
McDonald, William & Nancy Barker, of Franklin Tp.   28 Oct. 1808.
   R, A-292.
McDonald, William & Elizabeth Mead.   15 Feb. 1849.   MA, R, B-147.
McDougal, George M. & Amanda H. Ball.   27 Sep. 1854.   R, D-10.
McDougal, James O. & Laura H. Ball.   30 Sep. 1860.   MA, R,
   D-123.
McDougal, Richard & Julian Noel.   29 Nov. 1849.   MA, R, B-167.
McDowel, John & Elizabeth Price.   7 Jan. 1819.   R, A-41.
McDowel, William & Sarah Dever.   28 Nov. 1809.   R, A-298.
McDowell, Abraham (of Jackson) & Polly Higgins.   29 Jan. 1826.
   R, A-98.
McDowell (McDonald), Charles & Dorcas Nicholls.   16 June 1849.
   MA, R, B-153.
McDowell, John B. & Rebecca Rockwell.   29 Jan. 1859.   MA, R,
   D-80.
McDowell, R. S. & Ruth Brush (Bush).   7 June 1848.   MA, R, B-128.
McDowell, Samuel & Lucinda Chabot.   20 Sep. 1842.   MA, R, B-36.
McDowell, Samuel & Hannah Bennett.   15 Jan. 1828.   R, A-115, 119.

McDowell, Samuel & H. A. E. Crull. 4 Oct. 1855. D-22.
McDowell, William & Rebecca Halterman. 31 Jan. 1822. R, A-63.
McDowell, William & Ann Eliza Clingman. 5 Jan. 1830. R, A-139.
McDowell, William F. & Martha Ann (Jane) Holliday. 2 Feb. 1848.
    MA, R, B-115.
McDowell, Woodford G. & Cathereen Bennett. 20 Dec. 1828. R,
    A-127.
McElheny, John & Sarah Ketchum. 28 Sep. 1846. MA, R, B-93.
McElheny (McIlhinney), Marshall & Matilda Adderly. 3 July
    1841. MA, R, B-21.
McElhinney, John & Harriet Frescot (Prescott). 3 Feb. 1853.
    MA, B-258.
McElrath, John & Eliza Andrews. Ca 29 Apr. 1833 (among a list
    of others, not individually dated). R, A-174.
McEltree, John & Betsy Rollins. 1 Dec. 1818. MA, R, A-45.
McElwain, Hugh & Susanne McCall. 21 May 1857 by John Joseph
    Raus__, Aetna Furnace. R.
McElwait, Joseph & Barbary Funk. 16 Aug. 1832. R, A-166.
McEntee, Thomas & Matilda Salladay. 20 Apr. 1854. D-1.
McFadden, Charles & Mary Jane Harmon. 17 June 1855. R, D-19.
McFadden (McFadgin), William & Priscilla Hammett. 24 Jan. 1814.
    MA, R, A-329.
McFan, Kimber & Sarah Ann Chaffin. Andrew J. McFan att. ages.
    7 Dec. 1845. MA, R, B-82.
McFann, A. J. & Nancy Andre. 23 Dec. 1852. MA, B-255.
McFann, A. J. & Margaret Ann Munyan. Her father Jacob Munyan
    cons. 17 Dec. 1853. MA, D-3.
McFann, David & Rachel Hays. 22 Nov. 1840. MA, R, B-15.
McFann, James & Jane Scott. 23 Sep. 1839. MA, R, A-272.
McFann, John & Sabina Salone. 25 May 1851. B-211.
McFarlane, John & Sarah Sealing. 24 Dec. 1846. MA, R, B-96.
McFarlin, Benjamin & Hariet A. Ripley. 28 June 1844. MA, R,
    B-60.
McFerren, William & Emily Bennett. 27 May 1851. MA, B-209.
McGary, Morgan & Sarah Chesnut. 14 June 1846. MA, R, B-87.
McGee, Green & Franky E. McConky. 19 Dec. 1847. R, B-115.
McGhee, Patrick & Barbara Gilroy. 28 Nov. 1858. MA, R, D-80.
McGill, John & Ellen Shert (Shade). 24 Aug. 1843. MA, R, B-48.
McGilligan, Thomas & Hannah Devor. 7 May 1846. MA, R, B-88.
McGilligan, Thomas & Louisa B. Dever. His second marr., her
    first marr. 3 Apr. 1856. R, C-3, D-28.
McGlaughlin, William & Rachel Welch. 3 Jan. 1850. R, B-175.
McGlauglin, Hugh B. & Matilda Hartley. 26 Mar. 1851. MA.
McGowen, James & Catherine Smith. 24 Apr. 1860. MA, R, D-115.
McGraw, George & Adeline Yonker. 13 Nov. 1851. B-225.
McGraw, James & Ellender A. Shaw. 21 June 1855. R, D-19.
McGraw, Presly Washington & Charity Bond. Her pars. Stephen &
    Content Bond cons., witn. William McGraw, George Mitchell.
    2 July 1838. MA, R, A-256.
McGraw, Samuel & Cynthia Reeves. 29 Nov. 1855. R, D-25.
McGraw, William & Harriet Cowen (Conn). 29 Apr. 1849. MA, R,
    B-151.
McGuire (McGrine?), A. L. & Catharine McGrullin. 27 Feb. 1855.
    B-285.
McHenry, George & Nancy Pecone. 14 Oct. 1842. MA, R, B-35.
McHolland, Charles & Lucinda Adams. 9 Feb. 1829. R, A-128.
McIntyre, Daniel & Mary Jones. 6 Nov. 1838. MA, R, A-263.
McK, John Gill & Cynthia Ann James. 15 Apr. 1844. MA.
McKean, James & Eleanor Shuler (Sheek). 19 Apr. 1838. MA, R,
    A-255.
McKean, St. Clair & Minerva Johnson. 25 May 1833. MA.
McKee, John D. & Melissa Montgomery, both of Porter Tp. Her
    father William Montgomery cons. 8 Jan. 1834. MA, R, A-186.

McKenny, Daniel Jr. & Caty Sampson. 24 June 1808. R, A-288.
McKey, Samuel & Hester Huckworth. 16 Aug. 1855. R, D-20.
McKinney, Clem G. & Rachel Colegrove. 2 Aug. 1845. MA, R,
   B-75.
McKinney, Darius & Marg Egbert (Cybert?). 1 Aug. 1846. MA, R,
   B-90.
McKinney, George Jr. & Harriett Burriss. Stephen Lewis att. her
   age. George McKinney att. he had neither pars. nor guardian
   living, and is not an apprentice. 14 Feb. 1813. MA, R,
   A-331.
McKinney, George W. & Rachel Coale. Thomas Coale att. her age.
   22 Sep. 1839. MA, R, B-2.
McKinney, George W. & Mary Ann Wilcoxon. 26 Aug. 1840. MA.
McKinney, James & Gertrude Applegate. Cornelius Gallagher att.
   ages. 27 Jan. 1855. MA, R, D-13.
McKinney, John & Belinda Cooper. 3 Sep. 1819. MA, R, A-47.
McKinney, Lorenza D. & Icebinda Stockham. 12 Sep. 1841. R, B-24.
McKinney, Solomon & Elizabeth Green. 11 July 1811. MA, R,
   A-311.
McKinney, Solomon & Ruth Bayly (Bailey), both of Washington Tp.
   5 Nov. 1824. MA, R, A-84.
McKinney, William & Slaviah Hutton. 28 Oct. 1819. MA, R, A-47.
McKinney, William & Louisa Bliss. 18 Feb. 1841. R, B-15.
McKinney, William & Nancy Hodges. 3 May 1850. MA, R, B-185.
McKinzy, John & Mary Crow. 28 Aug. 1808. R, A-292.
McKnight, John & Mary Scofield. 23 Feb. 1860. MA, R, D-118.
McKonkey, Samuel & Susan Titus. 23 May 1851. MA, B-207.
McKowan, John & Angeline Shane. 21 Aug. 1835. MA.
McLaughlin, Dennis & Elizabeth McLain. 18 Sep. 1856. MA, R,
   D-35.
McLaughlin, Isaac & Angelina Smith, both of Washington Tp.
   30 Oct. 1831. R, A-156.
McLaughlin, James & Huldah Brown. 16 Sep. 1851. MA, B-230.
McLaughlin, James & Almira Springer. 14 May 1856. B-286.
McLaughlin, John & Verlinda Wilcoxen. 8 Sep. 1825. R, A-91.
McLaughlin, John & Jane Jones. 7 Feb. 1848. MA.
McLaughlin, Robert & Sophiah Bennet. 6 May 1847. MA, R, B-102.
McLaughlin (MacGloplin), Robert & Ann Pierce (Peirie). 13 July
   1856. He was born Ireland, res. Franklin Furnace. She was
   born Va., dau. of Harris & Ann Peirie. R, C-11, D-32.
McLaughlin, William & Mary Ann Landers. 17 Jan. 1826. R, A-95.
McLaughlin, William & Sallie Munion. Valentine Bussey att.
   ages. 27 Dec. 1858. MA, R, D-80.
McLaughton (Laughlin), Daniel & Elizabeth Utt. Her father
   Henry Utt cons., att. John Utt, witn. Henry Darlington,
   Elias P. Boyers. 1 May 1817. MA, R, A-27.
McLean, W. E. S. & Nancy Spencer. 20 Dec. 1851. B-226.
McCloud, Samuel J. & Elizabeth Watterhouse. 3 Sep. 1818. MA,
   R, A-39.
McMahon, Thomas & Margaret Conley. 25 Nov. 1855. R, D-27.
McManager, James W. & Dulcena Carter. 17 Dec. 1846. R, B-98.
McManaway, Joseph & Molinda Johnson. 7 Feb. 1856. R, D-26.
McManighel, Archibald & Virginia Belcher. M. B. Wild att. ages.
   11 Aug. 1855. MA.
McManis, Philip & Betsy White. 26 Sep. 1843. MA, R, B-63.
McMasters, Samuel C. & Margaret R. Cunning. 3 Dec. 1839. R,
   A-276.
McMimis, And. & Rebecca Bolton. 13 Apr. 1857. R, D-53.
McMullen, James S. & Susan Mears. 31 Mar. 1846. R, B-87.
McMullen, John G. & Ann Thomas. 27 Oct. 1846. MA, R, B-96.
McNamar, Nicholas & Anna Williamson. 1 Dec. 1824. R, A-86.
McNamer, Joseph & Mary M. Smith. 7 Nov. 1854. MA, R, D-12.

McNamer, Samuel & Barbery Humphreys. John Lute att. ages.
   15 June 1850. MA, R, B-181.
McNamer, William & Martha Snorgrass. His father John McNamer
   cons., witn. Samuel Humphreys. 12 Dec. 1839. MA, R, A-277.
McNatton, Joseph & Mary Jones. 16 Aug. 1832. MA, R, A-165.
McNaughton, George & Lydia Corriell. John Miller att. ages.
   2 Mar. 1848. MA, R, B-123.
McNaughton, John & Eliza Tipton. 9 Feb. 1843. MA, R, B-41.
McNeal, Giles & Elizabeth Feurt. Her father Peter Feurt att.
   she is over 18. 30 Oct. 1827. MA, R, A-110, A-117.
McNeal, Giles & Martha Feurt. 30 Oct. 1837. MA.
McNeal, John & Anna Johnson. 31 Dec. 1837. MA, R, A-250.
McNeal, Seymour & Margaret Beloat. 18 May 1831. MA, R, A-154.
McNeal, William & Matilda Willey. 1 July 1855. MA, R, D-19.
McNelley, James & Martha Monroe. 22 May 1845. MA, R, B-73.
McNelley, William & Mary Monroe. 14 Aug. 1848. MA, R, B-132.
Mcnhollan (Mulholland?), James & Betsy Taylor. 16 Nov. 1812. MA.
McNutt, Samuel & Ann E. Lucas. 14 Apr. 1857. R, D-51.
McPherson, Jesse & Lucretia Hush. Joseph Bunch att. ages.
   12 Mar. 1859. MA, R, D-84.
McQuillin, Samuel & Elizabeth Proctor. 25 Aug. 1857. R, D-64.
McSurely, Miles & Katharine McCan (McLain). 24 Jan. 1833. MA,
   R, A-173.
McVey, James & Ellenor Peyton. 9 Feb. 1809. R, A-293.
McVey, James L. & Emily Andrews. 10 Nov. 1836. R, A-222.
McWhorter, Hugh & Polly Smith. 12 Apr. 1815. MA, R, A-348.
Meacham, Milton M. & Clara A. Coyl. 29 Apr. 1851. MA, B-209.
Meachem, William T. & Mary Ann Hill. 31 May 1848. MA, R, B-124.
Mead, Daniel H. & Nancy Titus. He is 22 (23), born Scioto Co.,
   res. Harrison Tp., son of Hezekiah & Lydia Mead. She is 23,
   born Scioto Co., res. Harrison Tp., dau. of Stephen & Susan
   Titus. 14 June 1857. R, C-9, C-11.
Mead, Ebenezer & Emily M. Gaston. 27 Aug. 1834. R, A-184.
Mead, Ezra & Eastar Rickey. 29 Mar. 1832. R, A-162.
Mead, Hezekiah & Lydia Dodge. 21 Aug. 1828. MA, R, A-124.
Mead, James & Lydia S. Rickey. 24 Feb. 1837. R, A-239.
Means, Andrew & Mary Ann Thompson. 6 Feb. 1845. MA, R, B-68.
Mears, Joseph & Marian Thomas. 28 Oct. 1845. MA, R, B-87.
Mears, Samuel & Mary Armstrong. 31 Aug. 1859. MA, R, D-100.
Meats, John & Dorothy Pappel. 18 Nov. 1857. R, D-67.
Medley, Henderson & Polly Bertram (Butler?). His mother cons.,
   att. Malilee Davis. 8 May 1853. MA, B-279.
Medley, James & Jane Brown. 4 Dec. 1852. MA, B-278.
Mee, John & Eliza Hutchison. Her father cons., att. James
   Prichard. 3 May 1852. MA, B-275.
Meek, James & Mary Salladay. Her father Philip Salladay cons.,
   witn. Jesse Hitchcock, George Salladay. 25 Feb. 1807. MA,
   R, A-286.
Meek, Joseph & Dysa Foster. 5 Nov. 1828. MA, R, A-123.
Meek, William & Julia Tomlinson. 11 July 1850. MA, R, B-182.
Meier, Christian Johan & Maria Anna Elizabeth Runge. 29 Dec.
   1848. MA, R, B-138.
Meier, Lewis & Villabeder Karlo. 11 Oct. 1852. MA.
Meile, Antonio & Caroline Baldauf. 24 Mar. 1857. R, D-54.
Meister (Master), George & Nancy Bower (Bowen). 5 Feb. 1843.
   MA, R, B-43.
Melcher, Benjamin & Nancy Lloyd. 19 Oct. 1817. MA, R, A-30.
Melone, John & Lidea Jayne. 30 Mar. 1809. R, A-296.
Melone, John & Susannah Triggs. 7 Dec. 1811. MA.
Meloney, William A. & Rachel Wilson. 23 Oct. 1851. MA, B-220.
Melson, James & Zekiah Robinson (Robison). His father Jesse
   Melson cons., witn. Jeremiah Armstrong. 9 Apr. 1818. MA,
   R, A-36.

Menager, Peter & Lucretia Hart. 15 Oct. 1834. MA, R, A-191.
Menego, Augustus & Leona Hoby. Her pars. cons. 2 Dec. 1854.
MA, R, D-12.
Menigo, Peter & Paulina Martin. 21 Aug. 1849. MA, R, B-154.
Menser (Mensel), Wilhelm & Anna Martha Fasner. 28 Aug. 1843.
MA, R, B-47.
Mentz, Medor & Josephine Gist. Her father Georg Geist cons.
2 Nov. 1858. MA.
Mercer, Nottingham & Hannah Trexler. 1 Dec. 1814. MA, R, A-344.
Merley, August & Pherona Suitor. 14 July 1857. R, D-55.
Merma (Maiy?), Creed Francis & Mary Catherine Pint (?). 11 Jan.
1854. MA.
Merrill, Asa & Hannah Powers. 6 Jan. 1840. MA, R, B-3.
Merrill, James M. & Lydia A. Murphy, of French Grant. 15 Mar.
1842. R, B-30.
Merrill, John P. & Julia A. Moore. 8 Sep. 1848. R, B-130.
Merrill, Josiah G. & Sophia Hayward. 28 Oct. 1849. MA, R,
B-160.
Merry, James B. & Juliann Chabot. 25 Mar. 1852. MA, B-235.
Mershon, Henry & Elizabeth Holt. 9 July 1840. MA, R, B-10.
Mershon, Jackson & Jane McCleary. He is 22, born Adams Co.,
res. Scioto Co., son of H. & C. Mershon. She is 21, born
Scioto Co., res. Union Tp., dau. of Andrew & Mary McCleary.
6 Nov. 1856. R, C-5, D-39.
Mertz, Mathias & Rebecca Vilee. 26 June 1856. R, D-32.
Mesgrove, Abner & Lydia Goodridge. 23 Oct. 1831. R, A-157.
Messer, Charles C. & Nancy Cuppit. 7 Apr. 1859. MA, R, D-90.
Messerer, George & Elizabeth Holmien. 6 Sep. 1851. B-217.
Messing, Charles & Wilhelmina Haas. 12 Nov. 1859. MA, R, D-111.
Messmer, Anthony & Barbara Hinkle. 6 Aug. 1859. MA, R, D-107.
Metcalf, F. J. & Caroline Duduit. 28 Apr. 1850. MA, R, B-178.
Metzger, Adam & Caroline Cook. 13 Mar. 1844. MA, R, B-56.
Metzger, Jacob & Mary Baker. 16 Mar. 1853. MA.
Meyer, Anthony (Henry) & Margaret Lang. 4 Dec. 1851. MA, B-226.
Meyer, Benjamin & Caroline Hess. 1 Dec. 1857. R, D-66.
Meyer (Mezger), John Friedrich & Rosina Judith Mehl. 22 Jan.
1857. R, D-61.
Meyer, Karl & Rosina Nagel. 3 Sep. 1852. MA, B-247.
Meyer, Simon & Bette Stern. 20 Dec. 1858. MA, R, D-92.
Mick, Ezekiel K. & Barbara Ann Acre. 12 Mar. 1843. MA.
Middaug, Bird & Elizabeth Ann Jackson. 29 Jan. 1846. MA, R,
B-82.
Middaugh, Elijah & Mahala McAlister. 17 June 1847. MA, R,
B-103.
Midkirk, James & Lucinda Hammet. 30 Aug. 1808. R, A-292.
Mikirons, James M. & Lucelda Jane Scofield. 16 Aug. 1853.
B-267.
Milam, Malcolm & Rebecca Paton. 4 Aug. 1844. MA.
Milam, Russel & Susan Bennett. 3 Feb. 1853. MA, D-4.
Miler, Charles & Jane Arthur. Her father Lewis Arthur cons.
26 Feb. 1846. MA, R, B-84.
Miler, Ezekiel & Mary McNamer. 19 Jan. 1842. MA, R, B-28.
Miler, Ezekiel & Susan Wilson. 27 Sep. 1849. MA, R, B-158.
Miler, James & Mary Boanum. 15 Nov. 1842. MA, R, B-37.
Miler, Thomas & Mary Canter. Her pars. James & Elizabeth
Canter cons., witn. Lewis Canter. 15 Sep. 1836. MA, R,
A-226, A-234.
Miles, Benjamin R. & Rosa Gilbert. 21 Sep. 1857, by E. P.
Pratt. R.
Miles, Branson & Angeline Sargent. John W. Sargent of Franklin
Furnace cons., witn. Jesse Coyl, William Patterson. 10 Mar.
1831. MA, R, A-151.

SCIOTO COUNTY MARRIAGES

Miles, Francis M. & Catherine Littlejohn. 19 Aug. 1860. MA,
R, D-123.
Miles, Jas. & Conyada Stevenson. 3 Aug. 1856. R, D-37.
Millar, Charles & Rebecca Miller. 12 Oct. 1843. MA, R, B-49.
Millar, William & Sarah T. Mastin. 25 Nov. 1830. MA, R, A-148.
Miller, Adam B. & Eliza Seely. 18 Sep. 1839. MA.
Miller, Andrew & Eliza J. Jackson. 1 Dec. 1851. MA, B-231.
Miller, Andrew & Rosina Pealing (?). 18 Oct. 1853. MA.
Miller, Enoch & Julana Pool. 13 Dec. 1838. MA, R, A-249.
Miller, Henry G. & Jane Berryman. 12 Nov. 1828. R, A-126.
Miller, Isaac & Sarah Cunningham. Her mother Nancy Cunningham
cons., witn. William Peyton, John Burns. 3 Apr. 1839. MA,
R, A-267.
Miller, Jacob & Sarah Salsbury. 19 Feb. 1860. MA, R, D-114.
Miller, James A. & Isabella J. Downey. 15 Mar. 1860. MA, R,
D-118.
Miller, John & Jane F. Flanders. 5 Feb. 1846. MA, R, B-86.
Miller, John & Matilda Coryell. 11 June 1846. MA, R, B-91.
Miller, John & Sarah Ray. 13 May 1851. MA.
Miller, John (Johann Muller) & Cuniginde Lentz. 23 Mar. 1852.
MA, B-234.
Miller, John & Sarah Caravan. 6 Sep. 1855. R, D-20.
Miller, John & Margaret Bar. 20 Aug. 1860. MA, R, D-122.
Miller, John G. & Martha Eppihimer. 9 Sep. 1858. MA, R, D-78.
Miller, John W. & Margaret Powers. 24 Aug. 1850. MA, R, B-187.
Miller, Peter & Mary Weghorst. 24 Mar. 1855. R, D-16.
Miller, Timothy & Isabella Rose. 1 Mar. 1860. MA, R, D-132.
Miller, William & Amelia Renshahous. 26 Sep. 1851. MA, B-216.
Miller, William (Wilhelm Müller) & Catherine Rode. 19 July
1860. MA, R, D-121.
Miller, William H. & Loana Didwit. 19 June 1859. MA, R, D-98.
Miller, William V. & Juliana Maria Ransom. 17 Mar. 1831. R, A-151.
Miller, William V. & Samantha Copeland. 24 Apr. 1836. MA, R,
A-214, A-232.
Millholen, John & Elisabeth Jones. 31 Aug. 1854. R, D-10.
Millhollan, Charles & Sarah Tucker. 17 Feb. 1820. MA, R, A-58.
Millirons (Williams), Abraham & Rebecca Strait. 27 June 1855.
R, D-19.
Millirons, George W. & Margaret Manley. Sampson Millirons cons.
13 Dec. 1860. MA, R, D-124.
Millirons, James & Mahala Mault. 22 Aug. 1841. MA, R, B-22.
Millirons, Salathiel & Martha Norman. 19 Apr. 1849. MA, R,
B-153.
Millirons, Samuel & Elizabeth Toland. John & Elizabeth Toland
cons., witn. Adam Stumbaugh, Sophiah Stumbaugh, Cumfort
Stumbaugh. 19 Nov. 1829. MA, R, A-136.
Millirons, William & Mary Hall. Her father John Hall, of Green
Tp., cons., witn. Daniel Hall, Robert Hall. 21 Mar. 1822.
MA, R, A-65.
Millirons, William & Nancy Culp. 11 Nov. 1847. MA, R, B-113.
Mills, Nehemiah Jr. & Mary Tucker. Henderson Curry (Corray)
att. her age. 1 Apr. 1817. MA.
Minard, Daniel & Margaret Craigmiles. Archibald Hammond att.
ages. 26 Aug. 1853. MA, B-272.
Minard, David H. & Jane Reed. 14 Feb. 1836. MA, R, A-213.
Minard, George & Asha Hawk. Philip Isaminger cons., says "Acha
is my wife's sister and her father and mother being dead, she
is left under my care," witn. J. H. Ricker. 6 Dec. 1835.
MA, R, A-211.
Minard, Lorenzo & Cynthia Ann Beller. Ann Sims cons., witn.
Samuel & Elizabeth Millirons, Elias Beler. 19 May 1840.
MA, R, B-8.

89

Minch, Lewis & Samantha H. Farmer. 4 Jan. 1849. MA, R, B-138.
Minego, Harrison & Josephine Prothon. 13 May 1859. MA, R, D-102.
Minford, Robert & Amanda Steward. He is 26, born Ireland, res. Portsmouth, son of John & Mary Minford. She is 21, dau. of Morand & Mary Stewart. 31 Dec. 1857. C-10.
Minford, Robert J. & Elizabeth Greer. G. W. Ward att. ages. 8 Nov. 1854, by E. P. Pratt. MA, R.
Minford, William & Mary Ann Mapes. Her father Thomas Mapes cons., says she is 17 years 10 months old. 22 Aug. 1851. MA, B-214.
Mink, Rodolph & Laura Schuster. 20 Oct. 1848. MA, R, B-133.
Minor, John James & Margaret Johnson. 13 Feb. 1854. D-6.
Misner, Samuel N. & Eliza Jane Lee. 25 May 1853. MA.
Misner, Samuel N. & Martha J. Bayley. 11 July 1856. B-287.
Mitchel, Augustus & Parmelia Thornton. 8 Aug. 1847. R, B-104.
Mitchel, R. A. (Alexander) & Sarah Jane Miller. He is 22, born West Union, Oh., res. Portsmouth, son of Alex & Ellen Mitchel. She res. Clay Tp., born Ross Co., Oh., dau. of Anthony & Mary Miller. 13 Oct. 1856. R, C-1.
Mitchel, William & Sary Myers, of Nile Tp. 22 Mar. 1810. R, A-298.
Mitchell, Charles & Nancy M. Drake. 16 Aug. 1860. MA, R, D-123.
Mitchell, George & Ruhama Piles. 17 Feb. 1831. R, A-152.
Mitchell, George & Nancy Brumlee. 13 Sep. 1842. R, B-34.
Mitchell, George & Elizabeth Ann Noel. 14 Sep. 1842. R, B-34.
Mitchell, John & Sarah Jane Huston. Joseph Huston cons. 6 Nov. 1827. MA, R, A-234.
Mitchell, Lemuel & Nancy Jane Armstrong. 14 Sep. 1854. R, D-10.
Mitchell, Thomas J. & Nancy A. Tabor. 6 May 1851. MA, B-212.
Mittendorf, John F. & Caroline Kotter (Kutter). 10 Apr. 1852. MA, B-237.
Moer, Henry & Sarah Higgins. 25 Dec. 1834. MA, R, A-197.
Moler (Molder, Nolder), John & Mary Ann Mathews. Her mother Mary Mathews cons., witn. Reuben H. Mathews. John Moler Sr. cons., witn. James Carlon. 26 Feb. 1849. MA, R, B-141.
Molster, John F. & Amana Rose. 16 Sep. 1860. MA, R, D-122.
Molster, William H. & Susan Ann Bennet. His father Martin Molster cons. 12 Jan. 1859. MA, R, D-95.
Mondeary (Mandeerie), Peter & Mary Tearout. 17 Nov. 1849. MA, R, B-162.
Monegold, Jacob & Margaret Newcom. 15 Oct. 1848. MA, R, B-133.
Monk, George & Eliza Culp. 14 Dec. 1852. MA, B-257.
Monroe, Aaron & Elizabeth Wood. 7 May 1823. MA, R, A-75.
Monroe, Aaron & Sally Marshall. 9 July 1837. R, A-245.
Monroe, Dannel & Mather Stroud. 26 June 1806. R, A-12, A-280.
Monroe, George & Julia Pey. 27 Oct. 1860. MA, R, D-126.
Monroe, Jacob & Eliza Stilwell. 14 Feb. 1850. R, B-173.
Monroe, Jacob & Mercy White. 11 Sep. 1853. MA, B-272.
Monroe, James & Melissa Bennett. 16 Mar. 1837. MA, R, A-242.
Monroe, James & Catharine McNelly. 7 Aug. 1841, by John Dewitt, M.G. MA, R.
Monroe, Jesse & Elizabeth Wirt. 17 Mar. 1853. MA, B-258.
Monroe, John & Jane Fullerton. William Fullerton att. her age. 10 Apr. 1827. MA, R, A-105.
Monroe, John & Anne Conroy. 3 Sep. 1853. MA.
Monroe, Joseph & Nancy Snider. His father Charles Monroe cons., witn. Mark Snyder. 1 Oct. 1831. MA, R, A-155.
Monroe, Leonard (Aaron) & Mary McKee (McGhee). 11 Apr. 1839, by James Lawson, J.P. MA, R.
Monroe, Thomas & Rachel Rockwell. 20 Mar. 1845. MA, R, B-69.
Monrow, Charles & Patcy Jacobs. 8 Feb. 1810. R, A-300.

SCIOTO COUNTY MARRIAGES

Monrow, Ira & Nancy Higgins. His father Solomon Monrow cons.
2 Oct. 1833. MA, R, A-182.
Montgomery, Abraham A. & Permelia Norris. 27 Oct. 1830. MA.
Montgomery, Elis & Elizabeth Chapman. 4 May 1853. MA, B-264.
Montgomery, James & Sally Conklin. 22 Apr. 1818. MA.
Montgomery, John & Charlotte Snyder, both of Porter Tp. 14 Oct.
1819. MA, R, A-49.
Montgomery, McLain & Mary Montgomery. 29 Nov. 1860. MA, R,
D-171.
Montgomery, Milton & Melvina (Mellise) Chapman. His father
William Montgomery cons., witn. John D. McKee. Reuben
Chapman cons., witn. James Chapman. 30 Jan. 1834. MA, R,
A-190.
Montgomery, Robert & Harriet Long. 27 May 1827. R, A-131.
Montgomery, Sylvester K. & Levina Grey. 12 July 1848. MA, R,
B-127.
Montgomery, William & Nancy Beloat. George Beloat cons., "Sir,
you will issue licens for Wm. Montgumery and Nancy Beloat to
get married as I have done all in my power to prevent it and
it is all to no purpus, from your &c." 20 Dec. 1821. MA, R,
A-63.
Montgomery, William Henry & Jane Gaines. 22 Jan. 1846. MA.
Moony, John & Annettunia Wolfin. 24 Oct. 1854. R, D-11.
Moore, Allen & Nomi Carey. 8 Sep. 1810. R, A-303.
Moore, Allen & Hannah Bonser. 6 Feb. 1812. MA, R, A-316.
Moore, Allen & Emily Clark. 5 May 1833. MA, R, A-176.
Moore, Amanuel & Lavina Dole. 10 Feb. 1859, by E. P. Pratt.
MA, R.
Moore, Amos & Winneyford Calvert, both of Washington Tp.
25 Mar. 1832. R, A-161.
Moore, Charles & Parthenia Bliss. 2 Apr. 1837. R, A-247.
Moore, Cornelius & Eliza G. Frier. 8 Sep. 1835. R, A-205.
Moore, Cornelius & Margaret Thompson. 30 Apr. 1851. MA, B-208.
Moore, David & Cela Shelpman. 12 Mar. 1807. R, A-283.
Moore, Davis P. & Elizabeth A. Kendall. 22 Oct. 1850. MA,
B-192.
Moore, Ebenezer F. & Martha Jane Rodgers. 27 Oct. 1844. R,
B-63.
Moore, Edward & Virginia Barker. 3 Nov. 1858. MA, R, D-82.
Moore, Eren (Evan) & Cynthia Piles. 1 Apr. 1830. R, A-142.
Moore, Evan & Catharine Phillips. 15 Jan. 1829. R, A-126.
Moore, Forman & Anna Worley. 15 Feb. 1815. MA, R, A-346.
Moore, Foster & Delila Moore. He res. Adams Co. 23 Feb. 1809.
R, A-292.
Moore, George & Susan Maria Bennett. 30 Mar. 1848. MA, R,
B-128.
Moore, George W. & Amelia Eulett. William Stockham att. her
age. 2 June 1836. MA, R, A-219.
Moore, Hamilton & Maria J. Clark. 15 Aug. 1846. R, B-90.
Moore, Jackson & Martha Freeman. 12 Feb. 1843. MA, R, B-41.
Moore, Jacob & Lucinda Bacom. 25 June 1804. R, A-4.
Moore, James & Sally Hise. Catherine Hise, of Porter Tp. cons.
"for him to marry my Sarrow hise...", witn. William Moore,
John Louderback. 24 Aug. 1822. MA, R, A-69.
Moore, James & Mary Frost. 28 Jan. 1829. R, A-130.
Moore, James & Elizabeth Story. 15 Feb. 1849. MA, R, B-143.
Moore, Jeremiah & Elizabeth Cooley. 23 Dec. 1829. MA, R, A-138.
Moore, John & Nancy Jackson. 12 July 1806. R, A-12, A-281.
Moore, John & Ary Harrison. 8 Aug. 1816. R, A-22.
Moore, John (of Amos) & Vianna Carey. 19 Apr. 1829. R, A-131.
Moore, John & Mrs. Elizabeth Grubb. 17 Oct. 1833. MA, R, A-181.
Moore, John & Sophia Abbott. (10) May 1839 (1829). R, A-269.

SCIOTO COUNTY MARRIAGES

Moore, John & Nancy Larimer. William Larimer att. her age.
3 Nov. 1841. MA, R, B-25.
Moore, John & Sarah D. Wilhelm. 20 Sep. 1852. MA, B-247.
Moore, John A. & Mary Ann Woodyard. 4 Dec. 1842. MA, R, B-38.
Moore, John C. & Sarah A. Worley. 14 Feb. 1845. R, B-68.
Moore, John O. & Sarah Jane Scott. 20 Mar. 1856. R, D-27.
Moore, Joseph & Polly Lawson. 15 Jan. 1812. R, A-315.
Moore, Joseph & Isabel Elliott. 6 Aug. 1839. R, A-271.
Moore, Leroy S. & Sarah M. Elliott. 25 Nov. 1842. MA, R, B-37.
Moore, Levi & Amanda Gunn. Her father Samuel Gunn of Washington
(Tp.?) cons., witn. Zina Gunn, Apama Gunn. 29 Dec. 1814.
MA, R, A-344.
Moore, Levi & Elizabeth Deal. Her father Jnerl (?) Deal cons.
4 Apr. 1858. MA, R, D-76.
Moore, Levi & Mary Emma Dickison. 19 Apr. 1860. MA, R, D-116.
Moore, Loyed N. & Martha A. Dodds. 12 Nov. 1850. MA, R, B-192.
Moore, Milton & H. E. Waller. 6 Nov. 1849. R, B-166.
Moore, Philip & Amelia Collins. 15 Mar. 1811. R, A-310.
Moore, Philip & Cynthia Belli. 10 Jan. 1812. R, A-315.
Moore, Philip & Apama Gunn. 6 May 1816. R, A-20.
Moore, Philip & Margaret Smith. 8 Oct. 1829. R, A-135.
Moore, Samuel & Salley Oney (Oucy). 20 May 1817. MA, R, A-27.
Moore, Samuel W. & Isabella Ann Flanders. 4 (14) Mar. 1842.
MA, R, B-36, B-70.
Moore, Silas & Pertima Ann Dauson. 15 Apr. 1844. R, B-59.
Moore, Thomas & Mary Humphreys. Samuel Humphreys cons.
18 Mar. 1839. MA, R, A-267.
Moore, William & Katharine Hammet. 12 Aug. 1812. MA, R, A-320.
Moore, William, of Green Tp. & Elizabeth Snook. Her father
Philip Snook cons., witn. Alex Curran & James Moore. 4 May
1813. MA, R, A-326.
Moore, William & Emily Dollarhide. 6 Aug. 1838. MA, R, A-258.
Moore, William & Sarah Bentley. 22 Aug. 1851. B-214.
Moore, William & Elizabeth Ann Grimes. 28 Jan. 1853. MA.
Moore, William & Catherine Smith. 1 Mar. 1859. MA, R, D-82.
Moore, William & Emily Havens. 27 Mar. 1859. MA, R, D-89.
Moore, William M. K. & Elizabeth F. Smith. 11 Aug. 1847. R,
B-105.
Moore, William R. & Caroline Oldfield. 23 Feb. 1854. D-2.
Morford, Thomas W. & Adeline Snook. 11 Feb. 1849. MA, R, B-141.
Morford, William C. & Celinda Finton. Her mother Susan Finton
cons., her father being in California, att. John S. Baccus.
6 Nov. 1853. MA, D-3.
Morgan, David & Mary Jones. 5 Dec. 1854. MA, R, D-12.
Morgan, Ephraim & Eliza Farmer. 20 Dec. 1855. D-23.
Morgan, Joseph F. & Sarah Jane Wheeler. 9 Mar. 1853. MA, B-279.
Morgan, Richard M. & Eleanor Overturf. 15 July 1847. R, B-104.
Morgan, Samuel J. & Caroline Turner. 18 Jan. 1847. MA, R, B-97.
Morgan, Samuel J. & Nancy Holman. 12 July 1853. B-263.
Morgan, Thomas & Mary Williams. 24 Apr. 1850. MA, R, B-177.
Morgan, Thomas J. & Rebecca Creamer. 28 Oct. 1841. R, B-24.
Mork, Simen & Elisabeth Blagg. 11 Jan. 1850. R, B-168.
Morrell (More), Cyrus W. & Mary Worley. 19 July 1829. MA, R,
A-133.
Morris, John S. & Julia A. White. 9 Mar. 1851. MA, B-207.
Morris, Thomas & Phebe Wood. 3 Oct. 1826. R, A-100.
Morris, William & Nancy Ward. 12 Dec. 1837. MA.
Morrison, Benjamin F. & Mary A. McJunkins. 3 June 1858. MA, R,
D-94.
Morrison, David & Martha Mitchel. 12 Nov. 1835. R, A-208.
Morrison, George Washington & Albina Conklin. Her father
William Conklin cons., witn. Joseph L. Barber, Joseph Conk-
lin. 12 Apr. 1835. MA, R, A-200.

SCIOTO COUNTY MARRIAGES

Morrison, James & Malinda Conklin. William & Mary Conklin
cons. 14 Nov. 1829. MA, R, A-136.
Morrison, James & Lavina Warner. 17 Oct. 1847. MA, R, B-109.
Morrison, James M. & Maria L. Turner. He is 26, born Armstrong
Co., res. Porter Tp., son of Robert Morrison. She is 18,
born Porter Tp., dau. of William Turner. 16 Aug. 1857. R,
C-13, D-57.
Morrison, Joseph & Martha A. Berry. 3 July 1859. MA, R, D-96.
Morrison, William & Jane Munion (Morrison). His father James
Morrison cons. "about six months ago...has left Scioto Co.
for parts unknown, and William's mother is now dead.." att.
Lemuel Patton. 20 Jan. 1853. MA, B-256.
Morrison, William H. & Lucinda Blazer. George & Hannah Dewitt
cons. "for my son." 16 Apr. 1835. MA.
Morrow, Joel & George A. Gades. 9 Mar. 1856. R, D-27.
Morrow, Stephen C. & Oella V. Roberts. 6 Dec. 1858. MA, R,
D-93.
Morrow, Willson & Rachael Chandler. 13 Sep. 1840. R, B-11.
Morrow, Wilson & Naoma Chandler. 1 Aug. 1833. R, A-179.
Morse, Joseph & Sarah Wait. 2 June 1822. MA, R, A-67.
Morton, Henry A. & America D. Lowry. 24 July 1858. MA, R,
D-81.
Morton, James & Levina Miles. 9 Feb. 1844. MA, R, B-53.
Morton, John & Mary Day. 21 Sep. 1817. MA, R, A-30.
Morton, Joseph & Hannah Sarven (Lawer? Saneer? Larver?) 27 Feb.
1833. MA, R, A-173.
Morton, Willis L. & Caroline Bliss. 4 Aug. 1842. R, B-36.
Moseman, Constantine & Mary U. McAleer. 3 Aug. 1856. R, D-37.
Mosemann, John & Katharina Hetzer. 2 Feb. 1858. R, D-72.
Moser, Reuben A. & Rebecca Renolds. 22 Feb. 1849. MA, R,
B-142.
Moses, Alexander & Ester Freeberg. 13 Aug. 1860. MA.
Mosher, Philip C. & Ellen (Elenor) Stanford. A. J. Johnson
att. her age. 24 Sep. 1833. MA, R, A-183.
Moss, Andrew & Elizabeth Williams. 13 Sep. 1838. MA, R, A-259.
Moss, George & Letitia Brouse. 22 Sep. 1853. B-270.
Mossman, Hartley & Mary E. Fasheres. His father John Mosman
cons., att. Constantine Moseman, William Warnka. 14 Apr.
1858. MA, R, D-88.
Mott, Albanas & Nancy Loveland. 26 July 1853. MA, B-263.
Mougey, Charles & Jane Magnet. 31 Oct. 1846. MA, R, B-94.
Mouhat, James & Hannah White. He is 20, born Cincinnati, res.
Madison Tp., son of James Mouhat. She is 18, born & res.
Madison Tp., dau. of John White. 8 Feb. 1857. C-4.
Mountjoy, John & Elisabeth Sprouse. 9 Aug. 1855. R, D-20.
Mountjoy, William & Elizabeth Hile. He is 19, res. Washington
(Tp.?), son of Ranson Mountjoy. (Not dated - 1856?) C-6.
Moxley, John D. & Ann Kendrick. T. J. Graham att. ages.
17 Dec. 1839. MA, R, A-276.
Moxley, Nathaniel K. & Sophia McConnel. 29 Nov. 1848. R, B-135.
Moxley, Thomas S. & Susannah McConnell. 4 Dec. 1836. MA, R,
A-221.
Muckelwrath, William & Jane Liggett. 27 Mar. 1845. R, B-72.
Muckenrath, Hugh & Mary Ann Foster. 6 Feb. 1854. B-282.
Muhlhausen, Heinrich (Henry Milhisen) & Barbary Adams. 23 Jan.
1845. MA, R, B-67.
Muhlhauser, Gottlieb & Elizabeth Sponson. 23 July 1860. MA, R,
D-129.
Muhliman (Mehleman), John & Catherine Smith. 24 May 1860. MA,
R, D-119.
Mulholland, James & Mary Walsinger. Her father John Walsinger
cons., witn. Charles Mulholland. 12 Mar. 1843. MA, R, B-42.

Mullen, George A. & Mary Melvina Umphreys (Humphries). His
mother Margret Breathwell cons., witn James Mullen. John
Lute att.,"His mother wroute me aline to get his licens."
witn. Amos R. Throckmorton. 27 Apr. 1851. MA, B-206.
Mullen, James & Eliza Jane Snook. 18 June 1848. MA, R, B-124.
Mullen, Thomas & Mary Ann Winton. 16 June 1853. B-266.
Mumford, John & Sarah Jones. 1 Mar. 1834. MA, R, A-191.
Muncey, James & Parmelia Wallace. 19 June 1851. B-211.
Muncey (Mundy), Moses & Polly Wallis (Walls). Thomas Muncey
att. ages. 30 Apr. 1826. MA, R, A-97.
Muncey, Thomas & Elizabeth Wallas. 9 Apr. 1823. R, A-74.
Mungen (Meengen), Francis & Anestialeo Belico. 12 July 1854.
R, D-8.
Munk, William & Mary Angel. 27 Aug. 1845. MA, R, B-76.
Munn, David & Tabitha Frizel. 17 Dec. 1807. R, A-287.
Munn, David C. & Amanda Stilwell. 20 June 1839. MA, R, A-269.
Munn, David C. & Amanda Reed. 3 Nov. 1844. MA, R, B-64.
Munn, Ira H. & Eliza J. Rice (Price). 8 Oct. 1847. MA, R,
B-108.
Munn, J. L. & Evilina Munn. 7 June 1838. R, A-255.
Munn, James & Filina Olliver. 27 Mar. 1817. R, A-27.
Munn, Jasper & Rebecca Rice (Kiel). 8 Dec. 1853. MA, D-2.
Munn, Solomon & Jemima Bennett. Her mother Nancy Bennett cons.,
witn. Catharine Bennett, Benjamin Bennett. 13 July 1820.
MA, R, A-53.
Munn, William & Joanna Hitchcock. Jesse Hitchcock att. her age.
14 Feb. 1811. MA, R, A-308.
Munn, William W. & Maria Bonser. 27 Mar. 1853. MA, B-262.
Munnel, John & Lucinda H. Woodring (Wotring). 15 Mar. 1838.
MA, R, A-250.
Munnel, William & Christina Woodring. 2 Feb. 1843. MA, R, B-41.
Munrow, Thorndon & Mary Ann Squire. 7 Feb. 1850. R, B-170.
Munyan, Jacob & Rebecka Bradshaw. 12 Mar. 1835. MA, R, A-200.
Munyan, Jeremiah & Sally Ann Smith. 7 Sep. 1856. MA, R, D-36.
Munyan, Thomas & Sarrah Patton. 1 Apr. 1824. R, A-87.
Munyan, William & Lureena Abigail Bradshaw. Her father Isaac
Bradshaw cons., witn. T. J. McFann, John Clagg. 16 Mar.
1848, by A. J. McFann. MA, R.
Munyan, William & Elizabeth Perry. Her father A. Perry cons.
18 Mar. 1855. MA, R, D-16.
Murdock, Aaron & Jane Crowley. 4 June 1836. MA, R, A-219.
Murdock, Drake & Mahala Story. 22 July 1852. MA.
Murfin, James & Eliza Ann Turner. 29 Sep. 1835. R, A-205.
Murfin, James & Elizabeth S. Rodgers. 17 May 1842. R, B-30.
Murfin, James & Ruby Y. Gould. 22 Feb. 1849. R, B-141.
Murphey, James M. & Elizabeth Snook. 12 Feb. 1819. R, A-127.
Murphy, David W. & Cynthia Ann Givens. 8 July 1841. B-120.
Murphy, J. S. & Martha E. Fugate. 4 July 1854. B-284.
Murphy, James & Sarah Ann Collard. 25 Dec. 1842. MA, R, B-39.
Murphy, John & Mary Enright. 6 Jan. 1855. MA, R, D-14.
Murphy, John & Catherine Melroy. 8 Aug. 1860. MA.
Murphy, John M. & Elizabeth Hawkins. 15 Nov. 1840. MA, R, B-12.
Murphy, Madison & Mary Jane Herly. 25 Aug. 1854. R, D-10.
Murphy, Michael & Adaline Ormsby. 27 Jan. 1852. MA, B-228.
Murphy, Moses & Matilda Ferrell. 27 Aug. 1844. R, B-59.
Murphy, Recompense S. & Rachel Kelly. 30 July 1831. MA, R.
A-174 lists their marriage with 12 others, not individually
dated.
Murphy, Samuel & Susan Culp. 3 Nov. 1836. MA, R, A-221.
Murphy, Samuel & Sabina Basset. 1 Jan. 1850. R, B-165.
Murray, David N. & Harriet C. White. 14 May 1850. R, B-179.
Murray, David N. & Isabella McNairn. 7 May 1839. R, A-268.

SCIOTO COUNTY MARRIAGES

Murray, John & Ann Conley. 26 Sep. 1859. MA, R, D-101.
Murray, Newton & Ellen Updegraff. 26 Dec. 1843. MA, B-243.
Murray, Peter H. & Phillippi Davey. 18 July 1850. R, B-184.
Murrin, Frederick & Elizabeth Akerman. 3 June 1854. D-7.
Musgrave, Joseph & Mary Allison (Ellison). 23 Mar. 1852. MA, B-234.
Musgrave, Samuel & Evangely (Elizabeth) Martin. Joseph Musgrave att. ages. 30 Mar. 1852. MA, B-239.
Musgrove, Elijah & Martha Armitage. 23 May 1822. R, A-66.
Musick, Elexius & Belinda Payne. William M. Payne att. her age. 9 Feb. 1830. MA.
Musick, Martin (Mathias) & Eliza (Elizabeth) Hock. 12 Mar. 1843. MA, R, B-42.
Musser, John & Mary Jane Ball. 27 Dec. 1827. R, A-114, A-120.
Musser, John C. & Isabella Jones. 15 Nov. 1855. D-22.
Musser, Joseph T. & Esther Ann Ackerman. 26 Sep. 1851. MA, B-217.
Musser, William & Jane Simpson. 14 Aug. 1836. R, A-220.
Musser, William H. & Sarah J. Sturgeon. 1 June 1851. B-207.
Mussey, Francis B. & Mary Boynton. 28 Apr. 1847. MA, R, B-103.
Mussic, John & Frances Hock. 5 Jan. 1853. MA.
Mussick, Joseph & Katharine Daniels. 4 Dec. 1839. MA, R, A-274.
Mustard, David & Sarah Eulitt. 6 Dec. 1840. MA, R, B-14, A-275.
Mustard, George & Elinor Delia, of Seal Tp. 28 June 1810. R, A-304.
Mustard, Joseph & Sarah Cartar. 29 Nov. 1808. R, A-293.
Mustard, Robert & Margret (Mary) Williams. 16 Sep. 1843. MA, R, B-48.
Mustard, William & Jean Delea, of Seal Tp. 15 Feb. 1810. R, A-299.
Muttner, William & Mary Miller. 7 Sep. 1858. MA, R, D-78.
Myers, A. N. & Sarah E. Montgomery. 29 Oct. 1855, by E. P. Pratt, First Presby. R.
Myers, Allen & Judia Callahan. 18 Apr. 1854, by E. P. Pratt. R.
Myers, Cord (Court) & Mary Rehen (Rohen). John Runger att. ages. 10 Apr. 1853. MA, B-260.
Myers, James & Matilda Bennett. 6 Oct. 1836. R, A-223.
Myers, John & Sarah Ward (Loyd?). 1 July 1849. MA, R, B-155.
Myers, Joseph & Lucintha Tecker (Tucker, Hecker). He is 26, born Germany, res. Waverly, Pike Co., Oh. She is 19, born & res. Portsmouth. 16 Feb. 1855. R, C-2, D-48.
Myers, Samuel & Mary Fowler. He is 32, born Penn. She is 27. 14 Sep. 1856. R, C-5, D-38.
Myres, B. J. & Jane Dalton. 24 Feb. 1847. MA, R, B-99.
Myres, William & Mary Ann Larimore. 27 May 1849. MA, R, B-152.
Nail, Henry & Mary Maria Box. Her stepfather James Allison cons. 16 Aug. 1858. MA, R, D-78.
Nail, Jacob & Leah Halterman, of Vernon Tp. 27 June 1833. MA, R, A-179.
Nail, John Jr. & Lucinda Allison. Rachel Allison cons., witn. Eve Enslow, Thos. J. Enslow. 26 Mar. 1835. MA, R, A-203.
Nail, John & Rebecca Jane Searl. 11 (12?) Sep. 1856. MA, R, D-41. D-46 records same names, dated 8 Jan. 1857.
Nail, Joseph & Sarah Halterman, of Vernon Tp. 14 Aug. 1832. R, A-167.
Nail, Joseph & Rebecca Sullivan. 12 Nov. 1856. R, D-40.
Nail, Joshua & Loas Collis. 1 June 1847. MA, R, B-103.
Nail, Peter & Elisabeth McGarvy. 23 Mar. 1856. R, D-27.
Nail, Wesley & Mary Arthur. Her father Lewis Arthur cons., witn. Samuel Carrick. 13 Nov. 1842. MA, R, B-37.
Nail, William & Minerva Snodgrass. 14 Mar. 1844. MA, R, B-56.

95

Nail, William & Sarah Snorgrass. Her father Robert Snorgrass cons., witn. John Nail, John Snorgrass. 24 Nov. 1832. MA, R, A-172. A-172 shows his name Noel.
Nail, William & Maria Taylor. Her father Jeremiah Taylor cons. 4 July 1858. MA, R, D-81.
Nance, Peter & Catharine White. John White att. ages. 30 Aug. 1849. MA, R, B-190.
Naples, David & Caroline Benner. 26 July 1855. D-21.
Nash, William A. & Susan S. Forsythe. 1 Jan. 1857. R, D-48.
Neahaus, Herman & Charlotte Ruttger. 31 Mar. 1856. R, D-26.
Neal, Joseph & Rhody Johnson. 24 Mar. 1830. MA, R, A-143.
Neary, Edward M. & Elsa (Eliza) J. Sikes. He is 24, born & res. Harrison Tp., son of Mathew Neary. She is 20, dau. of Levi Sikes. 14 Feb. 1858. R, C-14, D-96.
Neel, Hudson & Ellen Ferrill. 10 Aug. 1844. MA.
Neff, Andrew & Juliana Smith. 14 Sep. 1832. R, A-167.
Neff, Isaac & Emeline Holms. His father George Neff, and her father Isaac Holmes cons. 11 Jan. 1852. MA, B-199.
Neff, John & Sarah Randell. 28 Mar. 1847. MA, R, B-100.
Neff, John & Emily Smith. 30 Nov. 1834 by Mark Bradburn, J.P. R.
Nelson, Anderson & Rebecca Jane Methews. 21 June 1855. MA, R, D-19
Nelson, Thomas & Elizabeth Mastin. 18 July 1815. R, A-281.
Nesmith, John & Emely Harley. 15 June 1854. D-2.
Neunberger, George & Eliza Gilpen. 28 Nov. 1860. MA.
Neuner, George & Margaret Davis. 24 Mar. 1856. R, D-28.
Neve (Neves), William & Ann Eliza Burt. 24 Mar. 1859. MA, R, D-90.
Neves, George & Elisabeth Cole. 19 Apr. 1857. R, D-50.
Nevin, Edwin H. & Ruth C. Little. 6 July 1837. R, A-242.
Nevins, John & Electa W. Young. 7 Sep. 1836. R, A-226.
Newcomb, James & Lucind Kirkendall. 30 Aug. 1857. R, D-64.
Newcomb, Philip & Lydia Bradshaw. 27 May 1850. MA, R, B-180.
Newcomb, Phillip & Lydia Young. Charles Young att. ages. 1 June 1844. MA, R, B-61.
Newell, John & Matilda Chamberlain. 30 Nov. 1848. MA, R, B-136.
Newland, Josiah E. & Maria Thompson. Her father Solomon Thompson cons. 30 Nov. 1859. MA, R, D-105.
Newland, William & Susan Lewis. 27 Oct. 1859. MA, R, D-107.
Newman, Bradford N. & Nancy Weldon. 30 Dec. 1838. R, A-263.
Newman, David S. & Mary M. Dever. 12 Feb. 1852. MA, B-238.
Newman, Hiram J. & Tobitha Holt. 18 Feb. 1858. R, D-83.
Newman, James & Elizabeth Edwards. 5 Nov. 1850. MA, B-193.
Newman, William & Allanda Duncan. 26 June 1853. B-263.
Newman, William P. & Nancy Jane Carraway. 17 Oct. 1858. MA, R, D-88.
Nice (Neec), William & Lydia Weaver. 15 Nov. 1812. MA, R, A-323.
Nicholas, Joseph & Margaret Rebeccah Rice. 16 Apr. 1840. R, B-9.
Nichols, David & Kezia Melson. 27 Oct. 1833. R, A-178.
Nichols, Elias & Sarah Nichols. 2 May 1839. MA, R, A-268.
Nichols, George & Anna Nichols (Melson). Her mother Keziah Nichols cons. 10 May 1838. MA, R, A-255.
Nichols, Henderson & Sopha Noel. 16 Dec. 1834. R, A-193.
Nichols, Hezekiah B. & Nancy Ann Noel. George Pollock att. ages. 18 Dec. 1851. MA, B-229.
Nichols, Horatio B. & Mary Rice. 16 Mar. 1848. MA, R, B-126.
Nichols, Jacob & Cynthia Walsinger. 3 June 1847. MA, R, B-102.
Nichols, James & Nancy Cahall. 26 Sep. 1839. MA, R, A-273.
Nichols, John & Mary Hutton. John Hamilton att. he heard both of her pars. att. her age over 18. 8 Sep. 1833. MA, R, A-178.
Nichols, John B. & Maria Merrill. 13 Feb. 1851. B-203.

Nichols, William & Esebel (Nancy) Harmon. 30 Aug. 1814. MA,
R, A-340.
Nichols, William & Elzira Heflen. 12 Nov. 1859. R, D-113.
Nichols, William J. & Nancy Myers. George Malone att. her age.
2 Aug. 1849. MA, R, B-154.
Nickells, Samuel P. & Polly K. Gates. Cons. of Mr. Gates.
14 Dec. 1852. MA, B-254.
Nickols, S. D. & S. J. Wheelock. 25 June 1855, by E. P. Pratt.
R.
Nicoles, David & Nancy Hutton. 11 Aug. 1808. R, A-289, A-291.
Nicoles, David & Mary Noel. 12 Aug. 1828. MA, R, A-129.
Nicoles, Joseph & Rachel Dysart. 22 Feb. 1809. R, A-293.
Nicoles, Thomas & Elizabeth McNamar. 9 Apr. 1807. R, A-284.
Nicoles, William & Nancy Hughs. 6 June 1809. R, A-295.
Niedermaire, Herman & Victoria Braunstein. 15 Nov. 1838. MA,
A-262.
Niedoeffer, Peter & Margaret Bender. 6 May 1848. MA, B-244.
Niemer, William & Elizabeth Dierker. 11 June 1845. MA, R, B-73.
Nixon, Samuel & Mary Brooks. 16 Jan. 1828. R, A-114, A-119.
Noel, Aaron & Catharine Orm. 30 June 1832. R, A-163.
Noel, Abraham G. & Mary Glaze. 5 Oct. 1815, by Benjamin Feurt.
MA, R.
Noel, Absolam & Mary Goldsberry. 11 Sep. 1855. D-21.
Noel, Absolim & Susanah Noel. 4 Jan. 1827. R, A-103.
Noel, Andrew & Sarah Pollock. 25 Mar. 1827. R, A-106 (shows
his name Veach).
Noel, Andrew & Laurette Coppage. 6 Nov. 1842. R, B-36.
Noel, Andrew & Sarah Crain. 30 Dec. 1845. MA, R, B-82.
Noel, David & Sarah Landers. 16 Oct. 1823. R, A-78.
Noel, David & Nancy Morgan. 12 Jan. 1828. R, A-116.
Noel, David & May Jane Zornes. 6 Apr. 1848. MA, R, B-126.
Noel, Ezra H. & Louisa Barber. 8 Jan. 1846. R, B-81.
Noel, Francis Volney & Angeline Huston. 3 July 1859. MA, R,
D-98.
Noel, George & Eliza Landers (Landry). Her father Adam Landry
cons., witn. David Noel. 9 Apr. 1826. MA, R, A-97.
Noel, Isaac & Maryann Orm. 30 Jan. 1823. R, A-72.
Noel, Isaac & Harriet Johnson. 27 Sep. 1832. R, A-168.
Noel, Jacob & Lucretia Hitchcock. 7 Apr. 1807. R, A-284.
Noel, Jacob & Anna Glover. 5 Sep. 1815. R, A-283.
Noel, James & Elizabeth T. Cody (Hody). 27 Oct. 1833. R, A-243.
Noel, John & Margaret (Peggy) Lowery. 2 Apr. 1815. MA, R,
A-347.
Noel, John & Anna Hammitt. 31 Oct. 1816. R, A-24.
Noel, John F. & Olive Kelly. 16 Feb. 1853. MA, D-1.
Noel, John H. & Sarah Ann Hayward. 1 Aug. 1852. MA, B-246.
Noel, John P. & Hannah V. Powers. W. H. Noel att. ages.
24 June 1860. MA, R, D-119.
Noel, Joseph & Polly Pollock. 4 Dec. 1828. R, A-124.
Noel, Joseph O. & Mary Jane Finton. 1 Jan. 1856 (1857). R,
D-44.
Noel, Mathias & Elizabeth Wright. 18 Mar. 1838. MA, R, A-253.
Noel, N. M. & Margaret Miller. 18 Oct. 1855. MA, D-22.
Noel, Nicholas & Nancy Frizel. 21 Sep. 1812. MA, R, A-318.
Noel, Peter & Susannah Feurt. Marey Feurt cons., witn. Gabriel
Feurt, Benjamin Feurt. 23 Oct. 1806. MA, R, A-282.
Noel, Peter & Maria Hogue. 25 Jan. 1827. R, A-102.
Noel, Peter Jr. & Mary Ellen Goolsbery (Goldsberry). 12 Aug.
1838. MA, R, A-258.
Noel, Philip & Massie Feurt. His father Peter Noel Sr. cons.,
att. Peter Noel Jr. 6 Apr. 1812. MA.
Noel, Philip & Elizabeth Thomas. 11 Apr. 1837. R, A-242.

Noel, Soloman, Jr. & Fanny Johnson. 23 Mar. 1821. MA, R, A-59.
Noel, Solomon & Mary Huston. 10 Apr. 1812. R, A-74.
Noel, Telemachus P. & Rebecca Briggs. Joseph H. Cole att. ages.
   27 Dec. 1860. MA, R, D-130.
Noel, William D. & Nancy Ann Prior. He is 20, born Pike Co., Oh.
   res. Morgan Tp., son of Aseraim & Mary Noel. 26 Mar. 1856?
   C-6.
Noel, William H. & Mary Huston. 29 Aug. 1860. MA, R, D-170.
Noel, Zeblin M. V. & Elizabeth Newman. 24 Apr. 1856. R, D-29.
Noell, Chesley & Amanda Pond. 11 Aug. 1853. MA, B-267.
Nogle, W. H. & Mary Ann Ruggles. He is 23, born Jackson Co., Oh.
   res. Portsmouth, son of John Nogle. She is 20, born Jackson
   Co., Oh., res. Portsmouth, dau. of Ben Ruggles. 2 Nov. 1857.
   C-13.
Nolan, James & Mary Andre. 2 Oct. 1856. D-40.
Noland, George B. & Sarah A. Brous. 16 Mar. 1844. MA.
Nolder, John & Mary Hutton. 13 Oct. 1856. MA.
Nolder, Samuel & Martha McCall. 6 Apr. 1858. MA.
Nolun, James & May Snedegar. 26 Oct. 1856, by H.W. Noris, J.P.
   R.
Norman, James & Sarah White. Reason Zarly att. she is 21 years,
   11 months, 18 days old. 9 Mar. 1812. MA.
Norman, Santford J. & Rhoda Arnold. 28 Feb. 1856. R, D-27.
Norman, William & Martha Holt. 12 Nov. 1829. MA, R, A-138.
Norman, William & Martha Flarety. 17 Jan. 1835. MA, R, A-195.
Norris, Amaziah & Lucinda Smith. 4 May 1857. R, D-52.
Norris, Henry W. & Catherine Moore. James Moore att. her age.
   4 June 1846. MA, R, B-89.
Norris, Stephen W. & Elvira Rogers. 30 Oct. 1850. MA, R, B-191.
Northrup, James H. & Mary Frances Mershon. 28 Feb. 1860. MA,
   R, D-119.
Norton, Charles & Almirah Holmes. Her father William Holmes
   cons., witn. Conrad Keller. 9 Feb. 1852. MA, B-234.
Notingham, Thomas & Elizabeth Liston. 3 Oct. 1816. R, A-23.
Notingham, William & Susanna Collins. 16 Nov. 1830. R, A-147.
Nottingham (Nethingham), John & Sarah Williamson. 31 May 1827.
   R, A-107.
Nottingham, William T. & Elizabeth Williamson. 4 Aug. 1850. R,
   B-185.
Nourot, Joseph & Leona Jaqot. 8 Feb. 1860. MA, R, D-121.
Nunley, Elijah & Lavina Young. 17 July 1858. MA.
Nurnberger (Barnberger), Frederick & Mary Walter. 4 Jan. 1851
   (1850). MA, B-196.
Nurse, Joshua & Elizabeth Brouse, both of Washington Tp. 9 Nov.
   1827 (1826?). R, A-102.
Nurse, Lewis & Nancy Vance. 20 July 1859. MA, R, D-100.
Nurse, Reuben & Sophia Bliss. 31 May 1820. MA.
Nurse, S. R. & Julia A. Hungerford. 3 July 1856. R, D-33.
Nurse, Samuel R. & Pheobe Burdick. 1 Mar. 1825. R, A-87.
Nurse, Samuel W. & Terresa Peyton. 28 May 1848. R, B-129.
Nurse, Uriah & Narcisse M. Bliss. 16 May 1830. R, A-143.
Nurss (Norris), Joshua & Eliza Noland. 20 Jan. 1839. R, A-264.
Nutting, Henry W. G. & Margaret Hamilton. 31 May 1829. MA, R,
   A-131.
Nye, William & Charlotte Green. 27 May 1858. MA, R, D-76.
Oakes, John W. & Mary Whitcomb. 11 Oct. 1848. MA, R, B-132.
Oakes, Phineas & Frances Duduit. William Duduit att. her age.
   5 Feb. 1826. MA, R, A-98.
Oakley, William & Keziah Lockerd. 21 Mar. 1839. MA.
Oaks, Francis J. & Frances H. Tracy. 18 Dec. 1845. R, B-81.
Oaks, Joshua & Temperance Marshall. 10 Jan. 1850. R, B-172.
Oaler, John & Mary Kenna. 25 Oct. 1851. B-219.

SCIOTO COUNTY MARRIAGES

Oard, John C. & Matilda Circle. 17 May 1849. R, B-150.
Oard, John E. & Jane Alliway. 6 Aug. 1844. R, B-61.
Oard, John E. & Caroline M. Andus. 13 Aug. 1853. MA.
Oard, John E. (F.) & Charlotte (Lovey I.) Clark. 24 Nov. 1840.
  MA, R, B-7.
Oard, Josiah & Elizabeth Hunt. 29 Oct. 1835. R, A-207.
Oard, William P. & Eliza Oard. Her father Joseph Oard cons.
  11 May 1831. MA, R, A-152.
Oax, John & Margret Ruth. 12 Nov. 1860. MA, R, D-135.
Oberly, John J. & Felicity Magnet. 15 Sep. 1851. MA, B-222.
O'Briant, Permenus & Sarah C. Hyder. 24 July 1849. MA, R, B-155.
O'Bryant (O'Brien), John & Mahala Colven. 7 Mar. 1849. MA,
  B-144.
Odle, Chauncy & Linda Clifford. 21 Jan. 1844. MA, R, B-54.
Odle, Moses & Eliza Jane Bayler. 21 Jan. 1841. MA, R, B-1.
Odle, Nelson & Sally Walker. 12 Nov. 1840. MA, R, B-7.
Oehlschleger, Peter & Agathe Fulmer. 31 Dec. 1857. R, D-67.
Oehlshläger, Jacob & Jacobine Heinisch. 9 Nov. 1859. MA, R,
  D-106.
Ogden, Jonathan & Nancy Rodgers. 20 June 1832. MA, R, A-164.
O'Harra, Richard & Mary Jane Williamson. 17 Nov. 1840. R, B-8.
Ohlschlager, George & Caroline Lintz. 20 Sep. 1860. MA, R, D-128.
Oldfield, William & Maria Hemstead (Hanstead). 14 Nov. 1816.
  MA, R, A-24.
Oldfield, William Jr. & Mary Elizabeth Gilbert. 27 Aug. 1846.
  R, B-92.
Oldfield, William & Ann E. Frazier. 19 Oct. 1847. R, B-109.
Oldham, Peter & Lucinda Davis. Her father Rezin Davis cons.
  16 May 1819. MA, R, A-46.
Olehi, John & Marah Ritter. 13 Nov. 1831. R, A-158.
Olehy, William & Mary Glaze. 23 May 1826. MA, R, A-96.
Olislayer, Sebastian & Barbary Killbell. 29 Aug. 1834. MA, R,
  A-184.
Oliver, Israel M. (James) & Mercy Noel. 5 Dec. 1851. MA, B-224.
Oliver, James M. & Mary C. Stilwell. 22 May 1845. R, B-72.
Oliver, John & Anna Kirkendall. 18 July 1815. MA, R, A-283.
Ollivar, John & Polly Munn. 1 June 1817. R, A-29.
Olney, John C. & Mary Louisa Veach. Silvester Veach att. ages.
  18 June 1848. MA, R, B-130.
O'Neal, Samuel & Lydia Hall. Her father James Hall cons., witn.
  Samuel Skelton, Josiah Lewis. 9 June 1839. MA, R, A-269.
O'Neil, William & Mary McCrumb. 29 (30) Nov. 1851. MA, B-223,
  B-230.
O'Neill, Andrew & Martha Jane Duvall. 31 Mar. 1853. MA, B-258.
Oppy, James & Elizabeth Thompson. 26 Jan. 1841. R, B-15.
Orcutt, Augustus G. & Mary Crull. 3 Apr. 1844. MA, R, B-58.
Orcutt, James W. & Mary Ann Collier. 20 Feb. 1844. MA, B-243.
Orm, George & Effa Ann Finton. 16 Sep. 1858. MA, R, D-79.
Orm, John Jun'r. & Philina Hayward. 23 Dec. 1830, by L. Wheeler
  J.P. R.
Orm, Nathan & Margaret Noel. Her father Philip Noel cons., witn.
  Philip Noel Jr. & Solomon Noel. 6 Feb. 1822. MA, R, A-65.
Orm, Thomas & Catherine Cunning. Jonas Pierce att. her age.
  31 May 1849. MA, R, B-151.
Orm, Thomas J. & Catharine Ray. 21 Jan. 1858. R, D-70.
Orman, Frederick & Mary Eliza Ann Lair. 6 Oct. 1838. MA, R,
  A-261.
Orms, Albert & Susannah Taylor. 8 Sep. 1833. R, A-180.
Orms, Loyd & Elizabeth Hayward. 20 Sep. 1827. R, A-102.
Ormsby, Jerome B. & Perilla F. Walker. 21 Oct. 1850. R, B-191.
Osborn, James & Sophia H. Rigg. 13 July 1847. MA, R, B-104.
Osborn, Michael W. & Elizabeth Parshley. 23 July 1857. R, D-55.

SCIOTO COUNTY MARRIAGES

Otis, Jonathan & Margaret Duffie. 15 May 1829. MA.
Otis, Jonathan & Catharine Hawkins. 25 Dec. 1830, by Ezra
  Osborn, J. P. MA, R.
Ott, Valentine & Catherine Rhodes. 15 May 1852. MA, B-239.
Oursler, John & Mary Kenner. 24 Nov. 1851. MA.
Outen, William & Manda Ann McGraw. His father Emanuel Outen
  cons., att. William McGraw. 4 May 1848. MA, R, B-124.
Overdier, David & Mary Moss. 16 June 1847. MA, R, B-105.
Overturf, Conrad & Rhoda Kendell. 20 July 1826. R, A-103.
Overturf, Conrad & Rachel Kendall. 23 Aug. 1838. R, A-257.
Owen, Rodrick & Nancy Adams. 23 Sep. 1821. R, A-60.
Owen, Timothy & Jane Dever. David Dever att. her age. 24 Mar.
  1825. MA, R, A-89.
Owens, Erasmus & Mary Ranall. 28 July 1853. B-263.
Owens, George W. & Amanda Coal. 1 Apr. 1830. R, A-140.
Ox, John & Catharine Rumble. 26 Sep. 1844. MA.
Pabst, Phillip & Christina Pabst. 29 Nov. 1860. MA, R, D-125.
Pacsoe (Besche?), John & Mary Startsman. 12 Mar. 1853. MA.
Page, John Clark & Martha Kiser. 11 Oct. 1858. MA, R, D-85.
Paine, Olney & Marian Bartley. 11 Dec. 1808. R, A-293.
Painer, John & Janet Urquhart. 18 Sep. 1855. R, D-20.
Palmer, John & Matilda Stewart. 4 July 1848. MA, R, B-131.
Palmer, John A. & Melinda Driver. 3 July 1845. MA, R, B-73.
Palmer, Roswell E. & Marey Cooper. 7 May 1854. D-1.
Pancake, Harvey & Jemima Culp. 4 June 1850. MA, R, B-180.
Pangburn, Thadeus & Polly Hunter. 20 Dec. 1821. MA, R, A-63.
Panna, Jackson & Elizabeth Mathena. 2 June 1857. MA, R, D-53.
Parker, John V. & Maria Ann Parker. 30 Dec. 1847. MA, R, B-112.
Parks, Joseph B. & Sarah Monroe. 25 Apr. 1852. MA, B-246.
Parks, William & Martha E. Anderson. Her stepfather Amos
  Holstead cons. 31 Jan. 1854. MA, D-2.
Parnell, James & Catherine Andrews. 29 May 1849. MA, R, B-149.
Parrish, Joshua & Elizabeth Marshall. 10 July 1805. R, A-5.
Parrish, Joshua & Catharine Miller. 3 Nov. 1807. R, A-287.
Parscal, Robert & Lucretia Coriell. 17 May 1849. MA, R, B-150.
Parshley, Daniel R. & Eliza Vessel. 30 Mar. 1834. MA, R, A-191.
Parsons, Edgar A. G. & Ann Burns. 30 Dec. 1847. MA, R, B-112.
Partee, Aquilla & Nancy Dillon, of Seal Tp. 18 Jan. 1811. R,
  A-307.
Partee, James & Elisabeth Cartar. 7 July 1808. R, A-290.
Partelow, George & Kesiah Tubbs. 18 Oct. 1835. MA, R, A-243.
Pascal, John W. & Celey C. West. 9 Mar. 1857. R, D-51.
Passmore, Charles D. & Amanda Phillips. 21 Aug. 1847. MA, R,
  B-105.
Paten, John & Mary Stuort. 29 Sep. 1855. R, D-20.
Patten, Elias & Caroline Ruth. 20 Nov. 1855. D-23.
Patten, James H. & Martha E. Stropes. 21 Oct. 1860. MA, R,
  D-129.
Patten, Jeremiah & Comfort Powell. 1 Mar. 1827. MA, R, A-104.
Patten, Jeremiah & Nancy Rardon. 8 Jan. 1831. MA, R, A-150.
Patten, John & Belinda Louderback. 28 Feb. 1828. R, A-115.
Patten, John H. & Minerve Randell. 22 May (Mar.?) 1830. R,
  A-142.
Patten, Lemuel & Salena Chamberlain. Wyett Chamberlain cons.
  17 May 1846. MA, R, B-87.
Patten, Milton & Ruth Ann Kinney. 14 Jan. 1853. MA.
Patten, Russell & Catherine Berry. 9 Jan. 1851. MA, B-200.
Patten, Samuel & Catharine Nichols. 23 Apr. 1855. MA, R, D-17.
Patten, Thomas & Lucy Johnson. 30 Apr. 1843. MA, R, B-44.
Patten, William & Virginia Barbee. 6 Sep. 1852. MA, B-277.
Patten, William S. & Eliza Cox. He was born Marietta, Oh.
  She is dau. of Lucinda Cox. 15 Dec. 1856. R, C-1, D-52.

100

SCIOTO COUNTY MARRIAGES

Patterson, Galbreath & Jane Barber. 6 Mar. 1825. R, A-89.
Patterson, Ira & Martha Halsted. 1 (18) July 1827. R, A-109.
Patterson, John & Elizabeth Loomis. 2 Mar. 1850. MA, R, B-173.
Patterson, Joseph A. & Margaret J. Currie. He is 23, born
  Steubenville, res. Portsmouth, son of Jas. & Mary Patterson.
  She is 18, born & res. Portsmouth, dau. of Thos. & Hannah
  Currie. 1 July 1856. R, C-1, D-33.
Patterson, Lauchlen & Sarah Kinner. 22 Dec. 1859. MA, R, D-103.
Patterson, Thomas M. & Callie Clugsten. 28 Dec. 1852. MA,
  B-254.
Patterson, Winthrup & Mary Louder. 17 Oct. 1859. MA, R, D-109.
Pattingale, Stephen & Lydia Beloat, both of Porter. 16 Feb.
  1837. MA, R, A-239.
Patton, Abner & Julian Hoyt. 19 May 1831. R, A-155.
Patton, George & Catharine Stewart. 23 Apr. 1851. MA, B-206.
Patton, James & Susannah Powell. 28 Oct. 1819. MA, R, A-47.
Patton, Jinnings & Ellenor Purdy. 2 Dec. 1852. MA, B-254.
Patton, Joseph & Melinda Edginton. Brice Edginton att. her age.
  17 Dec. 1820. MA, R, A-56.
Patton, Lewis & Elizabeth Patterson. 21 Oct. 1857. R, D-63.
Patton, Milton & Ruth Ann Keeney. 14 Jan. 1854. D-3.
Patton, Samuel & Elizabeth Patton. His brother Thomas Patton
  Jr. att. their father Thomas Patton cons. Her father James
  Patten cons., witn. Jeremiah Patten. 4 Dec. 1813. MA, R,
  A-330.
Patton, Thos. & Jane (Jinne) Lowry. 10 Feb. 1808. R, A-289.
Paul, Peris & Elizabeth Monroe. 16 Oct. 1834. MA, R, A-193.
Paull, John & Sally Ann Cole. 15 June 1853. B-279.
Payne, William & Darkis Watson. Josiah Virbeck att. her age.
  5 Dec. 1826. MA.
Payton, Charles & Martha Jane Gettys. Her mother (only surviv-
  ing parent) Sarah Gettys, of Junior Furnace, cons., witn.
  D. A. Glidden, Samuel Gettys. 17 Apr. 1845. MA, R, B-70.
Payton, Jackson & Julia Ann Hart. 14 Feb. 1860. MA.
Payton (Paxton), James & Catharine Fleming. 25 Dec. 1828. MA,
  R, A-125.
Payton, Samuel & Margaret James. 29 June 1837. MA, R, A-237.
Payton, William & Loanna Dudwit. 30 Sep. 1850. MA.
Pearce, Charles D. & Mary M. Glaze. 17 Oct. 1860. MA, R, D-147.
Pearce, John & Sarah Bradshaw. 11 Apr. 1833, by E. Truitt, M.G.
  of M. E. Church. MA, R.
Pearl, Bazil & Julia Ann Heath. 22 Feb. 1852. MA, B-231.
Pearl, Robert & Deborah Wells. 22 June 1851. MA, B-214.
Pearl, Robert & Mary J. Rickey. He is 17, born Jackson Co., Oh.,
  son of Robert & Nancy Pearl. She is 18, born & res. Scioto
  Co., dau. of John G. & Mary Rickey. 24 Jan. 1858. R, C-9,
  D-69.
Pearson, William & Priscilla McFaden. 4 Apr. 1816. MA, R, A-20.
Peatling, Edward & Mary Ann Tearl (Tyrell, Searl). 12 Apr. 1855.
  R, D-17.
Pechler, Peter & Susannah Crouse. Conrad Pechler att. ages.
  4 Aug. 1839. MA, R, A-271.
Peck, Nathan & Minerva Hall. 18 Nov. 1857. R, D-66.
Peck, William & Mary Hickey. 16 Dec. 1819. R, A-49.
Peck, William G. & Charlotte Moore. 19 June 1841. R, B-20.
Peck, William V. & Mary Ann Cook. 29 Apr. 1833? (This is in a
  list of marriages, not individually dated.) R, A-174.
Peck, William V. & Harriet E. McCollester. 19 Apr. 1858. R,
  D-76.
Peebles, John S. & Martha Steell. 10 June 1835. R, A-202.
Pelhank, Henry & Elizabeth Holt. 1 Feb. 1857. R, D-46.
Pemberton, William & Mary A. Cartwright. George M. Owens att.
  ages. 30 July 1851. MA.

101

Penn, Samuel & Catharine Thompson. He is 40, born Pike Co., Oh., res. Brush Creek, son of S. & Jane Penn. She is 32, born Adams Co., res. Brush Creek, dau. of Mathew & E. Williams, second marr. 8 Feb. 1857. R, C-5, D-46.
Pennington, Hardin & Elizabeth White. 12 Sep. 1846. MA.
Penwell, Isaac & Mary F. Berry. 26 Feb. 1848. (License from Ross Co.) MA.
Perkins, James & Jane Mills. 6 July 1831. MA.
Perry, Abraham & Lucinda Malone. 5 Feb. 1835. MA, R, A-200.
Perry, Abraham & Fanny Grover. 9 May 1841. MA, R, B-19.
Perry, Isaac & Katharine Louderback. 12 Oct. 1815. MA, R, A-16.
Perry, James & Elizabeth Worley (Worldley). 16 Oct. 1818. R, A-61.
Perry, Jeptha & Margarette Humphreys. 11 Feb. 1836. R, A-213.
Perry, John & Drusilla Null (Noel). Andrew Paulson & John Null att. ages. 18 Oct. 1805. MA, R, A-7, A-279.
Perry, Lindsey & Elizabeth Slimp. 9 Sep. 1845. MA, R, B-76.
Perry, Lindsey & Celia Slimp. 4 Feb. 1855. MA, R, D-15.
Perry, Lyman & Tobitha Noel. 17 Dec. 1846. MA, R, B-97.
Perry, Nelson & Ann Remecca Gillis. 28 Jan. 1845. MA.
Perry, Oliver & Mary J. Gillis. 6 Oct. 1851. MA.
Perry, Samuel & Margaret Lindsay. 22 Apr. 1813. R, A-325.
Perry, Samuel & Rachel Roberts. 29 Oct. 1837. MA, R, A-235.
Perry, Samuel & Rebecca Chandler. 19 May 1839. MA, R, A-269.
Perry, Samuel & Lydia Hamner. His mother Margaret Malone and Lydia's father J. N. Hamner cons. 17 Nov. 1858. MA, R, D-95.
Perry, Samuel & Catherine Littlejohn. 6 July 1860. MA.
Perry, William & Nancy McDonnell (McDonald). 22 Jan. 1818. MA, R, A-33.
Peter, Jacob & Rosa Wortz. 5 Apr. 1858. MA, R, D-85.
Peters, Isaac & Adeline Diduit. 7 Nov. 1845. MA.
Peters, John & Mary C. Fuller. 21 Dec. 1843. MA, R, B-51.
Peters, John & Sarah Slavens. 5 Oct. 1848. R, B-135.
Peters, Milton C. & Ruth Slavens. 5 Oct. 1851. MA, B-230.
Peterson, William & Maray Holcan (Holland). 26 Sep. 1805. R, A-8, A-279.
Pethoud, John & Mary Thompson. 14 Nov. 1822. MA, R, A-72.
Pethoud, John T. & Rebecca Steece. 10 Apr. 1853. MA, B-260.
Petry, John & Emily Lilly. 8 Apr. 1858. MA, R, D-74.
Petry, John & Susan Eifert. 15 Feb. 1859. MA, R, D-133.
Pettit, Allen & Nancy A. Hockenbery. Her father cons. 17 Dec. 1860. MA, R, D-124.
Pettit, George S. & Elizabeth Martin. 19 May 1844. MA, R, B-60.
Pettit (Pellet), John & Mary Francis Meredith. 20 May 1839. MA, R, A-269.
Pettit, John & Margaret Adams. His father Job Pettit cons. Her mother Emiline Adams cons. 2 Dec. 1858. MA, R, D-89.
Pettit, Samuel & Polly Yates. 27 Sep. 1830. MA, R, A-148.
Pewters, John & Jinny McDowll. 28 Jan. 1808. R, A-289.
Pewters, John & Betsy Price. John Graham att. ages. 10 Sep. 1812. MA, R, A-322.
Peyton, Henry & Ann Wiley. 26 July 1841. MA, R, B-21.
Peyton, Isaac & Rebecah Liston. 10 Aug. 1820. R, A-54.
Peyton (Payton), James & Susanna Smith. 1 June 1846. MA, R, B-87.
Peyton, John & Sarah Peyton. 3 Mar. 1849. R, B-142.
Peyton, William & Bridget Turner. 21 Oct. 1813. MA, R, A-327.
Pfander, Charles (Carl) & Elizabeth Gabler. 21 Nov. 1850. MA, B-196.
Pfeiffer (Favors), Constantino & Mary Legler. He is 24, born Germany, res. Portsmouth, son of Conrad Pfeiffer. She is 30,

born & res. Portsmouth, dau. of George Legler. 12 May 1856.
MA, R, C-7, D-31.

Phelps, George & Jennette Carter. 13 Sep. 1843. MA, R, B-49.

Phelps, J. E. & Angeline Mitchell. 14 June 1855. R, D-18.

Phelps, L. A. & Mrs. Jane Godfrey. He is 25, born Vermont, res.
Cincinnati, son of John & Elmira Phelps. She is 24, born
N.Y., res. Wheelersburg, dau. of Claney & E. Vanduson, second
marr. 11 Aug. 1856. MA, R, C-4, D-43.

Philips, James & Mary Brown. 29 Dec. 1833. R, A-184.

Philips, John & Mary Ledbetter (Laupetter). 25 Feb. 1854. MA,
D-6.

Philips, Samuel M. & Mary Brewer. 12 Feb. 1809. R, A-293.

Phillippi, George & Elizabeth Leser. 29 Oct. 1858. MA, R, D-86.

Phillips, Abner, of Jackson, Ohio & Hariet Robbins. Her guardian Thos. Aldrich cons., witn. Ezra Aldrich, of Bloom Tp.
29 Nov. 1823. MA.

Phillips, Allen B. & Jane Thomlison. 19 Oct. 1854. R, D-11.

Phillips, Craddock & Elizabeth Daniels. 27 Oct. 1860. MA, R,
D-129.

Phillips, John & Minerva Bennet. His mother Elizabeth Wood cons.
witn. Leonard T. Watkins. Her father Gilbert Bennet cons.,
witn. Samuel Bennett, Skelton Powell. 20 Sep. 1838. MA, R,
A-259.

Phillips, John S. & Hester Culp. 1 Dec. 1851. MA, B-243.

Phillips, Joshua & Elizabeth Custiss. 2 Aug. 1835. MA, R,
A-204.

Phillips, Levi P. & Mary Shane. 4 June 1838. MA.

Phillips, Theophilus & Mary Ann Stephenson. 14 June 1854. R,
D-4, D-8.

Phillips, William & Isabella Valance. 21 May 1849. MA, R,
B-148.

Phillips, William & Elizabeth Davis. Witn. Maria C. Phillips,
John E. Phillips. 5 Apr. 1858. MA, R, D-85.

Phipps, William & Mary Evans. 27 Apr. 1848. MA, R, B-126.

Pieper, Friedrich & Henrietta Schmale. 22 May 1849. R, B-149.

Pierce, Charles & Adeline Lawrence. 24 Mar. 1850. MA, R, B-174.

Pierce, Irven & Harriet Palmer. John Louderback att. ages.
16 Nov. 1845. MA, R, B-82.

Pierce, Joshua & Amanda Ausburn. He is 28, son of H. & Anna
Pierce. She is 17, born & res. Greenup Co., Ky. 26 Nov.
1856. R, C-3, D-45.

Pierce, Otis S. & Mary M. Cushman. 16 Oct. 1838. MA, R, A-261.

Piercefield, John & Mary Ann Friley. 11 Dec. 1859. MA, R,
D-113.

Piggott, John & Electa Squires. 4 Feb. 1836. MA, R, A-212.

Piggott, William & Sarah McConkey. Her pars. cons., att.
Walter Jenkins. 25 Aug. 1860. MA.

Piles, Absolam & Sabina Marshal. Samuel Marshall att. her age.
27 Oct. 1812. MA, R, A-322.

Piles, Clinton D. & Caroline H. Kendall. 9 Aug. 1849. MA, R,
B-156.

Piles, Henry & Sarah Elizabeth Martin. 23 Apr. 1846. MA, R,
B-88.

Piles, Isaac & Nancy Martin. 23 Dec. 1847. MA, R, B-112.

Piles, Jeremiah & Phibe Cole. 22 Mar. 1831. R, A-151.

Piles, John & Rachel Arnold. 19 Mar. 1818. R, A-35.

Piles, Samuel & Sary (Sally) Fartrass. 18 June 1846. MA, R,
B-88.

Piles, Washington & Susannah Rankin. 20 Nov. 1840. R, B-8.

Piles, William & Eleanor Brouce. 24 Apr. 1837. MA, R, A-240.

Piles, William & Maria Morrison. He was born Va. She was born
Va., res. Green Tp., dau. of James Morrison & Malinda Conklin.
20 Sep. 1857. R, C-13, D-62.

SCIOTO COUNTY MARRIAGES

Piles, William & Mary Ann Munion. Charles Price att. ages.
  11 Sep. 1858. MA, R, D-81.
Pillers, Samuel & Icy Vannorte. 22 Mar. 1835. MA, R, A-216.
Pincer, Frederick & Elizabeth Reller. 12 Mar. 1854. D-5.
Pinkerman, Charles & Elizabeth Smith. 18 July 1830. R, A-146.
Pinkerton, William & Rebecca Titus. Her father James Titus
  picked up affidavit (license). 21 Apr. 1853. MA, B-261.
Pitts, James & Keziah Tucker. His father Joseph Pitts cons.
  21 June 1832. MA, R, A-164.
Pitts, John O. & Mary Jane Cole. 3 Aug. 1856. R, D-34.
Pixley, Seymour & Eliza Smith. 30 Sep. 1827. MA, R, A-102.
Pixley, Simon & Elizabeth Orms. 19 June 1838. R, B-5.
Plater, John O. & Sally Smith. 22 Dec. 1852. MA, B-254.
Plum, Sam & Ava Blakeman. He is 40, born & res. Scioto Co.,
  son of William Plum, third marriage. She is 27, born Ky.,
  res. Jackson Co., Oh., dau. of Moses Blakeman, first marr.
  7 Oct. 1857. C-12.
Plumb, John Jr. & Nancy Plumb. John Plumb Sen'r. att. he is
  over 21, she is over 14. 13 Nov. 1833. MA, R, A-182.
Plumb, John & Christena Plumb. 7 Dec. 1833. R, A-177.
Plumb, John & Charlotte Blakeman. Her pars. cons., att. Isaac
  Fullerton. 21 Sep. 1842. MA, R, B-36.
Plumb, Samuel & Lovisa Snider. 6 Dec. 1835. MA, R, A-210.
Plumb, Samuel & Mary Shonkwiler. 26 Sep. 1850. MA, R, B-190.
Plumb, William & Elizabeth Marshall. 21 July 1808. R, A-290.
Plumb, William & Christain Shunkwiler. 31 Jan. 1816. R, A-18.
Poindexter, Thomas & Melvina Mundel. 25 Apr. 1850. MA, R,
  B-178.
Pollock, Andrew & Sarah Ann Patrick. 6 Jan. 1853. MA, B-255.
Pollock, David & Nancy Mustard. John Devers of Portsmouth att.
  ages. 11 Dec. 1806. MA, R, A-282.
Pollock, David & Mary Ann Smith. 22 Aug. 1839. R, A-271.
Pollock, George & Mary Newman. 24 Nov. 1852. MA, B-252.
Pollock, John & Marcy Noel. 13 Nov. 1806. R, A-282.
Pollock, John & Elizabeth Conrow. 29 July 1847. MA, R, B-107.
Pollock, Samuel & Lavisa Lucas. 27 Jan. 1842. R, B-29.
Pollock, Thomas & Jemima Ann Lucas. 4 Oct. 1842 (1841). MA,
  R, B-35.
Pollock, Thomas & Elizabeth Smith. 22 Jan. 1818. MA, R, A-34.
Pollock, William & Tabitha Conrow. 6 July 1848. MA, R, B-127.
Polock, John & Rosannah Noel. 9 Feb. 1837. R, A-240.
Pond, J. Evarts & Jeanie W. Baird. 18 Mar. 1858, by E. P. Pratt.
  R.
Pool, Aaron & Mary West. 6 Feb. 1840. MA, R, B-2.
Pool, Aaron & Hulda Coles. 4 Jan. 1844. MA, R, B-54.
Pool, Aaron & Eliza Dearman. 16 Apr. 1854. D-2.
Pool, Andrew & Elizabeth (Betsy) Rickets. 23 Jan. 1818. MA, R,
  A-36.
Pool, Calvin & Minervy Barber. 4 Oct. 1860. MA, R, D-125.
Pool, George E. & Martha Slattery. He is 19, born & res. Harri-
  son Tp., son of William Pool. She is 16, dau. of W. Slattery.
  His pars. & her pars. cons., att. Robert A. H. McCurdy.
  24 (22) Oct. 1857. R, C-14, D-63.
Pool, John & Susanna Crull. Her father William Crull cons.
  17 Sep. 1829. MA, R, A-135.
Pool, Levi & Sarah Ann Dodge. 29 Jan. 1840. MA, R, B-2.
Pool, Peter & Ada M. Aldrich. 14 Oct. 1824. MA, R, A-84.
Pool, William & Amy Dodge. 7 Jan. 1836. MA, R, A-211, A-227.
Porter, David C. & Catharine Pool. 14 Oct. 1849. R, B-159.
Porter, George R. (M.) & Rebecca Wolf. 7 Dec. 1834. MA, R,
  A-195.
Porter, Girrard & Mary Jane Rafesnyder. 12 Oct. 1843. MA, R,
  B-50.

104

SCIOTO COUNTY MARRIAGES

Porter, Philip & Polly Engle (Ingle), of Green Tp. Thomas
   Porter att. his age. 20 Nov. 1824. MA, R, A-90.
Porter, R. H. & Ruth A. Hannahs. 1 Mar. 1852. B-233.
Porter, Thomas & Anna Tophouse. Her stepfather George Jones
   and her mother Sally Jones, formerly Sally Tophouse, cons.,
   att. Daniel Tophouse. 27 Mar. 1823. MA, R, A-76.
Porter, William & Bathel (Rachel) Weeks. 4 Sep. 1806. R, A-282.
Porter, William & Mary Stapleton. 18 Apr. 1850. MA, R, B-177.
Porter, William & Angeline Pierce. 17 Feb. 1857 (15 Feb. 1858).
   R, D-169.
Porter, William & Ann Pearce. 4 Feb. 1858. R, D-68.
Porter, Zephaniah & Martha Musick. 21 Apr. 1836. MA, R, A-219.
Postelthwat, William H. L. & Elizabeth L. Heath. 28 Mar. 1852.
   MA, B-235.
Potter, William & Eliza Salladay. 28 Nov. 1847. R, B-110.
Potts, Charles & Fanny Bliss. 28 Mar. 1818. MA, R, A-35.
Powel (Pond), Samuel & Nancy (?) Hunelly. 11 Jan. 1850. R,
   B-171.
Powell, Bartholomew & Matilda Butcher. 31 Dec. 1846. MA, B-81.
Powell, Charles C. & Louisa Day. Benjamin Butterfield att. his
   age. 14 Feb. 1822. MA, R, A-64.
Powell, Henry B. & Emma Jane Kirkpatrick. 2 Sep. 1852. MA, B-246.
Powell, Hezekiah & Rosetta Squires. Her father Stephen Squires
   cons., witn. James Hammond. 7 Dec. 1833. MA.
Powell, Jacob & Rachel Enslow. 20 June 1842. R, B-31.
Powell, John & Matilda Chandler. 14 Mar. 1822. R, A-65.
Powell, John & Spicey Brock. His guardian Adam Stumbough cons.,
   witn. George Brock, Pleasant Brock. 29 Aug. 1826. MA, R,
   A-100.
Powell, John M. & Dorothy Trich. 20 Apr. 1849. MA, R, B-146.
Powell, Joseph W. & Huldah M. Linn. 3 Nov. 1849. MA, R, B-161.
Powell, Joshua & Nancy Chapman. He is 22, born Beaver Co., Pa.,
   son of Abraham Powell. She is 24, born Beaver Co., Pa., dau.
   of Luke Chapman. 28 Aug. 1856. MA, R, C-4, D-33.
Powell, Peter & Melvina Marshall. 21 May 1840. R, B-9.
Powell, Richard & Hannah Randall. 29 Sep. 1844. MA, R, B-64.
Powell, Silas D. & Amanda Farney. 10 Aug. 1853. MA, B-267.
Powell (Ponde), Theophilus & Elenore Hare. 20 Sep. 1850.
   B-192, B-215.
Powell, Thomas & Sophia Andre. 8 Jan. 1811. MA.
Powell, Vincent & Mary (Polly) Kelly. Her brother Charles
   Kelley att. her age. 30 May 1813. MA, R, A-326.
Powell, William & Sally Ross. Isaac Randall att. her age.
   16 June 1849. MA, R, B-156.
Power, John W. & Louisa Campbell. 30 Aug. 1848. MA.
Power, Twibill & Mary Ann Sweet. 23 Apr. 1848. MA, R, B-126.
Powers, Archey & Susanna Holman. 21 Sep. 1848. MA, R, B-131.
Powers, Ezekiel & Catharine Miles. 10 Mar. 1840. B-6.
Powers, Ezekiel & Sarah J. Dean. 30 Nov. 1851. MA, B-228.
Powers, Francis Jr. & Lucina Powell. 11 Aug. 1847. MA, R,
   B-108.
Powers, Robert J. & Mary Smith. 17 May 1849. MA, R, B-148.
Prather, Nelson & Mahala Noel. 25 Feb. 1840. R, B-1.
Pratt, Charles H. & Margaret Shelpman. 12 May 1855. R, D-18.
Pratt, Howard & Sarah Morton. 16 Feb. 1844. MA, R, B-53.
Pratt, John & Louisa Clemms. He is 23, born Germany, res.
   Ripley. She is dau. of Michael & Catherine Clemms. 25 Nov.
   1856. C-6.
Predeger, John George & Catherine Spanner. 4 Mar. 1859. MA,
   R, D-96.
Preiser, Blasins & Anna Schantcly. Her father J. Anton
   Schantcly cons. 30 Sep. 1852. MA.

105

SCIOTO COUNTY MARRIAGES

Prendergast, William & Mary Sullivan. 23 Nov. 1857. R, D-69.
Prescott, Henry & Martha M. Robinson. 21 Feb. 1851. MA, B-204.
Prescott, James & Pamelia J. Robinson. 3 Jan. 1850. R, B-166.
Prescott, James & Evaline Kline. 25 Feb. 1855. MA, R, D-15.
Prescott, James & Margaret Neve. 24 July 1859. MA, R, D-99.
Prescott, James B. & Lydia C. Boynton. 12 Nov. 1815. R, A-16.
Pressell, Daniel W. & Hester Ann Turner. 19 June 1844. R, B-62.
Preston, Nathaniel & Mary A. Holmes. 19 Feb. 1850. R, B-172.
Preston, Robert J. & Louisa M. Jennison. Her pars. Samuel &
    Ruth Jennison, of Rockville, Scioto Co., cons., witn. Samuel
    C. McMaster, W. B. Dodds. 26 Sep. 1833. MA, R, A-181.
Price, Andrew & Rachel Null. Her father Teter Null cons., witn.
    Isaac Null, William Price. 15 Apr. 1830. MA, R, A-141.
Price, Charles & Rachel Munion. 11 Oct. 1857. R, D-63.
Price, David & Rebecca Wade. 8 Aug. 1839. R, A-271.
Price, Isaac & Cintha Ann Moore. 25 June 1823. R, A-75.
Price, Jacob & Theressa Eblem. 10 Nov. 1860. MA, R, D-128.
Price, John & Elizabeth Scott. 6 Apr. 1850. MA, R, B-176.
Price, Madison & Mina Lindsey. 1 Jan. 1839. R, A-266.
Price, Merrit & Elizabeth Null. 24 Dec. 1828. R, A-128.
Price (Pine), Vinton & Minerva Bonser. 26 Mar. 1854. D-3.
Price, William & Mary Ann Hammet. 4 Aug. 1812. MA, R, A-321.
Prichard, James & Ellen McGill. 3 May 1852. MA, B-238.
Priest, John & Comfort McAuley. 1 Feb. 1852. MA, B-231.
Prince, Elias H. & Sophia Williamson. 27 Feb. 1831. MA, R,
    A-217.
Prince, John W. & Malinda Bagby. 13 Apr. 1860. MA.
Prior, Christopher Henry & Louisa Oblock. 24 Aug. 1859. MA,
    R, D-102.
Prior, John M. & Elizabeth McConky. 28 July 1857. R, D-57.
Prise (Price), Richard W. & Elisabeth Shufflin. 25 June 1857.
    R, D-54.
Pritchett, Theophilus & Frances Patillo. 2 July 1835. R, A-203.
Proebster, Johann Adam & Christiana Wallbrecht. 24 June 1812.
    MA.
Pryor, William & Electa W. Nevens. 31 Oct. 1848. MA, R, B-135.
Pucket, Thomas & Sophia Stumbo, of Vernon Tp. 28 July 1819.
    MA, R, A-47.
Purdum, John W. & Sarah Pursell. 10 Apr. 1855. R, D-17.
Purdum, W. W. & Lydia McNeal. 1 May 1850. MA, R, B-178.
Purdy, Allen & Hester Burt. Margaret Burt "assigns all my
    right and Claim of hur away to Mr. purdey as his propertey."
    Witn. Adam Utt Junr. 8 Apr. 1830, by Luther Wheeler, J.P.
    MA, R.
Purdy, Milton & Susan Elizabeth Bonser. 23 Dec. 1847. R, B-112.
Pursell, Thomas J. & Thomasin H. Spry. 17 Mar. 1857. R, D-52.
Purtee, Jared & Nancy Jayne Armstrong. 18 July 1837. MA, R,
    A-246.
Purtee, Richard & Matilda White. 20 Dec. 1838. MA, R, A-263.
Puthuff, Franklin & Elizabeth Alexander. His father Benjamin
    Franklin Puthuff cons. 6 June 1835. MA, R, A-202.
Putland, Edward & Elizabeth Wheeler. 22 Mar. 1858. R, D-75.
Putman, Abner & Emily Cole. 17 June 1844. MA, R, B-60.
Putman, Michael & Belinda Long. 12 July 1829. MA, R, A-132.
Pyatt, Jacob & Emily Jane Carter. Her father cons. 23 Sep.
    1847. MA, R, B-114.
Pyle, Henry Harrison & Sarah White. Her pars. cons. 14 Nov.
    1854. MA, R, D-12.
Pyle, James Nelson & Catharine M. Spriggs. Her father Peter
    Spriggs cons. 26 June 1852. MA, B-252.
Pyle, Jesse M. & Elizabeth A. Cox. 27 Feb. 1851 (1850). MA,
    B-203.
Pyle, Jonathan & Mary Shoop. 24 Sep. 1858. MA, R, D-83.

106

SCIOTO COUNTY MARRIAGES

Queen, William Jr. & Margaret Fout. 11 Oct. 1849. MA, R,
B-190.
Radcliff (Ratliff), David F. & Martha C. (Elizabeth) Poor.
3 June 1856. MA, R, D-32.
Radley, Jacob & Margaret Garrett. 12 Oct. 1841. MA, R, B-25.
Rafter, John & Frances Jones. 22 Sep. 1844. MA, R, B-62.
Ragsdail, Berry & Mrs. Sarah Chapman. His father Obediah
Ragsdail cons., witn. James Green, William Pearson. 30 June
1815. MA, R, A-283.
Rake (Rahe), John Henry & Mary Hulzmeier. 18 Dec. 1856. R,
D-44.
Rama, George W. & Hariet Johnson. 25 Feb. 1847. MA, R, B-99.
Ramsey, David & Tena Gebhardt. He is 24, born Penn., son of
David & Rebecca Ramsey. She is 19, born Scioto Co., dau. of
Lewis & T. Gebheart. 25 Dec. 1856. R, C-4, D-48.
Ramsey, George W. & Polly Barnett. 24 Apr. 1846. MA, R, B-88.
Ramsey, Robert & Julie Ann Bennet. 2 Mar. 1843. MA, R, B-45.
Ramsey, Samuel N. & Emely Douglass. 14 Apr. 1854. D-3.
Randall, Chanay C. & Nancy Sheldon. 5 Aug. 1842. MA, R, B-34.
Randall, Chaney M. & Nancy Wallace. 7 Apr. 1839. MA, R, B-6.
Randall, John & Lois Saint John Bloomer. Henry Bloomer att.
her age. 11 Dec. 1842. MA, R, B-38.
Randall, John & Samantha Newman. Her pars. Solomon & Elizabeth
Newman cons., witn. Peter Randall, Benjamin Randall. 21 May
1843. MA, R, B-45.
Randall, Peter & Margaret Lyra (Tiry). 25 Apr. 1844. MA, R,
B-58.
Randell, Benjamin & Nancy Craig. 12 July 1846. R, B-90.
Randles, John & Margret Gillilan (?). Presley Gillilan att.
ages and, "I am willing for my for the mach." 4 Jan. 1813.
MA.
Randolph, Perry & Jane Sayre. 27 Oct. 1854. B-285.
Rank, William & Nancy Stapleton. 20 Nov. 1850. MA, B-193.
Rankin, James A. & Hester Ann Williams. 4 Feb. 1841. R, B-14.
Rankin, William & Elizabeth Groninger. John Groniger att. her
age. Benjamin Rankin att. William is over 21. 28 July 1814.
MA, R, A-338.
Rankins, Burris B. & Sarah Williams. 27 Sep. 1849. R, B-158.
Rankins, William & Katharine Coner. 7 Sep. 1830. R, A-147.
Rannals, Edwards & Mary W. Kelly. 11 Jan. 1847, by __ Sampson,
J.P. R.
Ranshahous (Renshaw), Henry & Sarah Ann Skelton. Hannah Ransha-
hous cons., att. Thomas Stumbo. 13 Aug. 1853. MA, B-272.
Ransin, Liberty & Jane Elizabeth Fultz. Philip Newcomb att.
ages. 26 Mar. 1845. MA.
Ransom, Hiram & Rachel McDowell. 30 Sep. 1830. R, A-147.
Ransom, Samuel Ann Elvia (Eliza) Clingman. 26 Nov. 1826. R,
A-101.
Ransom, Samuel & Nancy Phillips. Her father Hezekiah Phillips
cons., witn. Mary Phillips, David Combs. 29 May 1831. MA,
R, A-154.
Rapp, Jacob & Eliza Nelson. 6 Sep. 1849. MA, R, B-164.
Rapp, Jacob & Mary Jane Giles. 17 Nov. 1852. MA, B-249.
Rardan, Philip & Mary McCowen. 9 Jan. 1840. R, B-1.
Rardon (Reardon), James & Mary Stump. 6 July 1809. R, A-296.
Raredon, Daniel & Rebeckah Ducy. 26 June 1807. R, A-284.
Raredon, George M. & Amanda Coale. Her father Thomas H. Coale
cons., witn. C. W. Veach, Henry Raridon. 20 Nov. 1847. MA,
R, B-114, B-118.
Raredon, Henry & Anna Buchanan. 5 Jan. 1844. MA, B-243.
Raredon, James & Mary Noel. 20 Dec. 1812. MA, R, A-323.
Ratcliff, Francis M. & Mary Jane Pearsefield. 10 Nov. 1855. MA,
D-22.

Ratcliff, Robert & Harriet Burt. 1 Sep. 1849. R, B-155.
Ratliff, John & Matilda Robinson. 13 Oct. 1851. MA, B-218.
Rauch, Peter & Barbara Painer. 12 Dec. 1853. MA, D-2.
Rawlins, Amer & Mary Jane Thompson. John Thompson cons., witn.
    William Thompson. 21 Nov. 1848. MA, R, B-145.
Rawlins, Charles & Susan Thompson. John Thompson cons.
    William Rawlins cons., att. James Thompson Jr., William
    Thompson, & Joseph Thompson. 5 Jan. 1843. MA, R, B-40.
Rawlins, Henderson L. & Sarah Thompson. John Thompson cons.,
    witn. James Thompson Jr., David Washburn. 21 Nov. 1848.
    MA, R, B-145.
Rawllings (Rollins), Charles & Elizabeth Perry, both of Green
    Tp. 9 Dec. 1813. MA, R, A-327.
Rawson, David & Susanna Triggs. 12 Aug. 1847. MA, R, B-106.
Ray, William & Harriot James. Her father cons., att. William
    Johnson. 5 Mar. 1853. MA, B-264.
Rayburn, Benjamin P. & Sebina Rollins. 25 Mar. 1852. B-235.
Raymond (Raynor), Philip & Lucretia Menager. 8 Oct. 1837. MA,
    R, A-236.
Raynold (Reynolds), George W. & Elizabeth Millar. Her father
    Abm. Millar cons., witn. Turner M. Mastin. 5 Jan. 1823.
    MA, R, A-71.
Raynor, William & Mary Barber. 7 Mar. 1833. R, A-174.
Raynor, William H. & Rhoda O. Kendall. 9 Sep. 1855. R, D-20.
Rea (Ray), Joseph & Olly Justice. 7 Dec. 1844. MA, R, B-67.
Read (Reed), William & Abigail (Mugail) Adams. 31 Dec. 1817.
    MA, R, A-36.
Rector, Frederick & Naomi Barton. 18 Sep. 1805. R, A-8, A-278.
Redd (Read) Travis & Mary Jaquett. 11 Nov. 1825. MA, R, A-93.
Redenger, M. & Mrs. E. Lodwick. He is 33, born Germany. She
    is 36, born Va., 2nd marr. __ Nov. 1857. C-13.
Redman, David & Jarusha Lucas. Her guardian Isaac McCanley
    cons. 26 Jan. 1860. MA, R, D-111.
Redmon, Simon G. & Catherine M. Omens. 28 Aug. 1860. MA, R,
    D-121.
Redoudey, Victor & Virginia Bernorden. 22 July 1856. B-287.
Redoutey, August (Aujuste) & Jane Boldman. 24 Dec. 1860. MA,
    R, D-139.
Reed, Calvin W. & Adelia Winkler. 12 Feb. 1857. R, D-46.
Reed, George H. & Margaret W. Walker. 3 Oct. 1849. MA, R, B-159.
Reed, Henry & Nancy Ann Babcock. 29 Mar. 1846. MA, R, B-88.
Reed, Lucius & Catherine P. Fitzmorris. 15 Oct. 1846. R, B-96.
Reed, Marshall & Louisa M. Chase. He is 24, born Penn., res.
    Jackson Co., son of John & Elizabeth Reed. She is 23, born
    Adams Co., dau. of Philip & Rosean Chase. 16 Oct. 1856. MA,
    R, C-5, D-39.
Reed, Matthias & Mary Ann Brown. 31 Jan. 1839. MA, R, A-264.
Reed, Pack & Loreno Dixen. 30 Sep. 1832. R, A-167.
Reed, Robert T. & Elizabeth Veach. 23 Sep. 1843. R, B-48.
Reed, Rodney & Jane Kelly. Her father Jacob Kelly cons. 13 Mar.
    1853. MA, B-261.
Reed, Samuel & Ellen Kinney. He is 24, born Pike Co., Oh., res.
    Portsmouth, son of William & Rebecca Reed. She is 24, born
    & res. Portsmouth, dau. of Washington & Mary Kinney. 20 (14)
    Aug. 1857. R, C-8, D-57.
Reed, Samuel D. & Nancy Joseph. 2 July 1854. R, D-8.
Reed, William & Rebecca White. 12 (14?) Apr. 1827. R, A-105.
Reeder (?), James D. & June Turn (Jane Turner?). 4 Oct. 1836.
    MA.
Reeder, James D. & Mary Jane O'Harra. 29 July 1858. MA, R, D-86.
Reeg (Rung, Roche), John & Charlotte Arnold (Ludia Ownoult).
    14 Sep. 1848. MA, R, B-131.

SCIOTO COUNTY MARRIAGES

Reeve, Volney & Theresa Vincent. 21 Oct. 1828. R, A-124.
Reeves, Benjamin F. & Calista Greensleve. 23 Feb. 1860. MA,
    R, D-112.
Reeves, Elijah & Mahala Nottingham. 5 Sep. 1820. MA.
Reeves, Hiram & Nancy Welsh (Walch). 9 Dec. 1830, by John Moore
    J.P. MA, R.
Reeves, Joseph & Margaret Jane Ishmael. 13 June 1828. R, A-124.
Reeves, Thomas & Polly Hoskinson. 5 Jan. 1822. R, A-64.
Reeves, William & Cynthia Ann Anderson. Her father Abner Ander-
    son cons. 26 Aug. 1850. MA, R, B-187.
Reeves, William L. & Serilda Gibson. Her father Samuel Gibson
    cons. 20 Oct. 1859. MA, R, D-107.
Reg, Adam & Margaret Dutes (?). 3 May 1857. R, D-57.
Rehlman, Frederick F. & Elizabeth Hanns. Henry Hanns att. ages.
    17 Aug. 1847. MA, R, B-106.
Rehur, Augustus & Sarah Ann Mapes. 1 Aug. 1850. B-245.
Reich, John & Sarah Herr. 6 June 1853. MA.
Reid (Reed), John & Rose Ann Mulhoren. 23 Jan. 1859. MA, R,
    D-77.
Reid, Thompson J. & Jane Fraizer. 27 Oct. 1860. MA. [A return
    without names, dated same day, shows a marriage was performed
    by Cornelius McCoy, J.P. It could be their marriage.]
Reigle, William & Ellen Culp. 16 Sep. 1855. R, D-25, D-29.
Rein, John A. & Eve L. Dernback. He is 25, born Germany, res.
    Cincinnati, Oh., son of Val & Mary Rein. She is 20, res.
    Jefferson Tp., dau. of Andres & Mary Dernback (Demback).
    13 Apr. 1857. C-10.
Reinhart, Nicholas & Elisabeth Knopf. 9 Sep. 1860. MA, R, D-122.
Reiniger, Frederick & Barbary Suiter (South, Suter). 14 Apr.
    1835. MA, R, A-199.
Reiser, John & Rosanna Reinedel. 26 Aug. 1857. R, D-61.
Reiser, John & Sophia Messerer. 27 Jan. 1858. R, D-68.
Reiter, Nicholas & Katharaine Kitting. 9 May 1835. MA, R, A-201.
Reller (Keller), Claimor Henry & Cathrina Cutter. He is "only
    son of John Henry and Elisabeta Reller from Ks. Hanober with
    Catarina Coetter, second daughter of Fredrig and Clara Elisa-
    betha Coetter on Harison furnas." 2 Apr. 1858. MA, R, D-71.
Rembert, John & Sarah Wheeler. 26 Aug. 1849. MA, R, B-156.
Remic (Remmick), George & Susanna Gifford. Her father Benjamin
    Gifford cons. 8 Aug. 1833. MA, R, A-179.
Remy (Ramey), William M. & Eleanor Smith. Her pars. Morgan
    Hampton & Mary Hampton cons., att. Charles B. Mason, Louis
    Smith. 15 Mar. 1855. MA, R, D-16.
Remy, William M. & Ruth Wilson. 2 Sep. 1860. MA, R, D-122.
Renfrau, Jackson & Sarah Runyan. 22 Feb. 1845. MA.
Renigar, George & Agnes Huddleson. 1 Jan. 1860. MA, R, D-111.
Renoad, John F. & Louisa E. Deemer. Her father Anderson Deemer
    cons. 1 Nov. 1849. MA, R, B-161.
Renshaw, John & Sarah A. Kinney. 29 Jan. 1852. B-231.
Reohn (Ream), Levi M. & Barbara Ulrich (Enrich). 4 Oct. 1849.
    MA, R, B-158.
Rese, Lafayette & Mary Ella Gorda (Gooden). 5 Nov. 1857. R,
    D-63.
Resley (Russley), James & Susan Roland. 2 Jan. 1835. MA, R,
    A-195.
Ress (Ross), George & Catharine Row. 23 June 1849. MA, B-244.
Retfier, Henry & Barbara Petusan. 27 Dec. 1849. B-245.
Reuder (Reiler), Frederick & Elizabeth Konig (Wys). 1 Dec.
    1851. MA, B-198.
Reuter (Rieter), Adam & Elizabeth Bumgarner. 19 Oct. 1849. MA,
    R, B-159.
Reuter, Frederic & Elisabeth Waller. 29 Jan. 1850. R, B-169.

Reuter, Friedrich & Catharina Coonsmann (Kunsmann). He is 25, born Germany, res. Portsmouth, son of John & Margaret Reuter. She is 22, born Germany, dau. of George & Mary Kunsmann. 14 Jan. 1857. R, C-1, D-60.

Reutzhauzen, Christian & Phillipean Bochner (Phebe Beakler). 26 Dec. 1843. MA, R, B-51.

Reynard, Jacob & Juletta Patterson. 24 Jan. 1830. R, A-141.

Reynolds, Abelard F. & Mary A. Jones. 27 June 1851. MA, B-210.

Reynolds, Abner A. & Elizabeth Ann Stevenson. 29 Nov. 1847. MA, R, B-110.

Reynolds, Church & Mary Downing (Downey). 6 Dec. 1842. MA, R, B-39.

Reynolds, Franklin & Elizabeth Elton Millar. 22 May 1827. MA, R, A-108.

Reynolds, G. & Amanda Coppage (Cartridge). 18 Feb. 1849. MA, R, B-142.

Reynolds, John & Sophiah Stewart. 22 July 1849. MA, R, B-153.

Reynolds, Lee L. & Martha Ann Jones (Janes). 12 Sep. 1852. MA, B-247.

Reynolds, Peter & Hannah S. Methena. 19 Oct. 1849. R, B-159.

Reynolds, Robert & Jane Reider. 29 Oct. 1821. MA, R, A-61.

Reynolds, Robert & Matilda Lopins. 30 Mar. 1854. D-1.

Rhoades, James Luther & Mary Ann Skelton. 16 Feb. 1858. R, D-88.

Rhoads, George & Katharine Miller. 23 Sep. 1840. MA, R, B-13.

Rhodes, Daniel D. & Mary Ann Leonard. 18 Feb. 1844. MA, R, B-53.

Rhodes, George & Annis Hicks. 20 Apr. 1854. D-1.

Rhodes, John & Maria Johnson. 10 June 1847. R, B-102.

Rice, Charles & Sarah J. Kirkpatrick. He is 23, born Carroll Co., res. Pike Co., son of John Rice. She is 19, born & res. Scioto Co., dau. of Jno. H. Kirkpatrick. 9 June 1856. MA, R, C-4, D-31.

Rice, Hiram & Malinda Canter. His father Charles Rice cons. 20 Oct. 1853. MA, B-271.

Rice, Jeremiah & Sarah Winn. 25 Oct. 1812. R, A-322, A-323.

Rice, Jesse & Mary Anderson. 18 May 1854. R, D-8.

Rice, John & Mary Jane Bennett. 22 Mar. 1854. D-3.

Rice, John H. & Mary Allison. 23 June 1854. D-2.

Rice, William M. & Elizabeth White. 14 July 1836. MA, R, A-219.

Richard, John & Maria Thompson. Silas Thompson att. ages. 30 Sep. 1860. MA, R, D-128.

Richards, Harrison & Rachel Anderson. Her father William Anderson cons., att. L. N. Higley. 2 Nov. 1860. MA, R, D-129.

Richards, Henry & Bulah Ann Edgington. 4 July 1847. MA, R, B-108.

Richards, J. W. & Martha Ann Fleck (Flick). 22 Oct. 1852. MA, B-277.

Richards, Jesse & Amanda Zornes. Her father Andrew Zornes cons. 23 July 1835. MA, R, A-205.

Richards, John & Mary Ann Darling. 20 Feb. 1845. MA, R, B-68.

Richards, Thomas & Susanna Yairs (Zairs? Lairs?). 18 June 1846. MA, R, B-87.

Richardson, John & Margaret Horn. 3 July 1835. MA, R, A-202.

Richardson, John W. & Elizabeth Spriggs. 18 Mar. 1852. B-240.

Richardson, Thomas & Margaret Crane. 27 May 1847. MA, R, B-102.

Richardson, William & Rosanna Hartley. 28 Jan. 1850. R, B-169.

Richardson, William P. (R.) & Elizabeth A. Allen. 27 May 1856. MA, R, D-42.

Richart, Harrison & Fanny H. Miles. 5 Jan. 1860. MA, R, D-104.

Richart, Henry F. & Sarah Kittle. 13 Dec. 1859. MA, R, D-105.

Richart, William & Ann Maria Clingman, both of Bloom Tp. 2 May 1826. R, A-96.

Richmond, Jackson & Matilda Mitchell. 27 June 1851. B-210.
Richt, Henry & Louisa Berstet. 17 July 1855. R, D-19.
Richter, Conrad & Catharina Rupert. 12 Jan. 1858. R, D-73.
Richter, Friedrich & Maria Stern. 29 May 1857. R, D-61.
Richy, William & Lucinda Thompson. 11 Sep. 1836. R, A-221.
Rickards, John & Rebecca Higgins. 16 Apr. 1834. R, A-189.
Ricker, Jacob H. & Mary F. Wood. 5 May 1840. R, A-270.
Rickerds (Record), Benjamin & Sabrina Killpatrick. 13 Jan.
    1830. MA, R, A-139.
Rickerich, Philip Peter & Caroline Maria Dennewitz. 8 Apr.
    1850. R, B-176.
Rickerig, Jacob & Catharina Seiling. 1 Dec. 1856. R, D-60.
Rickey, Ephraim & Anna Rockwell. Jacob Rickey cons., witn.
    Ezra Mead, Esther Mead. 19 July 1841. MA, R, B-23.
Rickey, Isaac Parker & Lydia Ann Henson. Her mother Elizabeth
    Henson cons., att. Samuel Henson, George Henson. His father
    Isaac Rickey cons. 25 Dec. 1859. MA, R, D-120.
Rickey, Jacob & Sarah Allen. 10 June 1838. R, A-255.
Rickey, Jacob & Abigail Kelly. Her mother Sarah Kelly cons., att.
    Jackson Kelley, Isaac P. Rickey. 25 May 1858. MA, R, D-89.
Rickey, John & Mary Wells. 6 July 1826. MA.
Rickey, Joseph & Sarah Snider. 1 Oct. 1831. R, A-155.
Rickey, Mordecai B. & Maria Steel. 12 Dec. 1848. MA, R, B-138.
Rickey, Thomas & Telina Rockwell. 8 Apr. 1854. D-2.
Riddlebarger, George W. & Isabell Ann Richeson. 17 Mar. 1852.
    MA, B-236.
Riddlebarger, William & Elvira Partridge. He is 21, born Jeffer-
    son Tp., res. Bloom Tp., son of J. & M. Riddlebarger. She is
    18, res. Bloom Tp., dau. of Dan & Elvina Partridge. 22 Dec.
    1857. R, C-12, D-74.
Ridenhour, Andrew & Margaret Adwell. 28 Aug. 1839. MA, R, A-272.
Ridenour, Frederick Jr. & Nancy Simmons. 28 Oct. 1838. MA, R,
    A-261.
Ridenour, Isaac & Betsy Eliza Diduit. 21 Oct. 1838. R, A-260.
Ridenour, Isaac & Maria Reed. Frederick D. Reed cons. 26 Feb.
    1834. MA.
Ridenour, John & Abigail Thomas. 1 Feb. 1835. R, A-197.
Ridenour, Samuel & Amelia Craine. 30 Jan. 1845. MA, R, B-67.
Ridenour, William & Catherine Halterman. 4 Nov. 1839. MA, R,
    A-273.
Rider, Henry J. & Mary Ann Peart. 10 Nov. 1837. MA, R, A-235.
Rider, Peter & Sarah Scott. 23 Nov. 1857. R, D-66.
Ridgely, William & Hannah Simmons. 20 Dec. 1810. R, A-307.
Rieder, Frederick & Catharine Redann. 28 May 1846. MA, R, B-86.
Riepenhof, Joseph & Catherine Rahrdt. 23 Nov. 1852. B-257.
Riesinger, Martin & Anna B. Strael (Strace). 30 Jan. 1860. MA,
    R, D-113.
Riesle, Adolph & Margaret Eck. 1 July 1852. MA.
Rife, Michael & Barbara Messer. 5 Nov. 1842. MA.
Rifinbunk, W. M. & Elizabeth Ann Johnson. 28 Nov. 1856. R, D-41.
Rigerish (Rickerich), John & Zelma Wheele. 1 Aug. 1860. MA, R,
    D-132.
Riggs, James W. & Mary E. Taylor. 17 July 1851. B-212.
Riggs, Stephen B. & Evadne Withers. 12 Oct. 1853, by E. P.
    Pratt. MA, R.
Rigly, John & Elizabeth Smith. 1 Oct. 1856. R, D-40.
Rigrich, John P. & Hester Williams. 7 Feb. 1853. MA.
Riker, Solomon B. & Susannah P. Stockham. 19 Mar. 1848. MA, R,
    B-122.
Riley (Kelly), George W. & Selah Kennedy. 4 July 1852. MA, B-241.
Riley (Kelly), John & Susan Smiley. Her father Nathaniel Smiley
    cons., witn. Moses Gerns. 21 Dec. 1845. MA, R, B-82.

Riley, Nathaniel & Tamar Lawwill. Her pars. Thomas J. & Sara
    Lawwill cons., att. James Howard. 8 Mar. 1855. MA, R, D-16.
Rinehart, John & Elizabeth Bradford. 17 Nov. 1851 (1850). MA,
    B-222.
Ring, Lawrence & Emeline Norris. 15 Apr. 1855. R, D-27.
Ripley, Wayne & Eliza Vigus. 26 Feb. 1844. MA, R, B-54.
Rippey, John & Elvira Orm. 3 Oct. 1848. MA.
Rissler (Kipler), John & Elliner Lelix. 4 Apr. 1836. MA, R,
    A-209, A-230.
Ritter, Frederick & Sarah (Sally) Campbell. Otha Dawson att.
    his age. 16 May 1811. MA, R, A-310.
Ritter, John (Johan Rupprect) & Mary Hock. 30 Sep. 1849. MA,
    B-244.
Roach, Jeremiah & Anna Rockwell. 14 Nov. 1837. MA, R, A-235.
Roach, John & Mary Snorgrass. Her father Robert Snorgrass cons.,
    witn. William Silvy, Rulaney Roach. His mother Elizabeth
    Roach cons., said his father is dead, witn. Rulaney Roach,
    John Kelley. 6 Sep. 1827. MA, R, A-109.
Roach, William & Salle M. Davidson. 25 Aug. 1859. MA, R, D-102.
Robberts, William & Nancy Connolly. 8 Sep. 1859. MA, R, D-101.
Robenson, Abraham & Rebeccah Logan. 22 Mar. 1814. R, A-334.
Roberts, Absalom & Matilda Fishburn. She att. she is about 30,
    has always been unmarried. 11 Dec. 1842. MA, R, B-38.
Roberts, C. W. & Mary Elizabeth Green. Her mother Susanna Green
    cons. 2 Dec. 1852. MA, B-278.
Roberts, John & Phoebe Jenkins. 11 Sep. 1828. R, A-122.
Roberts, John & Martha Dawson (Hewese). 13 Oct. 1850. MA, R,
    B-190.
Roberts, John J. & Mary Barker. 19 Sep. 1849. R, B-160.
Roberts, John W. & Mary Ann McCann. 22 Oct. 1853. MA, B-272.
Roberts, Lewis & Nancy Corns. 28 May 1834. MA, R, A-189.
Roberts, William & Elizabeth Warren. 23 June 1845. R, B-73.
Robertson, Andrew & Clara F. White. 15 Apr. 1859. MA, R, D-91.
Robertson, John & Fanney Horner. 13 Jan. 1824. R, A-80.
Robey, William & Mary Collins. Her father John Collins, of
    Alexandria cons., witn. Joshua Parrish. 9 Oct. 1807. MA,
    R, A-286.
Robins, Isaac & Phebe Darling. 15 Jan. 1831. MA.
Robinson, Andrew & Mahala Graham. 20 Feb. 1851. MA, B-203.
Robinson, Arthur & Amanda Utt. 28 Sep. 1845. MA, R, B-77.
Robinson, Henry & Amanda Degare. 19 Sep. 1849. MA, R, B-157.
Robinson, Hiram & Mary Ann Coon. 8 May 1842. MA, R, B-31.
Robinson, Horace & Mary Oliver. 10 Apr. 1853. MA, B-264.
Robinson, John B. & Elizabeth Rice. 28 Dec. 1848. MA, R, B-138.
Robinson, John M. & Hannah Bliss. 8 May 1851. B-208.
Robinson, Joshua V. Jr. & Malvina Scott. 17 Oct. 1843. R, B-49.
Robinson, Joshua V. Jr. & Martha B. Riggs. 10 Mar. 1853. R,
    D-161.
Robinson, Louis C. & Virginia Crichton. He is 35, born Indiana,
    res. Portsmouth, son of O. V. Robinson. She is 30, born &
    res. Portsmouth, dau. Cornelius McCoy, second marr. 18 Dec.
    1856. R, C-7.
Robinson, Lucien N. & Eliza Jane Riggs. 7 May 1839. R, A-268.
Robinson, Michal & Mary (Polly) Nail, of Bloom Tp. 12 Oct.
    1834. MA, R, A-192.
Robinson, William & Lucinda Hall. 19 Apr. 1832. MA, R, A-165.
Rockhold, John W. & Sophia E. Squires. 8 Mar. 1848. MA, R,
    B-116.
Rockwell, Benjamin & Katherine Bennett. Her father Robert
    Bennet cons., att. Thomas Bennet Jr. 5 Aug. 1819. MA, R,
    A-47.

Rockwell, Henry & Sophiah Millirons. Her father Michael Millirons att. she is in her 21st year, witn. Samuel Millirons, James M. Millirons, Selathial Millirons. 11 Sep. 1836. MA, R, A-245.
Rockwell, Isaac & Margaret Smith. 13 Sep. 1838. R, A-264.
Rockwell, James & Louisa Bennet. 4 Mar. 1846. R, B-84.
Rockwell, James & Elizabeth E. Shope. 5 Sep. 1859. MA, R, D-101.
Rockwell, John & Anna Allen. Ephraim Rickey att. her age. 28 Mar. 1841, by Isaac Fullerton. MA, R.
Rockwell, Joseph & Polly Bennett. 28 Jan. 1819. MA, R, A-42.
Rockwell, Leonard & Matilda Piles. 28 Nov. 1847. MA, R, B-110.
Rockwell, Lewis & Charlotte Squires. 24 Jan. 1836. MA, R, A-212, A-228.
Rockwell, Solomon & Cyntha Jane Godrich. 24 Feb. 1856. R, D-26.
Rodgers, James & Martha Mott. 30 Jan. 1851. MA, B-201.
Rodgers, Joseph & Mary Bradshaw. 17 Oct. 1847. MA, R, B-109.
Rodgers, Joseph C. & Isabelle Moore. 29 July 1848. R, B-130.
Rodgers, Leven & Delilah Dever. 18 Dec. 1855. D-23.
Rodgers, Levin & Elizabeth Calvert. Her mother Elizabeth Calvert cons. 6 Feb. 1827. MA, R, A-102.
Rodslaugh, Frederick & Elizabeth Reynolds. Simeon Canary att. ages. 13 Feb. 1852. MA.
Roe, James & Elizabeth Farney. 6 Jan. 1842. MA, R, B-28.
Rogers, Daniel & Jane Denney (Demsey). His father Levi Rogers cons. 30 Jan. 1839. MA, R, A-264.
Rogers, Elias P. & Susannah Spangle. 3 Mar. 1818. MA, R, A-34.
Rogers, Levi H. & Martha Shaffer. 22 Apr. 1837. MA.
Rogers, Samuel & Susan Snodgrass. 20 Dec. 1851. B-234.
Rogers, Thomas H. & Polly Boynton. Her father Asa Boynton cons., witn. Benjamin Locke. 1 Jan. 1822. MA, R, A-63.
Roland, John Richrd & Mary Kelly, both of Virginia. 23 June 1807. R, A-285.
Rolff, Gerhard & Laceta Dierky (Dekar). 1 June 1848. MA, R, B-125.
Rollin, William P. & Mary E. Dillon. Thomas J. Allen att. her age. 9 Sep. 1852. MA.
Rollins, Anthony & Nancy McGee. 3 Jan. 1837. MA, R, A-234.
Rollins, Eli & Sarah Black (Blagg). 6 Mar. 1853. MA, B-256.
Rollins, Elijah & Matilda Cable. 26 Nov. 1821. R, A-64.
Rollins, John & Rebecchy Piles. 1 Jan. 1824. R, A-80.
Rollins (Robbins), Joseph & Susan Patton. Her stepfather Louis Buman (Beuman) cons. 2 Feb. 1860. MA, R, D-106.
Roman, Thomas & Marth Dowas. 3 Feb. 1840. R, A-278.
Rose, Charles E. & Eveline Clugsten. 18 Dec. 1849. R, B-166.
Rose, Eli & Catharine Boldman. He was born Jefferson Tp., son of Israel & Mary Rose. She was born Jefferson Tp., dau. of Peter & S. Boldman. 10 (8) July 1856. R, C-5, D-33.
Rose, John & Mary White. 14 Nov. 1837. MA.
Rose, John & Anna Smith. 26 Aug. 1838. MA, R, A-258.
Rose, Peter & Mary James. 24 Oct. 1830. MA, R, A-147.
Rose, Richard & Patty Lewis. 14 Aug. 1820. R, A-54.
Rose, William H. & Eunice Johnson. 28 Mar. 1841. MA, R, B-19.
Rosebraugh, J. R. & Matilda Bishop. 7 Aug. 1857. R, D-57.
Rosebrough, Richard L. & Lucretia Hunt. Her mother Sally Hunt cons. 5 Nov. 1833. MA, R, A-178.
Ross, Charles & Scaniath Bail. 15 July 1851. MA, B-219.
Ross, Elias & Christina Turner. 24 Jan. 1831. MA.
Ross, Elza & Ann L. Batman. 15 Apr. 1847. R, B-101.
Ross, James F. & Elizabeth S. (T?) Hannahs. 21 May 1849. R, B-149.
Ross, Matthias B. & Elizabeth D. Tracy. 29 June 1843. R, B-47.

Ross, Samuel & Mary T. Russell. "Parents of both consented."
22 Mar. 1853. MA.
Ross, Samuel D. & Elizabeth Kinney. 7 Sep. 1847. R, B-106.
Ross, William & Catherine Burt. Her guardian J. Kindall cons.
6 Aug. 1852. MA, B-241.
Ross, William & Mary Hicombottom. 16 Nov. 1856. R, D-42.
Roth, John & Eve Hostetter. 21 May 1856. R, D-30.
Roth, Nicolaus & Mary Boose. 30 Jan. 1860. MA, R, D-112.
Rotherman, Anton (Anthony Rotherneil) & Christina Southpring.
12 Mar. 1840. MA, R, B-2.
Roundal (Kannals), Edward & Margaret (Mary) McNelly. 11 Jan.
1849. MA, B-139.
Rounsavell, David & Hester Clark. 11 Sep. 1823. MA, R, A-76.
Rouse, Henry C. & Levina J. Rutherford. 29 Sep. 1859. R, D-101.
Rouse, Reason & Martha Olehi. 23 July 1822. MA.
Rouse, Thomas & Elizabeth Weaver. 3 Jan. 1836. R, A-212, A-228.
Roush, Cornelius & Elizabeth Millirons. Her brother Adam
Millirons att. her age. 16 May 1813. MA, R, A-325.
Row, Christian L. & Caroline Baker. 28 Aug. 1859. MA, D-111.
Row, Henry & Mary Becken (Anna Maria Becker). 10 Apr. 1852.
MA, B-246.
Rowe, Charle & Martha Jeandau (Lundau). 12 June 1854. R, B-274.
Rowe, Charles & Lucina L. Squires. 30 Dec. 1847. R, B-121.
Rowland, Thomas & Charlotte Plumb. 8 June 1845. MA, R, B-73.
Rowley, Abraham & Josephine Taylor. 14 July 1839. MA, R, B-6.
Rowley, Edward & Elizabeth Ann Dever. 18 Jan. 1857. R, D-45.
Rowley (Rolse), George W. & Mary A. Carr. Charles Rowley att.
ages. 16 Feb. 1842. MA, R, B-28.
Rowley, Jackson & Emily Deavors. 24 Apr. 1856. R, D-29.
Rowley, Jesse & Cinthia J. Montgomery. 30 Jan. 1849. MA, R,
B-141.
Rowley, Josiah & Clarrissa Pile. 18 July 1858. MA, R, D-84.
Rowley, William & Nancy Dillon. 17 Feb. 1820. MA, R, A-58.
Royse, B. F. & N. A. Zorns. 24 June 1860. MA, R, D-120.
Royse, Benjamin & Rebecca Nicoles. 2 Apr. 1829. R, A-131.
Royse, Benjamin N. & Melinda Jane Shaw (Shew). 16 Oct. 1845.
MA, R, B-80.
Royse (Boyse), Frederick & Julian Heflin. 8 Sep. 1853. MA,
B-269.
Royse (Boyse), John N. & Sarah Pyatt (Pratt). Jno. H. Pyatt
cons., att. B. F. Temple. 8 Dec. 1853. MA, B-271.
Royse, Samuel R. & Nancy E. Hall. 8 July 1847. MA, R, B-107.
Ruburt (Ruppret), John & Elizabeth Gracian. 18 Nov. 1845. MA,
R, B-82.
Rückert (Rickup), John B. & Elizabeth Sherer. 2 May 1851. MA.
Ruckman, Abishai & Eliza Pool. 4 Nov. 1847. MA, R, B-110.
Ruckman, John & Sarah Carter. 19 July 1846. MA, R, B-89.
Rudmon (Redman), Frank & Ann Eliza Boldman. 27 June 1856. R,
D-32.
Rue, Jonathan & Nancy Powell. 28 Oct. 1841. MA, R, B-27.
Rulmann, Henry & Catharina Rahe. C. Meyer att. ages. 13 Jan.
1855. MA, R, D-14.
Rulofson, John & Catherine Morton. 28 May 1849. MA, R, B-150.
Runels (Reynolds), Calvin & Nancy Chesnut. 31 Mar. 1853. MA,
B-258.
Runge, Henry & Mary Anna Engle Reller. 29 Dec. 1848. MA, R,
B-138.
Runnelfield, Arnold & Jane Bailey. Aarom M. Bramble att. ages.
21 Aug. 1847. MA, R, B-105.
Rupe, John & Elizabeth McConnel. Her father John McConnel cons.
9 Oct. 1831. MA, R, A-157.
Rupprecht, Joseph & Magdalen Amann. 17 Aug. 1844. MA.

Rus (Rees), Anthony & Elizabeth Porn. 16 Feb. 1859. MA, R, D-82.
Rus, George & Barbary Raddle (Radell). 1 Apr. 1850. MA, R, B-179.
Rush, Burgat & Philipena Hurt. 15 May 1858. MA, R, D-88.
Russel, Thomas & Anna Hindman. 21 Mar. 1816. R, A-19.
Russel, W. B. & Rebecca L. Hibbs. 4 Aug. 1851. B-213.
Russel, William B. & Rhoda Heoredh. 1 June 1836. R, A-216.
Russell, A. B. & Augustine Vallaraider. 28 Oct. 1852. B-264.
Russell, Henry H. & Nancy Jane Grimes. 16 Nov. 1845. R, B-79.
Russell, James & Mary Barker. 8 Apr. 1859. MA, R, D-95.
Russell, John & Mary Jane Hill. 4 Feb. 1846. MA, R, B-83.
Russell, Lewis M. & Sarah Catherine Carpenter. He is 20, has
   no guardian. 25 Dec. 1854. MA, R, D-13.
Russell, Robert & Sarah A. Heoredth. 11 Oct. 1840. R, B-13.
Russell, William & Charlotte Ridenour (Redenfain, Redman).
   His father Thomas Russell cons., witn. James Walls, Joshua
   Walls. 16 Mar. 1833. MA, R, A-173.
Rust (Rush), John & Nancy Burriss. Moses Hayward att. ages.
   22 June 1843. MA, R, B-48.
Saddler, Henry & Sarah Martin. 14 July 1842. R, B-33.
Saddler, Henry B. & Elizabeth Bradford. 3 July 1839. MA, R,
   A-270.
Sadlar, Samuel D. & Lucetta Stumbaugh. 30 Sep. 1852. MA, B-277.
Sage, Samuel & Emma E. Robertson. Her father A. Robertson of
   Haverhill cons. 5 Oct. 1858. MA, R, D-83.
Sage, Stephen & Mary Winkler. He "will be 21 on Dec. 10, 1858."
   4 Nov. 1858. MA, R, D-79.
Sago (Lago), Michael & Dothy Spangler. Her father John Spangler
   cons. in a long letter, written in German, witn. Bennet
   Finton, Georg Leiuter, William C. Ludlow. 26 July 1837.
   MA, R, A-245.
Sailor, John & Catherine Hawkins. 17 Mar. 1829. MA, R, A-130.
Salesburry, John & Mary Liston. 10 Sep. 1811. R, A-313.
Salisbury, William & Ruth Myers. His mother cons. 3 Sep. 1812.
   MA, R, A-318.
Salladay, Daniel & Laura Nurse. 9 Mar. 1848. MA, R, B-122.
Salladay, David & Polly Sikes. John Sikes att. her age.
   24 Mar. 1814. MA, R, A-335.
Salladay, George & Pheobe Chaffin. 9 May 1812. MA, R, A-328.
Salladay, Ira & Eliza Norris. 14 Nov. 1839. MA, R, B-6.
Salladay, Jefferson & Adeline Grubb. Her father William Grubb
   if Vernon Tp., cons., witn. John H. Chaffin, William Grubb
   Jr. 1 July 1838. MA, R, A-259.
Salladay, John Miller & Martha Hayard. 11 May 1837. R, A-247.
Salladay, Josephus & Mary Hudson (Henderson). 23 Nov. 1843.
   MA, R, B-66.
Salladay, Silas C. & Caroline Nurse. 30 Dec. 1847. MA, R,
   B-114.
Sallady, Lemuel & Mary F. Berry. 7 Mar. 1850. R, B-174.
Sallady, Samuel & Sarah Gilkeson. 1 July 1806. R, A-281.
Salleday, Calvin & Catharin Berry. 20 Mar. 1856. R, D-26.
Salliday, Obadiah & Phoebe Nurse. 27 Sep. 1855. D-21.
Sallyards, Edward J. & Mariah J. Buffington. 14 May 1843. MA.
Sallyards, W. H. H. & Eliza Ann White. 4 Apr. 1850. MA, R,
   B-176.
Salsar, Joseph & Cinthia Ann Welch. 5 Mar. 1833. MA, R, A-173.
Salsbary, George & Nancy Brown. 22 Jan. 1850. R, B-169.
Salsbury, James & Nancy Kehoe, of Portsmouth. 19 Dec. 1819.
   MA, R, A-49.
Salsbury, Richard & Margaret McConkle. 11 Sep. 1855. D-21.
Salsbury, William & Julia Thompson. 18 Jan. 1848. R, B-113.

Salter, Jesse Boon & Mary Ann Hoover. 14 Aug. 1845. R, B-75.
Sampson, David Jr. & Nancy Bennett. Robbart Bennet cons., witn.
Dennis H. Hays. 21 Oct. 1823. MA, R, A-77.
Sampson, James & Peggy Bradford. His father cons. 2 Oct. 1817.
MA, R, A-30.
Sampson, William & Sarah Friley. Richard Friley att. ages.
31 July 1859. MA, R, D-107.
Samson, James & Elizabeth Wood. 28 Feb. 1855. MA, R, D-15.
Samson, Ralph & Huldah Brown. 13 Aug. 1826. MA, R, A-98.
Sanders, George C. & Sarah Hawkins. 13 Dec. 1842. MA, R, B-39.
Sanders, Henry & Matilda Welch. 6 Jan. 1859. MA, R, D-89.
Sanders, James & Maria White. 10 Apr. 1859. MA, R, D-94.
Sanders, Jonathan & Amanda Biggs (Briggs). 22 Oct. 1828. MA,
R, A-123.
Sanders, L. D. & Sarah Bennet. 28 Sep. 1856. MA, R, D-36.
Sanderson, John C. & Minerva Holt. 18 Mar. 1847. MA, R, B-100.
Sanford, Enoch & Mrs. Margaret Blundell. 11 Dec. 1814. MA, R,
A-341.
Santy, Francis & Aliana Rusia. 20 Apr. 1854. D-2.
Santy, Winbert & Cassy Jane Arnold. 4 May 1854. R, D-7.
Sapington, Elias & Polly Whitcomb. 26 Sep. 1830, by Luther
Wheeler. MA, R.
Sappington, Thomas & Jane Taylor. William Taylor att. her age.
4 June 1812. MA, R, A-321.
Sargent, John & Nancy Linn. 13 July 1823. MA, R, A-78.
Sargent, John & Deborah Thomas. 14 Dec. 1841. MA, R, B-26.
Saunders, Sylvanus & Polly Burk. Her mother Nancy Burk cons.,
witn. Samuel Vamoney, Jno. Clark. 18 Dec. 1816. MA.
Sauvageot, Jacephus & Catharine Faivre. He is 27, born France,
res. Portsmouth. She is 22, born France, res. Portsmouth.
17 Aug. 1856. R, C-2, D-49.
Savage, James Jefferson & Dorothy A. Hard (Ward). 11 Dec. 1853.
MA, D-5.
Sayre, Charles & Margaret Veach. 29 July 1847. MA, R, B-104.
Sayre, Daniel F. & Hannah Jones. 27 Aug. 1853. MA, B-267.
Sayre, William & Grace Ingils. 1 Nov. 1830. MA.
Sayres (Eseyers), Asa & Nancy Applegate. 26 Sep. 1816. R, A-23.
Scarff, Joshua & Nancy J. Bear (Beer). 25 Sep. 1838. MA, R,
A-260.
Schafer, Henry & Marie Kopf. 26 Jan. 1858. R, D-68.
Schander, Lucas & Margaret Zigler. 16 Dec. 1841. MA, R, B-26.
Schanhols (Sclionlold), George Frederick & Susannah Hoffman.
30 Jan. 1851. MA, B-200.
Scheeler (Schiller), John & Barbary Shaeffer. 9 Jan. 1851. MA,
B-198.
Scheill (Shall), John & Christene Baccus. 30 Mar. 1852. MA,
B-235.
Schellenger, Charles & Mary Jane Shultz. 31 Jan. 1859. MA, R,
D-82.
Schellinger, Lehman & Sarah Rollings. 19 Jan. 1856. D-24.
Schemmelpfenning, Hr. Fredrick & Margaret Bahrenburg. 24 Apr.
1848. MA, R, B-124.
Scherer, Michael & Anna Elizabetha Frische. 7 Oct. 1856. MA,
R, D-38.
Schmid (Smith), Michael & Christina Schmidt (Smith). Henry
Hauns att. ages. 20 Nov. 1849. MA, R, B-162.
Schmidt (Smith), George & Margaret Messerer. 18 Oct. 1851.
MA, B-220.
Schnitius, Bartholomew & Christine Hof. 31 Jan. 1856. R, D-25.
Schnorr, Benedick & Margaretha Stielhamer (Mary Stillhammer).
3 Jan. 1849. MA, R, B-137.
Schomburg, Louis & Elizabeth Dauber. 15 Jan. 1855. MA, R, D-14.

116

Schoonover, D. M. (G. W.) & Harriet Laughfert. 28 Sep. 1848.
MA, R, B-132.
Schoonover, Hiram & Debby Snowgrass. 7 Oct. 1852. MA, B-251.
Schoonover, James & Laura Wells. His father Hiram Schoonover
cons., witn. Timothy Wells. 15 Feb. 1844. MA, R, B-57.
Schoonover, John & Nancy Petit. His father Hiram Schoonover
cons. 7 June 1856. MA.
Schuler, Friedrich & Katharina Muller (Miller). 16 July 1857.
R, D-61.
Schum, Andrew & Magdaline Spunner. 12 Aug. 1857. R, D-62.
Schumpe, Henry & Catharine Louisa Mittendorf. F. Mittendorf
cons. 21 Aug. 1852. MA, R, D-9.
Schumpe, William & Maria Coriell. His father John C. Schumpe
cons. Her father Sela Coriell cons. 4 Nov. 1858. MA, R,
D-79, D-83.
Schuster, Conrad & Catharine Wirth. 31 Jan. 1850. R, B-170.
Schwartz, William & Elizabeth Fisher. He is 20, born Germany,
son of Jacob Swarts. His stepfather John Layher cons. She
is 19, born Germany, res. Portsmouth. 17 Feb. 1858. MA,
R, C-10, D-70. (Jacob Swarts may be brother - writing unclear.)
Scofield, William & Sureldah Dawson. 11 Jan. 1849. MA, R,
B-144.
Scoonover, Benjamin & Elizabeth Wheeler. 11 Mar. 1824. R,
A-81, A-88.
Scoonover, Isaac & Eliza Correll. 25 Dec. 1821. MA, R, A-64.
Score, Thomas & Mary Ann Swanter. 10 Nov. 1852. MA, B-278.
Scorour (?), James & Nancy E. Street. 17 Jan. 1856. R, D-26.
[Writing is barely legible.]
Scott, Alfred & Rachel Davis. 17 Mar. 1854. D-5.
Scott, Alfred & Cornelia Price. Her father John Price cons.
13 Dec. 1859. MA, R, D-102.
Scott, Andrew & Elizabeth Kelly. 2 Sep. 1842. MA.
Scott, B. B. & Elizabeth Squires. 30 Oct. 1854. R, D-11.
Scott, Benjamin B. & Dorothy Yeley. Her father Peter Yeley
cons., witn. Marshal C. Smith. 28 Apr. 1836. MA, R, A-216.
Scott, Benjamin B. & Ann Eliza Pile. 29 Jan. 1851. MA, B-201.
Scott, Benjamin B. & Julia A. Smith. He is 47, born & res.
Scioto Co., son of Robert & Elizabeth Scott, fourth marr.
She is 39, born & res. Scioto Co., dau. of Thomas & Hannah
Bennet, second marr. 14 Feb. 1858. R, C-9, D-74.
Scott, Henry & Elisabeth Dauber. 24 Aug. 1860. MA, R, D-122.
Scott, James & Kaziah McAuley. 10 Jan. 1850. R, B-167.
Scott, John & Catharine Fishburn. His father Hugh Scott cons.,
witn. Joseph Brant. Catharine is 19 years old the 18th of
August 1842. 31 July 1842. MA, R, B-40.
Scott, John & Levina Day. 28 Oct. 1847. MA, R, B-111.
Scott, John R. & Elmira Francis Mott. 2 Oct. 1858. MA.
Scott, Nathaniel & Sarah Horner (Homes). 23 May 1837. MA, R,
A-242.
Scott, Perry & Lucinda Bruner. 28 Oct. 1843. MA, R, B-51.
Scott, Peter & Maria Wilson. Her father David Wilson cons.,
witn. Joseph Brant. 18 July 1842. MA, R, B-40.
Scott, Robert & Elisabeth Burt. 12 Sep. 1810. R, A-305.
Scott, Thomas & Nancy Edwards. 20 Oct. 1850. B-196.
Scott, Uriah B. & Rebecca Davis. 17 Feb. 1851. MA.
Scott, William & Hanah Baker. 15 Jan. 1807. R, A-285.
Scott, William E. & Mary Bagbee. 4 Feb. 1847. MA, B-229.
Scott, William K. & Sarah J. Rose. 12 Jan. 1841. R, B-16.
Scurlock, Williamson & Martha J. Poor. MA dated 4 Mar. 1858.
MA, R, D-71.
Seahl, George & Catharine Koenig (Kanish). 10 Nov. 1851. MA,
B-222.
Seal, David & Pamley Danks. 2 Sep. 1858. R, D-78.

Seal, George & Jemima Perry. 2 June 1839. MA, R, A-269.
Searl, Miranda & Polly Coburn. His father Nathaniel Searl cons.
witn. John White. Moses & Mary Mault cons., say their dau.
Levina Coburn and her husband Jacob Coburn gave them Polly to
raise when not quite two years old. Levina is dead; Jacob
has left the country, and is probably dead also. Witn.
Solomon Dever, Jessee Mault. 22 Jan. 1829. MA, R, A-126.
Searl, Wyatt C. & Mercy White. Nathaniel Searl cons., witn.
Daniel White. 27 July 1834. MA, R, A-193.
Searls, Benjamin F. & Ann Murphy. John Murphy att. ages.
7 Nov. 1850. MA, B-199.
Sears, Nathan & Grace Newkirk. 20 Oct. 1818. MA, R, A-41.
See, Harvey & Clary Bend. 27 Mar. 1847. MA.
Seely, Amos & Sophia Bertrand. Her father Jno. Bertrand cons.,
att. Fras. Power, of French Grant. Witn. J. B. Bertrand.
29 Oct. 1835. MA, R, A-207.
Seibert (Saeberth), Henry & Sarah Needle (Nadle). 25 Oct. 1860.
MA, R, D-126.
Seibert, Jacob & Nancy Hodges. 19 Mar. 1845. MA, R, B-69.
Seibert, Thomas & Ellen Bramer. 13 Feb. 1845. MA, R, B-68.
Seidel, Heinrich (Henry Seattle) & Katherine Knight. 21 Sep.
1853. MA.
Seifert, Moses & Mary Menken. 3 Oct. 1856. MA.
Seifried, Alois & Mary Sturz (Plotz?). 12 Oct. 1857. R, D-66.
Selb, Remigius & Stantina Nagel. 21 Jan. 1859. MA, R, D-133.
Selfridge, Chester W. & Lucy E. Miles. 19 Sep. 1854. R, D-10.
Semon (Simmon), Joseph & Rose Bennarde. 25 Mar. 1858. MA, R,
D-74.
Senner (Senur), Robert & Mary McMasters. 1 Sep. 1848. MA, R,
B-130.
Senty (Santy), John Francis & Susanna Noel. 24 June 1848. MA,
R, B-124.
Serot, John B. & Elizabeth Andre. 11 Nov. 1819. R, A-49.
Serrot, Joseph F. & Emily A. Smith. 12 Sep. 1847. MA, R, B-108.
Serrot, Peter & Nancy Patton. 28 Jan. 1819. MA, R, A-44.
Seth, Hiram & Lavina Maple. He is 25, born Penn., res. Madison
Tp., son of Frances Seth. She is 17, born Penn., res. Jef-
ferson Tp., dau. of John Maple. 12 Jan. 1858. R, C-12,
D-70.
Seth, Jacob & Mary Rapp. 17 June 1848. MA, R, B-127.
Seth, Jacob & S. A. Ramsey. 17 Apr. 1855. R, D-17.
Seth, John & Jemima Bennet. 17 Oct. 1848. MA, R, B-133.
Sexton, John & Sarah Ray. Her father William Ray cons.
25 Apr. 1852. MA, B-239.
Sexton, John & Sarah Ann Williams. 18 Dec. 1853. MA, D-7.
Shabot, William & Sarah Smith. 5 July 1856. R, D-35.
Shafer, Henry & Nancy Long. 4 Aug. 1835. MA.
Shafer, John & Susan Winyard. 16 Sep. 1858. MA, R, D-85.
Shafer, Samuel & Elizabeth Wingard. 1 Apr. 1856. R, D-28.
Shaffer, Capatious & Susan Crouser. 8 Jan. 1857. R, D-46.
Shaffer, Charles N. & Eliza Ball. 10 Mar. 1824. MA.
Shaffer, George & Mary Lewis. Frederick Lewis of Alexandria
cons., said Mary was of age, witn. Ezekiel Blue. 15 Dec.
1814. MA, R, A-342.
Shaffer, George & Martha Wilcoxan, Washington Tp. 27 Sep. 1827.
R, A-110.
Shaffer, George & Elizabeth Hammerstein. 2 Apr. 1845. MA, R,
B-70.
Shaffer, Larken & Letia Ann Wells. 10 May 1849. MA, R, B-150.
Shaffer, Samuel & Mary Wait. 10 (16?) July 1848. R, B-127.
Shaffer, William & Sarah Bennet. 5 Nov. 1851. MA, B-230.
Shaffer, William F. & Hannah Clark. 24 May 1855. R, D-18.

Shaible, Friedrich (Frederick Shibla) & Julia Ann Barber.
27 June 1852. MA, B-239.
Shanaday, James & Martha McDonald. 24 Apr. 1854. D-2.
Shane, Levi & Lucinda Houchins. 19 Feb. 1838. MA, R, A-249.
Shane, William & Maria Williams. 26 Jan. 1850. R, B-169.
Shaner, David & Hanah M. Hitchcock. 28 Oct. 1858. MA, R, D-88.
Shaner, David & Elzina Vangorder. 6 Feb. 1860. MA, R, D-119.
Shaner, James & Susan Deamer. 18 Sep. 1859. MA, R, D-108.
Shaner, Peirsol & Sophia Laughlin. He is 43, born Beaver Co.,
    Pa., res. Madison Tp., son of David Shaner, second marr. She
    is 27 (26), born & res. Madison Tp., dau. of Jacob & Cynthia
    Bennet, second marr. 16 July 1857. R, C-8, C-11, D-64.
Shannon, Charles & Mary Ann French. 3 Nov. 1850. MA, R, B-191.
Shaw, Alexander & Mary Nichols. 2 May 1839. MA, R, A-268.
Shaw, Charles & Anna Wood, both of Nile Tp. 12 Nov. 1827. R,
    A-112, A-118.
Shaw, Johnathan & Nancy Royse. Benjamin N. Royse att. "I rec-
    eived a letter about two years ago stating that Samuel Royse,
    my brother and husband of said Nancy, was dead." 25 Dec.
    1858. MA, R, D-96.
Shaw, Joseph R. & Rachel Cornes. 26 June 1830. MA, R, A-143.
Shaw, William & Sibbee Lee. 10 Nov. 1825. R, A-93.
Shearer, George & Jane Berkshire. 21 Jan. 1841. MA, R, B-1.
Shearer, Joseph & Catherine Henken. 28 May 1849. MA, R, B-150.
Shearer, Joseph & Martha Fuller. 9 Dec. 1856. R, D-44.
Sheed (Sheid), John & Leny McKell. 16 Mar. 1847. MA, R, B-99.
Sheeley, Michael & Landersa (?) Wilson. 21 Aug. 1855. R, D-20.
Sheelman, Jno. & East India Dever. 21 July 1853. B-268.
Sheely, Henry Jr. & Narcisa Harris. 17 July 1831. R, A-154.
Sheldan, Samuel & Rachel Smith. 25 Feb. 1842. MA, B-120.
Sheldrake, Robert & Sally Hodge. 22 Sep. 1826. MA, R, A-101.
Shellieg, William & Mary Lambert. 22 Nov. 1855. D-23.
Shelpman, Cornelius & Eliza Pyle (Piles). 28 May 1843. MA, R,
    B-46.
Shelpman, Cornelius & Mary Kile. 26 Feb. 1852. B-233.
Shelpman, David & Margaret Marsh. 22 Feb. 1816. MA, R, A-19.
Shelpman, Isaac & Mary V. Brown. Her father P. N. Brown cons.
    20 Sep. 1860. MA, R, D-168.
Shelpman, Jacob & Peggy Dailey. 12 July 1814. MA, R, A-339.
Shelpman, Spicer & Susan Witherup. Abraham Snively att. ages.
    7 July 1850. MA, R, B-191.
Shelpman, William & Perthania Smith. 24 Nov. 1826. R, A-106.
Shelpman, William & Orella Bennett. 5 Jan. 1840. R, A-276.
Shelpman, William & Eliza Whitmore. 11 Feb. 1852. MA, B-231.
Shelton, Charles & Mary Jane George. 23 June 1844. R, B-61.
Shephard, Alexander & Maria Murphy. 27 Nov. 1850. MA, B-194.
Sheppard, Charlton & Margaret Eicher. 27 Nov. 1850. MA, B-194.
Sherer, John & Harrietta Sutter. Her father Georg Sutter cons.
    1 May 1852. MA, B-253.
Sherer, Valentine & Anna Catherine Stokes (Steker). 8 Jan. 1855.
    MA, R, D-13.
Shevlin, John & Margaret Wilch. 15 Dec. 1859. MA, R, D-118.
Sheward, Isaiah & Rachel Trexler. 23 Feb. 1815. MA, R, A-345.
Sheward, Nathan & Nancy Moore. 17 Oct. 1844. MA, R, B-63.
Shiel, Jacob & Margaret Brindle. 14 July 1841. MA.
Shields, Isaac & Mary Ann Liston. 16 June 1858. MA, R, D-86.
Shiery, Michael & Chestina Myers. 14 Aug. 1851. MA, B-216.
Shinalt (Canauts?), Thomas & Mary J. Philips. 5 Apr. 1850. MA,
    R, B-176.
Shipman, William J. & Elizabeth Ann Mitchell. 15 Jan. 1846. R,
    B-81.
Shober, George & Hannah Fisher. 26 Nov. 1847. MA.

Shoemaker, David & Harriet P. Kirkpatrick. 15 Sep. 1860. MA, R, D-128.
Shoemaker, Isaac & Margaret Brown. 30 May 1850. MA, R, B-180.
Shoemaker, Joseph & Salle Bonser. 30 Mar. 1820. R, A-57.
Shoemaker, Peter & Caroline Faller (Fuller). 2 Jan. 1841. MA, R, B-19.
Shoemaker, Samuel & Mary J. Taylor. 3 May 1854. D-3.
Shonkwiler, Daniel & Harriet Bennet. John W. Galford att. ages. 25 Dec. 1851. MA, R, B-274.
Shonkwiler, John S. & Mary Plum. 27 Apr. 1842. MA.
Shonkwiler, Simon & Phebe Monroe. 1 Nov. 1827. R, A-110, A-117.
Shonkwiler, William & Susannah Bennett. 11 Dec. 1851. B-226.
Shoop, David & Maria Russell. 2 Oct. 1858. MA, R, D-84.
Shope, Charles Wesley & Margaret Thompson. 20 Feb. 1838. MA, R, A-254.
Shope, Eli & Mary Titus. 1 May 1853. MA, B-265.
Shope, James & Armina Chatfield. John Shope cons., witn. Samuel Cable. 7 Nov. 1832. MA, R, A-170.
Shope, John & Elizabeth Chick. 25 Aug. 1847. MA, R, B-106.
Shope, John & Nioma Colvin. 21 Dec. 1846. MA, R, B-95.
Shope, Levi & Sarah Herrold. 9 Dec. 1849. R, B-171.
Shope, William & Margaret Call. Her father James Caul cons., witn. Hugh Call. 11 May 1815. MA, R, A-281.
Shoper, John Adam & Elenor Graves (Groves?). 13 Oct. 1829. R, A-135.
Short, James Harvey & Mary Crain. 21 Jan. 1853. MA, B-256.
Short, Stephen & Lydia McManis. 2 Oct. 1832. MA.
Shoup (Shupe), James & Julia O. Scott. Her father R. B. Scott cons., says she is of age, witn. Lawrence Shupe, Harrison Tp. 17 Apr. 1834. MA, R, A-201.
Shous, Jno. & Jerusia Adaline Hatt. 2 July 1853. B-266.
Show, James & Alma Wise. 15 Mar. 1853. B-259.
Showzer (Strawzer), Solomon & Lydia Ann Shook. George Andrews att. ages. 12 May 1852. MA, B-240.
Shufflin, E. G. & Penlope Barklow. 25 Feb. 1857. R, D-50.
Shulsh, John & Sarah Xentes (Antes). 14 Jan. 1830. R, A-138.
Shultz, John & Louisa Baker. 7 Oct. 1841. MA, R, B-25.
Shultz (Shutty), William R. & Agnes Orin (Asin, Farmer). 18 Dec. 1856. R, C-3, D-44.
Shunkwiler, George & Fanny Marshall. 1 May 1817. MA, R, A-28.
Shupe, David & Rachel Buckley. His pars. Jonathan & Mary Pyles cons. 28 Feb. 1859. MA, R, D-80.
Shupe, Lawrence & Polly Burt (Bennet). 27 Feb. 1834. R, A-188.
Shurdon, David B. & Jane Raynolls (Raynolds). 15 Dec. 1846. MA, R, B-95.
Shurtz, Andrew & Catherine H. Wheeler. 9 Jan. 1859. MA, R, D-82.
Shute (Shoot), Richard & Hannah McCarty. Her father Daniel McCartney cons. 31 Mar. 1814. MA, R, A-335.
Shuter, Henry & Isabel Kalder (Colder). 24 Oct. 1852. MA, B-249.
Shutt, John & Fanny Russell. 26 May 1825. MA.
Shutz (Sheelz, Streets), John & Izabell A. Parker. 25 May 1827. R, A-108.
Shwab (Swaab), Solomon & Caroline Coplands. 26 Nov. 1845. MA, R, B-79.
Sibert, John B. & Hannah Alloway. 2 Feb. 1855. MA.
Sickles, William & Corenthia Adeline Ripley. 2 Apr. 1835. MA, R, A-198.
Sidner, William & Amanda Craine. 27 Apr. 1841. R, B-18.
Sieck, Henry & Liza Welner. 10 Sep. 1854. R, D-10.
Sieck, John F. & Anna Marie C. Minke. 4 Dec. 1859. MA, R, D-106.

Siedfried, Jacob & Mary Anna Wolfel. 3 Apr. 1856. R, D-28.
Siefert, Hieronimus & Anastatia Brown. 20 Feb. 1854. MA.
Sigley, Daniel & Eliza Adkin. Her father David Adkin cons.,
    witn. George W. Adkin. 6 May 1833. MA, R, A-180.
Sikes, David & Rachel Virgin, of Porter Tp. 16 Jan. 1825. R,
    A-88.
Sikes, David & Katherine Rockwell. He was of Pike Co. 8 Feb.
    1837. R, A-239.
Sikes, Edward & Jemima Virgin. 31 Dec. 1818. MA, R, A-57.
Sikes, Hiram & Sarah Hoppis. John Hoppis cons., witn. John
    Snook, Katharine Hoppis. Sarah Sikes cons., witn. George T.
    Virgin. 8 Mar. 1827. MA, R, A-106.
Sikes, James & Lucinda L. Parks. 13 Jan. 1856. R, D-26.
Sikes, John & Polly Rockwell. Benjamin Rockwell att. her age.
    16 Apr. 1818. MA, R, A-38.
Sikes, Levi & Mary Keyes. 18 Feb. 1819. R, A-44.
Sikes, Melvin & Marun Seeley. 27 Jan. 1859. MA, R, D-79.
Silcox, R. S. & R. A. Varner. 11 Nov. 1847. R, B-109.
Sill, Richard & Polly Funk. 26 Mar. 1818. MA, R, A-37.
Silliman, George & Angeline Howard. 21 Oct. 1860. MA, R, D-135.
Sillimon, James & Mary Ann Snedecor. Her mother Elizabeth
    Snedecor cons., att. William Snedecor. (Not dated) 1856? MA.
Simmons, John & Esther Young. 25 July 1855. R, D-19.
Simmons, Stephen S. & Sarah Spangle. Her father Henry Spangle
    cons. 18 Dec. 1816. MA, A-25.
Simmons, Thomas L. & Matilda Fulks. 27 Oct. 1859. MA, R, D-106.
Simonis, J. & Nancy Shafer. 16 June 1852. MA, B-276.
Simons, Frances & Sarah A. Lewis. 14 Jan. 1858. R, D-73.
Simpkins, John & Loda Gillan. 16 July 1859. MA.
Simpkins, William & Jane Kidd. 6 Aug. 1859. MA, R, D-110.
Simpson, Cornelius W. & Susan Howe. 14 Oct. 1856. MA, R, D-38.
Simpson, Elias & Margaret Howard. 21 Apr. 1842. MA, R, B-31.
Simpson, James & Elizabeth J. Lewis. 4 Apr. 1839, by William
    Timmons, Minister. R.
Simpson, James Stackhouse & Pernina Chatfield. Her father R.
    Chatfield cons. 4 Oct. 1860. MA, R, D-126.
Simpson, John & Mary Noel. 3 Jan. 1805. R, A-3.
Simpson, Leonard & Margaret Dole. 18 June 1853. MA, B-279.
Simpson, Samuel G. & Raynetta Carter. 23 Sep. 1851. MA, B-216.
Simpson, Thomas & Melvina Castor. 17 Jan. 1847. R, B-97.
Simpson, William & Eliza Lewis. 4 Mar. 1837. R, A-239.
Sims, Robert & Julia M. Creighton. 10 Aug. 1859, by E. P.
    Pratt. MA, R.
Sinclear, Presly (Perry St. Clair) & Mary Mills, of Upper Tp.
    7 Feb. 1809. R, A-294.
Singer, Thomas & Elizabeth Downer. John McCormick att. her age.
    8 Feb. 1818. MA, R, A-35.
Sisler, Abraham & Elizabeth J. Moles. 10 Nov. 1850. B-193.
Sites, John & Margaret Speed. Barbara Tarhle (? German script)
    cons. 2 Nov. 1852. MA.
Skelton, Samuel Jr. & Cynthia Boynton. 5 Jan. 1847. MA, B-97.
Skidmore, Jackson & Cynthia Ann Garland. 23 Dec. 1852. MA,
    B-278.
Skidmore, John & Margaret Siberts. 14 Sep. 1859. MA, R, D-101.
Skifferson, Barry & Mary Haencey. He is 29, born Ireland, res.
    Portsmouth. She is 19, born Ireland, res. Portsmouth.
    2 Nov. 1856. R, C-2, D-49.
Skillings, Charles & Sally Baker (Barker). 10 May 1825. MA,
    R, A-90.
Slack, Harrison & Nancy Miller. Her father Jacob Millar cons.,
    att. G. M. Slack. 31 Aug. 1860. MA, R, D-129.

Slack, John S. & Rebecca Munnel. His father George W. Slack
cons., att. Harrison Slack. 24 June 1858. MA, R, D-88.
Slack, Samuel & Ruth Zaires. 27 Sep. 1849. MA, R, B-160.
Slack, Uriah & Sarah Bradford. Her mother Susannah Harris att.
her age. 22 Feb. 1827. MA, R, A-103.
Slack, William Johnson & Nancy C. Ferrel. His father George W.
Slack cons. 6 May 1852. MA, B-239.
Slateck, Madison & Lucinda May. 17 Mar. 1838. MA, R, A-253.
Slater, Samuel & Mary Colvin. 3 Oct. 1845. MA, R, B-80.
Slater, William & Priscilla Chapman. 26 May 1829. MA, R,
A-132.
Slattery, D. A. & Margaret Jones. He is 22, born & res. Harri-
son Tp., son of W. Slattery. She is 19, born Wales, res.
Jackson Co., dau. of William Jones. 17 Dec. 1857. C-14.
Slattery, Theodore & Sary Ann Pool. 20 July 1856. R, D-33.
Slattery, William & Lovina Hatch. 11 Sep. 1830. R, A-148.
Slattery, William & Mariah Stockham. Her mother cons., att.
Aron Stockham, Joseph H. Stockham, "further more that this
is a record of her age January 4, 1815." 4 Apr. 1835. MA,
R, A-198.
Slaughter, Richard E. & Mary Jane Hebsey (Kelsey). 22 May 1831.
R, A-152.
Slavens, James & Elizabeth Snedecor. 7 Apr. 1828. R, A-130.
Slavens, John & Rebeccah Crull. 25 Dec. 1828. R, A-127.
Slavens, Reuben H. & Julia Ann Sampson. 24 Sep. 1858. MA, R,
D-83.
Slavens, Stuart & Clarissa Schoonover. George Adams att. her
age. 26 July 1827. MA, R, A-108.
Sleeper, Parker & Margaret Sikes. 25 Jan. 1826. MA, R, A-97.
Slettery, John & Juliana Crull. 1 Jan. 1832. R, A-159.
Slimp, Alford & Ann Adelaide Chapman. 28 May 1856. MA, R, D-30.
Sloan, Patrick & Mary Jane Steal. 25 Jan. 1850. R, B-168.
Sloane, Peter P. & Melvina Lambert. 12 Sep. 1850. MA, B-191.
Sloat, John & Alice Ann Littlejohn. 20 June 1847. MA, R, B-103.
Sloat, Philip H. & Nancy J. Morrison. 15 Mar. 1849. R, B-149.
Slocum, Martin & Melissa Finney. 5 Feb. 1836. R, A-213, A-232.
Slocum, Moses C. & Elizabeth Squires. 4 Mar. 1822. MA.
Slocum, Samuel & Louisa F. Turner. 16 Sep. 1859. MA, R, D-110.
Slocumb, Cyrus & Perlina S. Wait. 16 Feb. 1851. MA, B-202.
Slocumb, Moses C. & Fanny Huddleston. 11 Mar. 1849. MA, R,
B-144.
Slocumb, Nathaniel & Mary Ann Turner. 26 Sep. 1849. MA, R,
B-157.
Slocumb, Uriah B. & Marietta Lair. 13 Feb. 1845. MA, R, B-69.
Sly, Joseph & Julia Ann Nearl. 13 Apr. 1856. R, D-29.
Sly, Samuel E. & Mary F. Buckley. 30 Nov. 1851. MA, B-224.
Sly, Tully Cicero & Cynthia A. Shope. 20 Feb. 1852. B-232.
Smalley, Thomas & Melvina Thompson. His father Abner Smalley
cons. 25 July 1852. MA, B-246.
Smalley, Thomas C. & Sarah Ann Price. Her father James Price
cons., witn. Josiah Smalley. 1 Dec. 1859. MA, R, D-105.
Smedley, George B. & Elizabeth W. Sullivan. 26 Jan. 1845. MA,
R, B-67.
Smedley, Isaac F. & Hannah Story. Her father William Story cons.
witn. George J. Smedley, George B. Smedley. 25 Feb. 1844.
MA, R, B-55.
Smiley, Richard & Louisa Culver. 31 July 1846. MA, R, B-90.
Smith, Abraham & Barbra Grogan. 3 Mar. 1833. MA, R, A-173.
Smith, Alxr. & Perthena Green Lee. 26 May 1817. R, A-29.
Smith, Alexander & Cynthia Hazelbaker. 25 Feb. 1852. MA.
Smith, Alexander & Elizabeth Brannum. 24 Mar. 1852. MA, B-237.
Smith, Alexander & Melissa Ann Willis. 7 Oct. 1858. MA, R,
D-78.

SCIOTO COUNTY MARRIAGES

Smith, Alfred M. & Charity Collins. 28 Oct. 1824. R, A-83.
Smith, Anthony & Julia Ann Haley. 12 Oct. 1826. MA, R, A-100.
Smith, Anthony & Electa Chaffin. 26 Dec. 1847. MA, R, B-113.
Smith, Benjamin & Esther Ann Bliss. 31 Oct. 1846. MA, R, B-93.
Smith, Charles & Elizabeth Dimner. 18 July 1850. R, B-183.
Smith, Charles & Mary McDowell. 20 Aug. 1859. MA, R, D-100.
Smith, Conrad & Anna Meyer. 29 Nov. 1853. B-282.
Smith, David & Mary Vastine. 25 June 1818. MA, R, A-39.
Smith, Eleazer & Harriet Bradshaw. 23 Jan. 1851. MA, B-200.
Smith, George & Minerva Howe. 18 Sep. 1851. MA, B-222.
Smith, George W. & Mary J. Watson. 26 May 1835. R, A-216.
Smith, George W. & Hannah Culp. 31 July 1845. MA, R, B-78.
Smith, Harper & Betsey Silvey. 21 Dec. 1834, by Mark Bradburn,
     J.P. MA, R.
Smith, Henry & Maria Carroll. John B. Carroll, of Clay Tp.,
     cons. 28 Feb. 1828. MA, R, A-115.
Smith, Henry & Elizabeth Radabaugh. 3 Feb. 1859. MA, R, D-77.
Smith, Isaac & Elizabeth Turner. 8 June 1815. R, A-281.
Smith, Isaac & Mary Eulitt. 17 Sep. 1829. MA, R, A-134.
Smith, Isaac & Amanda Garret. Her father Russel Garret, and
     Elizabeth Garret cons. 13 Dec. 1832. MA, R, A-172.
Smith, Isaac & Diane P. Wintersteen. 26 Dec. 1839. MA, R, A-275.
Smith, Isaiah & Trifena Noel. 1 Nov. 1832. R, A-168.
Smith, Isaiah M. K. & Christina Smith. 24 Dec. 1850. B-197.
Smith, Jacob & Elizabeth Barnhouse. 12 Apr. 1850. MA, R, B-181.
Smith, Jacob & Angaline Jones. 27 Dec. 1860. MA, R, D-124.
Smith, James & Louisa Cole. 13 Feb. 1812. R, A-317.
Smith, James & Jane Campbell. 6 Feb. 1818. MA, R, A-36.
Smith, James & Elizabeth Veach. 15 Jan. 1826. MA, R, A-104.
Smith, James & Polly Simpson. 12 June 1827. MA, R, A-107.
Smith, Jasper & Dianthy Hoit. 6 Apr. 1837. MA, R, A-243.
Smith, Joel H. & Melinda Erley. 24 Apr. 1835. R, A-200.
Smith, Joel W. & Christian Williamson. 28 Feb. 1850. R, B-172.
Smith, John & Mercy Stratton. 28 Sep. 1812. MA, R, A-318.
Smith, John & Nancy Cumston (Compton). Nathan Peyton att. her
     mother's cons. 10 Feb. 1814. MA, R, A-331.
Smith, John & Fanny Plumb. 27 Sep. 1827. MA, R, A-111, A-118.
Smith, John & Emesella Lemison (Euniscilia Tunison). 14 Feb.
     1828. MA, R, A-115.
Smith, John & Julian Searl. Her pars. Nathaniel & Rebecca Searl
     cons. 11 July 1830. MA, R, A-143.
Smith, John & Sarah Battles. 7 Mar. 1844. MA.
Smith, John & Phebe Ann Morgan. 7 Jan. 1847. MA, R, B-98.
Smith, John & Ann Loyd. (not dated) 1851. MA.
Smith, John & Sally (Sarah) Bennet. Jacob Smith att. ages.
     25 Dec. 1851. MA, B-235.
Smith, John & Margaret Smith. 15 Nov. 1860. MA, R, D-127.
Smith, John A. & Sarah Narley. 20 Nov. 1852. MA, R, B-273.
Smith, John C. (D?) & Drusella W. Wilcoxon. 25 Jan. 1827. R,
     A-114, A-119.
Smith, John F. & Mary Jane Orr. 2 Mar. 1854. B-283.
Smith, John W. & Maria Cook. 7 Aug. 1860. MA, R, D-122.
Smith, Jonathan & Bitha (Bethan) Melton. Anthony Smith att.
     ages. 20 June 1818. MA, R, A-39.
Smith, Joseph & Peggy Duncan. 17 Oct. 1834. MA, R, A-193.
Smith, Joseph & Margaret McCarty. Her father John McCarty cons.,
     witn. A. J. McFann, Joseph Smith. 12 June 1852. MA, B-241.
Smith, Joseph B. & Margaret Barnes. 17 July 1842. MA, R, B-33.
Smith, Joseph M. & Jemima Crull. 25 Apr. 1850. MA, R, B-178.
Smith, Joseph M. G. & Charlotte M. Hurd. 3 Nov. 1831. R, A-159.
Smith, Joseph W. & Cornelia M. Hancock. 17 Sep. 1845. R, B-77.
Smith, Joseph W. & Charlotte H. Paxton. Samuel A. Traugh att.
     ages. 31 Oct. 1859. MA, R, D-105.

123

Smith, Kilburn & Melissa Searl. Nathaniel Searl cons., att. her age over 18. 22 Feb. 1836. MA.
Smith, Kilburn H. & Mary Jane Perry. 15 June 1853. B-280.
Smith, L. P. N. & Rebecca T. Peebles. 10 Oct. 1839. R, A-276.
Smith, Laurence & Margaret Raugh. 16 Aug. 1859. MA, R, D-99.
Smith, Levi & Polly Pool. 7 Oct. 1828. R, A-122.
Smith, Levi & Mary E. Delong. 9 Feb. 1829. MA, R, A-127.
Smith, Levi & Sarah A. Redabaugh. 22 Oct. 1859. MA, R, D-104.
Smith, Louis & Ursela Waggner. 10 Dec. 1852. MA.
Smith, Marshall & Maria Ruckman. 11 May 1840. MA, R, B-4.
Smith, Mathew & Margaret Depoe. 25 Apr. 1839. MA, R, A-268.
Smith, Meek & Cynthia Ann McKinney. 16 Apr. 1841. R, B-20.
Smith, Melford & Jemimah McDaniel. 20 Nov. 1855. D-23.
Smith, Nathaniel F. & Maria Jeffords. 18 Dec. 1850. B-203.
Smith, Nathaniel F. & Rachel Johnson. 20 May 1860. MA, R, D-114, D-116.
Smith, Nelson & Julia Burt. 20 July 1844. MA, R, B-62.
Smith, Orson & Maria Whitmore. 22 Apr. 1819. MA, R, A-45.
Smith, P. B. & Jane Watkins (Walkins). 17 Jan. 1850. R, B-167.
Smith, Peter & Dorothy Thrush (Thenst? Thurst?). 12 Feb. 1840. MA, R, A-278.
Smith, Peter J. & Rebecca Moore. Forman Moore cons., att. her age. 31 Dec. 1840. MA, R, B-15.
Smith, Philip & Sarah Barnhouse. Edwin Knapp att. ages. 19 Apr. 1851. MA, B-206.
Smith, Reuben Junr. & Margaret Malone. 4 Dec. 1828. MA, R, A-125.
Smith, Robert & Margaret Ann Carrott. 21 June 1827. A-107.
Smith, Robert & Rebecca Smith. 29 June 1836. R, A-221.
Smith, Robert & Deborah Wilson. 4 Feb. 1841. MA, R, B-15.
Smith, Robert & Rachel Cole. 17 Jan. 1858. R, D-69.
Smith, Samuel & Mary Pollock. 11 Apr. 1850. MA, R, B-180.
Smith, Samuel M. & Viana Boldman. 8 Aug. 1858. MA, R, D-80.
Smith, Silas & Seela Ann Hazel. John Reed att. her age. 22 Sep. 1839. MA, R, A-273.
Smith, Stephen & Sarah Mills. 9 Aug. 1818. MA, R, A-40.
Smith, Stephen & Martha Fuqua. His father John F. Smith cons., witn. Cornelius Bradford, __ Burriss. 12 July 1838. MA, R, A-256.
Smith, Stephen & Rachel Scott. Lucinda Smith cons., witn. G. W. Smith, William Millirons says, "He has been actting and dooing for himself for abowt too years." 9 Nov. 1843. MA, R, B-52.
Smith, Stephen & Eliza Flarrity. 24 Dec. 1848. MA, R, B-136.
Smith, Stephen & Nancy Thompson. 23 Mar. 1848. MA, R, B-123.
Smith, Thomas & Martha MCan. 9 Mar. 1858. MA, R, D-73.
Smith, Thomas F. & Elizabeth McGer. Henry DeGroat att. ages. 10 Aug. 1849. MA, R, B-161.
Smith, Washington & Susan Trout. 16 Dec. 1849. R, B-164.
Smith, Washington & Vilina M. Perry. Her stepfather Isaac Malone and mother Margaret Malone cons. 11 Mar. 1859. MA, R, D-104.
Smith, William & Lydia Mustard. 2 Feb. 1815. R, A-344.
Smith, William & Sarah Burns. Her father Thomas Burns cons., witn. David Pollack, Michael Smith. 4 Aug. 1840. MA.
Smith, William & Orytha Thomas. 28 Oct. 1845. MA, R, B-87.
Smith, William & Lydia Snyder. 17 July 1853. B-265.
Smith, William & Anna C. Windell. 18 Aug. 1859. MA, R, D-108.
Smith, William E. & Margaret Ford. 27 Mar. 1856. R, D-26.
Smith, William S. & Phoeba Dawson. 4 July 1858. MA, R, D-88.
Smith, William T. & Emily Hamilton. 24 Apr. 1827. MA, R, A-106.
Smittle, William & Dorcus Smittle. 5 Feb. 1850. MA, R, B-172.

SCIOTO COUNTY MARRIAGES

Smothers, John & Jane Dauley. 4 Nov. 1847. MA, R. B-109.
Smothers, John & Cynthia Abigail Banes. 3 Oct. 1846. MA, R,
B-95.
Smyers, Frederick & Susan Crull. 9 Jan. 1812. R, A-315.
Smyth (Smith), Clarkson & Hannah Johnson. 25 May 1820. MA, R,
A-52.
Snedecor, John Jr. & Elizabeth Waltan. 1 Sep. 1839 (1837?).
R, A-273.
Snedecor, William & Polly Walton. 11 Feb. 1842. MA, R, B-30.
Snider, Benjamin & Serena Worley. His mother Elizabeth Snider
cons., witn. Martin A. Zornes. 24 Dec. 1840. MA, R, B-7.
Snider, Jacob & Polly Wilson. Her guardian Stephen Masters
cons., witn. Henry Snider, James Baccus. 29 July 1828. MA,
R, A-123.
Snider, James & Peggy Russell. 22 Mar. 1822. R, A-66.
Snider, James & Sarah Roberts. 23 Mar. 1820. MA, R, A-52.
Snider (Sinder, Linder), Leonhart & Justina Marquart. 4 Sep.
1855. R, D-20.
Snider, William M. & Mary E. Windell. 8 Feb. 1859. MA, R, D-78.
Snively, William & Mahala Wallace. 16 Apr. 1854. R, D-7.
Snively, William & Margaret J. Thomas. 2 June 1859. MA.
Sniverly, Abraham & Jane Smith. 21 Sep. 1855. D-21.
Snodgrass, James & Mahala Miller. 3 Nov. 1850. MA, B-193.
Snodgrass, John & Hannah Titus. Her father Tetus Titus cons.,
witn. Michael B. Coryell. 16 May 1825. MA.
Snodgrass, Robert & Minerva Canary. 16 Sep. 1838. MA, R, A-259.
Snodgrass, Willis & Margaret (Maria) Boys. He is 25, born & res.
Harrison Tp., son of W. & Hanna Snodgrass. She is 23, dau. of
Richard Boys. 23 Feb. 1858. MA, C-14.
Snook, Aaron & Elizabeth Hesler. 16 May 1822. MA, R, A-67.
Snook, Eli & Margaret Lee. 8 June 1843. MA, R, B-46.
Snook, Eli Wesley & Sophia Stumbo. 12 Apr. 1846. MA, R, B-85.
Snook, Isaiah & Polly Flemming. 21 Jan. 1827. MA, R, A-103.
Snook, James Harvey & Mary Kendall. 30 Oct. 1844. R, B-64.
Snook (Snuke), Jeremiah & Nancy Pitthone (Petod). 12 Dec. 1805.
R, A-10, A-280.
Snook, John & Barbary Hoppers (Hopps, Hoppas). 11 Mar. 1819.
MA, R, A-44.
Snyder, Andrew J. & Jane Dever. 26 Feb. 1850, by J. R. Turner,
and on 7 Mar. 1850 by Jeremiah Sailor. MA, R, B-172, B-174.
Snyder, Andrew J. & Mary Ann Johnson. 25 July 1852. MA, B-246.
Snyder, Henry L. & Jane Brown. 27 Jan. 1828. MA, R, A-116.
Snyder, John & Rosanna Chapman. 4 Jan. 1857. R, D-44.
Snyder, John S. & Sarah Mead. Judah Mead cons., att. Mehetable
Mead, Isaac Mead. 3 Jan. 1821. MA, R, A-57.
Snyder, Judah & Martha Rickey. 14 Mar. 1858. MA, R, D-74.
Sommer, Georg & Mary Glokner. 10 Jan. 1856. R, D-26.
Sommer, George & Mary Huchiens. 1 Nov. 1851. MA.
Songer, George & Mary F. Dawson. 29 Apr. 1852. MA, B-238.
Sonntag, Lewis & Caroline Suter (Schutts, Shuter). 9 May 1852.
MA, R, B-273.
Souder (Sanders, Louder), Samuel & Jane Williams. Enoch
Williams att. ages. 25 Mar. 1852. MA, B-236.
Southworth, Brison & Elizabeth Rickey. 2 Oct. 1860. MA.
Southworth, Elijah & Esther Rockwell. 1 Apr. 1847. R, B-102.
Southworth, Joseph & Cyinda Bennett. 19 Aug. 1852. MA, B-242.
Sowards, Charles C. & Catharine Hill. 18 Mar. 1837. MA, R,
A-240.
Sowash, Joseph & Mary Applegate. 27 July 1855. R, D-19.
Sowash, Robert G. & Catharine Degear. 26 Feb. 1852. MA, B-232.
Sowers (Lowers), Griffin & Rachel McLees. 4 July 1805. R, A-6.

125

Sownsby, Jacob & Catherine Faser. He is 30, born France, res.
Portsmouth, son of John Sownsby. She is 23, born France,
res. Portsmouth, dau. of John Faser. 9 Aug. 1856. C-6.
Spalding, Enoch & Sarah Ann Masters. Her mother Sarah Masters
cons. 27 Oct. 1830. MA, R, A-147.
Spangle, Henry & Margaret Jacobs. Her mother Hannah Jacobs, of
Jefferson Tp., cons., witn. George W. Lucas, N. B. Lucas.
13 Nov. 1829. MA, R, A-138.
Spangle, Jacob & Sarah (Sally) Johnson. 9 June 1816. MA, R,
A-21.
Spangler, Michael & Theressa May (Mai). 17 Apr. 1852. MA,
B-238.
Spellman, Harman & Mary Schaffer. 16 Mar. 1844. MA, R, B-57.
Spellman, Henry & Mary Relles. 18 Dec. 1842. MA, R, B-38.
Spence, Charles & Elizabeth Cochran. His father William Spence
cons., witn. John Spence. 26 Oct. 1836. MA, R, A-222, A-243.
Spencer, George T. & Sarah Jane Smith. 25 Dec. 1845. MA, R,
B-82.
Spencer, Isaac & Betsy Potter. 17 Dec. 1840. MA, R, B-7.
Sperl (Sperit), Johann Lemon Martin & Johanna Cattarina Webber.
6 Oct. 1844. MA, R, B-64.
Sponsel, Christopher & Elizabeth Horst. Her father cons.
24 Aug. 1847. MA, R, B-106.
Spradlin, Samuel & Sarah Ann Bennett. Her father Ira Bennett
cons. 25 Sep. 1852. MA, B-249.
Spragg, Caleb & Mary Jane Dunlap. 14 Nov. 1852. MA, B-249.
Spriggs, Benjamin F. & Eliza Dorch. 27 Oct. 1859. MA, R, D-112.
Spriggs, Jared & Charlotte Crull. 2 May 1844. MA, R, B-59.
Spriggs, Martin U. (A.?) & Mahala Brinard. 17 Mar. 1850. MA,
R, B-175.
Spriggs, Samuel & Emily Toppins. 16 June 1843. MA, R, B-46.
Spriggs, Teman & Mary Saney. 5 Feb. 1857. R, D-48.
Sprinkle, Elmadorus & Abagail Williams. 1 Jan. 1850. R, B-171.
Sprouse, John W. & Sarah Williams. 1 Oct. 1843. MA, R, B-48.
Sprowles, John & Christena A. Allen. 27 Oct. 1860. MA, R, D-126.
Spry, John W. & Louisa Davey. 2 May 1855. R, D-18.
Squire, Green & Margaret Noland. 5 Oct. 1845. MA, R, B-78.
Squire, John & Antoinette Vincent. Her father Anthony C.
Vincent cons., of French Grant. 8 Nov. 1823. MA.
Squire, Nathaniel & Elizabeth Mead. 9 June 1850. R, B-182.
Squires, Benjamin & Diane Robins (Roberts). Elijah Hudson att.
her age. 4 Jan. 1827. MA, R, A-103.
Squires, Ezra M. & Margaret Pool. His guardian Benjamin B.
Scott cons., att. Thomas J. Crull, John Squires. 4 Nov.
1860. MA, R, D-136.
Squires, Green B. & Lucy Kittle. 25 Aug. 1850. MA, R, B-188.
Squires, Henry (Harry) & Elizabeth Richards. Her mother
Elizabeth Williamson cons. 2 Feb. 1835. MA, R, A-196.
Squires, Jesse & Catherine Green. Richard Kiser att. ages.
25 Aug. 1858. MA.
Squires, John & Lucina Lamb. Her father Reuben Lamb, of Green
Tp., cons., witn. Edward Lamb, Willard Lamb. 30 Mar. 1822.
MA, R, A-65.
Squires, Lemuel H. & Elizabeth Bishop. 28 (27) Oct. 1839. MA,
R, B-12, A-274.
Squires, Robert T. & Rebecca McCowan. 30 Sep. 1847. MA, R,
B-110.
Squires, Thadious & Rhuama Pool. 28 Feb. 1828. R, A-116.
Squires, William H. & Jane M. Schoonover. 26 Dec. 1843. MA,
R, B-53.
St. Clair, John & Eliza Jane Lute. Her father Robert Lute cons.
10 May 1852. MA.

Stagg, Marlen (Martin) & Statis Combs (Corns). Joseph Staggs
cons., witn. James Thomas, Samuel Criswell. 3 Nov. 1829.
MA, R, A-135.
Staggs, Henry & Clarrissa Saxon. 3 Sep. 1858. MA, R, D-89.
Stahl (Seahl), Christian & Margaret Chilley. 28 Dec. 1852. MA.
Stam, Christian & Mary Eck. 12 July 1858. MA, R, D-86.
Stanford, Alexander J. & Nancy Gairy. 27 Nov. 1834. MA, R,
A-193.
Stanley, Isaac & Susannah Graves. 1 Jan. 1826. MA, R, A-104.
Stansbury, George L. & Mary Blair. 8 Nov. 1846. MA, R, B-97.
Stanton, John & Emma Carter. 29 Nov. 1860. MA.
Stanton, Solomon & Mary Ann Jackson. 12 Apr. 1838. R, A-252.
Stapleton, Henry & Ellen Degraut. 6 Dec. 1849. R, B-164.
Stapleton, William & Ann Goheen. 4 Dec. 1850. MA, B-223.
Starr, Jeremiah & Sally Scott. 13 Jan. 1825. R, A-86.
Starr, John & Elizabeth Sheeler (Wheeler). Her pars. David &
Jane Sheeler, of Bloom Furnace cons., witn. George B. Taylor.
16 Feb. 1840. MA, R, A-278.
Statham, Enoch & Catherine Anderson. Her father Elijah Anderson
cons., witn. Enoch M. Ewing. His mother, Priscilla Stathem
att. his age, witn. John Hoobler. 30 Jan. 1826. MA, R, A-95.
Stecklin (Stuckle), George Fredric & Elizabeth Schram. 28 Mar.
1850. MA, R, B-175.
Steece, Jacob & Louisiana Daniels. 7 Apr. 1842. R, B-32.
Steel, William B. & Julia Ann Oard. __ Apr. 1836. MA, R, A-214.
Steele, Thomas J. & Isabella Bruce. 17 Jan. 1844. MA, B-242.
Steinbergan, Charles & Levise Lucas. 7 Sep. 1809. R, A-297.
Stemshorn, Frederick & Lana Clause. 17 Oct. 1839. MA, R, A-273.
Stener, John & Mary Horn. 2 June 1856. B-287.
Stephens, Jacob & Mary Jane Lewis. 26 Aug. 1849. R, B-157.
Stephens, John & Margaret Loutherback. 13 Jan. 1857. R, D-44.
Stephens, John J. & Julia Bennett. John Bennett att. ages.
5 Aug. 1858. MA, R, D-85.
Stephens, William & Caroline Hawkins. 30 Jan. 1849. MA, R,
B-141.
Stephenson, Absolem & Sarah Bacon. 21 July 1817. R, A-29.
Stephenson, Chendenen & Anna Baily. 30 May 1848. R, B-128.
Stephenson, John & Rachel Wilson. 7 Feb. 1853. MA, R, D-7.
Stephenson, Robert D. & Sarah J. Parks. 10 Feb. 1857. R, D-47.
Sterling, Abraham & Corinda Johnson. 21 Feb. 1837. MA, R,
A-239.
Stevens, Calvin Jefferson & Cynthia Angeline Ripley. His mother
Charlotte Stevens cons., witn. Jordan Vigus, Wayne Ripley.
5 July 1844. MA, R, B-60.
Stevens, James & Nancy Brock (Buck). Aaron Hollingshead att.
ages. 10 May 1852. MA, B-240.
Stevens (Stewart), John & Elizabeth Williams. 12 Sep. 1844.
MA, R, B-63.
Stevenson, George & Hester Ann Montgomery. 29 Apr. 1833? (This
is in a list of couples, not individually dated.) R, A-174.
Steward, Alexander & Eunice Crawford. Her father William
Crawford cons., said she was over 14, witn. Ira Bennet.
29 July 1827. MA, R, A-102.
Steward, Henry & Emeline Shoemaker. 13 Aug. 1860. MA, R, D-129.
Stewart, Alexander & Sarah Shockley. 3 Dec. 1842. R, B-37.
Stewart, Amos (Annanias) & Dorcas Baccus (Bacuse). 13 Nov. 1825.
R, A-95.
Stewart, David & Elizabeth Adams. 9 Sep. 1845. R, B-77.
Stewart, George & Sally Conner (Counce?). 26 Dec. 1816, by
John Brown, J.P.   MA, R.
Stewart, Hugh & Elizabeth Duncan. 2 Jan. 1840. R, A-277.

Stewart, Hugh D. & Wilhelmina Bradford. His father Gilbert
  Stewart cons., att. Rufus R. Tucker. 6 Dec. 1860. MA, R,
  D-130.
Stewart, James & Sarah Ann Fishburn. 2 Sep. 1852. MA, B-246.
Stewart, John & Rebecca Street. 23 Jan. 1853. MA, B-259.
Stewart, John G. & Susan Maria Wilson. 16 Oct. 1856. R, D-39.
Stewart, John L. & Mercy Ann McNeal. 15 June 1854. D-1.
Stewart (Sturd), John W. & Polly Beloat. 11 Nov. 1827. MA, R,
  A-111, A-118.
Stewart, Manley & Mary Chapman. 28 Nov. 1849. MA, R, B-163.
Stewart, Nelson & Myra Chamberlain. 24 Dec. 1844. MA.
Stewart, Nelson & Laura F. Chamberlain. 5 Mar. 1850. MA, R,
  B-174.
Stewart, Paul & Susannah Wampler. 6 May 1847. MA, R, B-101.
Stewart, Stephen & Caroline Duduit. Her father W. Duduit cons.,
  witn. George Stuart, Jno. Stuart. 23 Mar. 1815. MA, R,
  A-347.
Stewart, Thomas & Elizabeth Cloud. 1 Oct. 1836. MA, R, A-223.
Stewart, William & Cynthia Chapman. 12 Nov. 1848. MA, R, B-140.
Stewert, Thomas & Pollie Culp. 27 Aug. 1857. R, D-59.
Stickrodh, Conrad & Rosanna Seal. 9 Oct. 1853. MA, B-273.
Stieber (Sheber), Frederick & Catherine Popra. 28 Oct. 1858.
  MA, R, D-83.
Stiles, Calvin & Miranda Jane Miles. Her stepfather J. F.
  Morton cons. 18 Dec. 1853. MA, D-2.
Stiles, Enos & Nancy Co. 3 Mar. 1850. R, B-191.
Stiles, George & Harriet Squires. 22 Nov. 1825. MA, R, A-93.
Stiles, George & Mary Ann Stewart. 4 Dec. 1828. R, A-128.
Stipp, William & Margaret Downing. 15 Aug. 1846. MA, R, B-90.
Stirling, James & Ann Marie Weldin. 23 Jan. 1834. R, A-186.
Stiver (Stiner), Peter & Anna Adams. 9 Nov. 1853. MA, B-269.
Stivers, Daniel & Jane Burt. 1 Apr. 1852. MA, B-236.
Stivers, Randall & Permelia Westfall. 6 Mar. 1851. MA, B-204.
Stockham, Aaron & Rhuhamy Sikes. 6 May 1811. MA, R, A-309.
Stockham, Aaron Jr. & Huldah McConnel. 18 Mar. 1837. MA.
Stockham, Aaron & Hannah Wisecup. 10 May 1838. MA, R, A-257.
Stockham, Aaron & Lucinda Piles. 28 Mar. 1840. MA, R, B-4.
Stockham, Aaron & Nancy Tucker. 15 Aug. 1853. MA, B-267.
Stockham, Allen & Sarah Crull. 2 Sep. 1855. D-21.
Stockham, Daniel P. & Margaret Bennett. Her father Thomas
  Bennet cons., witn. Caleb Bennet. 25 Mar. 1824. MA, R, A-81.
Stockham, David & Martha Wells. Her father Richard Wells cons.,
  witn. James Wells. 10 Sep. 1818. MA, R, A-40.
Stockham, David J. & Rebecca Larrimore. 30 Jan. 1847. MA.
Stockham, David J. & Mary A. Grimes. 8 May 1851. MA, B-208.
Stockham, Isaac & Margaret McCall. 8 Jan. 1839. MA, R, A-264.
Stockham, John & Nancy Cahall. Her father Franky Cahall cons.,
  witn. William Thompson. 9 July 1808. MA.
Stockham, John & Hannah Bennight. 25 Dec. 1823. MA, R, A-79.
Stockham, John & Catherine Price. 22 July 1839. MA, R, B-14.
Stockham, John & Calferna Chaffin. 20 Mar. 1845. R, B-70.
Stockham, Joseph & Hannah Bennet. 25 Mar. 1808. R, A-288.
Stockham, Joseph H. & Catharine A. Dewey. 7 Mar. 1843. MA, R,
  B-45.
Stockham, Makenzie & Lucetta Squires. 29 May 1851. MA, B-214.
Stockham, Richard J. & Sarah Rickey. John S. Rickey att. ages.
  16 Dec. 1847. MA, R, B-115.
Stockham, Richard J. & Rebecca Wells. 15 June 1853. MA, B-270.
Stockham, Thomas & Sophronia Chamberlain. 17 Feb. 1848. MA, R,
  B-116.
Stockham, William & Elenor Bennet. 25 Jan. 1816. R, A-18.
Stockham, William H. & Abigail Adams. 23 Jan. 1839. MA, R, A-265.

Stockham, William J. & Elizabeth S. Bennett. 18 Jan. 1849. MA,
R, B-147.
Stockham, William P. & Sarah Fields. 2 Mar. 1840. MA, R, B-2.
Stoddard, David & Salley Clark. Her pars. Samuel & Betsey
Maloan cons., witn. Alexander Crawford. 13 Jan. 1833. MA,
R, A-173.
Stoddard (Strodder), Elias R. & Christina Turner. 29 Apr. 1833?
(Their marriage is among a list of twelve, not individually
dated. There is a marriage affidavit of Jan. 24, 1831 for
Elias Ross & Christina Turner.) R, A-174.
Stombaugh, Peter & Rachel Anderson. 19 Mar. 1836. R, A-208.
Stone, James S. & Sarah Ann Morris. 5 Dec. 1855. R, D-25.
Stone, John R. & Susan Bisler (Rister). 9 May 1856. MA, R,
D-30.
Stone, Phenias & Sarah Evans. He is 24, res. Portsmouth, son of
P. & Anna Stone. She is 18, born Tipton, England, res. Ports-
mouth, dau. of James & Lydia Evans. 24 Dec. 1856. R, C-4,
D-43.
Stone, T. S. & Mary E. Locy. Her pars. Isaac & Phebe Locy cons.
His father Jason L. Stone cons. 31 Jan. 1855. MA, R, D-13.
Stone (Stour, Storre), William & Susannah E. Noel. 25 Sep. 1843.
MA, R, B-48.
Stonebraker, Joseph A. & Emily J. Cropper. Daniel F. Culley att.
ages. 11 May 1859, by E. P. Pratt. MA, R.
Stoner, Samuel & (no bride's name). David Stoner cons. 21 Aug.
1826. MA.
Stoner, William & Addean E. Maddock. 5 May 1858, by E. P. Pratt.
MA, R.
Storer, Asher & Elizabeth Storer. 2 Aug. 1832. R, A-166.
Storer, David & Deanna Macketee (Dianna McAtee). 20 Jan. 1820.
R, A-51.
Storer, David & Alvina Mott. 15 Jan. 1846. R, B-83.
Storer, Levi & Viola Woodruff. 14 Aug. 1851. B-213.
Storer, William & Elleanor Bonser. 28 Nov. 1852. MA, B-256.
Storm, Fielding & Emily Nichols. 30 Nov. 1829. MA, R, A-137.
Story, Francis & Sarah Hammond. 25 Apr. 1837. R, A-241.
Story, Richard & Catherine Hamilton. 25 Apr. 1858. MA, R, D-74.
Stout, Obadiah & Mary Roberts. Squire Wallace att. her age.
11 May 1840. MA, R, B-8.
Strain, Samuel & Irena Dawson. Sylvester Hughes att. that Moses
K. & Sally Dawson cons. 25 Mar. 1852. MA, B-236.
Strait, George & Ruthy Lewis. 26 Aug. 1860. MA, R, D-121.
Stram, John & Maymeliana Wieland. 12 May 1856. R, D-30.
Streaks (Striker?), Tiffin & Mary Haggerty. 8 Feb. 1854. D-5.
Street, James W. & Joanna Clark. 10 Nov. 1827. MA, R, A-112.
Strickland, Edward & Lydia Triggs. 17 Apr. 1856. MA, R, D-29.
Strickland, Edward & Martha Jane Katon. Her father T. T. Katon
cons. 18 Oct. 1859. MA, R, D-109.
Strickland, William & Elizabeth Lamb. 17 Dec. 1848. MA, R,
B-140.
Stricklett, Lewis & Elizabeth Ruggles. 24 Sep. 1829. R, A-136.
Strobel, John & Catherine Bennon (Bermon). 6 Dec. 1849. R,
B-163.
Strobel, Paul & Mary Oret. 13 Feb. 1858. R, D-74.
Strobridge, Phedrus & Margaret Laird. 5 Mar. 1816. MA.
Strohm, David & Frederica Reichert. 13 Sep. 1858. MA, R, D-83.
Struttner, Henry & Barbara Baum. 15 Feb. 1844, by Joseph O'Mealy,
Catholic Clergyman. MA, R.
Stuart, James & Hariet Shonkwiler. 27 Dec. 1849. R, B-169.
Stuart, Jefferson & Clarinda Canter. 14 Dec.(1855?). D-23.
Stucky, Orlando W. & Rachel Skonten. 8 Mar. 1857. R, D-50.
Stumbaugh, Thomas & Mary Ann Brock. 12 July 1833. MA, R, A-181.

SCIOTO COUNTY MARRIAGES

Stumbo, David & Joanna Janes. 14 Apr. 1853. MA, B-266.
Sturdy, George & Lidia Allard. 6 Apr. 1853. MA, B-259.
Sturgeon (Sturgill), Henderson & Arville Cutright (Cartright).
15 Feb. 1853. MA, R, D-14.
Sturgeon, John C. & Sarah Jane Helm. 21 Apr. 1842. R, B-30.
Suitor (Sinton?), Valentine & Elizabeth Winant. 7 May 1838.
MA, R, A-253.
Sullivan, Daniel & Bridget Dejnen (Degnen). 30 Apr. 1856. R,
D-28.
Sullivan, Florence H. & Eliza Ann Howes. 26 June 1844. MA.
Sullivan, George & Rebecca Carter (Canter?). 7 Nov. 1847. MA,
R, B-110.
Sullivan, George & Nancy Hensel. His father John Sullivan cons.,
att. William White. 13 Sep. 1853. MA, B-272.
Sullivan, James & Henriett Smith. 14 May 1844. MA, R, B-59.
Sullivan, James & Julia Ann Hudson. 20 Dec. 1846. MA, R, B-98.
Sullivan, Ml. & Hannah Neil. He is 35, res. Portsmouth, second
marr. She is 28, born Ireland, res. Portsmouth, first marr.
29 Jan. 1856. C-1.
Sullivan, Michael & Anne Campbell. 26 Nov. 1857. R, D-69.
Sullivan, W. & Catherine Nehol (Achol). 25 Apr. 1856. R, D-49.
Sultzman, Christian & Magdalene Seibold. 25 Feb. 1858. R, D-71.
Sulzmann, Christian & Catharine Betz. 21 July 1845. MA, R,
B-74.
Summer, Anthony & Christine Hensian. Jacob Sheeley att. her
age. 11 Nov. 1848. MA, R, B-134.
Summers, Madison & Manerva Thompson. His mother Susan Summers
cons. 16 Oct. 1859. MA, R, D-110.
Sun, John & Catharine Henderson. 1 July 1849. R, B-152.
Surmann, Jacob (Jacque) & Margaret Thiebaux. 5 June 1858. MA,
R, D-80.
Sutherland, Alexander & Margaret Coleman. He is 23, she is 19.
11 Sep. 1856. R, D-35.
Sutherland, Samuel & Thermuthus Mitchell. 28 Jan. 1840. MA, R,
A-277.
Sutherlin, George H. & Mary K. Tracy. 30 Nov. 1853. MA, D-5.
Sutterfield, John & Anna Smith. 14 Dec. 1839. MA.
Suttle, R. L. & Caroline C. Worley. 8 May 1855. R, D-18.
Swager, Isaac & June Broker. 24 Dec. 1857. R, D-68.
Swager, John & Rebecca Smith. 25 Dec. 1853. D-4.
Swaim, F. M. & Elisabeth Fixley. He is 20, born Athens Co., Oh.,
son of G. & Lucinda Swaim. She is 18, born & res. Scioto Co.,
Oh., dau. of Daniel & Martha Fixley. 24 May 1857. R, C-11,
D-54.
Swain, John G. & Louise Vincent. 20 July 1826. MA, R, A-99.
Swann, James H. & Sarah A. Webber. 18 June 1834. MA, R, A-190.
Sward, Francis M. & Caroline Shaley. 14 July 1860. MA, R,
D-120.
Swartz, John & Malinda Meningo. 20 Feb. 1850. MA, R, B-172.
Swartz, John & Caroline Smith. 9 May 1857. R, D-53.
Swartz, Joseph & Magdalene Engles. He is 23, born & res. Colum-
bus, son of Joseph Swartz. She is 19, born Germany, res.
Columbus, dau. of George M. Engles. 19 July 1856. C-7.
Sweet, Freeman & Caroline Cutler. 26 Feb. 1852. MA, B-233.
Sweet, Joseph & Malissa Bennett. 1 Sep. 1854. B-284.
Sweet, Samuel & Catharine Campden. 1 (10?) Sep. 1844. MA, R,
B-62.
Swift, Aurin R. & Mary J. White. 9 Sep. 1858, by E. P. Pratt.
MA, R.
Swintz, John & Louise Wise. 19 Sep. 1853. MA, B-281.
Swires, Stewart & Martha Jane Eckley (Jukley?). 12 Aug. 1853.
MA, B-273.

SCIOTO COUNTY MARRIAGES

Swoger, James & Margaret Snyder. 9 Nov. 1851. MA, B-243.
Swogger, William & Emily Clark. 15 Aug. 1851. MA, B-213.
Sword, Francis M. & Elizabeth Adams. 5 Nov. 1857. R, D-64.
Swords, William & Jannet Purdy. 27 Jan. 1846. MA.
Swords, William A. & Mary F. Ridenour. 16 Mar. 1830. R, A-140.
Swyer, Thomas & Elizabeth Swyers. 14 May 1851. MA, B-208.
Tabker, Henry & Mary Lewisman. 15 Aug. 1851. MA.
Tailor (Taylor), Jesse & Jane Mutter. 22 Aug. 1838. MA, R,
   A-257.
Talger, H. P. & M. Kugleman. 14 Nov. 1855. D-23.
Tanner, George & Mary A. Tanner. 30 July 1857. R, D-56.
Tarr, Benjamin F. & Harriet M. Hurd. 16 Aug. 1839. MA, R,
   A-273.
Tate, Mathew & Katherine Gilmore. 25 Dec. 1834. R, A-194.
Tatman, Peter & Rhuhama Holt. 12 June 1856. R, D-32.
Tauber, John & Margaret Dellert. 25 Sep. 1844. MA, R, B-63.
Tayler, Oliver C. & Mary W. Sturgeon. 11 Jan. 1860. MA, R,
   D-164.
Taylor, Coonrod & Elizabeth Ballard. 11 Jan. 1835. MA, R,
   A-197.
Taylor, Harvey & Eleanor Squires. 1 Dec. 1831. R, A-159.
Taylor, Harvey & Catharine M. Lacriox. Everett Hurd att. her
   age over 14. 7 Dec. 1846. MA, R, B-95.
Taylor, James & Mary S. Folsom. 29 Jan. 1834. R, A-187.
Taylor, James Ratliff & Eliza Jane White. 28 Sep. 1837. R,
   A-236.
Taylor, Jeremiah & Jane Searls. 25 Dec. 1838. R, B-6.
Taylor, John & Mary (Maisy) Moore. 16 Apr. 1812. MA, R, A-320.
Taylor, Levi & Mary Reese. 18 Oct. 1824. MA, R, A-84.
Taylor, Richard & Kesiah Pitts. 6 Nov. 1857. R, D-65.
Taylor, Robert & Harriet Grubb, of Wheelersburg. 6 Feb. 1844.
   R, B-54.
Taylor, Samuel & Abigail J. Gaston. 21 May 1851. B-217.
Taylor, Tandy & Nancy Corns. Her mother Elizabeth Corn cons.,
   witn. Jacob Spangle. 16 Dec. 1824. MA, R, A-85.
Taylor, Thomas & Eliza Culp. 1 Sep. 1851. MA.
Taylor, William & Hester Ann Robertson. 25 Jan. 1845. MA.
Taylor, Wyatt A. & Hellen Bonser. 26 Jan. 1854. B-282.
Teagarden, John M. & Margaret Wallace. 23 Mar. 1844. MA, R,
   B-56.
Teeters, George W. & Margaret Jane Reeves. 11 June 1846. MA,
   R, B-90.
Teller, Samuel & Kesiah Ann Wilson. 18 Sep. 1820. MA, R, A-55.
Tellerr, Valentine & Maria Oler. 1 May 1860. MA, R, D-131.
Temple, Taylor & Mary L. Coffrin. Her father G. W. Coffrin
   cons. 25 June 1860. MA, R, D-131.
Temple, William & Elizabeth Burt. 16 Sep. 1860. MA, R, D-138.
Terry, John P. & Susannah Waller. 29 Apr. 1833? (Theirs is
   among a list of marriages, not individually dated.) R, A-174.
Terry, Leroy G. & Ann A. Scott. 1 June 1848. R, B-125.
Teter, Joseph & Elizabeth Royse (Rice). 14 Sep. 1846. MA, R,
   B-92.
Teters, Michael & Polly Harbot. 11 Oct. 1853. MA, B-269.
Teters, William & Margaret Hodges. He is 24, born Scioto Co.,
   res. Twin Creek, son of William Moorehead. She is 19 (20),
   born Nile Tp., dau. of Moses & Elizabeth Hodges. 28 Jan.
   1858. R, C-8, C-12, D-72.
Tewkbury, Elbridge G. & Esther Shepherd. 19 June 1839. R,
   A-275.
Tewksbury, Moore R. & Sallie A. Baird. 27 May 1856, by E. P.
   Pratt. R.
Thacker, Rannel & Letty Adams. 4 May 1855. D-21.
Thayer, Cyrus & Maria Williams. 20 Dec. 1839. MA, A-275.

131

SCIOTO COUNTY MARRIAGES

Theobald (Teapold), Jacob & Barbara Myer. 14 Jan. 1860. MA,
    R, D-133.
Thockmorton, Amos R. & Elizabeth Lute. 10 Mar. 1850. R, B-175.
Thockmorton, Daniel F. & Pheobe Ellen Carpenter. 4 Mar. 1858.
    MA, R, D-75.
Thomas, Abraham & Mary Jones. He was born & res. Ky., second
    marr. She was born Ky., res. Portsmouth. 1 Sep. 1856. R,
    C-2, D-35.
Thomas, Amaziah & Margaret E. Morgan. 31 Mar. 1853. MA, B-258.
Thomas, Benjamin & Charity Thomas. 12 Jan. 1839. R, A-266.
Thomas, Daniel & Jane Williams. 6 Jan. 1844. MA, R, B-52.
Thomas, David D. & Elizabeth Williams. 20 Oct. 1858. MA, R,
    D-78.
Thomas, Henry & Melvina Pyle. Absalom Pyle cons., witn. Samuel
    Pyle, William Thomas. 7 Oct. 1835. MA, R, A-205.
Thomas, Isaac & America Barber. 9 May 1850. MA, R, B-179.
Thomas, Isaiah & Mary Jane Glover. 16 Feb. 1853. MA, B-257.
Thomas, Israel A. & Rebecca McLamore. 12 Dec. 1839, by J. R.
    Turner, M.G. MA, R.
Thomas, Jacob & Catherine Noel. 28 Jan. 1823. R, A-72.
Thomas, James Madison & Nancy Ann Johnson. His father John
    Thomas, of Greenup Co. Ky. cons., witn. Jno. Thomas Jr.,
    Eli Johnson. 16 Oct. 1838. MA, R, A-260.
Thomas, John & Americus Hesler. 6 Sep. 1842. R, B-34.
Thomas, John & Mary Owens. 21 Mar. 1844. MA, R, B-56.
Thomas, Jordon & Sarah Ann Estill. 24 Jan. 1860. MA, R, D-106.
Thomas, Joseph W. & Sarah A. Cable. 7 Feb. 1856. D-24.
Thomas, Larkin & Electa Jewett. William Jewett att. her age.
    14 Dec. 1842. MA, R, B-38.
Thomas, Manly & Mary Stewart. Abraham Thomas, of Green Tp.,
    cons., witn. Samuel French, Amos Stewart. Her father George
    Stewart, of Green Tp., cons., same witn. 30 Oct. 1823. MA,
    R, A-79.
Thomas, Martin Luther & Caroline Musser. 14 May 1843. MA, R,
    B-46.
Thomas, William & Mary Gilruth. 13 Apr. 1818. MA.
Thompson, Amaziah & Mary Sanford. 7 Jan. 1850. R, B-167.
Thompson, Andrew J. & Sarah Farley. Her father Henry F. Farley
    cons., witn. Joseph Barnburg (?), James Bennett. 1 Apr.
    1860. MA, R, D-114.
Thompson, Anthony & Mary Fuqua. 5 Apr. 1843. MA, R, B-43.
Thompson, David & Mahala Wheeler. 14 Dec. 1817. MA, R, A-31.
Thompson, David & Mary A. McCann. 22 June 1851. MA, B-210.
Thompson, Henry & Elizabeth Wallace. 28 Oct. 1847. MA, R,
    B-109.
Thompson, Isaac & Lucinda Newman. 3 Nov. 1843. MA, R, B-50.
Thompson, Jacob & Elizabeth Oppy. 12 June 1834. R, A-184.
Thompson, James & Susannah Malone. 24 May 1812. MA, R, A-320.
Thompson, James & Lucinda McCann. 2 July 1837. MA, R, A-245.
Thompson, James & Anna McCowan. 18 Dec. 1847. MA, R, B-111.
Thompson, James & Mary Gauk (Funk). 13 Aug. 1857. R, D-56.
Thompson, James B. & Maria Combs. Lewis Thompson att. his age.
    18 Nov. 1858. MA, R, D-95.
Thompson, John & Sally Malone. Richard & Susannah Malone cons.,
    att. Thomas Triggs. 13 Oct. 1814. MA, R, A-341.
Thompson, John & Belinda Sewell. 30 Oct. 1831. MA, R, A-157.
Thompson, John & Rebecca Hull. 14 June 1832. R, A-170.
Thompson, John & Anne Bennet. 22 Mar. 1833. R, A-175.
Thompson, John & Mary Welcher, both of Porter. 17 Mar. 1836.
    R, A-215, A-233.
Thompson, John & Ellen Thompson. 8 Aug. 1837. MA, R, A-246.
Thompson, John & Catharine Williams. 8 Oct. 1843. MA, R, B-49.

132

SCIOTO COUNTY MARRIAGES

Thompson, John & Hannah M. Austin. He is 24, of Sanilac Tp.,
Michigan. She is 18. Married 16 Apr. 1854 at Sanilac Co.,
Lexington, Michigan, by O. Maybee, J. P. Witn. William
Willson, Ensign Hill. R.
Thompson, Joseph Lewis & Susannah Beaty. 4 Sep. 1817. R, A-30.
Thompson, Mathew J. & Margaret Brison. 23 Sep. 1847. MA, R,
B-108.
Thompson, Mathew W. & Mary Ann Noel. 14 Jan. 1846. R, B-82.
Thompson, Milton & Elizabeth Highly. 5 Dec. 1833. MA, R,
A-185.
Thompson, Rees & Phoebe Nave (Howe). 11 Dec. 1806. R, A-283.
Thompson, Robert & Rebeccah Baccus. 20 July 1815. MA, R, A-282.
Thompson, Silas & Hannah Goheen. James Thompson att. his age.
26 Nov. 1858. MA, R, D-83.
Thompson, Solomon & Mary Edwards. 30 Mar. 1841. MA, R, B-19.
Thompson, Waddy & Cynthia Thomas. 17 Sep. 1810. R, A-306.
Thompson, William & Elizabeth Gibbs. 5 Jan. 1809. R, A-294.
Thompson, William & Ellen Shefflen. 23 Oct. 1848. R, B-133.
Thompson, William & Mary Jane Lewis. 21 Sep. 1851. MA, B-216.
Thompson, William & Elizabeth Walker. 11 Sep. 1853. MA, B-269.
Thompson, William & Maria Ford. 25 Nov. 1856. R, D-41.
Thornton, George W. & Dora Pelhenk. 16 Feb. 1860. MA, R, D-164.
Thornton, Henry G. & Cyrenia Ball. Her father David Ball cons.
19 Nov. 1845. MA, R, B-80.
Thornton, John H. & Sarah Glover, Wayne Tp. 18 Sep. 1809. R,
A-297.
Thoroman, James & Sarah E. Newlon. 2 Feb. 1859. MA, R, D-91.
Thoroman, William & Sally Tucker. Jno. Tucker cons. 19 Oct.
1815. MA, R, A-17.
Thorpe, Robert & Mary Homer. Edward B. Homer att. her age.
24 June 1838. MA, R, A-255.
Thrall, John & Margaret E. Edgington. 28 Oct. 1852. MA, B-256.
Throckmorton, Joseph & Lavina Ray. 29 Aug. 1851. MA, B-216.
Throne, Conrad & Rebeckah Norman. 11 Dec. 1806. R, A-282.
Thurman (Thoroman), James T. & Sophia G. Noel. (not dated) 1842.
R, B-30.
Thurston, Darius T. & Margrate P. Howell. 18 Apr. 1833. R,
A-176.
Tibbits, David A. & Mary Jane Bush. 5 Feb. 1843. MA, R, B-41.
Tidd, Elijah & Almira Ann Stockham. 28 Oct. 1847. MA, R, B-112.
Tidd, Moses & Catherine Cockrell. 11 Jan. 1816. MA, R, A-17.
Tillow, John & Jane Elizabeth Williamson. 18 Aug. 1847. R, B-105.
Timbrooks, James & Matilda Walterhouse. 9 Oct. 1828. R, A-122.
Timmonds, John & Katharine Funk. 16 Oct. 1817. MA, R, A-33.
Timmonds, John W. & Caroline Gebhardt. 12 Apr. 1855. R, D-17.
Tipton, William Senr. & Susan Cochran. 29 Mar. 1838. R, A-252.
Tirey (Terry), William W. & Betsey Bacy Bloomer. 26 Nov. 1826.
R, A-104.
Tirvy, Gorge & Mariam Sutter, Upper Tp. 18 Mar. 1809. R, A-294.
Titus, Arthur & Elizabeth Willis. 22 Dec. 1830, by Levi Sikes,
J.P. R.
Titus, Arthur & Harriet S. Chabot. 11 Oct. 1849. R, B-159.
Titus, Arthur J. & Harriet Bennett. 11 Sep. 1833. R, A-181.
Titus, Daniel & Eulalie Dodge. 14 Aug. 1847. MA, R, B-106.
Titus, G. B. & Susan Ann Bennet. 13 Oct. 1856. MA.
Titus, G. B. & Michal Crabtree. 20 June 1858. MA, R, D-88.
Titus, Isaac & Rachael Jones. 6 Sep. 1832. R, A-167.
Titus, James & Lydia Collis. 26 Dec. 1830. R, A-164.
Titus, Joseph M. & Mercy Mary Ann Feurt. Benjamin Feurt cons.,
witn. Stephen Chandler, Isaac Titus. 15 Nov. 1831. MA, R,
A-159.
Titus, Stephen & Susannah Rockwell. 28 Dec. 1831. R, A-161.

133

Titus, Tetus & Rhoda Taylor. 14 July 1822. MA, R, A-69.
Tobin, John & Ellen Coffey. 17 Feb. 1855. MA, R, D-15.
Toland, James & Sarah Mault, both of Madison Tp. 15 Mar. 1840.
    MA, R, B-9.
Toland, John & Harriet Burke. 30 Oct. 1848. R, B-137.
Toland, William & Marilda White. 21 Oct. 1843. B-51.
Toland, William & Elizabeth Ingram. George W. Morrow att. ages.
    27 June 1850. MA, R, B-182.
Tolbert, Reuben & Eleanor Musgrove. 19 Dec. 1830, by Asa
    Ballenger, J. P.   R.
Tolker, John Frederick & Margaret Wilbern. 27 Mar. 1843. MA,
    R, B-44.
Tolson (Holston), George & Susannah Hammet. 17 Feb. 1820. MA,
    R, A-51.
Tomlinson, Henry R. & Elenora E. Conwey. 28 June 1854. R, D-8.
Tomlinson, J. A. & Rachel Fout. 17 July 1854. R, D-9.
Tomlinson, Lewis & Josephine Herd. 10 Mar. 1848. B-229.
Tool (Pool), John W. & Levina Graves. 22 June 1833. MA, R,
    A-176.
Torbet, John & Catharine Bennet. Elijah L. Gaston att. ages.
    3 July 1830. MA, R, A-144.
Torrence, Benjamin F. & Aseneth J. Orcutt. 11 Dec. 1839. MA,
    R, A-276.
Tosser (Folser), John & Mary Thomas, widow. 13 Feb. 1834. MA,
    R, A-187.
Totten, Alexander & Mary P. Dick. 27 Jan. 1857, by E. P. Pratt.
    27 Jan. 1857. R.
Tover, John & Elizabeth Gagel. 15 Nov. 1846. MA, R, B-95.
Townsend, Peter & Nancy Zornes. 24 July 1845. MA, R, B-74.
Townson, William & Catharine Cook. 23 Nov. 1848. MA, R, B-144.
Tracy, Charles Oscar & Maria Kinney. 15 Dec. 1827. R, A-113.
Tracy, Charles P. & Isabella McClain. 20 Dec. 1858, by E. P.
    Pratt. MA, R.
Tracy, George & Mary Timmonds. 5 Aug. 1820. MA, R, A-54.
Tracy, James & Mary Ann Cooley. 18 May 1837. MA, R, A-241.
Tracy, John B. & Mary Eliza Brady. David Brady att. her age.
    14 May 1860. MA, R, D-131.
Tracy, John L. & Mary J. Nichols. 6 Jan. 1859. MA, R, D-93.
Tracy, Joseph & Mary Jane Freeman. 25 Mar. 1849. R, B-148.
Tracy, Samuel M. & Mary Daily. 13 Oct. 1822. R, A-69.
Tracy, Samuel M. & Margaret Thurston. 27 Oct. 1851. B-220.
Tracy, Uri & Harriet E. Lloyd. 4 Dec. 1851. B-225.
Tracy, Van Der Lynn & Annice B. Davis. 12 Apr. 1854. D-5.
Traler, Nelson & Rebecca Barnhart. 18 July 1859. MA, R, D-102.
Trane (Drane), James & Sarah S. Philips. Her mother Mary
    Phillips cons., witn. Abraham Degear, Harriet Degear, of
    Union Tp. 26 Jan. 1854. MA, D-7.
Travis, Abraham & Sarah Creamer. 21 Nov. 1835. MA.
Travis, Daniel & Mary Kirkendall. 22 July 1830. MA, R, A-144.
Travis, Joseph & Rachel Cramer. Francis (?) Cramer cons., witn.
    Robert Lucas. 30 Mar. 1809. MA, R, A-294.
Travis, Noah & Elizabeth Spangle (Spangler). 21 Jan. 1815. MA,
    R, A-345.
Travis, Noah & Hannah Jones. 18 May 1825. R, A-89.
Travis, Robert & Polly Cramer (Creamer). 22 July 1821. MA, R,
    A-60.
Traxler (Trexler), John & Louisa Price. Her father William
    Price cons., witn. Lemuel Lindsey, Isaac Price. 4 May 1825.
    MA, R, A-89.
Treat, John & Mary Hardin. 20 Feb. 1845. R, B-69.
Treat, John A. & Catharine E. Brown. 2 Apr. 1843. MA, R, B-44.
Trexler, Wellington & Ellen Evans. He is 28, born & res.

SCIOTO COUNTY MARRIAGES

Portsmouth, son of John Trexler. She is 19, born Illinois,
dau. of Wattson Evans. 14 Apr. 1858. MA, R, C-14, D-75.
Tribby, James L. & Lennina Wells. 7 (3?) Aug. 1851. B-219,
B-220.
Trichler, Philip & Elizabeth McJunkin. 1 Nov. 1860. MA, R,
D-126.
Trick (Prick, Frick?), Frederick & Keziah Wilkin. 4 Aug. 1855.
R, D-19.
Trickey, Samuel & Christina Bennett. 11 Oct. 1835. R, A-211.
Triggs, Hezekiah & Ellen Patten (Patun). 17 Apr. 1856. R,
C-3, D-28.
Triggs, Jacob & Sarah T. Chaffin. 12 June 1853. B-268.
Triggs, John & Hannah Melone. Thomas Triggs att. her age.
10 Sep. 1818. MA, R, A-41.
Triggs, Richard & Minerva Thompson. His father William Triggs,
and her father J. L. Thompson cons., witn. Lewis Thompson,
William Malone. 23 Feb. 1843. MA, R, B-43.
Triggs, William & Susannah Malone. 4 Feb. 1817. MA, R, A-26.
Triggs, William & Mary Malone. 14 Aug. 1823. MA, R, A-78.
Triplett, Benjamin F. & Henriette Fleming. 16 Sep. 1858. MA,
R, D-81.
Tritch, James & Missouri Barber. 12 Apr. 1849. MA, R, B-146.
Tritt, Jacob & Margaret Rickey. 23 Dec. 1858. MA, R, D-77.
Trotter, John C. & Eliza Lawrence. 7 July 1859. MA, R, D-108.
Truet, Anderson & Elizabeth Purnal. 23 Mar. 1815. R, A-348.
Truitt, George & Maryann Worley. 23 Jan. 1834. R, A-186.
Truitt, Jabez & Susanna Worley. 8 June 1837. R, A-246.
Truitt, James & Fanny Woodyard. 7 Jan. 1821. MA.
Truitt (Trewit), James & Airy Evans. 23 Aug. 1825. MA, R,
A-91.
Truitt, Jonathan & Polly Andre. 15 Dec. 1821. MA, R, A-64.
Truitt, Parker & Eleanor Moore. 15 June 1827. R, A-107.
Trumbo, Andrew & Jane Power. 23 Nov. 1837. R, A-249.
Tüchter, Ernst & Ann Marie Havekotte. 20 Mar. 1859. MA, R,
D-90.
Tucker, A. J. & Kiturah Woodruff. 17 June 1855. R, D-18.
Tucker, Abraham & Mary Eliza Dodds. 7 June 1836. A-219.
Tucker, Elijah & Nancy Pitts. 29 Oct. 1835. MA, R, A-210.
Tucker, James & Teresa (Luesa) Venort. 13 Nov. 1828. R, A-125.
Tucker, Joseph & Julia Ann Darlington. 29 Mar. 1838. MA, R,
A-252.
Tucker, Lewis & Nancy Steene (Sterne). 18 Oct. 1850. MA, R,
B-190.
Tucker, Samuel S. & Margaret Clark. 4 June 1859. MA, R, D-97.
Turley, John A. & Charlotte E. Robinson. 2 Jan. 1844. R, B-51.
Turner, Abraham & Mary Jane Wilson. (not dated) 1843. R, B-49.
Turner, Abram & Cassa Fossett. 2 Oct. 1851. B-217.
Turner, Adam C. & Sally Ann Stivers. Her father Robert Stivers
cons., witn. Randel Stivers. Becca Turner, widow of James R.
Turner dec'd. cons., witn. William Hoover. 22 Aug. 1845.
MA, R, B-81.
Turner, Daniel & Ellen Vale. 30 Oct. 1845. MA, R, B-78.
Turner, David & Mary Anderson. 2 Aug. 1855. R, D-19.
Turner, George W. & Sarah Ann Janes. 20 Apr. 1837. MA, R,
A-247.
Turner, Ira M. & Matilda Hankins. 23 Dec. 1845. MA.
Turner, James B. & Sary N. Miller. 20 Dec. 1829. R, A-137.
Turner, James N. & Eliza Hagerman (Hagum). Rebecca Turner
cons. 12 Apr. 1853. MA, B-259.
Turner, Jesse & Hannah Ogdon. 18 Jan. 1847. MA, R, B-98.
Turner, John L. & Delesa Brown. 29 Oct. 1843. MA, R, B-66.
Turner, John R. Jr. & Airy W. Smith. 8 June 1847. R, B-102.

135

Turner, Joseph & Orrilla Slocumb. 4 Sep. 1845. MA, R, B-77.
Turner, Levi & Josephine Slocumb. He is 25, born Porter Tp.,
    son of W. & Elizabeth Turner. She is 16, born & res. Porter
    Tp., dau. of Martin Slocumb. 1 Sep. 1857. R, C-13, C-14,
    D-63.
Turner, Perry & Susan Ann Bradford. 23 May 1849. MA, R, B-152.
Turner, Robert & Sarah Murphy. 6 July 1854. R, D-8.
Turner, Samuel G. & Phebe Whillson. 7 May 1820. R, A-53.
Turner, William & Elizabeth Flemming. Her father Isaac Flemming
    cons., witn. William Moore, David Watts. 13 Dec. 1814. MA,
    R, A-343.
Turner, William & Priscilla Vaughen. 19 Nov. 1845. MA.
Turner, William & Mary E. Daniels. 9 Feb. 1860. MA, R, D-117.
Turner, William G. & Diedamia Ball. 27 June 1832. R, A-164.
Tyler (Smith), Joseph & Mary Phillips. 4 Mar. 1854. R, D-7.
Tyree, Jerome B. & Margaret Ann Shoemate. 1 Mar. 1847. MA, R,
    B-99.
Tyrrell, John R. & Rachel Fenimore. 15 Nov. 1854. MA, R, D-12.
Tyson, Jacob & Mary Bennet. Her father Gilbert Bennet cons.,
    says she is of age. Both of Bloom Tp. 28 Dec. 1837. MA,
    R, A-249.
Ulen, Samuel & Margaret Ann Thomson. 1 Feb. 1829. R, A-127.
Ulrich, John & Catharine Houbert (Hubbard). 22 Oct. 1844. MA,
    R, B-65.
Underwood, Daniel & Caroline Brady. 28 Nov. 1858. MA, R, D-93.
Underwood, Joseph D. & Melvina Huffman. His mother Sarah Under-
    wood, of Greenup Co. Ky., cons., witn. Robert Huffman, Jacob
    Huffman. 15 Dec. 1859. MA, R, D-102.
Upham, Edward & Lucy Ann Gibbens. 7 Nov. 1838. MA, R, A-263.
Upp, David F. & Emily Marshall. 7 Feb. 1847. MA, R, B-100.
Upperman, George & Eliza Carroll (Carr). Her mother, Mrs. Eliza
    Carroll, only surviving parent, cons. 20 May 1832. MA, R,
    A-163.
Urquhart (Darquhat), Alexander D. & Clarissa Colegrove. 14 Nov.
    1851. MA, B-222.
Urquhart, George O. & Ann McKenzie. 1 May 1855. R, D-18.
Utioan, Emanuel & Belinda Cooper. Her mother Isabell Cooper
    cons., att. John McKinney. 6 Aug. 1828. MA, R, A-121.
Utt, Adam & Pricilla Bennet, of Franklin Tp. 20 Sep. 1809. R,
    A-297.
Utt, Adam Jr. & Jayne Burt. 29 Aug. 1823. R, A-78.
Utt, Henry & Nancy Bennett. 12 Nov. 1818. MA, R, A-41.
Utt, Henry & Sarah Elizabeth Banes. Her father A. B. Banes, of
    Morgan Tp., cons., says she is over 18. 29 Feb. 1844. MA,
    R, B-55.
Utt, Jacob & Jemimah Crull. 17 Aug. 1809. R, A-297.
Utt, Jacob & Peggy Utt, of Madison Tp. Her brother John Utt
    att. her age. 17 May 1812. MA, R, A-318.
Utt, Jacob & Rhoda Sheldon. 24 July 1843. MA.
Utt, James R. & Lavarien Gallian. 31 Aug. 1847. MA, R, B-106.
Utt, John & Martha Jane Valentine. He is 26, born Scioto Co.,
    res. Washington Tp., son of John & Elizabeth Utt. She is 18,
    born Pike Co., dau. of Jacob & Nancy Valentine. 14 Feb. 1858.
    R, C-9, C-11, D-71.
Utt, Joseph & Eliza J. Smith. He is 29, son of John & Elizabeth
    Utt. She is 16, dau. of Robert & Phoebe Smith. 18 Jan. 1858.
    R, C-9, C-11, D-69.
Utt, Peter & Barbara Brown. 2 Nov. 1840. MA.
Valadin, Dupartee & Elizabeth C. Mapes. 20 Mar. 1842. MA, R, B-32.
Valadine, Denny & Harriet F. Colvin. 30 Nov. 1848. MA, R,
    B-137.
Valentine, Jacob & Sally Stratton. 6 Mar. 1836. MA, R, A-214.

Valentine, John E. & Rebeca E. Utt. 2 Dec. 1855. R, D-64.
Valoday, Frances & Nancey Slater. 12 Aug. 1808. R, A-291.
Valodin, Francis & Temperance Burt. His father, F. Valodin
cons. "for my son Frances Valodin to be married to Miss
Burt, daughter to Major S. B. Burt", witn. Elijah A. Glover.
15 July 1824. MA, R, A-83.
Valodin, Jerome B. & Mary Jane Moore. 24 Dec. 1844. MA, R,
B-69.
Valodine, Denny & Sarah J. Patterson. 11 Sep. 1843. MA, R,
B-48.
Van Houtten, John & Keziah Monrow. 15 Feb. 1818. MA, R, A-33.
Vanbeber (Vanbibon), John & Patty (Polly) Trigs. 25 Jan. 1812.
R, A-319.
Vanbever, Jacob & Elizabeth McKinney. 4 Nov. 1824. R, A-84.
Vanbibber, Isaac & Mary Shope. 16 Dec. 1819. MA, R, A-50.
Vanbibber, James, of Greenupsburg, Ky., & Naomi B. White. Her
father Matthew White cons., witn. Edward White. 19 July
1836. MA, R, A-220.
Vanbibber, Jonathan & Eliza Crank (Frank). Vernon Township.
His father Jacob Vanbibber cons., witn. Richard Malone.
Her mother Anny Cowan cons. 6 Feb. 1829. MA, R, A-130.
Vanbibber, Noah (Joseph) & Mary Rice. 18 Dec. 1848. MA, R,
B-136.
Vance, Jerome B. & Elizabeth Shellig. 7 July 1858. MA, R,
D-87.
Vance, John M. & Ellen S. Sullivan. Her mother Ellen P. McGill
cons., att. John Sullivan. 20 Apr. 1852. MA, B-275.
Vance, Nelson & Eliza J. Weaver. 20 Nov. 1845. MA.
Vance, Philip L. & Lishena Russel. 20 Feb. 1847. MA, R, B-100.
Vanderford, William & Cornelia Jane Noel. 25 Jan. 1855. MA,
R, D-13.
Vandervort, James & Juley A. Fletcher. 30 Sep. 1856. R, D-37.
Vanduser, Thomas & Mary Hark. 7 Mar. 1840. MA, R, B-2.
Vangorder, Green & Isabella Moore. 11 Aug. 1846. MA.
Vangorder, Green & Rebecca Buckles. 2 May 1847. MA, R, B-101.
Vangorder, Green & Cynthia Heron. 20 Nov. 1851. MA, B-222.
Vangorder, Henry & Polly Shumway. 27 May 1834. MA, R, A-189.
Vangorder, Lewis & Louisa McAtee. 4 Feb. 1851. MA, B-201.
Vanhorn, James & Maryann Raber (Raver). 25 Feb. 1845. MA, R,
B-72.
Vankirk, Robert & Hannah Hood. 22 Oct. 1856. MA, R. D-40.
VanMeter, Andrew & Margery Kiddle (Riddle). 13 Nov. 1848. MA,
R, B-136.
Vannetten, James A. & Eliza Ann McDonald. 12 Feb. 1855. MA, R,
D-15.
Vannort, Charles & Elizabeth Horner. Her father Joseph Horner
cons. 11 Nov. 1824. MA, R, A-84.
Vannort, Charles & Mary Gilmore. 27 June 1835, at Jefferson Tp.
MA, R, A-202.
Vannort, Charles & Milly Clark. 2 May 1835. MA.
Vantine, Josiah & Polly Odell. 19 Mar. 1829. R, A-131.
Varner, James S. & Lavisa Collis. 18 Sep. 1845. MA, R, B-79.
Varner, John W. & Caroline Noel. 16 Oct. 1851. B-220.
Varner, Leo & Amelia Wilcorn. 14 Oct. 1851. MA, B-230.
Varner, Sampson & Maria Huston. 26 Nov. 1846. R, B-93.
Vaser, Petter & Polly Trimmer. 25 June 1811. MA, R, A-312.
Vastine, Abraham & Harriet Ives. 27 Jan. 1826. MA, R, A-95.
Vastine, Gabriel & Anna Gwathney. 6 Dec. 1842. R, B-38.
Vastine, John & Mary McLaughlin. 13 Apr. 1826. R, A-96.
Vastine, John & Massee Noel. 9 Mar. 1837. R, A-245.
Vastine, William & Mary Fulce. 1 Apr. 1843. MA, R, B-32.
Vaughters, John A. & Ada Jane Brouse. Samuel P. Cummins att.
ages. 18 Nov. 1860. MA, R, D-130.

Vaughters, William & Sophia Graham. 29 Oct. 1842. MA, R, B-36.
Vaughters, William & Mary J. Broison. 2 Nov. 1851. MA, B-221.
Veach, Benjamin & Eleanor Cable. 10 Mar. 1836. MA, R, A-231.
Veach, Charles W. & Elizabeth Burriss. 25 Mar. 1832, by John
  Moore, J. P. R.
Veach, Charles W. & Amelia A. C. Worley. 20 June 1850. R,
  B-181.
Veach, George W. & Phoebe J. Burdic. 23 June 1858. MA, R,
  D-82.
Veach, Horatio & Mille Ann Veach. 7 Mar. 1852. B-233.
Veach, John W. & Ann Plummer. 28 Dec. 1823. R, A-80.
Veach, Sylvester & Hariet Custis. 24 Mar. 1822. R, A-65.
Veach, Thomas & Sophia Mills. 20 June 1839. MA, R, A-269.
Veachell, Sylvester & Mary Frend. 9 Oct. 1852. B-248.
Venn, Joseph & Appolona Kraus. 21 July 1859. MA, R, D-100.
Verigan, Frances & Hannah Eppiheimer. Samuel Eppiheimer att.
  her age. 5 Jan. 1843. MA, R, B-40.
Vetter (Fetter), Joseph & Mary Lang (Long). He is 23, born
  Germany, res. Portsmouth, son of Andre & Mary Vetter. She
  is 24, born Germany, res. Portsmouth, dau. of George & Mary
  Lang. 20 Sep. 1857. R, C-10, D-62.
Vias (Uris), Jacob & Margaret Ann Clarke. 28 Mar. 1839. R, B-3.
Vignes, James & Mary Sayre. He is 30, born Adams Co., Oh., res.
  Portsmouth, son of Paul & Mary Vignes. She is 21, born & res.
  Meigs Co., Oh., dau. of David & P. Sayre. 4 Dec. 1856. C-1.
Vigus, Jordan & Caroline Ripley. 9 Apr. 1836. MA, R, A-218.
Vigus, Nelson & Rachel Spence. 2 Feb. 1845. MA, R, B-70.
Vilet, Benjamin & July Ann Masters. Her father George Masters
  cons., witn. William Campbell, Abraham Degear. 21 Jan. 1844.
  MA, R, B-53.
Vilet (Violett), Samuel & Eunice Phillips. Constance Vilet cons.
  "Eunice is my natural daughter and is nineteen years of age.."
  witn. John Vilet. 25 June 1818, by George Beloat. MA, R.
Vincent, Henry & Marianna Callow. 8 May 1856. R, D-29.
Vincent, Joseph T. & Lucy C. Pratt. 21 Oct. 1851. MA, B-219.
Vinson, Isaac S. & Rebeccah P. Johnson. His father Jesse Vinson
  cons., witn. John L. Vinson. 12 Aug. 1832. MA, R, A-165.
Vinson, John L. & Catharine Spangle. 11 Sep. 1832. R, A-167.
Violet, John M. & Caroline M. Dewey. 25 Mar. 1845. MA, R, B-69.
Violet, S. B. & Jane C. Slattery. 20 Dec. (1855?). D-23.
Violet, Sampson & Sarah Boydston. 18 Dec. 1810. MA, R, A-310.
Virback, Alva & Cynthia Gay (Gray). Her guardian Thos. Gilruth
  cons., witn. Josiah Verbick. 13 Dec. 1825. MA, R, A-94.
Virbeck, Benjamin F. & Asenath Baccus. His mother Elizabeth
  Virbeck cons., witn. Alva Virbeck. 27 Feb. 1840. MA, R, B-4.
Virgin, Abraham & Elizabeth Enslow. 22 June 1822. R, A-67.
Virgin, George T. & Aley Sikes. 30 July 1820. MA, R, A-54.
Virgin, Kinsey & Eliza Young. 13 Mar. 1831. MA. R, A-163.
Virgin, Rezin & Eliza Whitcomb, the widow of Caleb Whitcomb.
  11 Mar. 1827. MA, R, A-106.
Voglesong, William G. & Elizabeth Reynolds. 15 Mar. 1846. MA,
  R, B-84.
Vokle (Wogel), John George & Frances Schwab. 14 Feb. 1853. MA.
Vondersaal, Konrad & Catherine Spanner. 12 Aug. 1858. MA, R,
  D-79.
Voorheese, Samuel & Ann E. Barker. 18 June 1848. R, B-125.
Voorhes, Richard & Catherine Allen. 10 Mar. 1852. B-234.
Voorhese, Comodoor Decatur & Elizabeth Atkinson. 4 Sep. 1845.
  R, B-76.
Vulgamore, Jesse M. & Eveline Adams. He is 44, res. Jefferson
  Tp., son of Eliza Vulgamore. She is 31, born Madison Tp.,
  res. Jefferson Tp., dau of George & Frances Shonkwiler. Her

SCIOTO COUNTY MARRIAGES

third marriage, his first. 18 Dec. 1857. R, C-10, D-66.
Waddell, Charles & Eleanor Moore. 27 July 1813. MA, R, A-326.
Wadgins (?), Edmund & Polly Ockshire. 30 Jan. 1833. MA.
Waggoner, Jacob & Joanna Cochran. 13 July 1835. MA, R, A-203.
Waggoner, James & Lucinda Sanford. Her mother Huldah Sanford
  cons. 4 Apr. 1836. MA.
Waggoner, John & Elizabeth Keizer. 1 Oct. 1849. B-244.
Wagner, Henry C. & Matilda E. Hepler. 22 Feb. 1859. MA, R,
  D-87.
Wagner, Michael Joseph & Maria Louisa Phillippi. Both res.
  Portsmouth. 19 Aug. 1856. R, C-4, D-34.
Wagoner, Leonhard & Eva Rosina Kiedeisch. 16 Jan. 1853. R,
  B-274.
Wahlbrecht (Walbright), John & Catharine Wealthy. 9 Apr. 1850.
  MA, R, B-176.
Wait, David & Cecilia Lacroix. 18 Jan. 1823. R, A-73.
Wait, John H. & Melvina Sikes. 13 Sep. 1839. R, A-272.
Waite, Benjamin F. & Mary Smith. 19 Dec. 1830. R, A-149.
Waits (White), George & Mary Jane Louderback. He res. Franklin
  Fce., age 25, born Ohio. She is 21, born Green Tp., dau. of
  John & Betsy. 16 Nov. 1856. R, C-11, D-39.
Walbright, Christian & Mary A. Doty. 1 Jan. 1855. MA, R, D-13.
Walburn, Benjamin & Sebina Rollens. 24 Mar. 1852. MA.
Walden, Lewis D. & Mary McCormic. 15 June 1834, by Jacob Lair,
  J.P. R.
Walden, Richard & Margaret McNally. 23 Sep. 1841. MA, R, B-23.
Waldo, Jehial & Polly Lewis. 8 Oct. 1851. MA, B-243.
Waley, Levi & Almira Wait. 26 Dec. 1833. R, A-184.
Walker, David M. & Mary G. Cummings. 29 Dec. 1856. D-45.
Walker, George P. & Helen M. Nichols. 14 Oct. 1851. MA, B-220.
Walker, James & Nancy Kinney. 1 Jan. 1843. MA, R, B-40.
Walker, James & Sarah E. Carter. 2 Oct. 1856. R, D-37.
Walker, James R. & Patience Worley. 1 Sep. 1829. R, A-133.
Walker, John & Elizabeth Lewis. 8 Mar. 1849. MA, R, B-145.
Walker, John & Mary A. Smith. 12 June 1856. R, D-31.
Walker, John & Mary Wood. 8 Jan. 1860. MA, R, D-104.
Walker, Joseph & Eleanor Robison (Robinson). 9 Jan. 1817. MA,
  R, A-26.
Walker, Joseph & Katharine Thompson. 16 Jan. 1850. MA, B-206.
Walker, Peyton & Susanna Wallace. 1 Sep. 1853. MA, B-269.
Walker, Richard D. & Rachel Bush. 10 Nov. 1853. MA, B-281.
Walker, Thomas L. & Malinda M. Sutten. 17 Feb. 1857. R, D-45.
Walker, Washington W. & Sarah Emily Smith. Her father Alexander
  Smith cons. 3 Feb. 1853. MA, B-266.
Walker, William & Susan Bradford. 17 Dec. 1828. MA, R, A-125.
Walkertonshells, William & Sarah Ann Applegate. 21 June 1853.
  B-280.
Wallace, Aaron & Mercy Powell. Her stepfather and guardian
  Richard Powell cons., says she is 16. 7 Oct. 1852. MA,
  B-247.
Wallace, Amos & Eliza Calloway (Louisa Kallaway). 8 Aug. 1844.
  MA, R, B-61.
Wallace, Archibald & Abigail Crull. 25 Dec. 1856. R, D-43.
Wallace, Daniel & Mary Bufington. 20 June 1824. R, A-82.
Wallace, Esquire & Sally (Sarah) Roberts. 19 Feb. 1833. MA,
  R, A-172.
Wallace, James & Catharine Rankins. 9 May 1848. MA, R, B-126.
Wallace (Walls), John & Hester Ann Baldridge. 23 June 1850. MA,
  R. B-191.
Wallace, John & Mary Urquhart. 19 Mar. 1852. B-237.
Wallace, Richard Jr. & Polly Bussy. 22 Jan. 1846. MA, R, B-84.

139

Wallace, Riley & Emily Shelpman. His guardian Abraham Snively cons. 20 Mar. 1853. MA, B-260.
Wallace, Robert & Elizabeth Waggoner. 28 Mar. 1836. MA.
Wallace, Robert & Eliza James. 15 Apr. 1855, by M. McElhenny, J.P. R.
Wallace, Robert & Elizabeth Paines. 15 Apr. 1857. D-56.
Wallace, Samuel & Clarrissa N. Coriell. 8 Aug. 1839. MA, R, A-271.
Wallace, Samuel & Jane Baldridge. 7 June 1848. MA, R, B-128.
Wallace (Wallis), Squire & Perthene Eulitt. 17 Sep. 1829. MA, R, A-134.
Wallace, William & Mary Dodge. Lynds Dodge cons., att. Harris Dodge. 16 July 1843. MA, R, B-49.
Wallace, William & Sophronia Lair. 15 June 1847. MA, R, B-104.
Wallace, William & Mahala Samson. 18 Nov. 1849. R, B-162.
Waller, George A. & Jane Davey. 6 Oct. 1847. MA, R, B-108.
Waller, John & Mary Jane Baldridge. 26 July 1836 (1837). R, A-244.
Walls, Elias & Sabrah Harmason (Hannison). Elza Walls att. his age. 30 Aug. 1826. MA, R, A-92.
Walls, Elza & Louisa Walls. 29 Dec. 1859. MA, R, D-102, D-105.
Walls, George W. & Margaret Rankin. 5 Dec. 1841. MA, R, B-25.
Walls, James & Rosanna Pyle. 12 Feb. 1829. R, A-128.
Walls, Joshua & Sarah Bowers. Loyd Howard att. their ages, witn. Andrew Hunter. 10 Apr. 1806. MA, A-11, A-280.
Walls, Lemuel & Emily Walls. His father Levi Walls cons., witn. Elza Walls. 27 Sep. 1827. MA, R, A-112, A-118.
Walls, Nehemiah & Lucinda Calvin. 10 July 1828. MA, R, A-121.
Walls, Samuel & Sophia Pile. 1 Sep. 1825. R, A-92.
Walls, Thomas & Sarah Brown. Her father Othos (or O. Thos.) Brown says she was 21 the 29th of October last. Witn. Samuel S. Brown, John Brown. His father Levi Walls cons., says he was 21 the 22nd of August last. Witn. Lemuel Walls, Samuel S. Brown. 21 Dec. 1825. MA, R, A-87.
Walsinger, Henry W. & Maria A. Odle. Her father Moses Odle cons. 3 May 1859. MA, R, D-97.
Walsinger, John & Rachel Lovel. 1 Oct. 1804. R, A-2.
Walsinger, John & Sally Clifford. 1 Nov. 1820. MA.
Walter, Charles (Carl) & Mary Eifort. 17 Apr. 1858 (MA). MA, R, D-75.
Walter, Christian & Idel Kenny (Henry?). 12 Apr. 1855. R, D-17.
Walter, Frederick & Barbara Fesler. 2 Nov. 1851. MA, B-221.
Walter, Gotleib & Doratha Roth. 29 May 1859. MA, R, D-99.
Walters, Nathaniel & Elizabeth Davis. 23 May 1844. MA, R, B-58.
Walton, Hiram & Susan Kisar (Kizer). Her father cons. (James Kizer?--illegible), witn. John Snedecor Jr., Hiram Walton. 1 Sep. 1837. MA, R, A-273.
Walton, Job & Emeline Slavens. Her father cons. (not named). 11 Feb. 1842. MA, R, B-30.
Walton, Job & Nancy Winkler. 10 Jan. 1859. MA, R. D-82.
Wamsley, Alfred L. & Amanda J. Early. 9 Nov. 1848. R, B-133.
Wamsley, Isaac B. & Nancy Newman. 11 Feb. 1841. R, B-15.
Wamsley, John & Sarah Carraway. 19 May 1836. MA.
Wamsley, John A. & Nancy W. Smalley. 14 Feb. 1855. MA, R, D-15.
Wamsley, John B. & Sela A. Newman. 4 June 1857. R, D-54.
Wamsley, John M. & Drusilla Cartright. 25 Mar. 1850. MA, R, B-175.
Wamsley, John M. & Mary Kennedy. 26 Feb. 1851. MA, B-204.
Wamsley, Robert F. & Nancy Liston. 2 Aug. 1860. MA, R, D-130.
Wamsley, Samuel B. & Elizabeth A. Freeman. 30 May 1850. R, B-181.
Wangler, Ambrose & Ann Carr. 19 Jan. 1860. MA.

Ward, Cascias & Jane Cox. He is 25, both res. Portsmouth.
2 Feb. 1857. R, C-3, D-52.
Ward, George W. & Sarah Minford. 13 Jan. 1848. MA, R, B-121.
Ward, Isaac N. & Harriet H. Gifford. 17 Mar. 1858. MA, R,
D-73.
Ward, John A. & Eleanor Munn. 18 Jan. 1849. MA, R, B-140.
Ward, Philip & Lydia M. McAuly. 23 Aug. 1857. R, D-63.
Ward, Robert & Polly McKinsey. 10 July 1808. R, A-289.
Ward, Thomas & Sarah Anderson. 14 Dec. 1854. MA, R, D-12.
Ward, William P. & Maria Story. 16 Nov. 1846. MA, R, B-93.
Warden, Barnet & Francis Brigle (Wrigle?), from Greenup Co., Ky.
16 May 1807. R, A-284.
Warden (Ward), James L. & Maria M. Dunaway. 20 Mar. 1851. MA,
B-204.
Ware, David C. & Susan Chew. Joseph C. Henry att. her age.
7 May 1843. MA, R, B-71.
Ware, Jacob & Ann Auckerman. Frederick Huren att. ages.
25 Dec. 1859. MA, R, D-103.
Waring, Joseph & Peggie B. Martin. 12 Apr. 1860. MA, R, D-115.
Warnaker (Wermker), Christian & Barbara Geist (Christ). 12 Oct.
1847. MA, R, B-108.
Warne, Ellison & Mary Barber. 6 Sep. 1846. MA, R, B-91.
Warner, Frank & Catharina Der. 5 Jan. 1857. R, D-60.
Warner, John & Levina Louderback. Her father Michael Louderback
cons. 14 Dec. 1834. MA, R, A-194.
Warnick, William & Harriet Young. 6 Jan. 1833. R. A-174.
Warnike, Carl Wilhelm August & Charlotte Caroline Brantfast.
8 Oct. 1856. MA, R, D-60.
Warnock, William & Polly Forster. Her pars. David & Elizabeth
Forster cons., witn. Samuel Warnock, John Greenslate, of
Green Tp. 31 July 1806. MA, R, A-281.
Warren, Benjamin & Eliza J. Pickford. 15 July 1851. MA, B-211.
Warren, Clemont & Mary Barton. 17 Oct. 1805. R, A-8, A-278.
Warren, Francis & Nancy Rickey. His father Joseph Voirin cons.
1 May 1859. MA, R, D-97.
Warren, George (James) & Emeline Bradshaw. 7 July 1856. MA, R,
D-34.
Warren, James V. & Catherine Yeager. 17 Jan. 1849. MA, R,
B-149.
Warwick, John B. & Sarah Moulton. 14 Feb. 1860. MA, R, D-118.
Washburn, David & Eliza Thompson. William Rawlins att. ages.
3 Sep. 1846. MA, R, B-94.
Washburn, Lemuel & Cinthy Rawlins. 13 Oct. 1822. R, A-70.
Washburn, Lemuel & Nancy Yingling. 25 Jan. 1839. MA, R, A-265.
Washburn, Parmenis & Alabina Cable. 7 Nov. 1847. MA, R, B-112.
Washburn, Samuel & Rebecca Bennet. 30 Jan. 1823. R, A-73.
Waterbrook, Christian & Louisa Slater (Shuter?). 1 Aug. 1856.
R, D-34.
Waterhouse, Aaron & Emily Voohrease. 29 Apr. 1833? (Among a
list of marriages not individually dated) R, A-174.
Waterman, Jason C. & Josephine L. Waterman. 1 Dec. 1858. MA,
R, D-94.
Waters, Thomas & Matilda Cooper. 9 May 1848. MA.
Watkins, James & Eliza Ruckman. 13 July 1851. MA, B-211.
Watkins, Jefferson L. & Laura E. Glover. 16 Sep. 1852. B-249.
Watkins, Jefferson L. & Sarah A. Thornton. 21 June 1849. R,
B-153.
Watkins, John & Alicia B. Wallingsford. C.O. Browning att.
ages. 13 Apr. 1853. MA, B-266.
Watkins, John C. & Eleno Laforgy. 12 Mar. 1857. R, D-50.
Watkins, T. B. & Mary Ann Wiley. 1 Jan. 1854. D-7.
Watson, Andrew & Margaret Hoobler. 22 May 1845. MA, R, B-72.

141

Watson, Joseph & Dorcus Darby. Her brother Alva Virbeck att.
    her age over 18. 15 Sep. 1824. MA, R, A-85.
Watson, Joseph & Ellen Jones. 3 July 1854. R, D-8.
Watson, William H. & Amelia Westwood. 11 Feb. 1846. R, B-83.
Watt, David & Sarah Baccus (Baucas). 5 Mar. 1820. R, A-52.
Watt, James & Elizabeth Call. 23 Apr. 1815. MA, R, A-281.
Watt, John & Mary Halterman. 3 Apr. 1831. R, A-153.
Watt, William Atison & Mary Holt. 4 June 1840. R, B-9.
Watters, Daniel & Martha Nokes. 8 Dec. 1817. R, A-31. An
    affidavit dated 2 Nov. 1817 from Thomas Waters, father of
    Nathaniel Waters att. "he is a free man and can act and do
    for himself," witn. Alexander McHenry, Samuel Waters. No
    bride's name shown on MA.
Watts, James M. & Nancy Jane Collis. 18 Jan. 1860. MA, R,
    D-109.
Watts, John & Peggy Chambers, both of Brush Creek Tp. 11 Sep.
    1821. R, A-62.
Watts, William M. & Nancy Kittle. He is 43, born Greenbriar Co.
    Va., res. Webster, son of Samuel & E. Watts, second marr.
    She is 44, born Logan Co., Va., res. Jackson Co., dau. of
    James & H. Fullerton, second marr. 29 Apr. 1856. R, C-5,
    D-29.
Waugaman, Henry & Charity A. Thomas. Henry Thomas cons. 11 Oct.
    1860. MA, R, D-168.
Waugh, John & Augustine Duduit (Didaway). 15 Feb. 1813. MA, R,
    A-329.
Wear (Weir), David & Catherine Miller. 11 Apr. 1852. MA, B-237.
Wear, Marshall & Mary West. 9 Oct. 1859. MA, R, D-105.
Weatherow, William & Elizabeth Sidney. 9 Apr. 1846. MA, R,
    B-85.
Weaver, Elijah & Elizah Jones. 18 May 1825. R, A-90.
Weaver, James & Jerutia Emory. 18 Feb. 1819. MA, R, A-44.
Weaver, John & Barbara Dutengefer (Budinthaver). 29 Nov. 1849.
    MA, R, B-163.
Weaver, John & Mary Brocher. John Q. Weaver att. ages. 7 June
    1860. MA, R, D-115.
Weaver, John D. & Susan Burk. Her father William M. Burk cons.,
    witn. James Berry, John S. Burk. 21 Mar. 1822. MA, R, A-64.
Weaver, Joseph & Malinda Duwit (Dewitt, David). 1 May 1849.
    MA, R, B-147.
Weaver, Lucius E. & Maria Jane Coyle. 28 Sep. 1853. MA, B-273.
Weaver, Samuel & Eliza Clark. 26 Jan. 1838. MA, R, A-251.
Weaver, Thomas J. & Susanna B. Parkes. 5 Mar. 1850. R, B-173.
Weaver, William B. & Martha Miller (Myler, Miler). 19 Nov. 1846.
    MA, R, B-96.
Webb, James & Sarah Broom. 12 Dec. 1808. R, A-294.
Webb, John & Hester Eliza Lewis. Her father John Lewis cons.
    11 Apr. 1833. MA, R, A-174.
Webb, John & Sarah Zaine. 7 Feb. 1847. MA, R, B-98.
Webb, Moses & Orffa Chesnut. 19 Apr. 1840. R, B-4.
Webb, William & Anna Hodges. Her father George Hodges cons.,
    said she is nearly 17 years old, witn. Aaron D. Hodges,
    Samuel Corwine. 3 Apr. 1828. MA, R, A-116.
Webber, Isaac & Margaret Wales. Her father David Wales cons.
    2 June 1836. MA, R, A-215, A-233.
Weber, Benedick & Anna Ward. 22 Jan. 1850. R, B-168.
Weber, Philipp Jacob & Margaretha D. Lademann. 15 Mar. 1857.
    R, D-61.
Wedding, Nicodemus & Mary Ann Dennis. 31 Aug. 1840. MA, R,
    B-11.
Wedding, Thomas & Matilda Noel. 18 June 1842. MA, R, B-31.
Weeks (Wicks), Amos M. & Amanda Hundle. MA says "Father present"
    and is made out by David M. Wicks. 14 May 1848. MA, R, B-125.

SCIOTO COUNTY MARRIAGES

Weeks (Welch), Elmore & Eliza J. Mosert (Loner). He is 18,
born & res. Harrison Tp., son of Robert Weeks. She is 14,
born Penn., res. Harrison Tp., dau. of Cambel Loner.
31 July 1857. R, C-14, D-57.
Weeks (Wicks), Robert M. & Eliza Welch. 7 Aug. 1837. MA, R,
A-246.
Weesner, John & Agnes Watschner. 16 Oct. 1840. MA, R, B-8.
Weir, Absolem & Nancy Ann Dewise (Dwyer). 16 July 1853. MA,
B-266.
Weis (Wies), Philip & Mary Diehle. 21 May 1860. MA, R, D-121.
Weisenberger, David & Theresia Hemmlepp. 17 Dec. 1856. R, D-44.
Weishan (Wishon), John R. & Stacy Bicka (Bilkens). 7 Jan. 1851.
MA, B-199.
Weisharn, John & Elisabeth Dolt. 2 Dec. 1855. MA, R, D-13.
Welch, Charles & Mary Scott. Conrod Gilmore att. her age.
26 July 1841. MA, R, B-21.
Welch, David & Phebe Lair. 10 Sep. 1845. MA, R, B-76.
Welch, Elmore & Nancy Pyle. 12 Apr. 1849. MA, R, B-146.
Welch, James & Eliza Jane Pyle. His father James Welsh Sr.
cons., att. Harvey H. Pyle. 13 Aug. 1848. MA, R, B-131.
Welch, John & Nancy Worley. 16 Mar. 1812. MA.
Welch, John & Susan (Cline?). (Volume D has Cline; the return
does not look at all like Cline.) 23 Sep. 1856. R, D-40.
Welch, John O. (C.) & Caroline Jane Somerville. David Brooks
Jr. att. ages. 1 Aug. 1845. MA, R, B-75.
Welch, John W. & Abigail Snyder. He is 28, born Piketon, Oh.,
res. Jefferson Tp., son of Ben & Abigail Welch, second marr.
She is 17, born & res. Jefferson Tp., dau. of Mark & Elizabeth
Snyder, first marr. 2 Apr. 1857. R, C-10, D-53.
Welch, Johnston & Nancy Zorns. 4 Aug. 1842. MA, R, B-33.
Welch, Joseph & Hannah Conway (Conroy). 27 Sep. 1852. MA,
B-248.
Welch, Joshua & Lorane Louderback. 1 Nov. 1835. MA, R, A-209.
Welch, Robert & Fanny Beck. 6 July 1851. B-211.
Welch, William & Elizabeth Corns. 4 Mar. 1827. R, A-105.
Welden, William A. & Cleopatra Devore. 1 Jan. 1833. R, A-172.
Weller, Phillip K. & Eleanor Keatly (Keitly). 2 Oct. 1836. MA,
R, A-224, A-243.
Wells, James & Elizabeth Kinney, both of Portsmouth. 11 Nov.
1819. MA, R, A-48.
Wells, James & Eliphael Morris. 16 Jan. 1823. R, A-71.
Wells, John & Charity Kellogg. 18 Oct. 1849. MA, R, B-163.
Wells, Timothy & Elizabeth Anderson. Robt. Anderson cons.
10 Apr. 1853. MA, B-261.
Wells, Timothy & Sarah Anderson. He is 33, born & res. Madison
Tp., son of Richard & Laura Wells, second marr. She is 18,
born Pa., res. Jefferson Tp., dau. of Robert Anderson, first
marr. 10 Dec. 1857. R, C-10, C-11, D-70.
Wellsher (Welcher), Amzi & Mary Baccus. 28 Jan. 1827. MA, R,
A-103.
Welsh, Anthony & Fanny McGennis (MacGinnis). 27 May 1850. MA,
R, B-180.
Welsh, Ellmore & Roann Craig. 17 Sep. 1838. MA, R, A-259.
Welsh, Joshua & Mary Baker. 24 Jan. 1844. R, B-53.
Welsh, Thomas V. & Susan Salters. 15 Dec. 1850. MA, B-196.
Welty, Frank & Magdalin (Malinda) Bish. He is 25, born Germany,
res. Portsmouth, son of Charles Welty. She is 19, born Ger-
many, res. Portsmouth, dau. of John Bish. 7 July 1855 (1856).
B-286, C-6.
Wendall, Grafton & Sarena Howell. 31 Oct. 1859. MA, R, D-108.
Wendfield, John G. & Ruth A. Butler. 13 Dec. 1853. B-282.
Wents, George & Mary Ann Peters. Her father Henry Peters cons.,
witn. Wm. Salter. 29 May 1833. MA.

143

Wertz, Casper & Rebecca Dortch. 16 Jan. 1851. MA, B-245.
Wessel, John J. & Mary Stork. 12 Feb. 1835. MA, R, A-196.
West, Clark & Jane Hood. Mary West cons., witn. Even Jones,
    Aaron Pool. Her pars. Thomas & Rebeca (?) Hood cons., witn.
    Robert Wilson, Even Jones. 17 May 1843. MA, R, B-45.
West, Jabez & Pheby Robins (Roberts). 14 Feb. 1834 (?) by
    Jacob Ward, M.G. MA, R.
West, John & Eliza Allen. 5 Mar. 1857. R, D-51.
West, John W. & Mary Kearns. 19 Aug. 1855. MA, R, D-20.
West, N. A. & Mary Jane Long. 8 Oct. 1856. MA, R, D-37.
West, Pleasant & Elizabeth Combs. He was born & res. Jackson
    Co., son of Jobe & Phebe West. She was born & res. Scioto
    Co., dau. of David & S. Combs. 29 Jan. 1857. R, C-5, D-47.
West, Thomas & Hannah Cartright. Her pars. Jesse & Catherine
    Cartwright cons., of Caroline Furnace, Greenup Co., Ky., witn.
    A. Sheppard. 27 Nov. 1850. MA, B-194.
West, William & Sally Worley. 19 Apr. 1814. R, A-333.
Westfall, William C. & Permelia Collins. 22 Feb. 1842. MA, R,
    B-28.
Weston, Thomas & Cincia Charles. 4 Oct. 1860. MA, R, D-129.
Westwood, Daniel & Sophronia Musser. 29 Nov. 1847. MA.
Wetzel, James W. & Eliza Ann Goshen. 14 Aug. 1835. MA, R, A-204.
Wetzel, Onden & Cornelia Bredaker. 17 Oct. 1848. MA.
Whaley, Silas & Susanna Halderman. 8 Apr. 1818. MA, R, A-36.
Wheaton, Uriah & Margret Mackey. 11 Apr. 1809. R, A-294.
Wheeler, George & Ellen Wilson. 21 June 1846. MA, R, B-88.
Wheeler, George W. & Elizabeth A. Bennet. 25 Mar. 1860. MA, R,
    D-118.
Wheeler, Hyatt C. & Eliza Jane Hancock. 11 Mar. 1845. R, B-69.
Wheeler, Isaac H. & Sarah Burt. Her father Benjamin Burt Jr.
    cons. 16 Feb. 1837. MA, R, A-230.
Wheeler, Isaac H. & Elizabeth Burt. 22 Nov. 1856. R, D-42.
Wheeler, John & Rebecca Ann Carter. 17 Oct. 1852. MA, B-248.
Wheeler, Joseph & Lydia Stratton (Shelton). Her father Charles
    Stratton cons., witn. John Smith, Harriet Stretton, of
    Washington Tp. 29 Mar. 1818. MA, R, A-35.
Wheeler, Joshua & Elizabeth Jane Runkles. 11 Mar. 1846. MA,
    B-242.
Wheeler, Levi & Joann Bennett. 25 Sep. 1847. MA.
Wheeler, Nathan III & Nancy Chamberlin. Wyatt Chamberlin att.
    her age. 13 May 1812. MA, R, A-319.
Wheeler, Nathan & Nancy Stout. 21 Apr. 1846. MA.
Wheeler, Nathan & Manerva Bennett. 12 Nov. 1854. MA, R, D-12.
Wheeler, Portious & Jane Burnside. 13 May 1817. MA.
Wheeler, Samuel & Polly Ruckman. 8 July 1831. MA, R, A-166.
Whitcher, Frederick P. & Hannah Throckmorton. 29 Apr. 1833?
    (Among a list of marriages not individually dated.) MA, R,
    A-174.
Whitcomb, Caleb & Eliza Pool. 29 June 1825. MA, R, A-91.
Whitcomb, Dan Y. & Susannah Vincent. 18 Aug. 1825. MA, R, A-90.
White, Abel & Mahala Chamberlain. 5 Feb. 1851. MA, B-203.
White, Albert & Emily Wood. 19 Dec. 1838. MA, R, A-263.
White, Albert & Ethelinda Bracy. (Owen White signed the affi-
    davit on the next page. It is possible he was attesting the
    age of Albert White, and signed in the wrong place.) 27 Mar.
    1859. MA, R, D-90.
White, Anson & Hannah Bagley. His guardian G. W. Flanders cons.
    21 Nov. 1858. MA, R, D-86.
White, Asa & Catherine Peto. 18 July 1820. MA, R, A-53.
White, Asa & Elisabeth Erwin. 4 Oct. 1855. D-22.
White, Bethuel & Ruth (Lucy) Earl. 4 Aug. 1816. MA, R, A-23.
White, Columbia & Jerusha Ann Emory. 3 Dec. 1846. R, B-96.

White, Edward (John) & Catherine Kuhn (Koons). 27 Dec. 1840,
 by John Clingman, J.P. MA, R.
White, Edwin & Mary Ann Finney. 29 Mar. 1849. MA, R, B-144.
White, Enslow & Elizabeth Bower. 4 Sep. 1849. R, B-160.
White, George S. & Hannah Martin. 6 July 1824. R, A-82.
White, George W. & H. A. Barber. 17 Nov. 1850. MA, B-195.
White, Harvey & Lucy Rockwell. 17 Apr. 1833. MA, R, A-182.
White, Henry C. & Emily Jane Allen. 8 Nov. 1854. MA, R, D-11.
White, Homer & Sarah Jane Cassidy. 27 June 1855. MA, R, D-19.
White, Horace & Mary Eliza Pinkerman. John White att. ages.
 2 Apr. 1852. MA, B-236.
White, Ira (?) M. & Elizabeth Ann Moore. 28 Aug. 1852. MA.
White, Israel & Suzan T. Howard. 3 May 1837. R, A-242.
White, Jackson & Anna Graves. 5 Sep. 1844. MA.
White, James & Mildred Henshaw. 27 Oct. 1859. MA, R, D-108.
White, Jesse & Polly Campbell. 26 Mar. 1818. MA, R, A-34.
White, John & Sylva Wyman. 13 Nov. 1814. R, A-343.
White, John & Seby McCann. 9 Nov. 1836. R, A-221.
White, John & Margaret Long. 21 (17) Sep. 1843. MA, R, B-50.
White, John & Barbary Giss. 7 Mar. 1846. MA.
White, John Jr. & Emarelda Willson. He is 21, born & res.
 Madison Tp., son of John White. She is 15, born Jackson Co.,
 res. Madison Tp., dau. of Jas. Wilson. 26 Oct. 1856. MA, R,
 C-4, D-41.
White, John D. & Sophia Conway (Carrway). 4 Apr. 1844. MA, R,
 B-57.
White, Josiah & Elizabeth Pickance (Pikkens). 1 Feb. 1835. MA,
 R, A-196.
White, Leonard C. & Margaret C. Hart. 3 Dec. 1851. MA, B-224.
White, Manlius & Sarah Wagoner. 3 Sep. 1854. R, D-10.
White, Mathew & Naomi Barton. 16 Feb. 1812. R, A-317.
White, Milton & Martha Jane Taylor. 30 Aug. 1848. MA.
White, Nelson & Eliza Wilson. Her father James Wilson cons.
 15 Dec. 1853. MA, D-6.
White, Osborn & Maria Chamberlain. 4 Jan. 1838. R, A-248, B-5.
White, Patrick & Bridget Henry. 14 June 1858. MA.
White, Paul & Elizabeth Walker. 2 Mar. 1852. MA, B-246.
White, Tapley & Prudence Martin. 23 May 1811. A-312, R.
White, Thayer D. & Eliza Kimball, of Green Tp. 3 Jan. 1825.
 MA, R, A-86.
White, Uriah & Mary Huston. 5 July 1808. R, A-290.
White, Uriah Jr. & Amanda Morton. 22 Oct. 1843. MA, R, B-49.
White, Wayne & Nancy Biggs. Edward White att. ages. 19 Oct.
 1848. MA, R, B-134.
Whiteaker (Whitticer), James & Eliza Jane Horner. Her mother
 Nancy Thane cons., witn. Andrew Baley, Isaac Wollam. 3 July
 1845. MA, R, B-76.
Whitehair, John & Catherine Gimps. 1 Nov. 1858. MA, R, D-93.
Whitemore, Barnvard & Catharine Rider. He is 24, born Switzer-
 land, res. Portsmouth, son of George & E. Whitemore. She is
 20, born Germany, res. Scioto Co., dau. of Phillip & S.
 Rider. 15 Aug. 1856. C-7.
Whitier, Thomas & Jane A. Boynton. 19 Dec. 1821. R, A-62.
Whitman, Joseph & Minerva Copenhaver. 4 Jan. 1855. MA, R, D-17.
Whitmore, Amos N. (H.) & Betsey Lamb. 2 Oct. 1816. MA, R, A-23.
Whitney, John & Pemel Filch (Fitch?). 15 Nov. 1835. R, A-207.
Whitney, John & Arina Kelly. 21 Dec. 1843. R, B-51.
Whitney, William G. & Elcy M. S. Voorhees. 20 Mar. 1850. R,
 B-175.
Whitte, Henry & Mary Donewitz. 21 Mar. 1848. MA, R, B-121.
Wickline, Henry T. & Mary Slagle. 1 Mar. 1859. MA, R, D-77.
Widmer, Jacob & Susannah Rider (Reiter). 18 May 1851. MA,
 B-209.

Wiehle, John & Caroline Schnecker. 10 Jan. 1857. R, D-60.
Wiehle, William & Caroline Gabble. 18 June 1860. MA.
Wiget, Joseph & Lucinda Bender. 12 Nov. 1855. MA.
Wiggard, George O. & Ruth Cranston. 21 Nov. 1849. MA, R, B-164.
Wiggs, Jacob & Sarah J. Chaffin. 11 June 1853. MA.
Wigham, Silas & Elizabeth Overturf. 21 Aug. 1845. R, B-77.
Wikell, A. E. & Catharine Payton. 9 Aug. 1854. R, D-9.
Wikoff, Peter & Mahala Bradford. His father John Wikoff cons.,
    witn. James Wikoff. 1 Aug. 1822. MA, R, A-68.
Wilburn, Jackson & Lucinda Callahan. 3 June 1846. MA, R, B-87.
Wilburn, Thomas & Roxanna Gharky. 8 Oct. 1835. R, A-206.
Wilcox, Ephraim & Mrs. Mary Howard. 1 Jan. 1831, by Ezra Osborn
    J.P. MA, R.
Wilcoxan, Otho & Mary Earley. __ Feb. 1835. R, A-198.
Wilcoxen, Overton (Urtoin) & Sabina Shaffer. 13 Oct. 1831. R,
    A-156.
Wilcoxen, Thomas J. & Rebecca Smalley. 25 Dec. 1834. R, A-195.
Wilcoxen, Thompson & Cyenda Mitchell. 23 Dec. 1830, by William
    Givens, J.P. R.
Wilcoxon, Aquilla & Joanna Carrol. 25 Apr. 1835. R, A-201.
Wilcoxon, Caleb & Mary Setton. 18 Nov. 1819. MA.
Wilcoxon, George D. H. & Anna Hoskinson. Her father Josiah
    Hoskinson cons., witn. Jesse Cockrell. 30 Aug. 1815. MA, R,
    A-20.
Wilcoxon, John & Nancy Miller. 29 Sep. 1838. MA.
Wilcoxon, John E. & Indiana Woodyard. Her mother Jene (?) Wood-
    yard cons. 3 Apr. 1848. MA, R, B-121.
Wilcoxon, Joseph & Caroline Hunt. 25 Mar. 1839. R, A-267.
Wilcoxon, Levi & Abigail M. Mastin. 12 May 1844. MA, R, B-59.
Wilcoxon, Loyd & Elizabeth Feurt. 29 June 1815. MA, R, A-282.
Wilcoxon, Rezin & Hannah Hibbs. 12 July 1840. R, B-28.
Wilcoxon, Thomas Jr. & Sally Wilcoxen. 19 Oct. 1815. MA, R,
    A-20.
Wilcoxon, William Z. (F.?) & Catharine Ballad. 4 Apr. 1850. R,
    B-179.
Wild, Milton & Vilene Carter. Jacob Carter att. ages. 10 June
    1849. MA, R, B-151.
Wild, William G. & Darkis Sheats. 25 Dec. 1837. MA, R, A-251.
Wilhelm, Jacob & Amanda Day. Dudley Day att. her age. 3 June
    1829. MA, R, A-132.
Wilkin, Henry & Rebecca Hibbs. 15 Aug. 1850. R, B-186.
Wilkins, William M. & Sarah Barber. 20 Dec. 1847. MA, R, B-111.
Will, George W. & Hannah McClure. Her father cons. 1 May 1847.
    MA, B-245.
Willard, Cyrus & Elizabeth Davidson. 18 Apr. 1853. MA, B-261.
Willard, Mellen & Elizabeth K. Cameron. 22 Nov. 1860. MA, R, D-134.
Willcoxen, Walter & Elizabeth Deaver. 27 Dec. 1810. R, A-307.
Willcoxon, Caleb & Charlotte Jones. 29 Dec. 1844. MA, R, B-66.
Willcoxon, Caleb & Sarah J. Daniels. 24 Dec. 1853. MA, D-7.
Willcoxon, Levin & Margit Williamson. 23 Mar. 1809. A-296.
Willey, Henry & Sarah Glasford. 30 May 1852. MA, B-246.
Willey, James F. & Margaret McCreery (McKery). 17 Apr. 1851.
    MA, B-208.
Willey, Michael & Phebe Jones. 13 June 1841. R, B-22.
Williams, Amos & Ann Thomas. 8 June 1852. MA, B-241.
Williams, Daniel & Mary J. Price. 1 Mar. 1855. R, D-16.
Williams, David & Mahala Squires. Her father Samuel Squires
    cons., witn. John Roberts, James Hughs. 26 July 1832. MA.
Williams, David & Peggy Huddleston. James Hughes att. her age.
    24 Mar. 1822. MA, R, A-67.
Williams, David & Elizabeth Hesler. 11 Feb. 1858. R, D-70.
Williams, Ebanezer & Hannah Daniels. 1 Feb. 1860. MA, R, D-111.

SCIOTO COUNTY MARRIAGES

Williams, Eli & Sarah Davis. 23 Apr. 1806. R, A-12, A-281.
Williams, Evans & Catherine Edwards. 4 May 1852. MA, B-275.
Williams, Ewel & Eliza Jane Lodwick. 12 Nov. 1834. MA, R,
 A-206.
Williams, Ewel & Harriet Loveland. 10 May 1857. R, D-53.
Williams, Garrett & Sarah Ann Cockrell. 8 Feb. 1844. MA, R,
 B-54.
Williams, George Jr. & Lucy Boynton. 13 Nov. 1818. MA, R, A-42.
Williams, Henry & Jane Anderson. Her pars. John & Julian
 Anderson cons., witn. John Williams. 16 Jan. 1834. MA, R,
 A-185.
Williams, Isaac & Delilah McCall. 11 Dec. 1822. MA, R, A-72.
Williams, Israel & Mary Jane Blagg. 26 Oct. 1848. MA, R, B-137.
Williams, James & Mary Darlington. 5 Mar. 1820, by John Carney,
 Baptist Church. MA, R.
Williams, James & Jane Price. 16 Feb. 1836. MA, R, A-213, A-229.
Williams, James & Eliza Jane Timmonds. 1 Jan. 1854. D-6.
Williams, Jeptha & Belinda Lee. John Brown Sr. att. her age.
 6 Feb. 1821. MA, R, A-58.
Williams, Jesse & Lidea Shores, of Seal Tp. 11 Apr. 1810. R,
 A-299.
Williams, Jesse & Rebecca Moore. 19 Oct. 1826. R, A-101.
Williams, Jessy & Ann Daley, Seal Tp. 21 Mar. 1806. R, A-11.
Williams, John & Phebe Jones. Her father Benjamin Jones cons.,
 att. Richard H. Laire, says she is over 18. 4 Apr. 1822.
 MA, R, A-65.
Williams, John & Rebecca Newman. 9 June 1843. MA, R, B-46.
Williams, John & Jane Elizabeth Tison. 9 Jan. 1846. MA, R,
 B-83.
Williams, John & Elizabeth Goun. 29 Dec. 1859. MA, R, D-104.
Williams, Jonathan & Mary Lair (Jain). 19 Mar. 1846. R, B-85.
Williams, Joseph, of Gallia Co. & Elizabeth Richart. 16 Jan.
 1838. R, A-248.
Williams, Joseph & E. Sherman. 1 Dec. 1855. D-23.
Williams, Lewis W. & Sarah Jane Lee. 23 Sep. 1853. MA.
Williams, Lilbourn & Sarah Detty. His father George W. Williams
 cons., att. Jesse Carpenter. 4 Mar. 1858. MA, R, D-75.
Williams, Lorenzo D. & Susan Nelson. Enoch Williams att. ages.
 6 Nov. 1851. MA, B-224.
Williams, Robert & Comfort Lewis. 7 Aug. 1811. R, A-311.
Williams, Samuel & Sidney Ann Huston. 12 Apr. 1838. R, A-252.
Williams, Thomas & Catharine Kearns. 20 Jan. 1856. R, D-25.
Williams, Thomas & Mary Lenard. 28 Nov. 1858. MA, R, D-76.
Williams, William & Catherine Morrison (Morris). 22 Apr. 1824.
 R, A-87.
Williams, William & Delila Hunt. 8 Aug. 1839. MA, R, A-271.
Williams, William A. & Martha J. Crane. 18 May 1851. MA, B-207.
Williams, William E. & Martha Jane Bowers. 8 June 1853. MA,
 B-262.
Williamson, Allden Washington & Sarah Ann Gherky. 22 Dec. 1841.
 R, B-26.
Williamson, Cornelius & Elizabeth Pool. 22 Nov. 1827. R, A-112.
Williamson, Francis & Eve Mackeltree. His mother cons. 6 May
 1813. MA, R, A-325.
Williamson, James & Jane McKinley. 27 Sep. 1818. MA, R, A-61.
Williamson, James & Christina Shaffer. 22 Sep. 1829. R, A-136.
Williamson, James T. (I.) & Martha Lewis Cargal. Henry Silvey
 att. her age. James Smith att. his age. 3 Sep. 1838. MA,
 R, A-257.
Williamson, John & Eleanor R. Wilcoxon. 27 Feb. 1851. MA, B-203.
Williamson, John & Hannah A. Page. 4 Jan. 1853. MA, B-256.
Williamson, John & A. F. Lucas. 2 Aug. 1855. R, D-19.

147

Williamson, Joseph & Elizabeth Willcoxon. 27 Jan. 1820. R, A-52.
Williamson, Joseph & Elenor Moore. 1 Jan. 1825. R, A-85.
Williamson, Joseph & Catherine Shafer, both of Washington Tp.
15 June 1826. R, A-97.
Williamson, Leonard McGinnis & Ann Farington. 20 Apr. 1845. R,
B-70.
Williamson, Martin J. & Margaret Feurt. Peter Feurt cons.
24 Apr. 1824. MA, R, A-87.
Williamson, Peter & Rosanna Shaffer. 24 May 1827. R, A-106.
Williamson, Thomas & Lucinda Oard. 29 Dec. 1831. R, A-158.
Williamson, Thomas & Drusilla W. Smith. William Early att. ages.
12 July 1852. MA, B-240.
Williamson, William & Elizabeth Dysert. 10 Oct. 1816. MA, R,
A-23.
Willis, Fielding & Eliza Minard. 1 June 1856. R, D-31.
Willis, Harrison & Serena (Levina) Hard. Her pars. Jonathan B.
& Sophronia Hard cons., att. John Willis, French Grant.
17 Jan. 1841. MA, R, B-14.
Willis, Henry & Matilda Green. Her pars. Coonrod & Susan Green
cons., witn. William Barnett, George Crawford. John Willis
cons. 8 July 1846. MA, R, B-92.
Willis, William & Philora Morrison. He res. Franklin Furnace,
born Vernon Tp. She was born Lawrence Co., dau. of James
Morrison & Mary Conklin. Samuel Hart att. ages. 28 Sep.
1856. MA, R, C-11, D-39.
Williun (Wilhin?), Edward & Clarissa Duncan. 16 July 1846. MA,
R, B-89.
Willoughby, Hardin H. & Emily Spence. 12 May 1844. MA, R, B-58.
Willson, David & Catharine Ann Brant. 28 Nov. 1844. MA, R,
B-68.
Willson, George & Rachel Storey. 29 June 1826. R, A-99.
Willson, Joseph & Julia A. McDougle. He is 24, son of John &
Elizabeth Willson. She is 26, born Scioto Co., res. Morgan
Tp., dau. of A. & Mary Noel, second marr. 21 Jan. 1858.
R, C-13, D-75.
Willson, Moses M. & Lenah J. Dyre. 17 Dec. 1857. R, D-70.
Willson, William M. & Arenda Roberts. 15 June 1841. R, B-32.
Wilson, A. E. & C. O. Long. He is 42, born Germany, res. Ports-
mouth, son of Jacob Wilson. She is 40, born Germany, res.
Portsmouth, dau. of Frederick Oto, second marr. __ Nov. 1856.
C-6.
Wilson, Albert & Rebecca Howe (Horne?). 23 July 1850. MA, R,
B-183.
Wilson, Alexander & Elizabeth Farrell. 16 Oct. 1854. R, D-11.
Wilson, Benjamin & Elizabeth Jackson. 6 June 1848. B-126.
Wilson, Chancellor W. & Ellen Swift. 24 Mar. 1859. MA, R, D-89.
Wilson, Clark (Charles) & Sarah A. Swords. 23 Feb. 1852. MA,
B-232, B-275.
Wilson, Daniel & Mary (Polly) McConnel. 23 Aug. 1827. MA, R,
A-109.
Wilson, David & Elizabeth Overly. 25 Aug. 1850. R, B-187.
Wilson, George M. & Fanny Scott. 15 June 1859. MA, R, D-97.
Wilson, George M. & Lotty Willett. 1 July 1860. MA, R, D-131.
Wilson, George N. & Cynthia Batterson. 29 Feb. 1844. MA, R,
B-56.
Wilson, George W. & Mary E. Elisabeth Jones. 11 July 1857. R,
D-56.
Wilson, Hiram & Martha Wallace (Walles). 5 Dec. 1830. MA, R,
A-149.
Wilson, James & Levina Green. 3 May 1859. MA, R, D-91.
Wilson, James Jr. & Martha Brown. 21 Feb. 1825. R, A-86.
Wilson, James & Rebecca A. Wiley. 4 Jan. 1852. MA, B-198, B-227.
Wilson, James & Amanda Forney. 7 Jan. 1854. B-282.

SCIOTO COUNTY MARRIAGES

Wilson, Jeremiah & Emeline Lemmison. 3 Oct. 1840. MA.
Wilson, John & Sarah Bissel. 8 Oct. 1835. R, A-206.
Wilson, John & Mary Turner. 11 July 1844. MA.
Wilson, John & Susanna Bonzo. 12 Aug. 1852. MA, B-252.
Wilson, John & Elizabeth Morgan. His guardian Henry Sword cons.
  23 Apr. 1858. MA, R, D-73.
Wilson, John & Milly Weaver. 26 Oct. 1859. MA, R, D-108.
Wilson, John Henry & Lucy Ann Cassady. 11 Jan. 1853. MA, B-256.
Wilson, Joseph & Harriet Crawford. His father John Wilson cons.
  T. B. Finton att. her age. 15 Aug. 1842. MA, R, B-50.
Wilson, Levi F. & Mary Hartman. 13 Jan. 1848. MA, R, B-114.
Wilson, Martin V. B. & Mehaly A. Noel. He is 20, born Pike Co.,
  res. Scioto Co., son of U. & Jane Wilson. She is 19, dau. of
  Ab. & Susan Noel. 11 Nov. 1857. R, C-10, D-65.
Wilson, Nathan & Sarah Spriggs. 19 Apr. 1849. MA, R, B-147.
Wilson, S. C. & Frances S. Skelton. Her pars. John & Manerva
  Skelton cons., att. James Skelton, George E. Rutter. 20 Mar.
  1855. MA, R, D-16.
Wilson, Samuel & Esther Lee. 13 Apr. 1815. MA, R, A-348.
Wilson, William & Sarah Adams. 7 Aug. 1829. R, A-135.
Wilson, William & Mary Morgan, Union Tp. 16 June 1840. R, B-10.
Wilson, William & Julia Ann Blagg. Richard Jackson att. ages.
  7 June 1840. MA, R, B-11.
Wilson, William & Sarah Ann How. 11 Feb. 1853, by E. P. Pratt,
  Presbyterian Church. MA, R.
Wilson, William & Elizabeth Otenburger. 2 Nov. 1856. MA, R,
  D-41.
Windle, Jacob H. & Sarah Emmons. 14 July 1859. MA, R, D-101.
Winet, Abraham & Nancy Jones. 25 Oct. 1847. MA, R, B-109.
Winet, John & Mary Jane McDowell. 7 Mar. 1847. MA, R, B-99.
Wing (Winey), A. H. & Belinda Stilwell. 18 July 1850. MA,
  B-197.
Wingard, J. B. & Mary Johnson. 10 Jan. 1858. R, D-67.
Wingo, Russell & Elmira Creswell. 7 Feb. 1854. B-283.
Winkler, Asher & Lucretia Gregory. 23 May 1841. MA, R, B-22.
Winkler, Harris & Nancy Story. 11 Oct. 1838. MA, R, A-260.
Winkler, Isaac & Jane A. Williams. 20 July 1847. MA, R, B-107.
Winkler, John & Clarissa Lamb. 15 June 1832. R, A-170.
Winkler, John & Cynthia Chandler. 10 Mar. 1842. R, B-29.
Winkler, Robert & Maria Dever. 6 Dec. 1845. MA, R, B-80.
Winn, Thomas & Jane Neve. Her father George Neve cons. 24 Dec.
  1852, by E. P. Pratt. MA, R.
Winte, Harman Henry & Pauline Hemlep. 15 Jan. 1858. R, D-70.
Winter, Frederick & Filica Overly. 26 Mar. 1857. R, D-51.
Wirt (West), Nicholas & Sumantha (Martha) Goddard. He is 24,
  born Germany, son of Elizabeth West. She is 19, born Penn.,
  dau. of Jas. Goddard. 7 Mar. 1858. MA, R, C-14, D-72.
Wirt (West), Samuel & Nancy Saulsberry (Salisbury). 25 June
  1818. MA, R, A-38.
Wise, John & Mary V. Freshell. 26 Aug. 1858. MA, R, D-84, D-114.
Wisecof (Wisecap), Abraham & Julia Sanford. 25 Oct. 1841, by
  John Lawson. MA, R.
Wishon, Jacob & Nancy Rice (Riece). 10 Mar. 1835. MA, R, A-199.
Witte, Henry (Johann Heinrich Witt) & Amanda Cline. 22 Aug. 1852.
  MA, B-249.
Wittenmyer, William & Sarah Ann Turner. 26 May 1845. MA.
Wittman, John & Lucinda Anderson. 1 Feb. 1859. MA, R, D-78.
Wix (Wicks, Hicks), Henry & Rachel Jones. not dated 1853. MA,
  D-3 (has names only in the margin).
Wixom (Wickson), Nathan & Betsy Eliza Hadlock. 1 Nov. 1827. MA,
  R, A-111, A-117.
Wolcott, Henry & Elizabeth B. Richart. 28 Apr. 1860. MA, R,
  D-115.

149

Wolf, Andrew & Rebecca Skelton. Her father Samuel Skelton cons., att. her brother John Skelton. 10 Apr. 1830. MA, R, A-141.
Wolf, Andrew & Mary Salladay. 31 May 1829. MA, R, A-132.
Wolf, David & Elizabeth Shope. John Snedecor att. her age. 22 Aug. 1814. MA, R, A-338.
Wolf, David & Polly Cable. 6 Aug. 1816. MA, R, A-22.
Wolf, Elhenney & Rachel Cochran. 27 Nov. 1850. MA, B-195.
Wolf, Jesse & Nancy Horner. 28 Dec. 1815. A-17.
Wolf, John & Cassandra Melton. 16 Nov. 1826 (1825). MA, R, A-94.
Wolf, John & Mary Shultz. 25 Dec. 1860. MA, R, D-133.
Wolf, William & Cassandra Ball. He res. Lawrence Co., Oh. Her father David Ball, of Green Tp., cons., witn. David Ball Jr. 3 Oct. 1829. MA, R, A-146.
Wolfard, Airhart & Penelope Minard. 25 June 1845. MA, R, B-76.
Wolfard, Francis Joseph & Mary Murray. 8 Apr. 1834. MA.
Wolford, John & Mary Shope. 27 Oct. 1836. MA, R, A-221.
Wollem, Jacob & Catharine Dewitt. 18 May 1848. MA, R, B-129.
Wollman, Lewis & Mary Rausohind. 28 Jan. 1850. R, B-168.
Wonderly, Daniel & Louisa Tetus (Teters). 10 Mar. 1832. MA, R, A-163.
Wood, Daniel & Esther Paul. 25 Mar. 1838. MA, R, A-252.
Wood, E. H. & Anna E. Gilpin. He is 48, res. Washington Tp., second marr. She is 20, res. Washington Tp., dau. of L. R. Gilpin, first marr. 16 Dec. 1856. C-6, D-44.
Wood, Elijah & Milly Pyles. Her mother Mary Pyles cons., att. James Wood. 8 Mar. 1838. MA, R, A-252.
Wood, Francis & Lucinda Reu. He is 22; she is 18, born Jackson Co., res. Harrison Tp., dau. of Charles Reu & Hannah Cooper. 20 Mar. 1858. C-14.
Wood, Jackson B. & America White. 12 Jan. 1848. MA, R, B-113.
Wood, Jacob & Mary Lair. Her father Richard H. Laire cons., says she was 14 the 2nd of July last, witn. David Welch. 17 Feb. 1847. MA, B-229.
Wood, James & Syrena White. 13 __ 1851 (recorded 14 May). B-207.
Wood, Job & Mary Ann Farrar. 7 Feb. 1854. B-283.
Wood, John & Abigail Paul. 20 July 1823. MA, R, A-78, A-88.
Wood, John N. & Elizabeth S. Wikoff. 19 Dec. 1843. MA, R, B-52.
Wood, Jonathan E. & Sarah Richart. Her father John Richart cons. 20 Feb. 1852. MA, R, B-237.
Wood, Oliver & Emily H. Mytinger. 21 June 1855. R, D-19.
Wood, Richard & Elizabeth Philips. 8 Jan. 1837 (recorded 8 Feb. 1838). MA, R, A-248.
Wood, Robert, from Piketon & Jane F. Peebles, from Portsmouth. 26 May 1827. R, A-107.
Wood, Simian & Emeline White. 31 Oct. 1832. R, A-168.
Wood, William L. & Cornelia B. Andrews. 18 Feb. 1846. R, B-83.
Woodard, David & Betsy Rickey. 5 Nov. 1828. MA, R, A-123.
Woodford, Frederick & Mary Dillon. 31 Oct. 1833. R, A-178.
Woodring, William & Mary Ann Cunningham. 3 Apr. 1845. R, B-72.
Woodrough (Woodruff), Isaac & Mary Bostwick. 12 June 1849. MA, R, B-148.
Woodruff, Ananias S. & Martha Tucker. 26 Feb. 1846. MA, R, B-86.
Woodside, William J. & Sarah J. Kepler. John Dymond att. ages. 18 July 1860. MA, R, D-132.
Woodward, David S. & Margaret Cochran. 18 Sep. 1850. MA, R, B-192.
Woodworth, Laban & Katharine Elliott. 28 Sep. 1826. MA, R, A-99.
Woolford, Daniel Jr. & Castena Hoppis. 3 Feb. 1820. R, A-58.
Woolford, Erhart & Aramatha Shope. Her father John Shope cons., witn. John B. Wolford, Jno. Shope Jr. 22 Oct. 1839. MA, R, A-273.

Woolford, Frederick & Keziah Heartly. 7 July 1842. MA, R, B-32.
Wooten, William & Nancy Jane Betts. Her father Abram Betts cons.
   19 Feb. 1858. MA.
Worcester, Samuel H. & Elizabeth L. Baylor. 15 Aug. 1850. R,
   B-187.
Worden, Benjamin F. & Julia Cole. 27 Mar. 1842. MA, R, B-29.
Work, Benjamin & Felicity Kidd. MA stats she was married to
   Samuel Work around 16 years ago; he left around 13 years ago.
   Nine years ago he wrote to his father. His pars. believe he
   is dead. 17 Mar. 1849. MA, R, B-143.
Work, Samuel & Eliza Head. His father John Work cons. 25 Dec.
   1819. MA, R, A-50.
Worley, Anthoney & Sarah Ann Silvey. 24 Mar. 1832. R, A-160.
Worley, Elijah & Rebecca Zornes. His father Anthony Worley cons.
   witn. John Welch. 29 Dec. 1819. MA.
Worley, Isaac & Elizabeth Edison. 2 Nov. 1811. R, A-314.
Worley, Jacob & Susannah Bibby. 25 Feb. 1819. R, A-44.
Worley, James E. & Mary Ellen Scott. 22 Mar. 1840. R, B-3.
Worley, John & Sarah Bradford. 14 May 1844. MA, B-59.
Worley, John M. & Mahala Mariah Burris. 15 Sep. 1831. R, A-157.
Worley, Joseph & Lydia A. Stelson. 30 Mar. 1859. MA, R, D-90.
Worley, Morgan & Eliza Noel. 15 Mar. 1849. MA, R, B-146.
Worley, Moses & Sarah Harmon. 18 Aug. 1819. R, A-47.
Worley, Sylvester T. & Caroline Piles. 5 Apr. 1854. B-283.
Worley, Sylvester T. & Elizabeth J. Hicks. 10 Nov. 1858. MA,
   R, D-86.
Worley, William C. & Harriet Veach. 24 Oct. 1852. MA, B-250.
Worley, William C. & Mary A. Willard (Willett). He is 28, born
   Ohio, res. Portsmouth, son of William & Rebecca Worley,
   second marr. She is 19, born Ky., dau. of Isaac & E. Willett,
   first marr. 20 Mar. 1856. C-6, B-286.
Worster (Weisted), John & Susannah Goeblin. 21 Nov. 1850. MA,
   B-194.
Woten, John & Emily Canter. He is 21, born Jackson, Oh., res.
   Scioto Co., son of Nathan & Elizabeth Woten. She is 18, born
   & res. Scioto Co., dau. of William & Catharine Canter.
   16 Aug. 1857. MA, R, C-8, C-12, D-64.
Wotring, Jacob & Mary M. Byers. 7 Dec. 1841. R, B-25.
Wright, George & Juliann Smith. 21 June 1854. R, D-8.
Wright, Isaac & Rebeccah Noel. 2 July 1812. MA, R, A-321.
Wright, John & Mary Fletcher. 11 July 1806. R, A-281.
Wright, John M. & Malinda Evans. 10 Aug. 1848. MA, R, B-129.
Wright, Joseph & Rebecca Landers. Adam Landers cons., says
   Rebecca is over 18, att. William Wright. 25 Mar. 1830. MA,
   R, A-141.
Wright, William & Caty Noel. 21 May 1807. R, A-285.
Wright, William (Wilhelm Reichert) & Hannah Stout. 5 Sep. 1853.
   MA.
Wrigley, John & Jane Tytus. His father James Wrigley cons., att.
   William Holmes. 15 June 1860. MA, R, D-119.
Wyand, Philip & Agnes Frische. 18 Nov. 1848. MA, R, B-134.
Wyatt, David S. & Mary France Blake. 23 Mar. 1854. D-3.
Wyatt, Jacob C. & Latitia Shelpman. 8 Jan. 1849. MA, R, B-139.
Wyatt, Noridan C. & Nancy Wallace (Walles), both of Madison Tp.
   23 Jan. 1838. MA, R, A-248.
Wyeth, Walter N. & Isabella Wait. 9 May 1859. MA, R, D-96.
Wyett, Alcubiddes & Martha W. Wyett. 23 Mar. 1841. R, B-17.
Wymer, Daniel F. & Lucy L. Porter. 5 June 1859. MA, R, D-97.
Wymer, George W. & Mary F. Bramble. 31 May 1859. MA, R, D-97.
Wynn, Benjamin F. & Drusilla F. Welch. 4 Mar. 1858. MA, R,
   D-71.
Yates, Jonathan & Eliza Yates. 16 Aug. 1847. MA, R, B-105.

Yeager, Cornelius H. & Frances Johnson. 6 Dec. 1859. MA, R, D-104.
Yeager, George & Rosena Meyer. 6 Aug. 1860. MA, R, D-128.
Yeley, Dennis & Eliza Wait. Her father Benjamin Wait cons. 16 July 1835. MA, R, A-203.
Yeley, Henry & Rebecca Lindsey. Her mother Sarah Barchus cons., witn. Gershum Bennett, Huldah Bennett. 11 Aug. 1844. MA, R, B-62.
Yeley, James W. & Emma Lionberger. Edwin Fuller att. ages. 14 Oct. 1858. MA, R, D-81.
Yeley, Joseph & Elenor Slocum. 9 Mar. 1854. D-6.
Yingling, Christian & Patsy Lee. Her father John Lee cons., witn. Peter Lionbarger, Janes Henry. 20 Oct. 1814. MA, R, A-347.
Yoakley, John & Susan R. St. John. 23 June 1847. MA, R, B-104.
Yost, Ephraim & Elizabeth Jane Hood. Her pars. Robert & Nancy Hood cons., witn. Michael Howard. 3 Sep. 1840. MA, R, B-11.
Yost, John & Margaret Roberts. 26 Dec. 1860. MA, R, D-133.
Young, Charles & Nancy Bellamy. 28 Sep. 1837. MA, R, A-236.
Young, Conrod & Mary Swords. 24 Sep. 1842. R, B-35.
Young, Rev. Dan & Melvina Montgomery. 25 Apr. 1842. R, B-32.
Young, Findley & Christiana Storer. 10 Aug. 1848. R, B-129.
Young, Jacob & Mary Shepard. 13 Nov. 1854. MA.
Young, Jesse & Mary A. Clough. 10 May 1835. R, A-211.
Young, John & Barbara Rider. Her father Franz (?) Rider, of Bloom Tp., cons. 8 Mar. 1859. MA, R, D-92.
Young, Johnson & Elizabeth Dunlap. 2 May 1859. MA, R, D-91.
Young, Lewis H. & Adeline Frazier. 22 Dec. 1840. R, B-7.
Young, Samuel & Mary Funk. 20 Dec. 1813. MA.
Young, William & Nancy Buckles. 20 Oct. 1831. MA, R, A-158.
Young, William & Susan Newcomb. 11 July 1853. MA, B-265.
Young, William & Elizabeth Boyes (Boyce). 6 Dec. 1859, by W. E. Williams, J.P. MA, R.
Young, William H. & Margrat Jane Bartlow. 18 Jan. 1860. MA, R, D-113.
Young, William J. & Caroline Beloat. 15 Oct. 1854. R, D-11.
Younker, David & Margaret Lorina Costz (Corta). 15 Sep. 1854. R, D-10.
Zapf, Jacob & Sarah Wahl. 1 Aug. 1850. R, B-185.
Zarly, Reason (Rezen Surely) & Sarah (Sally) Mustard. 17 Nov. 1814. MA, R, A-342.
Zeek, Andrew & Laura Loomis. 20 Apr. 1853. B-261.
Zephyrs, Thomas & Mary Jones. 12 July 1844. MA, R, B-60.
Zessler, Frederick & Barbara A. Glass. 5 July 1853. MA.
Ziegler, Charles & Louisa Schulz. 27 Apr. 1850. R, B-178.
Ziegler, Henry D. & Mary Norris. 27 June 1844. MA, R, B-60.
Zinckhan, Michael & Margaretha Roth. 1 Apr. 1857. MA, R, D-61.
Zollars, Charles M. & Caroline McColm. 31 July 1853. B-266.
Zollars, Zephiniah B. & Lavina Miles. 19 Feb. 1840. MA, R, B-6.
Zollner, Philipp & Mary Scott. 9 July 1857. R, D-61.
Zornes, Asa & Mary Evans. 6 May 1852. MA, B-276.
Zornes, John & Melissa Worley. 11 May 1840. MA, R, B-4.
Zornes, Martin A. & Susannah Bibbey. 7 Dec. 1848. MA, R, B-137.
Zornes, R. T. & Martha Jane Walker. 2 June 1853. MA, B-265.
Zornes, William & Mary Nichols. 26 Nov. 1846. MA, R, B-94.
Zorns, Aaron & Nancy Brightman. 11 May 1837. MA.
Zorns, George W. & Mary Jane Cooper. 8 Jan. 1857. R, D-46.
Zorns, Martin & Nancy McKinney (M. Kinney). 25 Mar. 1824. R, A-80.
Zorns, Martin A. & Delilah Hall. 25 Feb. 1851. MA, B-202.
Zorns, Martin Alvy & Mary Ann Storer. 25 Apr. 1839. MA, R, A-270.

SCIOTO COUNTY MARRIAGES

Zorns, Thomas & Prudence Pettet. 1 Nov. 1813. MA, R, A-327.
Zull, Ezekiel & Kesiah W. Sheffland. 8 Feb. 1846. MA, R, B-83.
Zwicker, Henry & Johanna Bertram. 28 Apr. 1847. MA, R, B-101.
Zwickert, Henry & Catharina From. 30 Dec. 1856. R, D-60.

Batterson (cont.)
Helen 37
Battles, Sarah 123
Baucas, Sarah 142
Bauch, Margaret 50
Baukamp, Hannah 81
Baum, Barbara 53, 129
Bayler, Eliza Jane 99
Bayless, Adelaine 75
Jane 82
Bayley, Martha J. 90
Baylor, Elizabeth L. 151
Baynes, Margaret 9
Bayse, David 56
Joseph 12
Baze, Joseph 12
Beakler, Phebe 110
Beals, Asa Gideon 8
Bean, Emaline 36
Mary 45
Bear, Nancy J. 116
Beard, Rachel 6
Beatty, Rebeckah 75
Beaty, Susannah 133
Beauchamp, Anna 81
Mary Ann 18
Bebar, Orlenda 20
Bebee, Sarah Ann 14
Beck, Catharine 73
Fanny 143
John 8
Rebecca (Mrs.) 8
Bedal, Rebeccah 8
Beelenger, Francis 12
Beeler, George 10
Magdalena 13
Beer, Nancy J. 116
Beinger, Francis 12
Belcher, Joseph 8
Richard 8
Virginia 86
Beler, Elias 89
Belico, Anestialeo 94
Bellamy, Nancy 152
Beller, Cynthia Ann 89
Belli, Cynthia 92
Eliza 52
Lucretia 2
Beloat, Ann 80
Caroline 31, 152
George 30, 91, 138
George W. 8
Joseph 8
Lydia 17, 101
Margaret 87
Mary 47
Minerva 70
Nancy 33, 91
Polly 128
Belote, Mary 16
Belz, Catherine 12
Bend, Clary 118
Bender, Barbara 17
Catharine 3
Christiana 74
E. (Mrs.) 17
Elizabeth 34
Jacob 17
Lucinda 146
Margaret 97
Benesser, Mary 10
Benet, Thomas 128
Benight, Thaddeus 9
Bennarde, Rose 118
Benner, Caroline 65, 96
Hanah 27
Mary Ann 57
Bennet, Ann Eliza 60

Bennet (cont.)
Anne 132
Benjamin F. 9
Caleb 128
Catharine 134
Cias 65
Cynthia (Mrs.) 119
Eleanor 71
Elenor 128
Elisabeth 75
Elizabeth (Mrs.) 9
Elizabeth A. 144
Elizabeth Jane 65
Elizabeth M. 80
Emeline 38
Frances 7
Gilbert 9, 82, 103,
136
Hannah 128
Hannah (Mrs.) 117
Harriet 28, 120
Ira 127
Jacob 119
Jemima 118
John 9
Julia Ann 107
Katherine 112
Louisa 113
Margaret 82
Margery 75
Maria 22
Martha 9, 41, 72
Mary 136
Minerva 103
Nancy (Mrs.) 9
Olive 84
Polly 120
Pricilla 136
Rebecah 9
Rebecca 141
Robbart 116
Robert 112
Sally 123
Sally Ann 21
Samuel 8, 9
Sarah 116, 118, 123
Sarah M. 1
Sophiah 86
Susan Ann 90, 133
Thomas 75, 117
Thomas (Jr.) 112
William 8
Bennett, Amanda 32
Ann 26
Benjamin 94
Caleb 32
Catharine 94
Cathereen 85
Christina 135
Cias 65
Cyinda 125
Delila 28
Deniza 55
Eliza (Mrs.) 32
Elizabeth 36, 67, 76
Elizabeth Ann 48
Elizabeth E. 18
Elizabeth Jane 65
Elizabeth S. 129
Elizabethe 13
Emily 85
Fanny 4
Gershum 152
Gilbert 75
Hannah 84
Harriet 133
Huldah 152
Ira 126

Bennett (cont.)
Isora 52
James 132
Jane 75
Jemima 94
Joann 144
John 127
Julia 127
Katherine 112
Levina 74
Mahetabel 10
Malissa 130
Manerva 144
Margaret 128
Maria 32
Maria Jane 1
Martha 44
Mary 31, 57
Mary Jane 110
Matilda 95
Matthias 4
Melissa 90
Nancy 44, 116, 136
Nancy (Mrs.) 94
Orella 119
Patsy 58
Polly 113
Rebecca 37
Robert 112
Samuel 75
Samuell 103
Sarah 42, 45
Sarah Ann 56, 126
Susan 27, 88
Susan Maria 91
Susannah 120
Bennight, Hannah 128
Bennitt, Josiah 84
Bennon, Catherine 129
Benson, Delila 24
Martha 59
Benter, Lizzy 34
Bentley, Sarah 92
Beoker, Henry 13
Jacob 5
Berexman, Catrena 7
Bergman, Anna Catharine
7
Berkheimer, Johanna 75
Berkley, Amanda 71
Berkshire, Jane 119
Bermon, Catherine 129
Bernn, Margaret 73
Bernorden, Virginia 108
Berry, Biddy 50
Catharin 115
Catherine 100
Eliza Ellen 67
Elizabeth 32
James 142
Martha A. 93
Mary F. 102, 115
Berryman, Jane 89
Martha 40
Bershaw, Victor 13
Berstet, Louisa 111
Bertholf, Amelia Ann 7
Bertram, Johanna 153
Polly 87
Bertrand, Felicity 14
J. B. 118
Jno. 118
John St. 13
Julia 13
Rosanna 64
Sophia 118
Besche, John (?) 100
Besecon, Josephine 12

Besko, Hannah 72
Bets, Abraham 10
Betts, Abram 151
  Janes (?) 55
  Nancy Jane 151
Betz, Catharine 130
  Mary 12
Beuhoop, Henry (?) 8
Beuman, Lewis 13
  Louis 113
Bey, Margaret 46
Bez, Sophie 3
Bibbey, Ethelinda 8
  Susannah 152
Bibby, Elizabeth 65
  Sarah 8
  Susannah 151
Bicka, Stacy 143
Biggerstaff, Mary Ann 37
Biggs, Amanda 116
  Christiana 67
  Mary 11
  Nancy 71, 145
  Norval 40
Bilkens, Stacy 143
Billen, Caroline 29
Billman, Agatha (Mrs.)
  10
  John 10
  K. 10
Bingham, Sarah Jane 28
  Simeon 11
Birbeck, Alva 138
  Elizabeth (Mrs.) 138
Bish, John 143
  Magdalin 143
  Malinda 143
  Ruth A. 143
Bishong, James 72
Bishop, Elizabeth 126
  Margaret 35
  Matilda 113
Bishup, Mary 48
Bisler, Susan 129
Bissel, Sarah 149
Bisset, Maria 80
Bivins, Cynthia (Mrs.)
  56
  Cynthia Ann 56
  Joseph 56
  William F. 56
Black, Mahala 8
  Mary C. 4
  Nancy 39
  Sarah 113
Blackburn, Catharine 32
Blackford, Elenor 78
  Joseph 78
Blagg, Elisabeth 92
  Julia Ann 149
  Mary Jane 147
  Sarah 113
Blair, John 8
  Linchy 51
  Lucy 8
  Mary 127
Blake, Eliza 71
  Katherine 73
  Mary France 151
  Philip 32
Blakeman, Ava 104
  Charlotte 104
  Moses 11, 104
  Sarah Ann 28
Blankenship, Clarinda 78
Blazer, Lucinda 93
Blechner, Anna 7
Blind, Betsy 16

Bliss, Caroline 93
  Emily 39
  Esther Ann 123
  Fanny 105
  Hannah 14, 112
  Harriet 5
  Jonathan 11
  Louisa 86
  Maria 33
  Nancy M. 41
  Narcisse M. 98
  Parthenia 91
  Sally 62
  Sophia 98
Blodget, Esther 65
Bloomer, Betsey Bacy 133
  Henry 107
  Louis Saint John 107
  Lydia Margaret 35
Blue, Ezekiel 118
Blundell, Margaret
  (Mrs.) 116
Blyfe, Laurah A. W. 46
Boaltinghar, David 52
Boanum, Mary 88
Bochner, Phillipean 110
Bockhoofer, E. Henry 18
Boen, Mary 19
Boggs, Nancy 2
  Samuel 12, 56
Bogs, Lucinda 23
Boidston, Winney (Mrs.)
  12
Boil, Clssy 80
Boilston, Anna 19
Boldman, Ann Eliza 114
  C. (Mrs.) 12
  Catharine 60, 113
  Jane 108
  Mahala A. 66
  Peter 12, 113
  S. (Mrs.) 113
  Sarah 57
  Viana 124
Bolen, Nancy 54
Boling, H. 79
  H. (Mrs.) 79
Bolton, Rebecca 86
Bond, Charity 85
  Content (Mrs.) 85
  Sally 3
  Stephen 85
Bondurant, Selina D. 70
  Thomas 70
Bone, Mary 73
Bonner, Reuben 16
Bonser, Abigail 9
  Anne 62
  Elleanor 129
  Hannah 91
  Hellen 131
  Jane 43, 51
  Jane F. 4
  Lucretia 40
  Margaret 17
  Maria 94
  Matilda 51
  Minerva 106
  Rhoda 40
  Rhody 16
  Salle 120
  Susan Elizabeth 106
  Temperance 70
Bonso, Mary J. 24
Bonzo, Susanna 149
Boose, Mary 114
Boothe, Mary 44
Boren, A. H. 2

Boren (cont.)
  Elizabeth 2
  Elizabeth (Mrs.) 13
  Hannah (Mrs.) 2
  Stephen 13
Bostwick, Lucy J. 3
  Mary 150
  Rosanthe 3
Bottenness, Ellen 81
Boultenhous, Daniel 52
Bowen, Adam 84
  George 32
  Mary Ann 36
  Nancy 32, 87
  Rebecca 35
  Sarah 61
  Susannah 63
  Thomas 31
Bower, Catherine 48, 62
  Elizabeth 46, 145
  George 61
  John 62
  Lettitia (Mrs.) 61
  Nancy 87
  Polly 43
  Sarah 61
Bowers, Martha Jane 147
  Mary Ann 81
  Sarah 140
Bowman, Aaron 13
  Augusta 39
  Martha 25
  Mary 36
Bowyer, Lucinda 15
Box, Mary Maria 95
Boyce, Elizabeth 152
Boyd, A. A. 22
  Elisabeth 77
  Eliza 77
  Elizabeth (Mrs.) 13
  Jonathan 13
  Levina 13
  Mahala 53
Boydston, Anna 19
  Sarah 138
Boyer, Elmanda 30
  John 30
  Lucinda 15
  Martha D. 20
  Rachel 29
  William F. 34
Boyers, Elias P. 86
Boyes, Elizabeth 152
Boynton, Asa 77, 113
  Charles C. 71
  Cynthia 77, 121
  Elizabeth 39
  Jane A. 145
  Laura 64
  Lucy 147
  Lydia C. 106
  Mary 95
  Polly 113
Boys, Margaret 125
  Maria 125
  Richard 125
Boyse, Frederick 114
Bracy, Ethelinda 144
Bradburn, Catharine 16
  Mark 96, 123
  Mary 14
  Notingham 7
Bradford, Cornelius 124
  Elizabeth 112, 115
  Louisa 82
  Mahala 146
  Maria H. 42
  Mary 18

Bradford (cont.)
Melinda 37
Peggy 116
Richard 116
Sarah 26, 122, 151
Susan 139
Susan Ann 136
Wilhelmina 128
Bradshaw, Aveline 50
Emeline 141
Harriet 123
Henderson 63
Isaac 11, 14, 94
Lureena Abigail 94
Lydia 8, 96
Margaret 76
Mary 66, 113
Nancy (Mrs.) 14
Rebecka 94
Robert 14
Sarah 45, 101
Sarah Ann 11
Brady, Caroline 136
David 134
Mary 19
Mary Eliza 134
Phebe 34
Polly 19
Brainard, Eleazer 71
Bramble, Aarom M. 114
Mary F. 151
Bramer, Ellen 118
Brand, Sally 3
Brandau, Anna Catarina
(Mrs.) 72
Barbara Elisbeta 72
John 72
Brandow, Elisabeth 72
Brandy, Elizabeth 70
Branham, Susan 44
Brannum, Elizabeth 122
Susan 60
Brant, Catharine Ann 148
Joseph 117
Brantfast, Charlotte
Caroline 141
Bratt, Harriet (Mrs.) 15
John 15
Morris 15
Phoebe (Mrs.) 15
Braun, Mary 82
Braunstein, Victoria 97
Breadwell, William 15
Breathwell, Margret
(Mrs.) 94
Bredaker, Cornelia 144
Brediger, Elizabeth 76
Brewer, A. M. 1
Angelina E. 54
Mary 103
Briant, Sarah 56
Brice, John (?) 17
Brickdeschler,
Friederika 56
Briggs, Amanda 116
Mary 11
Mary Jane 19
Rebecca 98
Samuel 15
Brightman, Nancy 152
Brigle, Francis 141
Brinard, Mahala 126
Brindle, Margaret 119
Brison, Margaret 133
Britenham, Mary 71
Brittenham, Elizabeth 19
Mary 71
Brocher, Mary 142

Brock, Allin 15
Anna C. 14
Elizabeth 41
George 15, 16, 76, 105
Martha Jane 76
Mary Ann 129
Nancy 127
Pleasant 105
Sarah 43
Spicey 105
Thomas 15
Brodbeck, Anthony 41
Charlotte 41
Paul 41
Broison, Mary J. 138
Broker, June 130
Brooker, Jacob 16
Mary E. 39
Brooks, Betsey Ann 24
David 143
Elizabeth 18
James 16, 72
Mary 97
Sally 72
Broom, Sarah 142
Brouce, Hannah 41
Brouck, Lewis 17
Brous, Nancy 64
Sarah A. 98
Brouse, Ada Jane 137
Andrew 16
Eleanor 103
Elizabeth 98
Hannah (Mrs.) 16
Letitia 93
Brown, America 53
Anastatia 121
Barbara 136
Bienna 83
Caroline 29
Catharine E. 134
Catherine 40
Corbley M. 14
Cynthia M. 21
Delesa 135
Eliza 78
Elizabeth 34
Hannah 11
Hetty (Mrs.) 4
Huldah 86, 116
J. H. 16
Jane 87, 125
John 17, 21, 127, 140
John (Sr.) 147
John H. 16
Joshua 44
Lilly A. 31
Lois 44
Lou (?) 21
Louisa 3
Margaret 120
Martha 148
Mary 23, 82, 103
Mary (Mrs.) 8, 70
Mary A. 51, 63
Mary Ann 25, 108
Mary V. 119
Matilda 73
Nancy 17, 49, 115
O. Thos. 140
Othos 140
P. N. 119
Rachel 29, 70
Rebecca 17
Royal 17
Samuel 17
Samuel S. 140
Sarah 4, 14, 140

Brown (cont.)
Udocius 17
Vienaes 83
Browning, C. O. 141
Browns, Julia 55
Bruce, Isabella 127
Bruck, Lewis 17
Bruer, John (?) 17
Stephen 15
Brugger, Maria 56
Bruner, Abram 17
Elizabeth 17
Lucinda 117
Mary Ann 48
Mary E. 44
Owen 42
Brunken, Sophia 51
Brunn, Margaret 21
Brunner, H. 17
Mary 25
Mary (Mrs.) 17
Samuel 17
Brush, Amey 7
Ruth 84
Brust, Margaret 65
Sibilla 49
Buchanan, Anna 107
Buck, John 18
Margaret 60
Nancy 127
Nancy (?) 1
Sarah 51
Susannah 60
Buckels, Elizabeth 25
Buckles, Nancy 152
Rebecca 137
Buckley, Elizabeth 35
Mary F. 122
Rachel 120
Sarah Ann 7
Buckly, Thomas 7
Buckner, Jane 83
Buddick, Hannah 77
Budinthaver, Barbara 142
Buffington, Elizabeth 79
Margaret 40
Mariah J. 115
Bufington, Cornelia Ann
19
Mary 139
Buman, Louis 113
Bumgarner, Dan'l. 56
Elizabeth 109
Bumment, Josephine 46
Bumnt, Willis (?) 36
Bunch, Joseph 87
Bunion, Elizabeth 62
Bunnel, Hannah 20
Burcaw, Mary Ellen 23
Burdic, Phoebe J. 138
Burk, Cinthia 4
Eliza 22, 46
John S. 142
Louisiana 48
M. A. 55
Mary 4
Nancy 1, 46
Nancy (Mrs.) 116
Polly 116
Sally (Mrs.) 4
Sarah 72
Susan 142
William 4
William M. 72, 81, 142
Wm. N. (Cpt.) 52
Burke, Harriet 134
Harriet M. 47
Burkick, Phoebe 98

159

Burniel, Hannah 20
Burns, Andrew 19
  Ann 100
  Eleanor 4
  Eliza 56
  John 89
  Lizzie 17
  Mary 55
  S. 17
  Sarah 124
  Thomas 124
Burnside, Jane 144
Burris, Mahala Mariah
  151
  Margaret 50
  Sarah Jane 11
Burriss, Elizabeth 138
  Franky 64
  Harriett 86
  Horatio 8
  Joanna 61
  Nancy 8, 78, 115
Burroughs, Mary J. 26
Burrows, Linnea 38
  Rachel 78
Burt, Abigail 27
  Amanda 24
  Ann Eliza 96
  Anna 63
  Benjamin 12, 19
  Benjamin (Jr.) 144
  Catharine 45
  Catherine 114
  Ciny 29
  Elisabeth 117
  Elizabeth 131, 144
  Hannah 9
  Harriet 108
  Hester 106
  James W. 9
  Jane 128
  Jayne 136
  Julia 124
  Mahittabel 12
  Malissa 33
  Malvina 15
  Margaret 106
  Margaret (Mrs.) 19
  Mary 67
  Polly 120
  Rebecca 19
  S. B. (Maj.) 137
  Sarah 144
  Temperance 137
  Viny 29
Burton, James 15
  Mandana 15
Burtwell, Mary 24
Burwick, Hannah 20
Bush, Elizabeth 4, 37,
  60
  George 29
  Jude 2
  Jula 2
  Mary Jane 133
  Rachel 139
  Ruth 84
Busker, Catherine 56
Busmer, John 13
Bussey, Eve 78
  Jane 74
  John 19
  Valentine 86
Bussy, Polly 139
Butcher, Matilda 105
Butlar, Susan 49
Butler, Ann 59
  Lydia Ann 66

Butler (cont.)
  Mary 42, 84
  Polly (?) 87
  Ruth A. 143
Butt, William 20
Butterfield, Benjamin
  71, 105
  Ellen 17
Butz, Margaret 58
Byer, Christina 58
Byers, Cyenda 63
  Hannah 81
  Jane 54
  Margaret 9
  Mary 54
  Mary M. 151
  William (Sr.) 20
Cable, Alabina 141
  Eleanor 138
  Elizabeth 35
  George 57
  Levina 10
  Martha J. 9
  Matilda 113
  Melissa 75
  Polly 150
  Samuel 4, 120
  Sarah A. 132
Cabot, Claudious 81
  Madalin 14
Cacy, James (?) 22
Cadot, Eliza Jane 14
  Lewis J. 65
  Mary 56
  Mary Jane 47
  Mary Louise 74
Cady, Martha (Mrs.) 20
  Silas 20
Cahall, Franky 128
  Nancy 96, 128
Cahler, Rose 38
Calhoun, Clarissa 8
Call, Charles 66
  Elizabeth 142
  Harriet E. 69
  Hugh 120
  Lucinda 66
  Lucretia 53, 67
  Margaret 120
  Susan 45
  Thomas 66
Callahan, Judia 95
  Lucinda 146
Callen, Rose 38
Callow, Marianna 138
Calloway, Eliza 139
Caloway, Mille 28
Calver, Emily 79
Calvert, Elizabeth 21,
  27, 113
  Elizabeth (Mrs.) 113
  Eveline Ophelia 25
  H. B. 53
  Harriet E. 53
  Winneyford 91
Calvin, Lucinda 140
Cameron, Elizabeth K.
  146
  Mary C. 83
  Stephen 83
Camfield, Anna 76
Cammon, Curtis 58
Campbell, Anna 83
  Anne 130
  Charles F. 20
  Ellenor 13
  Elvira 83
  J. E. 31

Campbell (cont.)
  Jane 123
  John 20
  Katherine 31
  Louisa 105
  Mary 3
  Mary Ann 73
  Mary Jane 31, 32
  Polly 145
  Sally 70
  Sarah 70, 112
  Sevrekan (?) 73
  Thomas M. 28
  William 138
Campden, Catharine 130
Canary, Hillenah 56
  Lucy 12
  Minerva 125
  Simeon 113
Canauts, Thomas (?) 119
Canfield, Mary 59
  Orsemus 9
Cann, Arthur 28
Canter, Catharine (Mrs.)
  151
  Clarinda 129
  Elizabeth (Mrs.) 88
  Emily 151
  James 88
  Lewis 88
  Lucinda 46
  Mary 88
  Rebecca (?) 130
  Susana 46
  William 21, 151
Canterbury, Hugh 32
  John 55
  M. Wara (?) (Mrs.) 32
  Sarah A. 32
Caravan, Sarah 89
Caraway, Martha 46
Carder, Delilah 46
Carey, Nomi 91
  Susy 27
  Vianna 91
Cargal, Martha Lewis 147
Carl, Joanna 41
Carlile, Mary Catherine
  42
Carlon, James 90
Carly, Elizabeth 82
Carnes, Margaret H. 47
Carney, John 66, 147
  Rebecca 16
Carpenter, Jane 72
  Jesse 147
  Nancy 73
  Patsey 4
  Pheobe Ellen 132
  Sarah Catherine 115
Carr, Ann 140
  Eliza 136
  Jane 27
  Margaret 61
  Mary A. 114
  Nancy 22
Carraway, Nancy Jane 96
  Sarah 140
Carrick, Samuel 95
Carrol, Elizabeth 37
  Joanna 146
Carroll, Capy 11
  Eliza 136
  Eliza (Mrs.) 136
  James 22
  John B. 123
  Lexis 22
  Margaret 83

Cline (cont.)
  Daniel 25
  E. (Mrs.) 25
  Jane 57
  Susan (?) 143
Clingman, Ann Eliza 85,
  107
  Ann Elvia 107
  Ann Maria 110
  C. (Mrs.) 47
  Catharine 47
  Catherine 47
  John 72, 145
  Samuel 47
Clise, Catharine 68
Cloud, Elizabeth 128
  Nancy Ann 6
Clough, A. 62
  Mary A. 152
Clugsten, Callie 101
  Eveline 113
Co, Nancy 128
Coal, Amanda 100
  Hester 25
Coale, Amanda 107
  D. W. 68
  Rachel 86
  Thomas 27, 86
  Thomas H. 107
Coburn, Jacob 118
  Levina (Mrs.) 118
  Polly 118
Cochenane, Liza 46
Cochran, Andrew J. 23
  Elizabeth 126
  Joanna 139
  Margaret 150
  Nancy 26
  Rachel 150
  Susan 133
Cockerell, Mary 83
  Mary Frances 13
  Susan 77
Cockral, Elizabeth 82
Cockran, Sally 44
Cockrel, Mary Ann 50
Cockrell, Catherine 133
  Harriet 26
  Jesse 146
  Lucinda D. 16
  Nancy 34, 67
  Patsy D. 68
  Sarah Ann 66, 147
  Susan 79
  Susannah 50
Cody, Elizabeth T. 97
Coetter, Catarine 109
  Clara Elisabetha
    (Mrs.) 109
  Fredrig 109
Coffey, Ellen 134
Coffman, Catherine 21
Coffrin, G. W. 131
  Mary L. 131
Coheenes, Catharine 4
Cohrine, James (?) 26
Coil, Ann 49
  Clary 80
Colbine, Rosena 28
Colbit, Mary 18
Colder, Isabel 120
Cole, Alzina 31
  Amos B. 26
  Caroline 6
  Edmund 1
  Elisabeth 96
  Emily 106
  Fanny 1

Cole (cont.)
  Frances Ann 2
  Harriet 11
  Julia 151
  Laura 27
  Louisa 123
  Martha E. (Widow) 26
  Mary (Mrs.) 26
  Mary Jane 104
  Nabby 31
  Nancy 68
  Phebe (Mrs.) 1
  Phibe 103
  Polly 57
  Rachel 124
  Sally 17
  Sally Ann 101
  Sarah 17
  Silas W. 26
  Thomas 26
Colegrove, Amanda 29
  Clarissa 136
  Cynthia 84
  Levina 37
  Matilda Jane 61
  Rachel 86
Coleman, Elizabeth 50,
  79
  Margaret 130
  Mary Ann 22
Coles, Hulda 104
Colgan, Elenor 56
  William 56
Colgin, Susannah 7
Colines, Mary 8
Collar, Elizabeth (Mrs.)
  27
  Enos 27
Collard, Mary 75
  Sarah Ann 94
Colley, Edward 6
  Mahala 6
Collier, Eliza Jane 50
  Elizabeth 84
  Margaret 84
  Marriet 84
  Mary A. 50
  Mary Ann 99
  Matilda 19
  Thomas 50
  Thomas (Jr.) 50
Collins, Amelia 92
  Charity 123
  E. A. 27
  Elizabeth 7, 8
  John 112
  Mary 8, 112
  N. (Mrs.) 27
  Nancy 18
  Permelia 144
  Susan 70
  Susanna 98
Collis, Ambrose 27
  Catherine S. 32
  James 27
  Lavisa 137
  Loas 95
  Louisa (Mrs.) 27
  Lydia 133
  Nancy Jane 142
  R. T. 27
  Regal T. 32
  Rhoda 24
Colven, Mahala 99
Colvin, Esther 79
  Harriet F. 136
  John 21, 84
  Mary 29, 50, 122

Colvin (cont.)
  Nioma 120
  Sophia 38
  William 27
Colwell, Amanda 36
Com, Jesse G. (?) 32
Combs, Amanda 62
  Ann 24
  David 70, 107, 144
  Elizabeth 144
  Maria 132
  S. (Mrs.) 144
  Sarah 70
  Statis 127
Comer, Emma 2
  Henry 4
Compliment, Catherine 42
Compton, Nancy 123
Comstock, George G. 29
Concklin, Eutheba 71
Conely, James 29
Coner, Katharine 107
Coney, Ann 1
Conklin, Albina 92
  Electa 34
  Joseph 92
  Luceba 4
  Malinda 93, 103
  Mary 28, 148
  Mary (Mrs.) 93
  Sally 91
  William 92, 93
Conley, Ann 95
  Bridget 58
  Juliana 9
  Margaret 86
Conn, Harriet 85
  Mary 57
Connally, Ann 70
  Peter 70
Connell, Samuel (?) 22
Conner, Mitelday 50
  Sally 127
  William 50
Connolly, Catherine 42
  Nancy 112
Conroy, Mary 34
Conrow, Elizabeth 104
  Sarah 57
  Tabitha 104
Conroy, Anne 90
  Hannah 143
  Thomas 28
Conway, Hannah 143
  Sophia 145
Conwey, Eleanor E. 134
Cook, Caroline 88
  Catharine 134
  Hugh 48
  Louisa 19, 69
  Maria 123
  Mary Ann 101
  Mercie 48
  Mercy (Mrs.) 48
  Nancy 24
  Roseann 53
  Sarah F. 40
Cool, Mary Elizabeth 32
Cooley, Elizabeth 91
  Mary Ann 134
Coolman, Edward 73
Cooly, Welthy A. J. 39
Coon, Mary Ann 112
  Peter 73
Coonel, Theressa 34
Coonsmann, Catharina 110
Cooper, Amanda 19
  Ann 69

163

Crull (cont.)
Jemima 123
Jemimah 136
John 32
Julia 27
Juliana 122
Marjory J. 67
Mary 73, 99
Mary J. 68
Nancy 9, 73
Polly 19
Rebeccah 122
S. 27
Sarah 128
Susan 125
Susanna 104
Thomas J. 126
William 82, 104
William M. 36
Crump, Matison 1
Culler, Rebeckah 60
Culley, Daniel F. 129
Culp, Cornelius 33
Eliza 90, 131
Ellen 109
Hannah 9, 123
Hester 103
Jemima 100
John 71
Martha Ann 57
Nancy 89
Phebe Ann 69
Pollie 128
Ruth 69
Sarah 70
Susan 94
Culver, Louisa 122
Cummings, Mary G. 139
Susannah 37
Cummins, S. T. 14
Samuel P. 137
Cumpston, Louisa 3
Cumston, Nancy 123
Cunning, Catherine 99
Margaret R. 86
Cunningham, Elizabeth 14
Hester 75
Marcella 74
Margaret Anne 55
Mary Ann 150
Mary Jane 11
Nancy 14
Nancy (Mrs.) 89
Sarah 89
Cuppit, Nancy 88
Curby, Cyanthian 60
Curey, Sarah (?) (Mrs.) 44
Curly, Mary 48
Curran, Alex 92
Currens, Catherine 38
Currie, Elenor 84
Hannah (Mrs.) 49, 101
Margaret J. 101
Mary E. 49
T. S. 49
Thos 101
Curry, Henderson 89
William 26
Curtis, Laura E. 60
Cushing, Mary Jane 16
Cushman, Mary M. 103
Custis, Hariet 138
Custiss, Elizabeth 103
Cutler, Caroline 130
Fanny 22
Jane 53
Cutlip, Mary 18

Cutright, Arville 130
Eliza Jane 42
John 41
Ruth 41
Cutshaw, Elizabeth 44
Cutter, Cathrina 109
Rebeckah 60
Cuykendall, John 31
Cybert, Marg (?) 86
Cyrus, Eleanor A. 56
Dailey, Peggy 119
Daily, Mary 134
Dain, Harriet 36
Daley, Ann 147
Dalson, Kaziah 66
Dalton, Jane 95
Danels, George 25
Daner, Barbara 46
Daniel, Catharine 44
Gabel 34
Mary E. 57
Sabol 34
Daniels, Abysina P. 36
Elizabeth 103
Hannah 146
Katharine 95
Louisiana 127
Martha 82
Mary 17
Mary E. 20, 136
Rebecca 82
S. H. 34
Sarah J. 146
Scienda 19
Danks, Pamley 117
Dannis, Michael (?) 34
Darby, Dorcus 142
Darling, Diana (Mrs.) 84
Eliza 80
James C. 84
Mary Ann 110
Melissa 82
Phebe 112
Sarah 84
Darlington, Belinda 39
Hannah 56
Henry 86
Julia Ann 135
Mary 40, 147
Mary B. 53
Melinda 62
Minerva 26
Darquhat, Alexander D. 136
Dasher, Catherine 47
Dauber, Elisabeth 117
Elizabeth 116
Dauley, Jane 125
Daum, Barbara 44
Daupel, Daniel 33
Dauson, Pertima Ann 92
Dautstral, Mary 46
Davey, Jane 140
Louisa 126
Phillippi 95
David, Malinda 142
Davidson, Elizabeth 146
John (Jdg.) 60
Salle M. 112
Davis, A. C. 73
Annice B. 134
Barbara A. 1
Caroline 50
Elizabeth 56, 103, 140
Elizabeth A. 10
Elizabeth H. 10
Lucinda 99
Lucy Ann 45

Davis (cont.)
Mahala 40
Malilee 87
Margaret 96
Mary Jane 67
Nancy 44
Rachel 117
Rebecca 19, 117
Rezin 99
Sarah 147
Semantha A. 66
Serilda 73
William 62
Davisson, Adaline 26
John 35
Joseph 28
Margaret 21
Davy, Susan A. 18
Dawes, William (?) 38
Dawnor, Nancy 63
Dawson, Anastatia 34
Catherine 5
Delilah 38
Irene 129
John 44
Martha 112
Mary F. 125
Mirenda 20
Moses K. 129
Nancy 63
Otha 112
Phoeba 124
Pulaski 34
Sally 129
Sureldah 117
Day, Amanda 146
Dudley 146
John 35
Levina 117
Louisa 105
Mary 93
Rebeck 38
Dayley, John 47
Dayton, Ruhama 80
DeBlau, Augustus 35
DeGroat, Henry 124
Deal, Elizabeth 92
Jnerl (?) 92
Deamer, Susan 119
Dean, Caroline M. 80
Cynthia M. 6
Elizabeth 54
Irene 50, 74
Lucy 47
Nancy 11
Phebe 80
Sarah J. 105
Dear, Amanda 48
Mary Jane 34
Dearing, Elizabeth B. 51
Dearman, Eliza 104
Deaver, Eliza 17
Elizabeth 146
George 48
Deavers, Mary 43
Deavors, Emily 114
Debar, Orlenda 20
Debow, Louisa 76
Washington 75
Deegins, B. B. 36
Degar, Mary 47
Degare, Amanda 112
Catharine 14
Eliza 83
Degear, Abraham 134, 138
Catharine 125
Harriet 134
Mary 22

Degear (cont.)
  Susan Ann 43
Degere, Mary 47
Degnen, Bridget 130
Degraut, Ellen 127
Degrot, Mary 44
Deitrich, Elizabeth
  (Mrs.) 30
  John 30
  Mary 30
Dejnen, Bridget 130
Dekar, Laceta 113
Delea, Jean 95
Delia, Elinor 95
Dellert, Margaret 131
Delong, Mary E. 124
Demback, Andres 109
  Eve L. 109
  Mary (Mrs.) 109
Demmer, Anderson 109
  Louisa E. 109
Demsey, Jane 113
Dennewitz, Caroline
  Maria 111
Denney, Jane 113
Denning, Newton B. 36
Dennis, Lucy 6
  Mary Ann 142
Denny, Charity 36
Densmore, Henry 39
  Marthy (Mrs.) 39
  Samuel 39
Depoe, Margaret 124
Der, Catharina 141
Dernback, Andres 109
  Eve L. 109
  Mary (Mrs.) 109
Dernlerin, Magdalene (?)
  60
Derris, John K. 37
Derstence, Magdalene 60
Detty, Sarah 147
Dever, A. (Mrs.) 36
  David 100
  Delilah 113
  East India 119
  Elizabeth Ann 114
  Hannah 53
  Jane 100, 125
  Louisa B. 85
  Maria 149
  Mary 13, 33
  Mary Jane 41
  Mary Jones 41
  Mary M. 96
  Sarah 84
  Solomon 33, 118
  William 36
Devers, Eliza 17
  John 104
Devor, Hannah 85
Devore, Cleopatra 143
Dewey, Abigail J. 48
  Caroline M. 138
  Catharine A. 128
  Eliza 38
  Harriet 16
  Rosanna P. 14
Dewise, Nancy Ann 143
Dewit, Sophia 18
Dewitt, Catharine 150
  Eliza 25
  Emily 69
  George 93
  Hannah (Mrs.) 93
  John 90
  Malinda 142
Dick, Mary P. 134

Dickey, Elizabeth 21
Dickison, Mary Emma 92
Dickson, Mary Ann 76
  Sarah R. 3
Didaway, Augustine 142
Diduit, Adeline 102
  Betsy Eliza 111
Didwit, Loana 89
Dieckman, Heinrich 37
Diehle, Mary 143
Dierker, Elizabeth 97
Dierky, Laceta 113
Dieterick, Henry 66
Digers, Lydia 24
Dillen, Caroline 29
  Susanna 2
Dillon, Almira Louisa 21
  Elizabeth 54
  Fielden H. 37
  Mary 150
  Mary E. 113
  Nancy 100, 114
  Sarah 61
Dimner, Elizabeth 123
Dix, Mary 84
Dixen, Loreno 108
Dixon, Charilla 64
  Eveline 1
  Henry 37
Dobbs, Matilda 11
Dodds, Martha A. 92
  Mary Eliza 135
  Sarah Jane 40
  W. B. 106
  William 66
  William T. 37
Dodge, Amy 104
  Eulalie 133
  Harris 34, 140
  Lucretia 44
  Lydia 87
  Lynds 140
  Margaret 2
  Mary 140
  Sally 32
  Sarah 53
  Sarah Ann 104
Dodson, Julianna 48
Dolch, George 38
  Melinde 73
  Sally 8
Dole, E. 71
  Lavina 91
  Margaret 121
  Mary L. 45
  Rhozinna C. 71
  Rosina C. 71
  Sally (Mrs.) 10
  Samuel 30
  Sarah 13
  Selina 30
Doll, Margaret 40
Dollarhide, Emily 92
Dollerhide, Ritty 69
Dolt, Elisabeth 143
Donason, Maria 65
Donewitz, Mary 145
Donley, Josiah 38
Donohoe, Mary 50
  S. M. 41
Doonsberger, Catharine
  15
Dorch, Eliza 126
Dorrell, Eliza 30
Dortch, Doli 63
  Dorothy 63
  Frances 61
  Rebecca 144

Dortch (cont.)
  Susannah 38
  William 38
Doty, Mary A. 139
Dougherty, Ann 33
Douglas, James 38
  William 4
Douglass, Emely 107
Dowas, Marth 113
Dower, William (?) 38
Downer, Elizabeth 121
Downey, Isabella J. 89
  Margaret 67
  Mary 110
  Mary Jane 9
  Samuel 9
  Sarah (Mrs.) 67
Downing, Elizabeth 14
  Margaret 128
  Mary 110
Draine, Sarah 72
Drake, Nancy M. 90
  Permelia J. 79
Dray, Daniel 38
Drennan, Daniel 39
Driver, Melinda 100
Drumlee, Nancy 90
Drury, Elizabeth 54
  Ruth 7
Dubbard, Elijah 17
Ducate, Roselle 53
Ducy, Rebeckah 107
Duduit, Agaliha 49
  Anges 49
  Augustine 142
  Carline 88
  Caroline 128
  Frances 98
  John 47
  Mary Catherine 47
  Virginia 29
  W. 128
  William 47, 98
Dudwit, Loanna 101
Duffie, Margaret 100
Dugan, Lydia 52
  Nancy 71
  Thomas (?) 33
Duggan, Thomas 52
Dulany, Elijah 39
Dullenfoher, David 17
Dunahue, Elizabeth 33
Dunaway, Maria M. 141
  Martha J. 68
  Sarah M. 75
Duncan, Allanda 96
  Clarissa 148
  Elizabeth 51, 127
  Joseph 43
  Mary 43
  Mimy 51
  Peggy 123
Dunham, Elizabeth 24
Dunkin, Eliza A. 37
Dunlap, Elizabeth 152
  Mary Jane 126
  Rozisa 62
  Sarah Ann 23
  T. M. 20
Dunn, Berthena R. 37
  Charity 36
  Elizabeth Jane 82
  Nancy 36
Dunsmore, Martha (Mrs.)
  39
  Samuel 39
Dupey, Lucy 61
Dupuy, Moses 45

Dusan, Malinda 71
Dusing, Susannah Maria 12
Dutengefer, Barbar 142
Dutes, Margaret (?) 109
Dutiel, Frances 39
  Jane 3
  Jane Ann (Mrs.) 39
  Sophia 3
Dutremont, Abigel 31
Duvall, Martha Jane 99
Duvendack, Adam 18
  Maary 18
Duwit, Emily 69
  Malinda 142
Duyer, Maery 48
Dwyer, Nancy Ann 143
Dymond, John 150
Dyre, Lenah J. 148
Dysart, Rachel 97
Dysert, Elizabeth 148
Earl, Lucy 144
  Ruth 144
Earley, Malinda J. 28
  Mary 146
Early, Amanda J. 140
  Lovina 54
  William 148
Eastburn, Philip 40
Easton, Turner 40
Eaton, Hannah 53
Eblem, Theressa 106
Eck, Elisabeth 59
  Eva 75
  Margaret 111
  Mary 127
Eckhart, Catherine 47
Eckley, Eli 56
  Martha Jane 130
  Mary (Mrs.) 56
  Sarah E. 56
Edar, Martha 43
Eddenstone, Isabella J. 84
Edgington, Bulah Ann 110
  Margaret E. 133
  Mary Ann 25
  Thomas 40
Edginton, Brice 101
  Melinda 101
Edison, Elizabeth 151
  Jas. 54
  Margaret 54
Edwards, Adaline 15
  Catherine 147
  Celia A. 26
  David 40
  Elizabeth 96
  Joseph 42
  Katharine (Mrs.) 40
  Mary 133
  Nancy 117
Egbert, Marg 86
Eicher, Margaret 119
Eifert, Susan 102
Eifort, Mary 140
  Mary A. 7
  Sabastian 62
  Suranna 53
Eisman, Hester 35
Eldred, Mary Margaret 78
Eldridge, Esther 7
Elick, Elizabeth 25
Ellcesser, Franz 41
Elliott, Elizabeth 50
  Hannah (Mrs.) 22
  Isabel 92
  Katharine 150

Elliott (cont.)
  Sarah M. 92
Ellis, Anna 11
  Elizabeth Ann 45
  Rachel 26
Ellison, Felix 39
  Mary 95
  Mary A. (Mrs.) 39
  Mary Jane 68
  Samartha A. 39
  Sarah 24
  Virginia C. 42
Elsiser, Mary 10
  Waldburk 41
Ely, Caroline 51
  Rebecca 64
Emerich, Mary 54
Emery, Abiah P. 83
  Samuel 83
Emlet, Mary 33
Emmons, Lucinda 45
  Rebecca 34
  Sarah 149
Emory, Elizabeth J. 34
  Jerusha Ann 144
  Jerutia 142
Engallage, Louisa 72
Engle, Polly 105
Engles, George M. 130
  Magdalene 130
Enrich, Barbara 109
Enright, Mary 94
Enslow, Abraham 41
  David 14, 41
  Elizabeth 138
  Emily 14
  Eve 95
  Hannah 70
  Hannah A. 29
  Rachel 105
  Thos. J. 95
Enyar, Maery 48
Eppeheimer, Julia Ann 36
Eppenhimer, Mary 12
  Samuel 12
Eppiheimer, Hannah 138
  Samuel 138
Eppihimer, Martha 89
Erley, Melinda 123
Errot, Charlotte 38
Ervin, Rosana 27
Erwin, Elisabeth 144
Eseyers, Asa 116
Estel, Theresa 55
Estill, Sarah Ann 132
Estophy, Salony 42
Eulett, Amelia 91
Eulit, Emaline 24
  Isaac 24
  Mary (Mrs.) 24
Eulitt, Ellen 38
  Isaac 6, 38
  Mary 123
  Mary (Mrs.) 38
  Perthene 140
  Sarah 95
Evans, Airy 135
  Ann 40, 68
  Anthony 76
  Eleanor 3
  Ellen 134
  Henry H. A. 23
  James 129
  Jemima Elon 52
  Lucinda 76
  Lydia (Mrs.) 129
  Malinda 151
  Margaret E. 67

Evans (cont.)
  Mary 40, 55, 103, 152
  Nancy 29
  Sarah 129
  W. L. 42
  Wattson 135
Evens, Ester 55
Everett, Edward 48
  Rebecca 67
  Sally 65
Evins, Rosana 27
Evridge, Sintha 28
Ewing, Enoch M. 127
Fae, Philipp 43
Faedner, Fanny (?) 53
Fagel, Mary 37
Failer, Alfred 46
Faivre, Catharine 116
Faller, Caroline 120
Farington, Ann 148
Farley, Betsey 4
  Catherine 67
  Henry F. 132
  Sarah 132
Farmer, Agnes 120
  Anna (Mrs.) 43
  B. J. 75
  Blackson 43
  Eliza 92
  Eveline (Mrs.) 25
  Maria (Mrs.) 43
  Mary 42
  Mary (Mrs.) 42
  Nancy 40
  Samantha H. 90
  Sarah 66, 74
  William 42
  William S. 42
Farney, Amanda 105
  David R. 43
  Elizabeth 67, 113
Farrar, Mary Ann 150
Farrell, Elizabeth 148
Farrer, Mary J. 78
Farrington, Sarah Jane 31
Fartrass, Sally 103
  Sary 103
Faser, Catherine 126
  John 126
Fasheres, Mary E. 93
Fasner, Anna Martha 88
Faurty, Elizabeth 4
Faverty, Abigail A. 20
  Elizabeth 28
  Elizabeth (?) 4
  Gallentine A. 43
  Joseph 43
  Reason 43
Favors, Constantino 102
Feazel, William E. 78
Fenimore, Rachel 136
Ferguson, Abigal 61
  Elizabeth 83
  John 17
  Margey 17
  W. W. 55
Ferqua, Nancy 24
Ferrel, Ellen 79
  Nancy C. 122
Ferrell, Matilda 94
Ferres, John 43
Ferrill, Clarrissa 68
  Ellen 96
Fesler, Barbara 140
Fetter, Andre 138
  Joseph 138
  Mary (Mrs.) 138

Feurt, Benjamin 13, 15,
    30, 35, 48, 97, 133
  Elizabeth 87, 146
  Gabriel 17, 97
  Isabella 33
  L. (?) 46
  Lanah 35
  Levenia H. 45
  Marey 97
  Margaret 26, 148
  Martha 87
  Mary 43
  Mary Ann 2
  Mary D. 17
  Massie 97
  Mercy 30
  Mercy Mary Ann 133
  Nancy 14
  Peter 30, 35, 87, 148
  Rachel 13
  Sarah 48
  Susannah 97
Feurtt, Peter 14
Fiche, Maria (?) 8
Field, James 43
  Margaret P. 28
  Mary (Mrs.) 43
  Mary F. 14
  Nancy Ann 36
Fields, Catharine 49
  Emaline A. 37
  Mary M. 51
  Phebe C. 14
  Sarah 129
Filch, Pemel 145
Filsley, Mary A. 52
Finch, Wallace M. 29
Fink, Margie B. 6
Finney, Bridget 44
  Julianna 36
  Margaret 44
  Mary Ann 145
  Melessa 64
  Melissa 122
  Sarry 73
  Thomas 44
  William 64
Finton, Bennet 115
  Celinda 92
  Effa Ann 99
  Elizabeth 70
  Mary Jane 97
  Orriett 62
  Susan (Mrs.) 92
  T. B. 149
  Teresa 68
  W. J. 8
Fischer, Barthelomaus 44
Fishburn, Catharine 117
  Matilda 112
  Sarah Ann 128
Fisher, Elizabeth 117
  Hannah 119
  Lucretia 2
  Lucretia (Mrs.) 44
  Margaretta 44
Fitch, Elias 44
  Laura 68
  Nancy 71
  Pemel (?) 145
Fitzmorris, Catherine P.
    108
  John 44
  Ruth 29
Fixley, Daniel 130
  Elisabeth 130
  Martha (Mrs.) 130
Flaherty, Margret 46

Flanders, Elisabeth 14
  G. W. 144
  Isabella Ann 92
  Jane F. 89
  Lucy 39
  Mary 33
  Parmelia 29
  Sarah Belle 76
Flarety, Martha 98
Flarrity, Eliza 124
Fleck, Martha Ann 110
Fleming, Catharine 101
  Henriette 135
  Hester 37
  Sally 30
Flemings, Polly 26
Flemming, Elizabeth 136
  Isaac 136
  Polly 125
Fletcher, Juley A. 137
  Mary 151
  Sally 82
  Varina G. 83
Flick, Margaret 60
  Martha Ann 110
Flinn, Ellen 57
Flower, Mary P. 11
Flowers, John 47
  Mary (Mrs.) 47
  Mary A. 47
Fog, R. E. W. 46
Folser, John 134
Folsom, Mary S. 131
Forcett, Isaac 43
Ford, C. W. 51
  Margaret 124
  Maria 133
Forney, Amanda 148
Forny, Jane F. 7
Forster, David 141
  Elizabeth (Mrs.) 141
  Polly 141
Forsythe, Nancy F. 31
  Susan S. 96
Fort, Mary Ann 2
Fortner, Mary 67
Fortress, Hester 27
Fortride, Lissette 49
Fossett, Cassa 135
Foster, Alex 31
  Dysa 87
  Jane 57
  Job 45
  Joshua 65
  Margaret 6
  Mary Ann 93
  Polly 76
  Susannah 43
  W. S. 65
Foulner, Fanny 53
Fourt, Henry 43
Fout, Elizabeth 65
  Lydia 12
  Margaret 107
  Rachel 134
Fowler, Constina 51
  Mary 95
  Mary Ann 40
  Susan 4
Fox, Catharine 74
  Nancy 80
Fraizer, Jane 109
Francis, Susan 49
Frank, Eliza 137
Frawly, Mary 42
Frazer, William C. 46
Frazier, Adeline 152
  Ann E. 99

Frazure, Delilah C. 75
Free, Mary 54
  Susannah 8
Freeberg, Ester 93
Freeland, Mary Jane 81
  Sarah Jane 81
  Susannah 54
Freeling, Mary Jane 81
  Sarah Jane 81
Freeman, Angeline 40
  Elizabeth A. 140
  Isme 46
  Martha 91
  Mary Jane 134
  Michael 46
  Nancy 70
Freidenmacher, Harriet
    12
French, Jeremiah 20
  Mary 20
  Mary Ann 119
  Samuel 132
Frend, Mary 138
Frescot, Harriet 85
Freshell, Mary V. 149
Freund, Louise 42
Frick, Frederick (?) 135
Frier, Eliza G. 91
Friley, Mary Ann 103
  Sarah 116
Frische, Agnes 151
  Anna Elizabetha 116
  Mary 73
Frizel, Nancy 97
  Tabitha 94
From, Catharina 153
Front, Elizabeth E. (?)
    22
Frost, Mary 91
Fugate, Martha E. 94
Fuget, C. 47
  Cloe (Mrs.) 47
  Margaret 61
Fukel, Maria (?) 8
Fulce, Mary 137
Fulks, Matilda 121
Fuller, Caroline 120
  Caroline H. 29
  Constantina 49
  Edwin 152
  Frances H. 57
  Jane M. 63
  John 59
  Martha 119
  Mary C. 102
  Mary F. 33
Fullerton, Adaline 44
  Bacey Ann 47
  Eliza 44
  H. (Mrs.) 142
  Isaac 11, 104, 113
  James 44, 142
  Jane 90
  John 9, 47
  Lucy 54
  Nancy 9
  Roxe Ann 47
  Susan 9, 51
  William 90
Fullmer, Fanny (?) 53
Fulmer, Agathe 99
Fultz, Jane Elizabeth
    107
Funk, Barbary 85
  Hester 61
  John 47
  Katharine 133
  Margaret (Mrs.) 47

Funk (cont.)
   Margaret Ann 78
   Margret 78
   Mary 132, 152
   Melvira Ann 23
   Polly 121
Fuqua, James 43
   John M. 6
   Martha 124
   Mary 132
   Nancy 55
   Sarah M. 51
Furnace, Caroline 144
Gabble, Caroline 146
Gabler, Elizabeth 102
Gaboudel, Louis 47
Gades, George A. 93
Gagel, Elizabeth 134
Gahr, Charlotte (Mrs.) 47
   Valentine 47
Gaines, Catharine 43
   Jane 28, 91
Gairy, Nancy 127
Gale, Harriet 41
   Susan B. 46
Galford, John W. 120
Gallagher, Cornelius 86
Gallant, Patrick 48
   William 48
Gallian, Lavarien 136
Gallup, Abigail 62
   George W. 17
Gammon, Elizabeth 39
Gandy, Sarah 83
Gappan, Hester A. 46
Gappen, Mary Ann 64
Gard, Nancy 1
Gardner, Ellen 67
   George W. 18
   Mary Evelina 52
Garey, Prudence 38
Garland, Cynthia Ann 121
Garliner, Martha A. 82
Garret, Amanda 123
   Elizabeth 1, 123
   Russel 123
Garrett, Margaret 107
Garring, Cecilia 43
Garvin, Margaret Ann 41
Gaston, Abigail J. 131
   E. L. 9, 48
   Elijah L. 134
   Emily M. 87
   Frances Anna 56
   Joseph L. 48
Gates, (?) 97
   Bethia (Mrs.) 48
   E. (Mrs.) 48
   Polly K. 97
   Samuel P. 48
   Wilson 48
Gauk, Mary 132
Gay, Cynthia 138
   Mary Ann 23
   Thomas 23
Gebhardt, Caroline 133
   Jane Ann 44
   Lewis 107
   T. (Mrs.) 107
   Tena 107
Gebheart, Lewis 107
   T. (Mrs.) 107
   Tena 107
Gehouht, Eliza 15
Geist, Adam 49
   Barbara 141
   George 88

Gellim, Razilly 6
Gelruth, Minerva 70
Gelson, Elizabeth 45
Gennis, Hannah 4
Gentry, Effie Marie 52
George, Elizabeth F. 25
   John 21
   Lucretia Jane 6
   Mary Jane 119
   Robert A. J. 6
   Rosanna 21
Gerdes, Wilhelmina Sarah 10
Gerns, Moses 111
Gerwood, Sybil A. 42
Gessenger, Arabell B. 36
Gettys, Martha Jane 101
   Samuel 101
   Sarah (Mrs.) 101
Ghalliher, Katharine 67
Ghar, Charlotte 40
Gharky, George H. 49
   Roxanna 146
   W. 22
Gherky, Sarah Ann 147
Ghornley, Margaret 83
Ghrams, Jesse G. (?) 32
Gibben, Caroline 18
Gibbens, Lucy Ann 136
Gibbons, Harriet M. 17
Gibbs, Elizabeth 133
   Ellen 31
   James 5
Gibson, Rich 50
   Samuel 49, 109
   Serilda 109
Giddis, Wilhelmina Sarah 10
Giekler, John 49
Gies, Sybille 74
Giess, Maria 72
Gifford, Benjamin 109
   Catherine 27
   Harriet H. 141
   Jerusha 16
   Margaret Ann 36
   Martha Jane 39
   Mary M. 39
   Sarah Helen 36
   Susanna 109
Giffords, Caroline 57
Gilbert, Effie Ann (Mrs.) 49
   Giles 49
   M. Emma 3
   Mary Elizabeth 99
   Rose 88
   Susan 49
Gildeson, Sarah 115
Giles, Margaret A. 1
   Mary Jane 107
   Sarah J. 49
Gililan, Hana 54
Gilkison, Jane 14
Gillan, Loda 121
Gillenwater, Elizabeth 10
Gillenwaters, Leonard 47
   Mary 47
Gillett, Jane 5
Gilliam, Eliza 31
Gillilan, Margret (?) 107
   Presley 107
Gillim, Kazilla 6
Gillis, Ann Remecca 102
   Julia 6
   Mary J. 102

Gillis (cont.)
   Polly 23
Gilliume, Victoria 76
Gilmore, Conrod 143
   John 24
   Katherine 131
   Mary 137
Gilpen, Eliza 96
Gilpin, Anna E. 150
   L. R. 150
Gilroy, Barbara 85
Gilruth, Helen H. 39
   James 39
   Mary 132
   Thos. 138
Gimps, Catherine 145
Gims, Peggy 39
Ginatt, John B. 49
Ging, Katharine 69
Giss, Barbary 145
Gist, Josephine 88
   Maria 72
Givens, Cynthia 32
   Cynthia Ann 84, 94
   Sarah E. 18
   William 146
   William (Jr.) 18, 82
Glace, Andrew 61
Glasford, Sarah 146
Glass, Barbara A. 152
   Caroline 1
Glaze, Andrew 10
   Anna 80
   Elizabeth 10, 40
   Eve 50
   Mary 26, 31, 97, 99
   Mary Jane 24
   Mary M. 101
   Rachel 50
   Rhoda 50
Glidden, Caroline H. 29
   D. A. 101
   Joseph M. 80
   Mary G. 31
   Nancy A. 31
   S. S. 36
Glockner, Atelaiunta 53
Glokner, Mary 125
Glover, Ann M. 70
   Anna 97
   Azel 76
   Elijah A. 137
   Laura E. 141
   Margaret 47
   Mary Jane 132
   Nancy A. 47
   Sarah 133
   Sarah Jane 76
Goble, Hannah 35
Godare, Mary 51
Goddard, Jas. 149
   Martha 149
   Sumantha 149
Godderd, James 51
   Mary 51
Godfrey, Jane (Mrs.) 103
Godrich, Cynthia Jane 113
Goeblin, Susannah 151
Gohean, Catherine 4
Goheen, Ann 127
   Hannah 133
Goldsberry, Mary 97
   Mary Ellen 97
Golson, Polly 52
Gonkler, Mary Ann 13
Gooden, Daniel 18
   Mary Ella 109

Hamilton (cont.)
  Margaret 45, 98
  Reuben 54
  Sarah 15
Hamlibb, Hannah W. 13
Hammack, Mary 55
Hammerstein, Elizabeth
  118
Hammet, Katharine 92
  Lucinda 88
  Mary Ann 106
  Susannah 134
Hammett, Elizabeth 43
  Lucy 36
  Priscilla 85
Hammitt, Anna 97
Hammon, James 52
Hammond, Archibald 89
  James 105
  Sarah 129
Hamner, J. N. 102
  Lydia 102
Hamon, Rachel A. 55
Hampton, Mary (Mrs.) 109
  Morgan 109
Hancock, Cornelia M. 123
  Eliza Jane 144
  Laura T. 49
Handricks, Sarah Ann 39
Hanen, Eliza 60
Haney, Lucinda 71
Hanford, Mary Ann 67
Haning, Adel 48
Hankins, Matilda 135
Hanna, John 39
Hannahs, Elizabeth S.
  113
  Elizabeth T. (?) 113
  Ruth A. 105
  Sarah J. 28
Hannaman, Nancey 37
  Susannah 40
Hannison, Sabrah 140
Hanns, Elizabeth 109
  Henry 109
Hanson, Mary 37
Hanstead, Maria 99
Harbet, John 56
Harbot, Polly 131
Hard, Adeline 35
  Cynthia 69
  Dorothy A. 116
  Edwin 35
  Jonathan B. 148
  Levina 69, 148
  Lucy 73
  Lucy J. 35
  M. 55
  Mary 10
  Serena 148
  Sophronia (Mrs.) 35,
  148
Hardin, Ann 25
  Elizabeth 64
  Mary 134
  Nancy 51
  Sarah 42
Hare, Elenore 105
Hark, Mary 137
Harley, Emely 96
Harmason, Sabrah 140
Harmire, Mary 33
Harmon, Esebel 97
  Esther Ann 15
  Henry (?) 59
  Isabel 3
  Isabella 12
  Marther 65

Harmon (cont.)
  Mary Jane 85
  Nancy 97
  Sarah 151
Harness, Adam 55
Harper, Eveline 73
  Foloura 60
  H. E. 60
  Henderson 73
Harr, Elizabeth 5
Harris, Elizabeth 32
  Francis (Sr.) (Mrs.)
  22
  Francis E. 22
  Luruhama 66
  Narcisa 119
  Susannah (Mrs.) 122
Harrison, Ary 91
  Belinda 42
  Viene 22
Harrisson, Clarrisa 53
Harrst, Belinda 42
Hart, Julia Ann 101
  Lucretia 88
  Margaret C. 145
  Mary Jane 28
  Samuel 148
Harter, Clarinda 30
Hartley, Lucy 31
  Matilda 85
  Rachel 68
  Rosanna 110
  Sarah 30
Hartman, Catharine 13
  Catherine 27
  Jemima 7
  Kunegunda 24
  Mary 149
Harvey, Elizabeth 71
  Emeline 35
  Lucinda 71
Haskins, Eliza 74
  Hester Ann 5
Hasted, Elizabeth 12
Hatch, Alice 30
  Lovina 122
  Ruby G. 7
Hatfield, Catherine 13
  Cynthia Ann 17
  Martha A. 1
Hatt, Jerusia Adaline
  120
Hatton, William 56
Haubert, Anna (Mrs.) 10
  Catherine 10
  Louisa 47
  Margaret 73
  Nickolas 10
Hauka, John 69
Haukenheimer, Bena 68
Hauns, Henry 116
Havekotte, Ann Marie 135
Havenor, Whilemena 44
Havens, Emily 92
Haverty, Joseph 15
Hawk, Asha 89
  Eliza 39
Hawkins, Caroline 127
  Catharine 100
  Catherine 115
  Elizabeth 94
  Martha 70
  Milly 46
  Polly 59
  Sarah 116
Hay, Margaret 71
Hayale, Mary Elizabeth 6
Hayard, Martha 115

Hayden, Emma F. 66
Haynes, Elizabeth 3
Hayns, Josiah 35
Hays, Dennis H. 116
  Rachel 85
Hayse, Rhoda 9
Hayward, Elizabeth 99
  Hannah 9
  Julia 23
  Moses 115
  Philina 99
  Sarah Ann 97
  Sophia 88
Hazel, Seela Ann 124
Hazelbaker, Abraham 57
  Cynthia 122
  Juliann (Mrs.) 57
  Matilda 79
Hazlebaker, Cynthianne 4
Head, Eliza 151
  Sophronia 61
Headlock, Lydia 67
Heartly, Keziah 151
Heath, Cecilli 32
  Elizabeth L. 105
  Emily 56
  Eunice 36
  Hiram 72
  Julia Ann 101
  Maria 32
Hebsey, Mary Jane 122
Hecker, Lucintha 95
Hedhen, Mary 71
Heev, Sally 49
Heflen, Elzira 97
Heflin, John N. 114
  Julian 114
Heflinger, Elizabeth 55
Heid, George 57
Heied, Michael 59
Heinisch, Jacobine 99
Helm, Sarah Jane 130
Helmer, Elizabeth 32
  Margrate 51
Helmreich, Katharine 61
Helms, Hannah 46
Hemlep, Pauline 149
Hemmlepp, Theresia 143
Hemmlipp, Eda 8
Hempstead, Jane 77
  Margaret Jane 48
Hemstead, Maria 99
Henderson, Catharine 130
  Margaret J. 31
  Mary 115
Henken, Catherine 119
Hennis, Dorcas Ann 31
  Sarah 47
Henry, Anne 39
  Bridget 145
  Francis 76
  Idel (?) 140
  Janes 152
  Joseph C. 141
  Julian 83
Hensel, Nancy 130
Hensener, Wilhelm 53
Henshaw, Jerusha 10
  Mildred 145
Hensly, Mahala 2
Henson, Andrew J. 61
  Elizabeth (Mrs.) 111
  George 111
  Jackson 48
  Lydia Ann 111
  Mary 61
  Mary (Mrs.) 48
  Mary Jane 48

Henson (cont.)
  Nancy Sophronia 61
  Samuel 48, 111
  W. J. 61
Heorald, William 58
Heoredth, Sarah A. 115
Hepler, Matilda E. 139
Herbert, Anna 2
Herd, Josephine 134
Herell, Elizabeth (Mrs.)
  58
Herly, Mary Jane 94
Herman, Hanna 37
Herodth, Emily Frances
  80
Heron, Cynthia 137
Herr, Sarah 109
Herrold, Sarah 120
Herron, Frederick 4
  Maria 47
Heslar, Barbary 73
Hesler, Americus 132
  Elizabeth 125, 146
  Hannah 77
  Hester 51
  Mary 58
  Mary Jane 58
  Nancy 74
  Polly 4
  Sarah Sumantha 36
Hess, Caroline 88
Hetlinger, Mathaus 57
Hetzer, Katharina 93
Heuberth, Anna 2
Heuth, J. B. 57
Heutzman, Barbara 59
Hew, Sally (?) 49
Hewese, Martha 112
Hey, George 56
  Jacob 56
Hibbard, Maria 42
Hibborn, John 57
Hibbs, Aaron 58
  Hannah 146
  Rebecca 146
  Rebecca L. 115
Hibshear, Mary 74
Hice, Barbary 55
Hickey, Mary 101
Hickinbottom, Louisa 11
Hickle, Charlotte C. 13
Hickman, Delilah 58
  Sarey 10
Hicks, Annis 110
  Berry 22
  Elizabeth J. 151
  Henry 149
  J. W. 66
  James 58
  John W. 58
Hicombottom, Mary 114
Hides, Candice 60
Hied, Christina 66
Higgans, Eunice 4
Higgins, Anna 16
  Elizabeth 9
  John 9
  Katharine 13
  Maria 27
  Polly 84
  Rebecca 111
  Sarah 90
Higgs, Hester 63
Highland, Andrew 45
Highly, Drusilla 28
  Elizabeth 133
Higins, Nancy 91
Higley, L. N. 110

Hile, Elizabeth 93
Hill, Andre 59
  Catharine 125
  Catherine 59
  E. A. 69
  Elizabeth 23
  Hannah 67
  Jacob 23
  Jane (Mrs.) 59
  John 59
  Mary Ann 87
  Mary Jane 115
  Nathan 59
Hillbrecht, Hanna 49
Hiltz, Ludivica 10
Hilz, Caroline 36
Hin, Catharin (?) 4
Hindman, Anna 115
Hiner, Sally 57
Hinkle, Barbara 88
Hinkley, Anne 4
Hinton, James M. (?) 64
  Lucretia 46
  William 44
Hipsher, Katherine 36
Hirron, Stephen M. 58
Hise, Catharin 4
  Pegge 78
Hiss, Catharine 91
  Sally 91
  Sarrow 91
Hitchcock, Eliza L. 25
  Hanah M. 119
  Isibel 24
  Jesse 6, 24, 78, 87,
    94
  Joanna 94
  Joanna B. 24
  Lavina 74
  Lucretia 97
  Lydia 43
  Maria E. 76
  Matilda 74
  Nancy Keller 78
  Rebecca 57
Hoble, Catharine 54
Hobstater, Phillipina 10
Hoby, Leona 88
Hock, Catharine 75
  Eliza 95
  Elizabeth 95
  Frances 95
  Mary 112
  Phillip (?) 59
Hockenbery, Nancy A. 102
Hodd, Hannah 137
Hodge, Margaret 5
  Maria 64
  Nancy 72
  Sally 119
Hodges, A. D. 3, 59
  Aaron D. 30, 142
  Anna 142
  Belinda 25
  Elizabeth (Mrs.) 52,
    131
  George 142
  Jemima 65
  Lucinda 52
  Mary 82
  Melinda 25
  Moses 59, 131
  Nancy 3, 78, 86, 118
  Phebe 12
  Polly 30
  Ransom 3, 52, 59
  Rebecca 29
  Robart D. 25

Hodges (cont.)
  Robert 59
  Sally (Mrs.) 25, 65
  Susey 25
Hody, Elizabeth T. 97
Hoeh, Phillip (?) 59
Hoeredh, Rhoda 115
Hof, Christine 116
Hoffman, Mary 41
  Rosina 41
  Susannah 116
Hoffner, Elisabeth 68
Hofstedter, Mary 69
Hogan, Eliza A. 68
  Rosan 53
Hogue, Maria 97
Hoit, Dianthy 123
Holbert, John 60
  Maria (Mrs.) 60
  Mary Jane 55
  Nancy 69
Holcan, Maray 102
Holland, Maray 102
  Mary 41
Holley, Sophronia 62
Holliday, Ann 60
  Jane 85
  Martha Ann 85
Hollingshead, Aaron 15,
  66, 127
Holman, Nancy 92
  Susanna 105
Holmes, Almirah 98
  Flora A. 65
  Harriet (Mrs.) 60
  Isaac 96
  J. 60
  John J. 44
  Malissa 17
  Marilda 69
  Mary A. 106
  W. C. 65
  William 69, 80, 98,
    151
Holmien, Elizabeth 88
Holms, Candas 75
  Emeline 96
Holsinger, Eliza J. 42
Holstead, Amos 100
  Catharine 60
Holston, George 134
Holt, Cynthia Ann 57
  Eliza A. 4
  Elizabeth 88, 101
  Ellendor 12
  Henry 60
  Julia Ann 12
  Martha 98
  Mary 142
  Matilda Jayne 67
  Minerva 116
  Rhuhama 131
  Sarah J. 57
  Sarah Jane 12
  Tobitha 96
Holtness, Susannah 30
Holybee, Anne 68
Home, Lucinda 3
Homer, Edward B. 133
  Mary 133
Homes, Elizabeth (?) 20
  Sarah 117
Honel, Aaron 16
Hoobler, John 127
  Margaret 141
Hood, Abigail 18
  Caroline 43
  Elizabeth Jane 152

Hood (cont.)
Emeline 62
Hannah 137
Jane 144
Lucy 27
Nancy 62
Nancy (Mrs.) 152
Rebeca (?) (Mrs.) 144
Robert 62, 152
Thomas 144
Hoor, Abigail 18
Hoothday, Elizabeth
(Mrs.) 52
John 52
Hootsley, Elizabeth
(Mrs.) 52
John 52
Hoover, Mary Ann 116
Rebecca 51
William 135
Hopkins, Ann 67
Carls 61
Hoppas, Barbary 125
Hoppers, Barbary 125
Hoppis, Castena 150
Catherine (Mrs.) 63
Delila 41
Hannah 59
John 121
Katharine 121
Mary 63
Sarah 121
Willim 63
Hopps, Barbary 125
Horn, George 61
Margaret 110
Mary 127
Horne, Jane 48
Rebecca (?) 148
Horner, Catherine (Mrs.)
61
Eliza Jane 145
Elizabeth 137
Fanney 112
Harriet 1
Henrietta 5
Joseph 20, 137
Nancy 150
Phebe 54
Richard 61
Sarah 117
Hornes, Elizabeth 20
Hornung, Elizabeth 46
Horst, Elizabeth 126
Hoskinson, Anna 146
Josiah 21, 146
Julia 38
Mary Emma Dent 21
Polly 109
Hosted, Elizabeth 12
Hoster, Carienia 30
Hostetter, Eve 114
Hottes, M. 8
Houbert, Catharine 136
Eva 22
Houchins, Lucinda 119
Mary 47
Hough, Isaac 23
Hour, George A. 61
Houser, Christina 8
Houtchins, Julia 53
How, Sarah Ann 149
Howard, Angeline 121
James 112
Laura 33
Loyd 140
Margaret 121
Mary (Mrs.) 146

Howard (cont.)
Mary Adeline 56
Michael 152
Rachel 16
Rhody 17
Suzan T. 145
Howe, Amanda 19
Caroline 78
Minerva 123
Phoebe 133
Rebecca 148
Susan 121
Howel, Belinda 34
Elizabeth 68
Howell, Emeline 27
Israel H. 23
Jonathan (Sr.) 62
Margrate P. 133
Sarah 27
Sarena 143
William 12
Howes, Eliza Ann 130
Howlans, John 72
Hoyt, Julian 101
Hubbard, Catharine 136
John 81
Louisa 81
Mary 73
Nicholas 59
Ruth 61
Hubbart, Anne 33
Hubble, Rosina 62
Hucher, Adeline 36
Huchey, Ann Louisa 65
Huchiens, Mary 125
Huckworth, Hester 86
Huddleson, Agnes 109
Huddleston, Cynthia Ann
25
Eliza 41
Ermina 29
Fanny 122
Joseph 39
Julia Ann 45
Mary 63
Nancy Maria 12
Peggy 146
Zire 39
Hudson, ---ler 62
Charles T. 63
Elijah 126
Julia Ann 130
Lavina 23
Mary 115
Mary L. 3
Huebner, Mary Ann 17
Moritz 17
Hues, Anna 81
Katharine 83
Huester, Augustin 51
Huffin, Sophia 41
Huffman, Cecelia 14
Jacob 136
John 63
Mary (Mrs.) 63
Melvina 136
Robert 136
Hugar, Mary A. 50
Hughes, Anna 82
James 146
Martha 62
Nathan 4
Sylvester 129
Winneford 35
Hughey, Charlotte (Mrs.)
78
Mariah 78
Samuel 78

Hughs, James 39, 146
Job 39
Margaret 34
Martha 39
Nancy 97
Hulce, Lucinda 67
Hull, Isaac (Jr.) 9
Isaac (Sr.) 9
Jane 9
Rebecca 132
Huls, Cynthia A. 24
Hulzmeier, Mary 107
Humbolt, Katharine 36
Humphreys, Barbery 87
Elizabeth 73, 74
Margaret 72
Margarette 102
Mary 92
Samuel 87, 92
Humphries, Mary Melvina
94
Hundle, Amanda 142
Hunelly, Nancy (?) 105
Hungerford, Jane 78
Julia A. 98
Lucinda 63
Hunsucker, Sarah 65
Hunt, Caroline 146
Delila 147
Elizabeth 73, 99
Emily 31
Julia 55
Lucretia 113
May Jane 41
Sally 52
Sally (Mrs.) 113
Hunter, Andrew 18, 140
Harriet (Mrs.) 15
Lancy 9
Nancy 18
Polly 100
Hurd, Charlotte M. 123
Harriet M. 131
Mary Y. 29
Huren, Frederick 141
Hurt, Everett 131
Philipena 115
Husbee, Louisa 7
Huse, Hanah 83
Keziah (Mrs.) 64
Hush, Lucretia 87
Huston, Angeline 97
Cecilia A. 27
Elizabeth 27
Elizabeth (Mrs.) 27,
81
Elizabeth L. 7
Hellen M. 81
Joseph 90
Julia 3
Maria 137
Mary 98, 145
Mary E. 25
Mary M. 2
S. J. 81
Samuel 27
Sarah Jane 90
Sidney Ann 147
Sydney Anne 3
Hutchinson, Josephine B.
70
Hutchison, Maria 87
Hutton, Eliza A. 16
John 64
Mary 96, 98
Nancy 97
Rachel 41
Ruth 29

Hutton (cont.)
Sarah 10, 61
Slaviah 86
Hyatt, Marilla 73
Hyder, Elizabeth A. 81
Sarah C. 99
Hyett, Mary Elizabeth 6
Ickenberg, Fredrica 66
Ilch, Barbary 18
Iman, Matilda 18
Ingals, Abigal 43
Ingils, Grace 116
Ingle, Polly 105
Ingles, Elizabeth 69
Susanah 23
Ingram, Elizabeth 134
Ingrum, Amanda 45
Irvin, Louisa 52
Irwin, Elizabeth 2
Julia Ann 2
Margaret 37
Samuel W. 41
William 41
Isaminger, Ann B. 53
Philip 89
Ishmael, Margaret Jane
109
Ives, Harriet 137
Jackson, Charlotte 25
Elisabeth (Mrs.) 25
Eliza J. 89
Elizabeth 148
Elizabeth Ann 88
Evan 25
John 40
Joseph 65, 77
Mary 45
Mary Ann 127
Minerva 7
Nancy 91
R. (Mrs.) 65
Rachel 40
Richard 149
Sarah 35
William 40, 54, 65
Jacobs, Hannah (Mrs.)
126
Margaret 126
Patcy 90
Jacquese, Elizabeth
(Mrs.) 65
Peter 65
Jaeger, Luisa 8
Jaiky, Magdalina 10
Jain, Mary 147
James, Cynthia Ann 85
Eliza 140
Elizabeth 26
Eve 41
Harriot 108
James 66
Jonathan 65, 67
Josiah 65, 73
Margaret 101
Mary 113
Olivia 65
Janes, Hiram (?) 8
Joanna 130
Martha Ann 110
Mary (Mrs.) 39
Sarah Ann 135
Janson, William H. 67
Jaqot, Leona 98
Jaquett, Mary 108
Jatho, Carl 65
Jayne, Lidea 87
Jaynes, Caroline 8
Elizabeth 26

Jaynes (cont.)
Eunice 63
Sally Jane 41
Jeandesboz, Charles
Francis 65
Jeaugenot, Margt. 57
Jefferson, Willhelmina
70
Jeffords, Eliza Jane 60
Maria 124
Mary A. 53
Miranda 38
Pheby 66
Sarah Jane 6
Jenkins, Colvin 66
Emily 30
Lovina 2
Mary 34, 61
Nancy 20
Phoebe 112
Sarah (Mrs.) 66
Susan 20
Walter 103
Jennison, Louisa M. 106
Ruth (Mrs.) 106
Samuel 106
Jewett, Electa 132
William 132
Johnson, (?) 18
A. J. 93
Adam 67
Anna 87
Corinda 127
Eli 132
Elizabeth 25
Elizabeth Ann 111
Eunice 113
Fanny 98
Frances 152
George 65
Hannah 125
Hariet 107
Harriet 97
Jane 45
John 66
Lavina 67
Lucy 100
Margaret 90
Margaret T. 66
Maria 110
Mary 22, 64, 65, 149
Mary Ann 125
Minerva 85
Molinda 86
Nancy 43
Nancy Ann 132
Phebe 50
Rachel 124
Rebeccah P. 138
Rhody 96
Rosana 51
Sally 126
Sarah 9, 56, 126
Sarah Ann 7
Sarah C. 67
William 108
Johnston, Anna 27
Catharine 59
Ellen 65
Levi 27
Mary C. 32
Jondebow, Josephine 53
Jones, Alasanna 45
Amazetta 71
Angaline 123
Anna Maria 42
Benjamin 147
Charlotte 146

Jones (cont.)
David 31
David J. 67
Dianna 43
Elisabeth 89
Elizabeth 33, 46, 71
Elizah 142
Ellen 142
Emily 55, 56
Esther 68
Even 144
George 105
Gweny 55
Hannah 116, 134
Hester Ann 84
Hiram 8, 32
Isabella 47, 95
Jane 86
John (Sr.) 67
Jonathan (?) 67
Lucretia Ann 31
Luna 69
Margaret 30, 122
Margaret T. 66
Martha 77
Martha Ann 110
Mary 28, 35, 85, 87,
92, 132, 152
Mary A. 110
Mary Abigail 31
Mary E. Elisabeth 148
Mitilday 75
N. L. 68
Nancy 29, 149
Patience T. 35
Phebe 146, 147
Polly 51
Rachael 133
Rachel 76, 149
Rebecca 1, 9, 32
S. G. 68
Sally (Mrs.) 105
Sarah 32, 94
William 68, 122
Winfred 55
Jonsin, Daniel L. 66
Jopland, Charley 66
Joseph, Nancy 108
Joses, Frances 107
Journey, Mary A. 65
William 65
Jowete, William 66
Jukley, Martha Jane (?)
130
Junkin, David W. M. 68
M. 77
Mary (Mrs.) 77
William 77
Justice, Olly 108
Kah, Joseph 68
Juliana 69
S. (Mrs.) 68
Kahal, Edward 54
Elizabeth 54
Kallaway, Louisa 139
Kampelman, Barney 28
Kanish, Catharine 117
Kankan, Catherine 74
Kannals, Edward 114
Kaps, Elizabeth 70
Karger, Ernstine 74
Karl, Lorens 22
Karlo, Villabeder 87
Karr, Rebecky 11
Katon, Martha Jane 129
T. T. 129
Thomas 14
Keadauk, Catherine 31

Lair (cont.)
 Philipena 7
 Richard H. 150
 Samantha 63
 Sarah 48
 Sophronia 140
Laird, Margaret 129
Laire, Mary 150
 Richad H. 150
 Richard H. 147
 Richard M. 73
 Squire 66
Lairs, Susanna (?) 110
Lalendorf, Serena Kidd
  11
Laman, David 73
Lamb, Betsey 145
 Clarissa 149
 Edward 126
 Elizabeth 129
 Lucina 126
 Mary 24
 Murdwell 33
 Persis L. 23
 Reuben 126
 Willard 126
Lambert, Abegail 69
 Mary 119
 Melvina 122
 Sarah 76
Lampe, Charlotte 62
Lancaster, Ransom (?) 73
Lance, Henry 74
Landers, Adam 151
 Eliza 97
 Mary Ann 86
 Rebecca 151
 Sarah 97
Landry, Adam 97
 Eliza 97
Lane, Minerva 5
 Susanna Charlotte 20
Laneharten, Catherena 13
Lang, George 138
 Margaret 88
 Mary 138
 Mary (Mrs.) 138
Lantz, Rebecca 12
Largent, Comfort 83
Larimer, Nancy 92
 William 92
Larimore, Mary Ann 95
Larkin, Aury 7
Larrimore, Rebecca 128
Larver, Hannah (?) 93
Laten, Elizabeth 50
Lattermann, Mary 10
Lauble, Mary 74
Lauderback, Mary 12
Laughfert, Harriet 117
Laughlin, Daniel 86
 James 74
Lauty, Mary 41
Law, Janes (?) 78
Lawder, Jully 69
 Sally 69
Lawer, Hannah (?) 93
Lawhorn, Melissa 55
Lawhorne, Elizabeth 42
Lawhun, John B. 42
 Martha Jane 42
Lawrence, Adeline 103
 Eliza 135
Lawson, Charlotta 54
 Christina 70
 James 90
 John 24, 59
 Maria 17, 69

Lawson (cont.)
 Mary Jane 77
 Minerva 24
 Nancy 35, 77
 Polly 92
 Ruth 71
 Sarah 24
 Susan 81
 Susannah 44
Lawwill, Sara (Mrs.) 112
 Tamar 112
 Thomas J. 112
Layher, John 117
Layman, Magdalene 79
LeForge, Eleanor 16
Leach, Polly 63
Leadbetter, Rhoda 28
Leadenham, Mary 68
Ledbetter, Mary 103
Ledensmith, Christean 80
Leduke, Lidia 16
Lee, Belinda 147
 Deany 8
 Eliza Jane 90
 Elizabeth 27
 Esther 149
 John 35, 55, 152
 Margaret 125
 Mary 69
 Patsy 152
 Perthena Green 122
 Sarah Jane 147
 Sibbie 119
 Susan Catharine 23
Leetes, Fiate 75
Leeth, Elizabeth 33
Legler, Eleonora 16
 George 103
 Joseph 75
 Mary 45, 102
 Rosa 16
Lehman, Margaret 11
 Marie 42
Leighty, John 74
Leiuter, Georg 115
Lelix, Elliner 112
 Julia 47
 Sally 112
Lell, Doretz 36
Lellich, Julia 47
Lemison, Emesella 123
 Mary B. 42
 Rosita Ann 75
Lemmison, Emeline 149
Lemon, Lemuel 56
 Nancy 56
Lemons, Durfoilece 81
Lenan, Catherine 45
Lenard, Mary 147
Leniger, John 38
Lentz, Cuniginde 89
Leonard, Elizabeth 64
 Margaret 34
 Mary 10
 Mary Ann 110
 Nancy 6
 Sarah 20
 Susannah 34
Leryfa, Catharine 57
Leser, Elizabeth 103
Lesler, Frances 63
Lewis, Ann 55
 Catherine 9, 34
 Comfort 147
 David 75
 Eliza 121
 Elizabeth 72, 139
 Elizabeth J. 121

Lewis (cont.)
 Elsa 7
 Eve 32
 Frederick 60, 118
 Henry 9
 Hester Eliza 142
 Jane 42, 66
 Jemima 61
 John 142
 John C. 78
 Josiah 99
 Liza 22
 Louisa 5
 Lydia 52
 Margaret 26, 34
 Mary 21, 48, 118
 Mary A. 74
 Mary Jane 127, 133
 Nancy 20, 39
 Nancy Ann 78
 Patty 113
 Polly 139
 Ruthy 129
 Sally 60
 Sarah 63
 Sarah A. 121
 Sary Ann 39
 Sophia 58
 Stephen 86
 Susan 96
 Thomas C. 6
Lewisman, Mary 131
Lichner, Ann M. 34
Liden, Bridget 22
Liggett, Jane 6, 93
 Sarah Ann 1
Liles, Thomas 41
Lill, Dauherty 36
Lilly, Emily 102
Limley, Catharine (?) 38
Linden, John (?) 74
Linder, John (?) 74
 Leonhard 125
Lindsay, Margaret 102
Lindsey, Beaulah 30
 Catharine 38
 Dulina 71
 Eliza 27
 Harriet 20
 Lemuel 134
 Mina 106
 Nancy 40
 Orrissa W. 24
 Rebecca 152
 Sarah 6
 Urania 6
Link, Caroline 82
Linn, Huldah M. 105
 John 76
 Nancy 116
Lintz, Caroline 99
 Corinna 73
Linz, Catharine 49
Lionbarger, Mary 35
 Peter 35, 152
 Peter (Jr.) 35
Lionberger, Emma 152
Liston, Elizabeth 98
 Margaret 61
 Mary 78, 115
 Mary Ann 119
 Nancy 140
 Perry 76
 Rebecah 102
Little, Ruth C. 96
Littlejohn, Alice Ann
  122
 Catherine 89, 102

Littlejohn (cont.)
Elizabeth 5
Henry 4
Joseph 19
Lucinda 28
Margaret 19
Mary 5
Nancy 4
Peggy 39
Valentine 6
Littleton, Sarah 60
Livery, Josephine 13
Livesay, Moses 75
Livingston, Margaret 18
Lixsal, Letha Ann 29
Lloyd, Harriet E. 134
Nancy 87
Locey, Filina 18
Lockart, Delitha 25
Locke, Benjamin 14, 113
Eliza 66
Lockerd, Keziah 98
Locy, Isaac 129
Mary E. 129
Phebe (Mrs.) 129
Lodge, Martha 2
Lodwick, E. (Mrs.) 108
Eliza Jane 147
Ellen 58
Jane Elizabeth 69
Martha 71
Loffborough, Catharine
E. 19
Logan, Eliza 52
Mary 65
Rebeccah 112
Logler, Joseph 75
Loner, Cambel 143
Eliza J. 143
Long, Belinda 106
C. O. (Mrs.) 148
Eliza 64
George 138
Harriet 91
Levina 49
Margaret 145
Mariah Jane 51
Mary 138
Mary (Mrs.) 138
Mary Jane 144
Nancy 118
Valentine 77
Longwith, Mary J. 59
Longworth, Henry 59
Susan (Mrs.) 59
Loomis, Elizabeth 101
Laura 152
Lucy Jane 37
Mary 47
Lope, Elizabeth 7
Lopins, Matilda 110
Lorburger, Fosbrager
(Mrs.) 77
Fred 77
Fredricka (Mrs.) 77
Lord, Abner 77
Eliza 77
Elizabeth 77
Ezra F. 77
Nancy 61
Lordier, Mary Jane 72
Loth, Rosina 25
Louder, Mary 101
Mary Anna 50
Samuel 125
Louderback, Belinda 100
Betsy (Mrs.) 139
Catherine 71

Louderback (cont.)
Elizabeth 58
Hannah 59
John 91, 103, 139
Katharine 102
Lavina 57
Levina 141
Lorane 143
Louisa 42
Mary Jane 139
Matilda 4
Michael 141
Polly 51
Sarah Jane 19
Loughlin, Sophia 119
Loutherback, Margaret
127
Lovel, Rachel 140
Loveland, Harriet 147
Lucinda 29
Nancy 93
Low, Margaret 78
Lowe, Nancy 9
Lower, Elizabeth 46
Francis 9
Lowers, Griffin 125
Lowery, Elizabeth 2
Margaret 97
Peggy 97
Lowry, America D. 93
Jacob 78
Jane 101
Jinne 101
Mahulda 73
Mary (Mrs.) 78
Loyd, Ann 123
Sarah (?) 95
Lucas, A. F. 147
Abigail 25
Ann E. 87
George W. 126
Jarusha 108
Jemima Ann 104
Lavisa 104
Levisa 24
Levise 127
N. B. 126
Nancy A. 37
Rebeccah 58
Robert 20, 134
Ziar 22
Lucher, Lewis W. 78
Ludlow, William C. 115
Ludwig, Louisa 70
Lupius, Mary Elizabeth 6
Lusk, Mary Ellen 37
Lute, Eliza Jane 126
Elizabeth 132
John 87, 94
Robert 126
Luther, Barbara 59, 69
Margaret 29, 79
Margarita 12
Lutz, Abraham 79
Lynch, Elizabeth 42
Robert 23, 42
Lyons, Lucy Jane 12
Lyra, Margaret 107
MCan, Martha 124
MJunkins, Mary Ann 82
William T. 82
MacGinnis, Fanny 143
MacGloplin, Robert 86
Machmanagel, Catherine
52
Mackeltree, Catherine 40
Eve 147
Macketee, Deanna 129

Mackey, Margret 144
Maddock, Addean E. 129
Mary (Mrs.) 7
Mary J. 7
William 7
Madison, Jane 4
Magnet, C. E. (Mrs.) 65,
79
Clotilda 65
Felicity 99
J. N. 65, 79
Jane 93
Mai, Theressa 126
Mail, Francis 60
Maiy, Creed Francis (?)
88
Malcolm, Elizabeth 32
Malcom, Sophia Rice 76
Mallen, Mary Ann 14
Maloan, Betsey (Mrs.)
129
Samuel 129
Malone, Esther 79
George 97
Hannah 53
Lucinda 102
Margaret 124
Margaret (Mrs.) 102
Mary 135
Richard 39, 132, 137
Sally 132
Susannah 132, 135
Susannah (Mrs.) 132
William 135
Maltimore, Eliza 21
Rebecca 66
Mandeerie, Peter 90
Manges, Clarissa Ann 73
Manley, Margaret 80, 89
Manly, Esther 71
Jas. 79
M. A. (Mrs.) 79
Mann, Elizabeth 22
Manny, Caroline 11
J. 11
Mapes, Elizabeth C. 136
Mary Ann 90
Sarah Ann 109
Thomas 90
Maple, John 118
Lavina 118
Mar, Ann 57
March, Mary E. 40
Mary James 44
Mark, Martha 16
Markum, Loise 66
Marquart, Justina 125
Marret, Ruth 50
Marsh, Anne 26
Margaret 119
Mary 15
Ruth 47
Sarah M. 1
Marshal, Sabina 103
Marshall, Caroline 38
Elisabeth 35
Elizabeth 100, 104
Ellen 35
Emily 136
Fanny 120
Melvina 105
Narcissis 2
Nelson 21
Sally 90
Samuel 103
Temperance 98
Ziare 78
Marshel, Eliza 44

Marshel (cont.)
  Frances 62
Marsid, Thomas J. (?) 80
Martain, Friedrich 75
  Mary 75
Marteness, Maryann 79
Martin, Aidy (Widow) 28
  Ann 84
  Anny 68
  Catherine 58
  Elizabeth 95
  Evangely 95
  Hannah 145
  Jacob 81
  James J. 50
  Jane 21, 73
  Lavina 40
  Malinda 81
  Mary 6, 51, 71
  Mary Elizabeth 50
  Miami 77
  Nancy 5, 103
  Paulina 88
  Peggie B. 141
  Prudence 145
  Sarah 115
  Sarah Elizabeth 103
  Tobitha 45
  William 81
  William H. 81
Martten, Friedrich 75
  Mary 75
Masch, Mary E. 40
Maseh, Mary 15
Mason, Charles B. 109
  Elizabeth 4
Massey, Diana 5
  Polly 1
  Thomas 1
Master, George 87
Masters, Catherine 7
  George 61, 138
  Harriet 40
  July Ann 138
  Malinda C. 10
  Martha A. 77
  Sarah (Mrs.) 126
  Sarah Ann 126
  Stephen 125
Mastin, Abigail M. 146
  Elizabeth 96
  Mary 81
  Rebecca M. 70
  Sarah 10
  Sarah T. 89
  Turner M. 108
Mathena, Elizabeth 100
Matheny, Elizabeth 36
Mather, Ebenezer 80
Mathers, Ann Eliza 52
Mathew, Elizabeth 63
  Mary Ann 53
Mathews, A. 67
  Ann Eliza 52
  Catherine 67
  Julia A. 81
  Lucinda 29
  Mary (Mrs.) 90
  Mary Ann 90
  Reuben H. 90
Matson, Mary A. W. 77
Matthews, Eliza 81
  Rulaney 83
Mault, Jessee 118
  Lucinda 58
  Mahala 89
  Mary (Mrs.) 118
  Moses 118

Mault (cont.)
  Sarah 134
May, Lucinda 122
  Theressa 126
Maybee, O. 133
Mayhue, Elizabeth 63
Maze, L. D. 82
  Matilda 16
McAleer, Mary U. 93
McAlister, Mahala 88
McArthur, Allen C. 33
McAtee, Dianna 129
  Louisa 137
  W. T. 65
McAuley, Anna 1
  Comfort 106
  Kaziah 117
  Polly 26
  Rachel 28
McAuly, Lydia M. 141
McBride, Elizabeth
  (Widow) 76
McCague, Mary 7
McCall, Califurnia 28
  Delilah 147
  Elizabeth 78
  Louisa 16
  Margaret 128
  Margaret A. 11
  Maria 39
  Martha 98
  Sarah A. (Mrs.) 82
  Susanne 85
McCama, Mary 64
McCan, Katharine 87
  Mary Jane 45
McCanley, Isaac 108
  James 34
  Melinda 34
McCann, Lucinda 132
  Margret 4
  Mary 45, 46
  Mary A. 132
  Mary Ann 112
  Sarah A. 64
  Seby 145
McCartney, Daniel 120
  Hannah 120
McCarty, Daniel 120
  Hannah 120
  John 123
  Margaret 123
McCauley, Mahala 34
McChesney, Richard 83
McClain, Isabella 134
McClary, Mary 83
McCleary, Andrew 88
  Emeline 15
  Jane 88
  Mary (Mrs.) 88
  Matilda 27
  Nancy 59, 73
McCleland, Memima 40
McClene, Mary 48
McClese, Ruhama 67
McCloud, David 27
  Elizabeth 27
  Margaret (Mrs.) 27
  Samuel J. 14
McClovis, Mary Ann 67
McClung, Letitia 31
  Rhode 45
McClure, Hannah 146
  Mary 48
McClury, Letitia 31
McColey, James 83
McCollester, Harriet E.
  101

McCollister, Elizabeth 7
  Mary 51
  Nancy 29
  Ruth A. 33
  Sarah 22
McColm, Caroline 152
  M. 83
McConkey, Sarah 103
McConkle, Amanda 20
  Margaret 115
McConky, Elizabeth 106
  Franky E. 85
McConnel, Abraham 43
  Elizabeth 114
  Huldah 128
  John 114
  Mary 148
  Polly 148
  Sophia 93
McConnell, Jane 68
  Nancy 44
  Susannah 93
McCormic, Mary 139
McCormick, John 121
  Susannah (Mrs.) 59
McCowan, Anna 132
  Rebecca 126
McCowen, Mary 107
McCown, Abigail 14
McCoy, Cornelius 109,
  112
  Harriet 13
  James 13
  Miriam 40
  Pearson 13, 57
  Phebe 29
  Sarah U. 28
McCrary, Alexander 83
McCreary, Eleanor Bigham
  72
McCreery, Margaret 146
McCrumb, Mary 99
McCuffrey, Margaret 19
McCurdy, Margaret 79
  Robert A. H. 104
McDaniel, Jemima 124
McDermet, David 84
McDermit, Sarah 82
McDonald, Charles 84
  David 83
  Eliza Ann 137
  John 53
  Martha 119
  Nancy 53, 102
McDonnell, Nancy 102
McDougal, Nancy 62
  Richard 62
McDougall, Aseaneth 36
McDougle, Julia A. 148
McDowell, Eliza 49
  Eliza M. 33
  Elizabeth 67, 71
  Harriet 62
  Louisa 36
  Martha 32
  Mary 123
  Mary Jane 149
  Rachel 107
  Samuel 62
  William F. 42
McDowll, Jinny 102
McElhenny, M. 140
McFadden, Clementa 55
McFaden, Priscilla 8,
  101
McFadgin, William 85
McFan, Andrew J. 85
  Emily 35

McFan (cont.)
 Kimber 35
McFann, A. J. 94, 123
 A. Jackson 11
 James 61
 T. J. 94
McGarvy, Elisabeth 95
McGee, Effa 79
 Nancy 113
McGeene, Catharine 23
McGennis, Fanny 143
McGer, Elizabeth 124
McGhee, Mary 90
McGiddis, Eliza J. 42
McGill, Ellen 106
 Ellen P. 137
McGlone, Francis 62
McGowen, James 2
 Mary J. 2
McGraw, Manda Ann 100
 Martha 1
 Sarah 75
 William 75, 85, 100
McGrine, A. L. (?) 85
McGrullin, Catharine 85
McHenry, Alexander 142
McIlhinney, Marshall 85
McIntire, Patsey 16
 Sally 16
McIntyre, Joseph 30
 Margaret 30
McJunkin, Elizabeth 135
 Jane 35, 77
McJunkins, Mary A. 92
McK'ney, Washington 25
McKean, James M. 69
 Nancy 25
McKee, Arthur 62
 James 91
 John D. 91
 Mary 62, 90
 Taxy 34
McKeever, Elizabeth 47
 James 49
 Sophia 49
McKell, Leny 119
McKelroy, Margaret 69
McKenzie, Ann 136
McKery, Margaret 146
McKindall, Sarah Jane 43
McKinley, Jane 147
 Sarah 44
McKinney, Cynthia 9
 Cynthia Ann 124
 Elizabeth 137
 George 86
 Harriet 54
 John 136
 Mary 78, 82
 Mary Ann 21
 Nancy 152
 Phebe 17
 Sarah Jane 43
McKinsey, Polly 141
McLain, Elizabeth 86
 Katharine 87
 Martha Jane 28
McLamore, Rebecca 132
McLane, Ann 39
McLary, Elizabeth 71
 Mary E. (Mrs.) 71
McLaughlin, Adaline 38
 Angeline 46, 51
 Mary 54, 137
 Rachel 77
 Samuel 38
McLean, Mary 74
 Nancy 75

McLees, Rachel 125
McLoud, Margaret 1
 Martha Jane 28
McMahon, Sarah 47
McMan, Sarah 47
McManagale, Clarinda 37
McManaghiel, Levina 52
McManegel, Mary 81
McManighel, Catherine 52
 James 52
McManis, Lydia 120
McMannus, Angeline 1
McMaster, Samuel C. 106
McMasters, Eliza 37
 Maria 5
 Mary 118
McMullan, Susannah 77
McMurry, Nancy 37
McNairn, Isabella 94
 Mary 71
McNally, Eliza J. 30
 Margaret 114, 139
 Mary 114
McNaly, Mary 27
McNamar, Elizabeth 97
McNamer, John 87
 Mary 88
 Sobina 12
McNeal, Ann 64
 Caroline W. 45
 Giles 30
 Lydia 106
 Margaret (Mrs.) 48
 Mercy Ann 128
 Nancy 6
 Susan 48
McNelly, Catharine 90
 Elizabeth 13
 Hannah (Mrs.) 30
 Mary F. 35
McNetty, Hannah (Mrs.)
 30
McNott, Harriett 24
McNutten, Harriett 24
McQuality, Eliza 40
McQuerry, Margaret 73
Mead, Abigail 15, 37
 Elizabeth 47, 84, 126
 Esther 71, 111
 Ezra 15, 111
 H. 17
 Hannah 12
 Hezekiah 87
 Isaac 71, 125
 James 54
 Jane 18
 Joshua 71
 Judah 47, 125
 Lydia 12
 Lydia (Mrs.) 87
 Mehetable 125
 Nancy 43
 Rachel 9, 48
 Rebecca 37
 Sarah 2, 125
Meakley, Martha A. 76
Mears, Susan 86
Mechant, Jacob 80
Mecheny, Samuel B. 83
Meddough, Mary Jane 73
Meengen, Francis 94
Mehl, Rosina Judith 88
Mehleman, John 93
Meister, Mary 24
Melane, Ann 39
Melcher, Benjamin 3
 Eunace 43
 Eunice A. 3

Melcher (cont.)
 Mary C. 66
Melone, Hannah 135
 Lydia 75
 Polly 65
Melroy, Catherine 94
Melson, Ann 17
 Anna 96
 Eleanor 74
 Jesse 17, 87
 Joseph 17
 Kezia 96
 Martha 70
 Martha (Mrs.) 74
 Mary 21
 Susannah 16
Melton, Bethan 123
 Cassandra 150
 Mitha 123
Menager, Lucretia 108
Mender, Ellen 50
Meningo, Malinda 130
Menken, Mary 118
Mensel, Wilhelm 88
Mentel, Elizabeth 16
Meredith, Mary Francis
 102
Merker, Hannah T. 15
Merret, Elizabeth 50
Merrill, Maria 96
Merriman, Julia Ann 57
Mershon, C. (Mrs.) 88
 Cassey J. 54
 H. 88
 Jerusha 60
 Mary Ann 83
 Mary Frances 98
Mesmer, Josephine 59
Messer, Barbara 111
 Margaret 75
Messerer, Christina 51
 Margaret 116
 Sophia 109
Messman, Rosina 73
Metcalf, Caroline 77
Methena, Hannah S. 110
Methews, Rebecca Jane 96
Metz, Margaret 10
 Phebe 74
Mews, Matilda 16
Meyer, Anna 123
 C. 114
 Henry 88
 Rosena 152
Meyers, Karoline 70
 Mary 54
Mezger, John Friedrich
 88
Mickey, Ann 11
Middaugh, Mary Jane 64
Mila, Mena 69
Milam, Edward 75
 Elizabeth 3
 Mary Mahala 35
Milard, Permina 14
Mile, Margaret 57
Miler, Amanda 67
 Emily Jane 21
 Martha 72, 142
 Mary 21
 William 21
Miles, Branson 35
 Catharine 105
 Fanny H. 110
 Lavina 152
 Levina 93
 Lucy E. 118
 Miranda Jane 128

178

Milhisen, Henry 93
Millar, Abm. 108
  Elizabeth 108
  Elizabeth Elton 110
  Jacob 121
  Nancy 121
Miller, Ann E. 66
  Anthony 90
  Caroline 13
  Catharina 65
  Catharine 65, 100
  Catherine 142
  Cornelius 56
  Elizabeth 25, 75
  Friedrich 13
  Hiram 7
  Jacob 121
  John 87
  John D. 72
  Juliett 31
  Katharina 117
  Katharine 110
  Louisa (Mrs.) 13
  Mahala 125
  Malinda 14
  Margaret 97
  Martha 142
  Mary 15, 95
  Mary (Mrs.) 90
  Mary Jane 22
  Matilda 34
  Nancy 65, 121, 146
  Phebe 84
  Rachel 7
  Rebecca 89
  Sarah Jane 90
  Sary N. 135
  Sophia 73
  Susanna 22
  Thomas T. 14
Millholland, Charles 40
Millirons, Elizabeth
  (Mrs.) 89
  James M. 113
  Mary 57
  Michael 33, 113
  Michael (Jr.) 33
  Salathiel 4
  Sampson 89
  Samuel 89, 113
  Sarah 33
  Selathial 113
  Sophiah 113
  William 124
Mills, Jane 102
  Margaret S. 38
  Mary 121
  Sarah 42, 124
  Sophia 138
Minard, Cynthia A. 72
  Eliza 148
  Elizabeth 24
  Louisa 79
  Maria 58
  Penelope 150
Mindle, Ellen 50
Minech, Mary 53
Minego, Mary 53
Minford, John 90
  Mary (Mrs.) 90
  Sarah 141
Ministt, Mary 3
Minke, Anna Marie C. 120
Minnego, Elizabeth 56
Minrups, Marianne 58
Minster, Mary 3
Mitchel, Alex 90
  Alexander 90

Mitchel (cont.)
  Ellen (Mrs.) 90
  Martha 92
Mitchell, Angeline 103
  Cyenda 146
  Eliza 6
  Elizabeth Ann 119
  George 85
  Mary 34
  Matilda 111
  Thermuthus 130
Mittendorf, Catharine
  Louisa 117
  F. 117
Mock, Katherine 54
Molder, John 90
Moler, Drusilla 44
  John (Sr.) 90
Moles, Elizabeth J. 121
Mollies, Elizabeth 13
Molster, Martin 90
Monday, Betsy 52
Monin, Mary 26
Monk, Eliza 3
  William 49
Monroe, Aaron 90
  Charles 90
  Elizabeth 101
  Else 61
  Gracey 35
  Martha 27, 87
  Marthy Jane 73
  Mary 87
  Mary J. 74
  Nancy 72
  Phebe 120
  Sarah 100
Monrow, Keziah 137
  Patty 5
  Polly 5
  Rebeccah 37
  Solomon 37, 91
Montgomery, Cinthia J.
  114
  Hester Ann 127
  Josephine 67
  Mary 23, 29, 91
  Mary Ann 9
  Melissa 85
  Melvina 152
  Nancy 16
  Sarah 61
  Sarah E. 95
  William 23, 85, 91
Montgumery, Wm. 91
Moor, Lozina 26
Moore, Allennor 75
  Amos 91
  Ann Marie 49
  Barbary 32
  Casander 27
  Catherine 36, 98
  Charles 82
  Charlotte 101
  Cintha Ann 106
  Cyanda 7
  Cynthia 21
  Delila 91
  Eleanor 135, 139
  Elenor 148
  Eliza 23, 62
  Elizabeth 57
  Elizabeth (Mrs.) 4
  Elizabeth Ann 43, 145
  Emily 14, 74
  Forman 124
  Isabella 137
  Isabelle 113

Moore (cont.)
  James 92, 98
  Jemima 46, 69
  John 109, 138
  Julia A. 88
  Julia Anna 47
  Julianna (Mrs.) 47
  Keziah 70
  Latitia 19
  Letitia 1
  Maisy 131
  Maria 82
  Mariah 65
  Mary 25, 131
  Mary Jane 137
  Nancy 58, 81, 119
  Orphy 80
  Patience 59
  Phebe 77
  Philip 22, 52
  Rachael 43
  Rebecca 124, 147
  Rebecca T. 23
  Sintha 52
  William 91, 136
Moorehead, William 131
Moran, Elenora 79
  Margaret 53
More, Allennor 75
  Cyrus 92
Morford, Elizabeth 83
  Sarah Ellen 25
Morgan, Ann Elizabeth 29
  Anna 76
  Barbary 64
  Civilia Ann 76
  Eleanor 80
  Elizabeth 149
  Isam 60
  Isim 1
  Lucy Ann 22
  Margaret 20
  Margaret E. 132
  Maria L. 57
  Maria T. 57
  Mary 31, 149
  Mary B. 1
  Mary E. 60
  Nancy 97
  Peggy 18
  Phebe Ann 123
  Rachel 68
  Ruth A. 43
  Sarah 50
Morison, Washington 28
Morrell, Jerusha M. 40
Morris, Catherine 147
  Eliphael 143
  Sarah Ann 129
Morrison, Catherine 147
  Emma 77
  James 93, 103, 148
  Jane 93
  Maria 103
  Martha 79
  Nancy J. 122
  Philora 148
  Rachel (Mrs.) 82
  Robert 93
  Sarah Jane 75
  William 93
Morrow, George W. 134
  Hester 80
Morten, Margaret 66
Morton, Amanda 145
  Catharine (Mrs.) 81
  Catherine 114
  J. F. 128

Morton (cont.)
J. H. 81
James (?) 80
John G. 81
Letitia 68
Sarah 105
William B. (?) 81
Moseman, Constantine 93
Mosert, Eliza J. 143
Mosier, Leah 43
Mosman, John 93
Moss, Mary 100
Sally Ann 84
Mossman, Augusten 55
Hartley 55
John 55
Mary Polena 55
Mosure, Leah 43
Mott, Alvina 129
Elmira Francis 117
Martha 113
Melissa F. 63
Motz, Elizabeth 56
Mouhat, James 93
Moulder, Drusilla 44
Moulton, Mary B. 34
Sarah 141
Mountjoy, Elenor 84
Ranson 93
Muas, Suzan 26
Mudgate, Rebecca 52
Mueller, Elizabeth Cook
13
Mulholland, Charles 93
James (?) 87
Mulhoren, Rose Ann 109
Mullen, James 94
William 23
Muller, Caroline 13
Freidrich 13
Johann 89
Katharina 117
Louisa (Mrs.) 13
Wilhelm 89
Mulligan, Edward 28
Mary 28
Mullins, Elizabeth 13
Foster 13
Muncey, Thomas 94
Mundel, Melvina 104
Mundy, Moses 94
Munion, Catherine 80
Elizabeth 62
Jane 93
Mary Ann 104
Rachel 106
Sallie 86
Munk, Dauswell 79
Matilda 79
Munn, Eleanor 141
Elenor 53
Evilina 94
Hannah 19
James (Sr.) 19
Lucretia 62
Melinda 32
Nancy 83
Peggy 19
Polly 99
Solomon 19
Munnel, Rebecca 122
Munnell, Lucinda 13
Munrow, Gracey 35
Munyan, Elsy 19
Jacob 85
Margaret Ann 85
Sally 54
William 14, 19

Munyon, Ellse 78
Murfin, Anna 21
Hannah 27
James 78
W. D. 75
Warren D. 25
Murphin, Abigail 73
Murphy, Ann 118
Bridget 33
D. W. 11, 18
Ellen 34
Fanny 58
John 118
Lydia A. 88
Maria 119
Martha 64
Mary 82
Moses 44
Nancy 19
Rebecca 64
Sarah 136
Sophia F. 26
Murray, Mary 150
Murse, Lucy 19
Mus, Matild 16
Musgrave, Joseph 95
Sarah 72
Musgrove, Eleanor 134
Mary Ann 56
Musick, Martha 105
Musser, Barbary Ann
(Mrs.) 38
Caroline 132
Eleanor 10
Martha Elizabeth 38
Sophronia 144
Mustard, Hannah 38
Lydia 124
Nancy 104
Sally 152
Sarah 33, 152
Sarah (Mrs.) 38
William 38
Muster, Mary 24
Mutter, Jane 131
Mye, Lena 71
Sina 71
Myer, Barbara 132
Margaret 57
Mary 31
Myers, Chestina 119
Lucinda 30
Margaret 73
Mary 14
Nancy 97
Ruth 115
Sary 90
Myler, Martha 142
Myres, Elizabeth 61
Mytener, Catharine 77
Mytinger, Emily H. 150
Nadle, Sarah 118
Nagel, Caroline 50
Catherine 10
Rosina 88
Stantina 118
Nagle, Catharine 38
Isaac 77
Sarah J. (?) 77
Nail, Eliza Jane 37
John 96
Mary 112
Minerva 35
Philipina 10
Polly 112
Rachel 63
Sarah 52
Napp, Edman 6

Narley, Sarah 123
Nave, Phoebe 133
Nearl, Julia Ann 122
Neary, Mathew 96
Needle, Sarah 118
Neff, George 96
Nehol, Catherine 130
Neil, Hannah 130
Lucy 28
Nelson, Eliza 107
Elizabeth 53
Susan 147
Nensian, Christine 130
Neowell, Lucinda 9
Nethingham, John 98
Neucun, Lydia 57
Neve, George 149
Jane 149
Margaret 106
Nevens, Electa W. 106
Neves, William 96
Newcom, Margaret 90
Newcomb, Philip 107
Susan 152
Newkirk, Grace 118
Newlon, Sarah E. 133
Newman, Elizabeth 98
Elizabeth (Mrs.) 107
Lucinda 132
Mary 104
Molissia 49
Nancy 22, 140
Rebecca 147
Samantha 107
Sela A. 140
Solomon 107
Newton, Lucy 59
Niblick, Sidney 82
Nicholas, Marey 64
Nicholls, Dorcas 84
Nichols, Anna 96
Catharine 100
Elizabeth 59
Emily 129
Helen M. 139
J. 5
Keziah (Mrs.) 96
Mary 26, 119, 152
Mary Ann 41
Mary J. 134
Mary L. 13
Nancy 59
Sarah 96
Nickles, Anna 55
Nickols, Isabel 61
Nicoles, Rebecca 114
Ruth 65
Nicols, Samuel 68
Nirrmand, Henry (?) 59
Noel, A. 148
Ab. 149
Aman (?) 15
Ann E. 15
Anna 21
Aseraim 98
Caroline 6, 137
Catherine 132
Caty 151
Cornelia Jane 137
David 75, 97
Drusilla 102
Eliza 151
Elizabeth Ann 90
Ellen 47
Jacob P. 78
Jemima 46
Joanna 36
Julian 84

Patten (cont.)
Rebecca 12
Rebecca A. 23
Rutha 6
Thomas 28
Thomas (Jr.) 6
Patterson, Druzilla 38
Elizabeth 101
Ellen 37
Fanny 27
Jas. 101
Juletta 110
Mary (Mrs.) 101
Sarah J. 137
William 88
Patton, Elizabeth 101
Julia Ann 4
Lemuel 93
Mary Ann 56
Nancy 59, 118
Rachel 28
Sarrah 94
Susan 113
Thomas 28, 101
Thomas (Jr.) 101
Patun, Ellen 135
Paul, Abigail 150
Esther 150
Mary Jane 27
Olive 73
Perris 73
Paulson, Andrew 102
Paupetter, Mary 103
Pawkett, Joseph 43
Paxson, Cassandra 5
Paxton, Charlotte H. 123
James 101
Payne, Belinda 95
Betty F. 66
William M. 95
Payton, Catharine 146
Elizabeth 16
James 102
Mary (Mrs.) 60
Ruhama (?) 80
Sarah 69
William 60
Pealing, Rosina (?) 89
Pearce, Ann 105
Pearl, Cynthia 51
Nancy (Mrs.) 101
Robert 101
Pearsfield, Margaret P.
28
Pearson, William 107
Peart, Mary Ann 111
Peasefield, Mary Jane
107
Peatling, Elizabeth 78
M. (Mrs.) 78
William 78
Pebbles, Rebecca T. 124
Pechler, Conrad 101
Peck, Mary C. 34
Pecone, Nancy 85
Peebles, Elizabeth 57
Jane F. 150
Nancy Ellen 27
Rachel R. 54
Peirie, Ann 86
Ann (Mrs.) 86
Harris 86
Pelhank, Elizabeth 5
J. 40
Louisa 13
Nany 40
Pelhenk, Dora 133
Pellet, John 102

Pendall, Nancy 56
Penfield, John 15
Penn, Jane (Mrs.) 102
Nancy Jane 21
S. 102
Pennington, Jane 76
Mary Ann 81
Penrod, Mary 79
Penroot, Mary 79
Peral, Elizabeth 33
Perry, A. 94
Ann 2
Ann Eliza 39
Bula 30
Elizabeth 30, 94, 108
Hannah 63
Jemima 118
L. 46
Liza 11
Louisa 11
Margaret 84
Maria 44
Mary 45
Mary Ann 76
Mary Jane 124
Polly 79
Samuel 11
Susannah 23
Vilina M. 124
Peter, Barbara 1
Peters, Henry 143
Mary Ann 143
Priscilla C. 11
Peterson, Elizabeth Jane
83
Mary 80
Petit, Mary Jane 35
Nancy 117
Peto, Catherine 144
Petod, Nancy 125
Pettet, Prudence 153
Petting, Elizabeth 78
M. (Mrs.) 78
William 78
Pettit, Elizabeth 10
Job 29, 102
Petusan, Barbara 109
Pew, Emely 63
Pewtheren, John 31
Pey, Julia 90
Peyton, Ellenor 87
Hannah 36
Nathan 123
Renda 70
Sarah 102
Terresa 98
William 89
Pfeiffer, Conrad 102
Phelps, Elmira (Mrs.)
103
John 103
Philbin, Katherine 49
Philips, Elizabeth 150
Mary (Mrs.) 134
Mary J. 119
Sarah S. 134
Philliips, Hezekiah 107
Mary 107
Phillippi, Maria Louisa
139
Phillips, Amanda 100
Annie 63
Asa (?) 63
Catharine 91
Elizabeth 42
Eunice 138
Fanny 38
John 38

Phillips (cont.)
John E. 103
Julia Ann 23
Maria C. 103
Mary 136
Piat, Rebecca (?) 6
Piatt, Minerva 29
Pickance, Elizabeth 145
Pickerel, Jane 24
Pickford, Eliza J. 141
Pierce, Amanda 58
Angeline 105
Ann 86
Anna (Mrs.) 103
Charlotte 63
H. 103
Jonas 99
Sarah 58
Pierpoint, Larken 23
Sarah Ann 23
Pierson, Emily 74
Pierve, Elizabeth 5
Horace 5
Piesons, Laura 10
Piggott, Electa 83
Electa (Mrs.) 66
John 66
Mary 66
Pikkens, Elizabeth 145
Pile, Ann Eliza 117
Clarrissa 114
Minerva 79
Rebecca 6
Sophia 140
Piles, Caroline 151
Catherine 22
Cynthia 91
Elenor 79
Eliza 119
Elizabeth 63
Jeremiah 8
Lucinda 128
Matilda 113
Rebecchy 113
Ruhama 90
Pinkerman, Mary Eliza
145
Pint, Mary Catherine (?)
88
Pitthone, Nancy 125
Pitts, Joseph 104
Kesiah 131
Nancy 135
Pixley, Seymour 72, 75
Pliment, Bethia 52
Plotz, Mary (?) 118
Plowman, Sally 63
Plum, John 11
Mary 120
Mary J. 11
William 104
Plumb, Charlotte 114
Christena 20, 104
Fanyny 123
John 11, 20
John (Sr.) 104
Mary J. 11
Nancy 20, 104
Plummer, Ann 138
Mary 20
Polis, Theresa 45
Pollack, David 124
Pollock, Ann 53
Catharine Ann 19
George 96
Mary 124
Polly 97
Sarah 97

Shonkwiler (cont.)
Frances (Mrs.) 138
George 138
Hariet 129
Mary 104
Nancy 36
Shook, Lydia A. 50
Lydia Ann 120
Shoop, Mary 106
Shoot, Richard 120
Shope, Aramantha 150
Cynthia A. 122
Elizabeth 150
Elizabeth E. 113
James 24
Jno. (Jr.) 150
John 120, 150
Lucinda A. 11
Mary 137, 150
Mary Ann 24
Nancy 16
Sally 20
Ursula 34
Shores, Lidea 147
Short, Elizabeth 30, 78
Elizabeth N. 31
Shoush, Scioto 17
Showmaker, Abigail 16
Emily Dulcina 16
Susan 9
Shred, Rosina 7
Shroud, Ann Rebecca 84
Shufflin, Elisabeth 106
Shuler, Eleanor 85
Rosena 76
Shultz, Elizabeth 42
Henty 42
Mary 150
Mary Jane 116
Shumway, Harriet 84
J. Q. 48
Polly 137
Sylvanus T. 62
Shunkwiler, Christain 104
Eveline 1
Shupe, Abigail 13
James 120
Lawrence 120
Margaret 39
Shurtz, Mary Jane 60
Shuter, Amelia 10
Caroline 125
Louisa (?) 141
Shutty, William A. 120
Siahl, Margaretha 5
Siberts, Margaret 121
Sidney, Elizabeth 142
Francis J. 55
Sarah Ann 17
Sidnor, Catherine 16
Siel, Christina 49
Signor, Mary 64
Sikes, Aley 138
Eliza J. 96
Elsa J. 96
John 115
Levi 96, 133
Margaret 122
Mary Eliza 5
Melvina 139
Polly 115
Rhuhamy 128
Sarah 7, 121
Silas, Thomas 41
Sill, Mary L. 71
Naoma 83
Silvey, Betsey 123

Silvey (cont.)
Henry 147
Sarah Ann 151
Silvy, William 112
Simmon, Joseph 118
Simmons, Hannah 111
Nancy 111
Orinda P. 72
Sarah 63
Simonton, Elizabeth 16
Matilda 58
Simpkins, Fanny 59
Simpson, Ann 66
Ellenora 46
James 46
Jane 95
John 75
Mariah 26
Polly 123
Sintha 75
Sims, Ann 89
Singer, Catherine 72
Sinn, Catherine 10
Sisler, Nancy 4
Skellenger, Eliza 84
Skelton, Barbary 76
Frances S. 149
James 149
John 149, 150
Manerva (Mrs.) 149
Mary Ann 76, 110
Rebecca 150
Samuel 99, 150
Sarah Ann 107
Skidmore, Elizabeth 58
Jane 62
Sarah E. 24
Skinner, Polly 71
Zabra 40
Skonten, Rachel 129
Skouter, Mary 63
Skouton, Solomon 78
Slack, G. M. 121
George W. 122
Harrison 122
Mary 75
Mary Ellen 46
Susannah 59
Slagle, Mary 145
Slater, Louisa 141
Nancey 137
Samuel 38
Slattery, Jane C. 138
Juliann 32
Louise Ann 37
Martha 104
W. 104
Slaughler, Rosater 43
Slavens, Elisabeth (Mrs.) 23
Emeline 140
James 23
Margaret 26
Rosanna 23
Ruth 102
Sarah 102
Slaver, Ann M. 12
Sleev, Sally (?) 49
Slimp, Celia 102
Elizabeth 102
Sirena 24
Syrenia 35
Sloat, Louisa 63
Slocum, Elenor 152
Slocumb, Clarinda 46
Clarissa 44
Josephine 136
Laura 54

Slocumb (cont.)
Martin 136
Orrilla 136
P. S. (Mrs.) 2
Slupf, Mary 38
Sly, Francis E. 80
Martha Ann 75
Smalley, Abner 122
Josiah 122
Nancy W. 140
Rebecca 146
Smart, Elizabeth 58
Mary Jane 79
Metilda (Mrs.) 83
Smedley, Elizabeth L. 4
George B. 122
George J. 122
Joanna 11
Rachel 40
Smiley, Nathaniel 111
Susan 111
Smith, Airy W. 135
Alexander 139
Alice 64
Amanda 22
Angelina 86
Anna 49, 113, 130
Anthony 123
Any Winneford 15
Barbary 49, 83
Betsey 67
Betsy 22
Caroline 76, 130
Caroline J. 81
Catharine 43
Catherine 2, 28, 85, 92, 93
Christina 116, 123
Clarkson 125
Cynthia 76
Drusilla W. 148
Eleanor 109
Eleanor A. 56
Eli 53
Eliza 104
Eliza Ann 60
Eliza J. 136
Elizabeth 15, 16, 17, 21, 22, 33, 72, 104, 111
Elizabeth F. 92
Ellen 71
Emelia 22
Emily 57, 72, 96
Emily A. 118
Emma 22
Fatama 2
Fetamar 2
G. H. 41
G. W. 124
George 116
Godfrey 49
Henriett 130
Hester F. 67
Jacob 123
James 147
Jane 125
John 28, 144
John (Jr.) 28
John F. 124
Jonithan 49
Joseph 123, 136
Julia A. 117
Julia Ann 5
Juliana 96
Juliann 151
Katharine 33
Lawrence C. 25

187

Swartz, Joseph 130
Margaret 56
Swaunim, Harriet 81
Swearingen, Levina 55
Sweet, Eliza 76
Elizabeth Ann 73
Jane 83
Mary Ann 105
Rachel 82
Susan 75
Swift, Ellen 148
Swobbeary, Eliza 82
Sword, Henry 149
Swords, Eliza 49
Mary 152
Sarah A. 148
Violet 6
William 44
Swyers, Elizabeth 131
Sylva, Rachel 14
Tabor, Nancy A. 90
Tanner, Mary A. 131
Tarhle, Barbara 121
Taylor, Annis E. 70
Betsy 87
Conrad 69
Elizabeth 70
George B. 127
H. 64
Hannah 28
J. 18
Jane 116
Jeremiah 18, 96
Jesse 131
Josephine 114
Maria 96
Martha 12
Martha Jane 145
Mary 2
Mary E. 111
Mary J. 120
Peggy 23
Pertrina 24
Rachel Lucetta 18
Rebece 62
Rhoda 134
Susannah 99
William 116
Teapold, Jacob 132
Tearl, Mary Ann 101
Tearout, Mary 90
Tecker, Lucintha 95
Telen, Nancy 27
Temple, B. F. 114
Terry, Nancy 40
Teters, Louisa 150
Margaret 75
Tetus, Louisa 150
Thane, Nancy (Mrs.) 145
Thenst, Dorothy (?) 124
Thiebaux, Margaret 130
Thienpont, Eml. 38
Thocmorton, Mary 2
Thomas, Abigail 111
Abraham 132
Amanda 82
Ann 86, 146
Charity 132
Charity A. 142
Cynthia 133
Deborah 116
Elcey 20
Elizabeth 97
Henry 142
James 127
Jesse L. 75
Jno. (Jr.) 132
John 132

Thomas (cont.)
Joseph 64
Levina 29
Margaret 48
Margaret J. 125
Marian 87
Mary 31, 61, 75
Mary (Widow) 134
Mary Jane 11
Orytha 124
S. C. 68
Sarah M. 64
William 132
Zerilda 80
Thomason, Druzilla 8
Thomlison, Jane 103
Thompson, Amanda 46
Ann 14, 78
Ann B. 37
Anna 12
Caroline C. 54
Catharine 21, 102
Eliza 141
Elizabeth 4, 54, 55,
99
Elizabeth Ann 18
Ellen 132
George 46, 57
J. L. 135
James 35, 54, 133
James (Jr.) 108
John 54, 108
Jos. L. 54
Joseph 108
Joseph L. 35
Julia 115
Katharine 139
Lewis 132, 135
Lucinda 111
Manerva 130
Margaret 46, 91, 120
Margaret (Mrs.) 46
Maria 96, 110
Maria L. 48
Mariah 23
Martha 46
Mary 102
Mary Ann 87
Mary Jane 108
Matthew J. 5
Melvina 122
Minerva 135
Nancy 76, 124
Rees 35
Sarah 35
Sarah A. 2
Sarah E. (Mrs.) 5
Sarah Ellen 13
Silas 110
Solomon 96
Sophia 57
Susan 108
William 108, 128
Thomson, Margaret Ann
136
Thoreman, Hester 10
Thornton, Permelia 90
Sarah A. 141
Thoroman, Andrew 66
James T. 133
Mary D. 64
Thomas 66
Throckmarten, Suzana 30
Throckmorton, Amos R. 94
Foster 30
Hannah 144
Throne, Rebeccah 75
Thrush, Dorothy 124

Thurst, Dorothy (?) 124
Thurston, Margaret 134
Tilton, Mary 52
Timberlake, Catherine 67
Timbrook, Rebecca 15
Timmonds, Eliza Jane 147
H. Amanda 76
M. A. J. 76
Mary 134
Timmons, Sarah 70
William 121
Wm. 55
Tims, Harriet 61
Peggy 39
Tindall, Mary 16
Tippon, Margaret 31
Tipton, Cassa 83
Eliza 87
Elizabeth 63
Ellen 40
Lurania 30
Tiry, Margaret 107
Tise, Anna Mary 72
Tison, Jane Elizabeth
147
Titus, Elizabeth 27, 56
Green 58
Hannah 125
Isaac 133
James 27, 104
Mary 120
Nancy 87
Rebecca 104
Sarah 80
Stephen 87
Susan 86
Susan (Mrs.) 87
Tetus 125
Tobins, Anna 58
Eliza Mary 51
Todd, Benjamin 48
Toland, Catherine 8
Elizabeth 89
Elizabeth (Mrs.) 89
John 89
Mary 69
Tomlinson, John 6
Julia 87
Nancy 6
Sally 70
Tomlison, Mary 41
Tophouse, Anna 105
Daniel 105
Sally (Mrs.) 105
Toppins, Emily 126
Michael 21
Townsend, Rachel Mariah
4
Rhoda 4
Sarah Ann 46
Townson, Daniel 57
Tracy, Anne Maria 35
Charles P. 5
Elizabeth D. 113
Esther 25
Frances H. 98
Mary K. 130
Mary R. 66
Millie E. 46
Noah 2
Trask, John (?) 46
Traugh, Samuel A. 123
Travis, Mary (Mrs.) 48
Sarah 48
Scureman (?) 48
Trent, Mary (?) 21
Trett, Mary 33
Trewit, James 135

Trexler, Elizabeth 9
Hannah 88
John 134, 135
Rachel 119
Susanna 65
Trich, Dorothy 105
Triggs, Elizabeth 78
Hester 63
Lydia 129
Mariah 49
Sally 22
Susanna 108
Susannah 87
Thomas 132, 135
William 135
Trigs, Patty 137
Polly 137
Trimmer, Polly 137
Trout, Elizabeth E. (?)
22
Susan 124
Troxler, Catharena 12
Truitt, E. 101
Trumbo, Rebecca 70
Trutt, J. M. G. (?) 22
Try, Eliza 61
Tubbs, Eliza 2
Kesiah 100
Tucker, Ann 37
Caroline 61
Elizabeth Jane 37
Jno. 133
John 37
Keziah 104
Lucintha 95
Margaret 20
Martha 150
Mary 84, 89
Nancy 128
Rufus R. 128
Sally 133
Sarah 89
Tumbleson, Urch 70
Tunison, Euniscilia 123
Turn, June 108
Turner, Anne 58
Becca (Widow) 125
Bridget 102
Caroline 92
Christina 113, 129
Cynthia 15
Elizabeth 18, 81, 123
Elizabeth (Mrs.) 136
Hester Ann 106
J. R. 125, 132
James R. 135
Jane (?) 108
John L. 3
Levina 70
Louisa F. 122
Manarcissa M. R. 11
Maria L. 93
Martha J. 2
Mary 8, 149
Mary Ann 122
Mary L. 2
Matilda 48
Nancy P. 65
Narissa M. R. 11
Rebecca 16, 33, 135
Sarah Ann 149
Sarah P. 26
W. 136
William 93
Tyree, Lyra (?) 18
Mary 18
Tyrell, Mary Ann 101
Tyson, Jacob 82

Tyson (cont.)
Sarah 15
Tytus, Jane 151
Ullem, Hannah 47
Ulrich, Barbara 109
Umble, Elias 63
Joseph 63
Umphreys, Mary Melvina
94
Sarah Ann 21
Underwood, Sarah (Mrs.)
136
Uooting, Winnie 44
Updegraff, Ellen 95
Uris, Jacob 138
Urquhart, Alexander 57
Isabella 81
Isabella (Mrs.) 83
Janet 100
Margaret Ann 83
Mary 139
Robert 83
Usbee, Louisa 7
Usher, Katharine 58
Usua, Elizabeth 79
Utt, Adam (Jr.) 106
Amanda 112
Elizabeth 86
Elizabeth (Mrs.) 136
Hannah 65
Henry 6, 30, 86
Henry (Jr.) 30
John 86, 136
Lucretia 9
Margaret 51
Mary 25
Mary Ann 79
Peggy 136
Rebeca E. 137
Vicy 30
Valadin, Argate 74
Vale, Ellen 135
Valentine, Jacob 136
Martha Jane 136
Nancy (Mrs.) 136
Vallaraider, Augustine
115
Valodin, Esther 59
F. 137
Frances 137
Oret 44
Vamoney, Samuel 116
Vanbibber, Eleanor 18
Jacob 18, 137
Jacob (Jr.) 18
Joseph 137
Lavina 74
Vanbibon, John 137
Vance, D. 77
Isabella 103
Nancy 98
Vandervort, Ann 14
Vanduson, Claney 103
E. (Mrs.) 103
Vanduzen, Sophia 54
Vangorder, Elzina 119
Melvina 48
Polly 66
Vanhorn, Phebe 68
Vannort, Isabel 64
Mary 15
Matilda 64
Sally 10
Vannorte, Icy 104
Vantine, Betsy 36
Polly 56
Varnager, Charlote 41
Varner, Emily 35

Varner (cont.)
Mary Jane 34
R. A. 121
Sarah C. 49
Vastine, Louisa A. 29
Mary 123
Vaughen, Priscilla 136
Veach, Elizabeth 108,
123
Harriet 151
Helen M. 43
Lucretia 57
Margaret 116
Mary Louisa 99
Mille Ann 138
Sarah 26
Silvester 99
Venhon, Aveline A. 12
Venort, Luesa 135
Teresa 135
Verbeck, Lydia 36
Verbick, Josiah 138
Vern, Seraphine 56
Vernier, Mary 57
Vessel, Eliza 100
Phebe 78
Vessell, Nancy 83
Vetter, Andre 138
Mary (Mrs.) 138
Vickers, Mary Jane 46
Nancy Jane 46
Victor, Elizabeth 38
Vigers, Sarah 21
Vignes, Mary (Mrs.) 138
Paul 138
Vigus, Eliza 112
Hulda 78
Jordan 127
Sarah 21
Vilee, Rebecca 88
Vilet, Constance 80, 138
John 80, 138
Maria 80
Sarah 32
Vincent, Anthony C. 126
Antoinette 126
Eliza Ann 47
Louise 130
Lucy 23
Mary 24
Susannah 144
Theresa 109
Vinson, Catherine 5
Jesse 138
John L. 138
Violet, John 80
Maria 80
Violett, Samuel 138
Virback, Alva 36
Virback, Alva 142
Josiah 101
Sena 36
Virgin, George T. 121
Jemima 121
Rachel 121
Voelkel, John 56
Voirin, Joseph 141
Voohrease, Emily 141
Voorhees, Belinda 66
Elcy M. S. 145
Malinda 66
Narcissa 5
Vulgamore, Eliza (Mrs.)
138
Waatts, Sophia 27
Wachco, Otilda 82
Wadabrok, Charlotte 81
Waddle, Joanna 37

191

Wade, Rebecca 106
Wadkins, Louisa 17
Wagerly, Mary 78
Waggner, Ursela 124
Waggoner, Christeane 4
  Elizabeth 140
Wagoner, Sarah 145
Wahl, Sarah 152
Wair, Olive A. 56
Wait, Abigail 9
  Almira 139
  Benjamin 152
  Caroline 78
  Eliza 152
  Isabella 151
  Mary 118
  Melissa 19
  Nancy Jane 49
  Perlina S. 122
  Philosse 19
  Reuben 15
  Sarah 93
Walbright, John 139
Walburn, Elizabeth 37
Walch, Nancy 109
Waldrick, Elizabeth 77
Walduk, Elizabeth 77
Waler, David 142
  Margaret 142
  Susannah 131
Wales, Maria 65
Walk, Margaret 71
Walker, Elizabeth 10,
  35, 133, 145
  Loreta 22
  Margaret W. 108
  Martha Jane 152
  Mary 41, 43
  Mary A. 70
  Perilla F. 99
  Sally 99
Walkins, Jane 124
Wall, Catherine 41
  Catrina 41
Wallace, Catherine 61
  Eleanor 77
  Elizabeth 132
  John 66
  Mahala 125
  Margaret 131
  Martha 148
  Nancy 107, 151
  Parmelia 94
  Squire 129
  Susanna 139
Wallas, Elizabeth 94
Wallborn, Mary 1
Wallbrecht, Christiana
  106
Wallbright, Louise 72
Waller, Elisabeth 109
  H. E. 92
  Margaret 25
  Mary 43, 71
Walles, Elizabeth 68
  Martha 148
  Nancy 151
Wallingford, Mary 27
Wallingsford, Alicia B.
  141
Wallis, John 68
  Polly 94
  Squire 140
Walls, Amazilla 22
  Arcade 33
  Elizabeth 68
  Elza 140
  Emily 140

Walls (cont.)
  Fanny 17
  James 115
  Joshua 115
  Lemuel 17, 140
  Levi 17, 140
  Louisa 140
  Mary Ann 22
  Polly 94
  Rachel 43
  Thomas 17
Wallsinger, Elizabeth 3
Walsinger, Cynthia 96
  John 93
  Mary 93
Waltan, Elizabeth 125
Walter, Carl 140
  Mary 98
Walterhouse, Matilda 133
Walton, Hiram 140
  Polly 125
  Rachel 24
Wampler, Susannah 128
Ward, Anna 142
  Dorothy A. 116
  G. W. 90
  Jacob 84, 144
  Nancy 32, 92
  Sarah 95
  Sarah J. 13
Warden, Margaret 5
Warner, Lavina 93
Warnka, William 93
Warnock, Samuel 141
Warren, Daniel 83
  Elizabeth 112
  Emily 35
  James 141
  Mary E. 69
  Polly 83
  Susan 52, 65
Washburn, David 108
Washeo, Elizabeth 73
Waterman, Josephine L.
  141
Waters, Margaret 68
  Nathaniel 142
  Samuel 142
  Thomas 142
Watkins, Elizabeth 73
  Hannah 55
  Harriet 60
  Jane 124
  Judah (Mrs.) 39
  Leonard T. 103
  Rebecca J. 39
  Thomas 39
Watschner, Agnes 143
Watson, Darkis 101
  Mary J. 123
  Rhoda 74
Watterhouse, Elizabeth
  86
  Mariah 14
Watts, David 136
  E. (Mrs.) 142
  Fanny 17
  Naancy 26
  Samuel 142
Waw, Rebecc 30
Wayley, Margaret 15
Wayne, Mary 49
Weaks, Eliza 24
Wealthy, Catharine 139
Weatherwax, Sarah E. 77
Weaver, Elijah 61
  Eliza J. 137
  Filora Ann 41

Weaver (cont.)
  John 50, 61
  John Q. 142
  Lydia 96
  Mary 61
  Milly 149
  Rebecca 50
  Susannah 67
  Therisa 63
Webb, Elizabeth 78
  Jacob 39
  Mary F. 77
Webber, Johanna
  Cattarina 126
  Lois 63
  Mary 17
  Sarah A. 130
Weber, Anna Margaretha
  75
  Therisa 63
Weeks, Bathel 105
  Rachel 105
  Robert 143
Wees, Mary 44
Weesner, Catharine 5
Weghorst, Mary 89
Weisted, John 151
Welb, Margaret 59
Welch, Abigail (Mrs.)
  143
  Ben 143
  Cinthia Ann 115
  David 150
  Dilly 70
  Drusilla F. 151
  Eleanor 75
  Eliza 143
  Elizabeth 29, 42
  Harriet 73
  Hennrietta 45
  James 29
  John 151
  Louisa 44
  Mary 29, 49
  Matilda 116
  Rachel 85
  Sarah 29
  Solomon 29
Welcher, Amzi 143
  Mary 132
Weldin, Ann Marie 128
Weldon, Nancy 96
Weller, Philip K. 3
Wells, Deborah 101
  Evangely 81
  James 128
  Laura 117
  Laura (Mrs.) 143
  Lennina 135
  Letia Ann 118
  Martha 128
  Mary 111
  Rebecca 128
  Richard 128, 143
  Sarah 38
  Timothy 117
Welner, Liza 120
Welsh, Amanda 29
  James 29
  James (Sr.) 143
  Nancy 31, 109
Welsher, Harriet 57
Welty, Charles 143
Wermker, Christian 141
Werts, Harriet 36
West, Amy (Mrs.) 20
  B. G. 20
  Celey C. 100

Wills, Hannah 16
Willson, Eliza 5
  Elizabeth (Mrs.) 148
  Emarelda 145
  John 148
  Phebe 136
  Susanah 15
  William 133
Wilson, Amanda 63
  Amy 32
  Ann 67
  Catharine 72
  Charles 148
  Charlotte 80
  Cornelia 5
  David 117
  Deborah 124
  Diana 17
  Eliza 145
  Elizabeth 64
  Ellen 144
  Hannah 59
  Jacob 148
  James 145
  Jane (Mrs.) 149
  Jas. 145
  Jemima 73
  John 149
  Julia Ann 3
  Kesiah Ann 131
  Landersa (?) 119
  Louisa M. 38
  Louise Jane 67
  Louiza 18
  Margaret 33, 84
  Maria 117
  Martha 21, 45
  Mary 12, 39
  Mary Ann 30, 60
  Mary Jane 67, 135
  Moses 5
  Nancy 66, 72
  Pamelia 33
  Phebe 58
  Polly 125
  Rachel 87, 127
  Rhoda 76
  Robert 144
  Ruth 109
  Sarah 71, 76
  Sarah Jane 43
  Smith 18
  Susan 88
  Susan Maria 128
  U. 149
  Willing D. 74
Winant, Elizabeth 130
Wind, Maria 69
Windell, Anna C. 124
  Mary E. 125
Windgate, Rebecca 52
Windle, Anna 14
  Rebecca 11
Winet, Mary 69
  Rosanne 10
Winett, Roane 3
Winey, A. H. 149
Wingard, Elizabeth 118
Wingle, Anna Maria 81
  Louisa 81
Winkler, Adelia 108
  Harriet 51
  Mary 115
  Nancy 17, 58, 140
  Sina 45
Winn, Sarah 110
Winter, Christina 78
  Frederick 79

Winter (cont.)
  Magdeline 22
Wintersteen, Diane P. 123
Winton, Mary Ann 94
Winyard, Susan 118
Wirt, Elizabeth 90
Wirth, Catharine 117
  Margaret 51
Wirtz, Casper 46
Wise, Alma 120
  Louise 130
  Mary 78
Wisecap, Abraham 149
Wisecup, Hannah 128
Wishon, Cassey J. 54
  Hannah 14
  John R. 143
  Temperance 49
Witherow, Maria E. 63
Withers, Evadne 111
Witherup, Fanny 50
  Susan 119
Witherwax, Ann 74
Witmer, Remina 41
Wits, Magdalena 2
Witt, Johann Heinrich 149
Wittick, Jemine 41
Wogel, John George 138
Wolf, Anna G. T. 7
  Elizabeth 49
  Polly 18
  Rebecca 104
  Ruth 33
  Theodora 72
Wolfe, Jonathan 23
  Mary Ann 79
Wolfel, Mary Ann 121
Wolfin, Annettunia 91
Wolford, Catharine 12
  John B. 150
Wollam, Isaac 145
Womack, J. A. 80
Wood, Anna 119
  Caroline 77
  Elizabeth 75, 90, 116
  Elizabeth (Mrs.) 103
  Emily 144
  Fanny 62
  Jacob 41, 45
  James 150
  Jemimah 56
  Mary 139
  Mary Ann 37
  Mary F. 111
  Myle 45
  Phebe 92
  Polly 41
  Sally 15
  Sarah 17
  Sarah A. 64
  Simeon 17
Woodring, Christina 94
  Lucinda H. 94
  Margaret 19
  Sarah 25
Woodruff, A. S. 55
  Charlotte 7
  Electa S. 21
  Isaac 150
  Kiturah 135
  Mary Jane 21
  Nancy E. 46
  Picket 21
  Viola 129
Woods, Hugh 56
  Juliann 12

Woods (cont.)
  Rebecca 9
Woodyard, Fanny 135
  Indiana 146
  Jene (Mrs.) 146
  Mary Ann 92
Woolever, Sarah 25
Woolford, Elizabeth 9
  Mary 36
  Susannah 9
Woolry, Phebe 31
Woolsey, Jane 34
Wooting, Winnie 44
Work, John 151
  Samuel 151
Workman, Matilda 47
Worldley, Elizabeth 102
Worley, Amelia A. C. 138
  Anna 91
  Anthony 151
  Caroline C. 130
  Catharine E. 64
  Elizabeth 102
  Frances 82
  Hester Ann 41
  Lidia 54
  Louise F. 54
  Lydia 26
  Margaret 27, 40
  Mary 92
  Maryann 135
  Matilda 13
  Melissa 152
  Nancy 19, 143
  Patience 139
  Phebe Sallie 83
  Rebecca (Mrs.) 151
  Rebecca J. 6
  Sally 144
  Sarah 2
  Sarah A. 92
  Serena 125
  Susan 63
  Susanna 135
  William 151
Worth, Regina 49
Wortz, Harriet 36
  Rose 102
Woten, Elizabeth 151
  Nancy 50, 69
  Sarah 69
Wotring, Lucinda H. 94
  Sarah 25
Wright, Celina 71
  Cerena 71
  Elizabeth 97
  Hannah 1
  William 71, 151
Wrigle, Francis (?) 141
Wrigley, James 151
Write, Hannah 24
Wurth, Catharine 41
  Magdalena 2
Wyatt, Anna Melvina 6
Wyett, Martha W. 151
Wykoff, Matilda 39
Wyman, Sylva 145
Wymer, Martha E. 35
Wys, Elizabeth 109
Xentes, Sarah 120
Yairs, Susanna 110
Yates, Eliza 151
  Isaac 30
  Katherine 45
  Mehealy 29
  Polly 102
Yeager, Catherine 141
  H. P. 58

www.ingramcontent.com/pod-product-compliance
Lightning Source LLC
Chambersburg PA
CBHW050711280326
41926CB00088B/2920